ROUTLEDGE LIBRARY EDITIONS: VIRGINIA WOOLF

Volume 5

VIRGINIA WOOLF

VIRGINIA WOOLF
A Guide to Research

THOMAS JACKSON RICE

LONDON AND NEW YORK

First published in 1984 by Garland Publishing Inc.

This edition first published in 2018
by Routledge
2 Park Square, Milton Park, Abingdon, Oxon OX14 4RN

and by Routledge
711 Third Avenue, New York, NY 10017

Routledge is an imprint of the Taylor & Francis Group, an informa business

© 1984, Thomas Jackson Rice

All rights reserved. No part of this book may be reprinted or reproduced or utilised in any form or by any electronic, mechanical, or other means, now known or hereafter invented, including photocopying and recording, or in any information storage or retrieval system, without permission in writing from the publishers.

Trademark notice: Product or corporate names may be trademarks or registered trademarks, and are used only for identification and explanation without intent to infringe.

British Library Cataloguing in Publication Data
A catalogue record for this book is available from the British Library

ISBN: 978-1-138-54104-7 (Set)
ISBN: 978-1-351-01117-4 (Set) (ebk)
ISBN: 978-1-138-47601-1 (Volume 5) (hbk)
ISBN: 978-1-138-47602-8 (Volume 5) (pbk)
ISBN: 978-1-351-10621-4 (Volume 5) (ebk)

Publisher's Note
The publisher has gone to great lengths to ensure the quality of this reprint but points out that some imperfections in the original copies may be apparent.

Disclaimer
The publisher has made every effort to trace copyright holders and would welcome correspondence from those they have been unable to trace.

VIRGINIA WOOLF

GARLAND REFERENCE LIBRARY
OF THE HUMANITIES
(VOL. 432)

VIRGINIA WOOLF
A Guide to Research

Thomas Jackson Rice

GARLAND PUBLISHING, INC. • NEW YORK & LONDON
1984

© 1984 Thomas Jackson Rice
All rights reserved

Library of Congress Cataloging in Publication Data
Rice, Thomas Jackson.
　Virginia Woolf : a guide to research.

　(Garland reference library of the humanities ;
vol. 432)
　　Includes indexes.
　　1. Woolf, Virginia, 1882–1941—Bibliography.
I. Title. II. Series: Garland reference library of the
humanities ; v. 432.
Z8984.2.R5　1984　　016.823'912　　83-48264
[PR6045.072]
ISBN 0-8240-9084-5 (alk. paper)

Printed on acid-free, 250-year life paper
Manufactured in the United States of America

TO
CARRIE MICAELA RICE

CONTENTS

Preface	ix
Introduction	xiii
Periodical Abbreviations	xix

Part 1: Primary Bibliography
- A. Major Works
  - i. Novels — 3
  - ii. Short Fiction — 4
  - iii. Miscellaneous Writings — 6
- B. Autobiographical Writings, Diaries, Letters, and Documents — 10
- C. Manuscript Transcriptions and Scholarly Editions — 12
- D. Concordances — 15

Part 2: Secondary Bibliography
- E. Bibliographies — 19
- F. Biographies, Memoirs, Reminiscences, Interviews — 23
- G. Book-Length Critical Studies and Essay Collections — 39
- H. General Critical Articles or Chapters — 63
- J. Studies of *The Voyage Out* — 98
  - i. Books and Essay Collections — 99
  - ii. Critical Articles or Chapters — 99
- K. Studies of *Night and Day* — 102
- L. Studies of *Jacob's Room* — 104
- M. Studies of *Mrs. Dalloway* — 108
  - i. Books and Essay Collections — 109
  - ii. Critical Articles or Chapters — 110
- N. Studies of *To the Lighthouse* — 122
  - i. Books and Essay Collections — 123
  - ii. Critical Articles or Chapters — 124

- P. Studies of *Orlando*
    - i. Books and Essay Collections — 137
    - ii. Critical Articles or Chapters — 138
- Q. Studies of *The Waves* — 143
    - i. Books and Essay Collections — 144
    - ii. Critical Articles or Chapters — 146
- R. Studies of *The Years*
    - i. Books and Essay Collections — 153
    - ii. Critical Articles or Chapters — 154
- S. Studies of *Between the Acts* — 158
- T. Studies of the Short Stories — 163
- U. Studies of the Autobiographical Writings
    - i. Books and Essay Collections — 168
    - ii. Critical Articles or Chapters — 169
- V. Studies of the Biographies — 174
- W. Studies of the Feminist Tracts — 176
    - i. Books and Essay Collections — 177
    - ii. Critical Articles or Chapters — 177
- X. Studies of the Essays
    - i. Books and Essay Collections — 181
    - ii. Critical Articles or Chapters — 183
- Y. Studies of the Miscellaneous Writings — 191
- Z. Dissertations on Virginia Woolf — 192

INDEXES
- Author Index — 217
- Title Index — 230
- Subject Index — 239
- Virginia Woolf's Works: Index of Commentaries — 251

PREFACE

This guide to Virginia Woolf's writings and their critical reception is the third such bibliography on a modern British novelist I have published in the Garland Reference Library series (*James Joyce* and *D. H. Lawrence* appeared in 1982 and 1983, respectively). All three guides are fundamentally similar in intention, scope, and organization, chiefly because they were originally conceived, some twelve years ago, as chapters of a much larger bibliographical survey of modern British novelists. That this proved to be impractical is more a sign of my naiveté than of the growth of scholarship on these figures over the last decade (the explosion of Joyce, Lawrence, and Woolf studies has been going on, with little sign of abatement, for approximately the last thirty years).*

Publishing the guides to these three novelists separately has given me the opportunity to adapt some of the finer points of organization and coverage to the special nature of the authors' works and to the particular kinds of scholarship devoted to their writings. I have consistently aimed, in each case, to provide both the student and the professional scholar with the most *usable* format for exploring the critical approaches to the given author, making these guides, I believe, the most useful starting point for new research and scholarship. With Joyce and Lawrence, for example, this involved preparing separate listings of foreign-language publications, to promote the largely-neglected study of their international reputations. With Woolf, however, whose international reception is more limited and more adequately surveyed, all foreign-language scholarship has been fully integrated into this guide's secondary bibliography. Unlike the first two guides, moreover, this volume contains a checklist of dissertations on Virginia Woolf, since there is no such listing presently available (there are dissertation lists for Joyce and Lawrence). Finally, I have added a fourth index, primarily because many of the studies of Woolf have proven more difficult to classify than those of Joyce and Lawrence. The general critical books and articles on Woolf regularly devote substantial space to the discussion of specific titles, while the studies of individual works or genres often show a disconcerting propensity to range among a variety of titles, all resisting my attempts to categorize them absolutely. Nonetheless, I have assumed that a topical organization is essential to any research guide, have consistently entered such books and articles in the most appropriate section of this bibliography, and have, by the cross-references, the sectional headnotes, and the additional master index of commentaries on Woolf's works indicated the diversity of scholarship available for the concentrated study of any particular Woolf title.

Thus, I have sought to produce a simply-organized guide that makes easily accessible a diversified body of information on a complex author. To do so, I have necessarily had to be selective. I have, however, included all English and foreign-language books, essay collections, monographs, pamphlets, and special periodical issues concerned with Woolf and her works. These titles I have entered, *regardless of merit,* because they are conspicuous and I have always felt that one purpose of a research guide is to tell its user that some peculiarly rhapsodic admirations or apoplectic condemnations of Woolf are devoid of judgment or sympathy. I have been more selective with articles and chapters appearing in periodicals or in studies not exclusively concerned with Woolf since, while they are great in number, they tend toward considerable duplication and, at best, modest refinement of the same ideas. I have selected articles and chapters which offer original information and points of view or which best represent certain repeated themes in Woolf criticism. I have also included a number of discussions of Woolf from standard surveys of fiction or of the modern period (again, because they are conspicuous), since a reader with limited access to a major research library will need to rely heavily or exclusively on these titles. If I have erred in this matter of selection, I believe I have been perhaps too generous rather than too restrictive.

In my annotations, throughout this guide, I have sought a balance between description and, in many cases, evaluation of a publication, feeling that a lengthy précis of a study without a judgment of its value guides the user as little as a brief and insipid evaluation which omits any mention of what the title is about. I have generally

Preface xi

avoided an extended abstract of a book's thesis in the annotations, feeling that such condensations are comprehensible, if at all, only to someone who already knows the work and most users of this volume will know only a few of the titles included here well enough to profit from such abstracts. In the annotations throughout I have indicated various patterns among the critical responses to Woolf's works, and the numerous relations of her critics to each other, to critical theory, or to their time. My final intention for the annotations, then, is that the user who "reads through" this guide should be able to trace the historical development of Woolf's critical reception and recognize the chief tendencies, concerns, and needs of contemporary Woolf criticism.

No such work as this can be completed without incurring numerous debts. For their help in translating I thank David Danow, Masako Dorrill, and Marianne Wachter. For their comments and suggestions on the bibliography, in its various permutations over the last several years, I thank my editors Ralph Carlson, Duane DeVries, and Theodore Grieder. For assembling the index, I thank Dawn Bailey and Sharon S. White. For preparation of the final typescript, I thank Carol Cutsinger. For their encouragement and interest, I thank my wife, Diane, my children, and particularly my daughter Carrie who, like this guide, came third and has benefitted, I hope, from the lessons learned in "doing" the first two.

Note

*For my two-volume guide to research on the modern English novel, generally, and on thirty-five novelists, see *English Fiction 1900–1950* (Detroit: Gale Research Co., 1979, 1983). The "explosions" in Joyce and Lawrence scholarship could be said to date from the publication of similar anthologies of major critical essays: *James Joyce: Two Decades of Criticism,* ed. Seon Givens (New York: Vanguard, 1948) and *The Achievement of D. H. Lawrence,* ed. Frederick J. Hoffman and Harry T. Moore (Norman: Univ. of Oklahoma Press, 1953). The Woolf industry has developed more gradually, marked by the important studies published by Daiches in 1942 (see G16), Bennett in 1945 (G7), Blackstone in 1949 (G9), and Hafley in 1954 (G31). Yet, I would argue that the most substantial impetus to Woolf scholarship was provided by Erich Auerbach's discussion of *To the Light-*

house as the representative twentieth-century novel, with only asides on Joyce's *Ulysses* and Prousts' *A la recherche du temps perdu,* in his distinguished survey of the "representation of reality in Western literature": *Mimesis* (published in German in 1946, in English translation in 1953; see N7).

INTRODUCTION

Virginia Woolf: A Guide to Research is a selective annotated bibliography of works by and about Virginia Woolf. It consists of three parts: (1) the primary bibliography—which contains separate bibliographies of Woolf's major publications, of her autobiographical writings and correspondence, of her manuscripts, and of concordances to her writings; (2) the secondary bibliography—which contains international bibliographies of bibliographical, biographical, and critical publications concerning Woolf generally or her individual works; and (3) Indexes—which include a useful, topical, and thematic subject index for the guide and a comprehensive index to commentaries on Woolf's works. The balance of this introduction will explain more fully the principles of selection, arrangement, and annotation for each of these sections of the volume.

The Primary Bibliography
(Sections A through D)

Section A of the primary bibliography is a three-part listing of all Woolf's major works (novels, short fiction, miscellaneous writings). Original publication data are provided for all titles, with brief factual annotations and contents for collections. Section B is a selective listing of Woolf's posthumously published autobiographical writings, diaries, letters, and personal documents, with brief factual and descriptive annotations. Section C lists all scholarly editions and transcriptions of Woolf's manuscripts and typescripts, and section D lists the available concordances to Woolf's fiction. Cross-reference numbers in the annotations, in this primary section of the bibliography, generally send the user to important textual commentaries on and introductions to a title, which are themselves entered and annotated elsewhere in the guide. Sectional headnotes likewise contain numerous cross references to titles of related interest which are to be found in other sections of the volume.

The Secondary Bibliography (Sections E through Z)

By far the largest part of this volume, the secondary bibliography consists of twenty sections. Section E (bibliographies), is a broad but selective listing of previous primary and secondary bibliographies concerning Woolf, as well as essay-surveys of Woolf's critical reputation. Annotations describe the nature of the bibliographies and evaluate their accuracy and usefulness. Section F (biographies, memoirs, reminiscences, and interviews) is a generous, but again selective, listing of major biographical sources, published as books, articles, chapters, special journal issues, or essay collections. The annotations in this section describe and often evaluate the title and, when appropriate, provide some comment on the nature and duration of a memoirist's relationship with Woolf. For the most part, this section omits brief notes and incidental mentions in published writings or in letters, as well as essays, articles, or notes since assimilated into larger studies.

Section G (book-length critical studies and essay collections) is a comprehensive bibliography of critical books, essay collections, special journal issues, monographs, and pamphlets concerned with Woolf and her works generally, or with more than *two* of her works or genres. Studies limited to two of Woolf's works or genres are entered in each of the two appropriate sections on the individual works and genres (sections J through Y—see below). Annotations are more detailed in this section, giving the general drift of the title's thesis, surveying its chief points, and evaluating both its contribution to Woolf's international critical reputation and its practical usefulness to the student of Woolf. Dissertations are not considered published books for the purposes of this bibliography and are not included in this section, unless subsequently published. (For a checklist of dissertations, see section Z).

Introduction

Section H (general critical articles, or chapters) is a generous selection of critical essays and discussions of Woolf generally, or, again, of more than *two* of her works or genres, published in periodicals, special issues of journals, essay collections, or general studies of English and world literatures, of modern writers, of the novel, and so on. For the most part, this listing excludes both brief notes and essays, articles, or notes later assimilated into larger studies which are entered and annotated elsewhere. It does, however, include a selection of pedestrian surveys, obviously not because they are meritorious, but because they are readily found in most general library collections and can be helpful if the user realizes their superficial or derivative nature and has no access to a larger research library. Most of the entries, however, survived the selection process by merit and their inclusion should indicate implicitly their value. Thus, the majority of annotations in this section are brief, factual, and descriptive rather than evaluative.

Sections J through Y are extensive, annotated checklists of studies of Woolf's novels (sections J through S), short stories (section T), autobiographical writings (section U), biographies (section V), feminist tracts, (section W), essays (section X), and miscellaneous writings (section Y). Sections J through Y generally consist of two subsections: "Books and Essay Collections" and "Critical Articles or Chapters" on the given work or genre. Each of these fifteen sections on Woolf's individual works opens with a lengthy introductory headnote, referring the user to *essential* textual, bibliographical, biographical, or critical commentaries to be found in publications entered and annotated in other sections of this bibliography (e.g., each of the headnotes for the sections on Woolf's novels identifies those general studies of her fiction, found in sections G and H, that significantly consider the given novel). A comprehensive listing of commentaries on Woolf's individual works, by title, will be found in the concluding index for this volume: "Virginia Woolf's Works."

As with sections G and H, the principles for selection and annotation vary within the subsections on Woolf's individual works. The listings of book-length studies, essay collections, special journal issues, monographs, and pamphlets are comprehensive, and those of articles and chapters are generous yet selective. Dissertations, again, are not considered published books, or entered in the bibliographies (see section Z). The few available study guides or student "cribs" are included, however, not because of their merit but to make the record of book-length studies as complete as possible. Annotations for books entered in sections J through Y are detailed and evaluative; for articles they are concise and generally descriptive.

Section Z (dissertations on Virginia Woolf) is a comprehensive checklist of international dissertations wholly or largely concerned with Woolf. The entries identify the author, title, degree-granting institution, and date of the dissertation. The brief annotations refer the user to any published version of the dissertation, entered elsewhere in the guide, or to any published abstract of the dissertation.

Indexes

This bibliography concludes with four indexes: authors, titles, subjects, and Virginia Woolf's works—index of commentaries. The subject index should be a particularly useful means for tracing specific figures (literary and historical), ideas, places, themes, and titles in Woolf criticism. In a way, it suggests a number of alternative topical arrangements that might have been used for organizing this volume and should give the user further options for research within the bibliography. The final index provides the user with comprehensive listings of substantive commentaries on Woolf's individual works, by title, both to supplement the topical organization of this guide and to make practicable a truly exhaustive study of the available research on any particular title.

Foreign-Language Publications

While no attempt has been made to list the numerous translations of Virginia Woolf's works into a number of languages in the primary bibliography (for this information, see Kirkpatrick [E7]), as many foreign-language books, essay collections, special journal issues, monographs, pamphlets, and dissertations, and significant essays and chapters as could be located have been entered and annotated in the secondary bibliography of this guide. Fortunately, only

Introduction   xvii

a relatively small number of these publications finally proved to be inaccessible for annotation (all such entries are noted as "not seen"). All titles available in English translation were annotated from the English editions, with original foreign-language publication data provided in the annotation. The languages of all foreign-language publications are also identified in the annotations. Translations are provided only for the titles of works published in less-familiar languages or for titles posing potential difficulties, though in a more-familiar language, on the assumption that the user of this guide will have a modest knowledge of French, German, Italian, and Spanish. This same assumption was made for the occasional quotations provided in the annotations for foreign-language publications.

Cross-References

Cross-reference numbers are used throughout in entries to send the user to a main entry for a work or collection from which a particular title is extracted, in headnotes to refer the user to other titles which discuss a particular work or topic, and in the indexes. Cross-reference numbers found in the annotations for collections indicate the titles included in the collection that are entered and annotated elsewhere. Cross-reference numbers in the annotations throughout will also direct the user to a prior annotation for the same entry, to the published version of an unpublished dissertation (section Z only), or to a title described in or relevant to the annotation.

Abbreviations and Reference Terms

Abbreviations are used throughout this bibliography for Virginia Woolf's name (VW) and for the titles of her two most frequently discussed works of fiction: MRS. DALLOWAY (MD) and TO THE LIGHTHOUSE (TL). Abbreviations are not used, however, in entry titles, in quotations, or whenever there appears to be a possibility for confusion. For journal abbreviations, see the list that follows.

The most frequently used, and perhaps unfamiliar reference terms are "passim" ("throughout the work" and "here and there") and "cf." (within parentheses—indicates a comparison made by the author of the book or article annotated). Quotations within the annotations are from the work annotated unless otherwise attributed.

Dates of Coverage and Item Count

The terminal date of this bibliography was 1 January 1984. The total number of entries is 1,358.

PERIODICAL ABBREVIATIONS

Only a limited number of abbreviations have been adopted for the most frequently cited periodicals in this guide. These abbreviations have been used consistently throughout the bibliography, except when the periodical itself is the main entry. That is, special issues are classified as "essay collections" and entered alphabetically, by the name of the periodical.

BNYPL	*Bulletin of the New York Public Library*
CE	*College English*
ConL	*Contemporary Literature*
DA	*Dissertation Abstracts*
DAI	*Dissertation Abstracts International*
L&P	*Literature and Psychology*
MFS	*Modern Fiction Studies*
PMLA	*Publications of the Modern Language Association of America*
RS	*Research Studies*
TCL	*Twentieth Century Literature*
TSLL	*Texas Studies in Literature and Language*
UTQ	*University of Toronto Quarterly*
VQR	*Virginia Quarterly Review*

Part 1
Primary Bibliography

A. MAJOR WORKS

This slightly annotated, chronological checklist provides initial English and American publication information for VW's principal writings and for posthumously published anthologies, collections, and selections of her works. The annotations supply contents for collections (*complete* for story collections, *selective* for essay collections), original separate publication dates for collected writings, cross-references to whole or partial reprintings, and other important publication information (including cross-references to textual commentaries and publishing histories). For VW's posthumously published autobiographical writings, diaries, and letters, see section B below. For scholarly editions and transcriptions of her manuscripts, see section C below. And for full bibliographical data on all VW's publications, through 1979, see Kirkpatrick's bibliography (E7).

The following section is subdivided into three parts:

A, i.   Novels (A1-A9)
A, ii. Short Fiction (A10-A16)
A, iii. Miscellaneous Writings (A17-A39)

A, i. Novels

A1 THE VOYAGE OUT. London: Duckworth, 1915. New York: Doran, 1920.
    For manuscript information see C2. For textual commentaries see G41, H121, J2, J6, J9, and J15.

A2 NIGHT AND DAY. London: Duckworth, 1919. New York: Doran, 1920.
    For textual commentary see H121.

A3 JACOB'S ROOM. London: Hogarth, 1922. New York: Harcourt, 1923.
    For textual commentary see H121.

A4 MRS. DALLOWAY. London: Hogarth; New York: Harcourt, 1925.
    For textual commentaries see M36, M38, M47, M51, and M81. Also see A16, A20, and T6.

A5 TO THE LIGHTHOUSE. London: Hogarth; New York: Harcourt, 1927.
    For manuscript information see C7. For textual commentaries see N28 and N62.

A6 ORLANDO: A BIOGRAPHY. New York: Crosby Gaige; London: Hogarth, 1928.
    For manuscript information see C9. For textual commentary see P15.

4   Fiction

A7   THE WAVES. London: Hogarth; New York: Harcourt, 1931.
         For manuscript information see C6. For textual
         commentaries see Q24-Q26, Q30. And for a con-
         cordance see D2.

A8   THE YEARS. London: Hogarth; New York: Harcourt, 1937.
         For manuscript information see C3. For textual
         commentaries see R3, R7, R9, R11, R19, R20, and
         R24.

A9   BETWEEN THE ACTS. London: Hogarth; New York: Harcourt, 1941.
         For manuscript information see C5. For textual
         commentary see S18. And for a concordance see
         D1.

A, ii. Short Fiction

Listed here are all uncollected stories, separately published stories,
and story collections, including posthumous publications. Dates for
previous periodical publication of individual stories in the collections are provided in the annotations. For fuller publication data,
see Kirkpatrick (E7). Also see C8.

A10 THE MARK ON THE WALL. Richmond, Engl.: Hogarth, 1917.
         Contains the title story (revised and reprinted
         in A12 and A13) and Leonard Woolf's "Three Jews."
         First publication of the Woolfs' Hogarth Press.

A11 KEW GARDENS. Richmond, Engl.: Hogarth, 1919.
         Separately published story, reprinted in A12
         and A13.

A12 MONDAY OR TUESDAY. Richmond, Engl.: Hogarth; New York: Har-
     court, 1921.
         Contents:
             "A Haunted House"
             "A Society"
             "Monday or Tuesday"
             "An Unwritten Novel" (1920)
             "The String Quartet"
             "Blue and Green"
             "Kew Gardens" (above)
             "The Mark on the Wall" (A10)
         All stories except "A Society" and "Blue and
         Green" reprinted below.

A13 A HAUNTED HOUSE, AND OTHER SHORT STORIES. London: Hogarth;
     New York: Harcourt, 1944.
         Contents:
             "A Haunted House" (A12)
             "Monday or Tuesday" (A12)
             "An Unwritten Novel" (A12)

"The String Quartet" (A12)
"Kew Gardens" (A11, A12)
"The Mark on the Wall" (A10, A12)
"The New Dress" (1927)
"The Shooting Party" (1938)
"Lappin and Lapinova" (1939)
"Solid Objects" (1920)
"The Lady in the Looking-Glass: A Reflection" (1929)
"The Duchess and the Jeweller" (1938)
"Moments of Being: 'Slater's Pins Have No Points'" (1928)
"The Man Who Loved His Kind"
"The Searchlight"
"The Legacy"
"Together and Apart"
"A Summing Up"
Four stories reprinted in A16.

A14 NURSE LUGTON'S GOLDEN THIMBLE. London: Hogarth, 1966.
Uncollected and previously unpublished children's story, discovered in 1965.

A15 A COCKNEY'S FARMING EXPERIENCES. Ed. Suzanne Henig. San Diego, Calif.: San Diego State Univ. Press, 1972.
Two uncollected and previously unpublished early stories (c. 1892). Includes the title story and the unfinished "Experiences of a Pater-familias."
See T15.

A16 MRS. DALLOWAY'S PARTY: A SHORT STORY SEQUENCE. Ed. Stella McNichol. London: Hogarth, 1973. New York: Harcourt, 1975.
Seven stories, four previously collected, directly or thematically related to VW's novel, MD. Contents:
"Mrs. Dalloway in Bond Street" (1923)
"The Man Who Loved His Kind" (in A13)
"The Introduction"
"Ancestors"
"Together and Apart" (in A13)
"The New Dress" (in A13)
"A Summing Up" (in A13)
See T20.

A, iii. Miscellaneous Writings

For full contents of the various essay collections listed here, as well as complete listings of VW's contributions to books, periodical publications, translations, and other miscellaneous nonfiction, see Kirkpatrick (E7). Also see C1, C5, C10, and X48.

A17 *STAVROGIN'S CONFESSION* AND *THE PLAN OF THE LIFE OF A GREAT SINNER*, BY F. M. DOSTOEVSKY. Trans. S. S. Koteliansky and Virginia Woolf. Richmond, Engl.: Hogarth, 1922.
    VW's and Koteliansky's first, and most significant collaborative translation.

A18 MR. BENNETT AND MRS. BROWN. London: Hogarth, 1924.
    Separately published essay, first in the "Hogarth Essays" series. Previously published in 1923, in an earlier version, and, in its present version, as "Character in Fiction" (1924). Collected in A28, A31, A32, and G49. Also see F48 and H16.

A19 THE COMMON READER. London: Hogarth; New York: Harcourt, 1925.
    Collects twenty-five biographical and critical essays, including the title essay, "Defoe," "Addison," "Jane Austen," "Modern Fiction" (reprinted in A31, G44, and N1), "JANE EYRE and WUTHERING HEIGHTS," "George Eliot," "The Russian Point of View," and "Joseph Conrad." All essays reprinted in A32.

A20 "Introduction." In MRS. DALLOWAY. New York: Modern Library, 1928. Pp. v-ix.
    VW's important revelation that Mrs. Dalloway "was originally to kill herself, or perhaps merely to die" at the novel's end. Reprinted in G44.

A21 A ROOM OF ONE'S OWN. New York: Fountain Press; London: Hogarth, 1929.
    Extracts reprinted in A31.

A22 THE COMMON READER: SECOND SERIES. London: Hogarth, 1932. Published as THE SECOND COMMON READER. New York: Harcourt, 1932.
    Collects twenty-six biographical and critical essays, including "ROBINSON CRUSOE," "THE SENTIMENTAL JOURNEY," "Beau Brummell" (also separately published, 1930), "Mary Wollstonecraft," "Dorothy Wordsworth," "George Gissing," "The Novels of George Meredith," and "The Novels of Thomas Hardy." All essays reprinted in A32.

A23 FLUSH: A BIOGRAPHY. London: Hogarth; New York: Harcourt, 1933.

A24 THREE GUINEAS. London: Hogarth; New York: Harcourt, 1938.
     Extracts reprinted in A31.

A25 ROGER FRY: A BIOGRAPHY. London: Hogarth; New York: Harcourt,
     1940.

A26 THE DEATH OF THE MOTH, AND OTHER ESSAYS. Ed. Leonard Woolf.
     London: Hogarth; New York: Harcourt, 1942.
          Collects twenty-eight biographical and critical
          essays and sketches, including the title sketch,
          "Street Haunting: A London Adventure" (also
          separately published, 1930), "Henry James"
          (three essays), "George Moore," "The Novels of
          E. M. Forster," "The Art of Biography," "A
          Letter to a Young Poet" (also separately pub-
          lished, 1932), and "Professions for Women"
          (reprinted in A31; also see C3). All titles
          reprinted in A32.

A27 THE MOMENT, AND OTHER ESSAYS. Ed. Leonard Woolf. London:
     Hogarth, 1947. New York: Harcourt, 1948.
          Collects thirty biographical and critical
          essays and sketches, including the title
          sketch, "On Being Ill" (also separately
          published, 1930), "THE FAERY QUEEN,"
          "Sir Walter Scott" (two essays), "DAVID
          COPPERFIELD," "Notes on D. H. Lawrence,"
          "Roger Fry" (also separately published,
          1935), "The Art of Fiction," and "The
          Leaning Tower" (reprinted in A31).
          All titles reprinted in A32.

A28 THE CAPTAIN'S DEATH BED, AND OTHER ESSAYS. Ed. Leonard Woolf.
     New York: Harcourt; London: Hogarth, 1950.
          Collects twenty-five biographical and critical
          essays and sketches, including the title essay,
          "Oliver Goldsmith," "Ruskin," "The Novels of
          Turgenev," "Leslie Stephen" (reprinted in N1),
          "Mr. Bennett and Mrs. Brown" (see A18), "Re-
          viewing" (also published separately, 1939),
          and "Walter Sickert" (also published separ-
          ately, 1934). All titles reprinted in A32.

A29 GRANITE AND RAINBOW: ESSAYS. Ed. Leonard Woolf. London:
     Hogarth; New York: Harcourt, 1958.
          Collects twenty-eight biographical and critical
          essays, including "The Narrow Bridge of Art,"
          "Hours in a Library" (also separately published,
          1958), "Life and the Novelist," "A Terribly
          Sensitive Mind," "Women and Fiction," and "The
          New Biography" (reprinted in A31). All essays
          reprinted in A32.

A30 CONTEMPORARY WRITERS. Comp. Jean Guiguet. London: Hogarth, 1965. New York: Harcourt, 1966.
    Collects six of VW's general essays on reviewing and literary criticism, and forty of her critical essays and reviews on contemporary authors (e.g., Bennett, Butler, Douglas, Forster, Galsworthy, Huxley, Lawrence, Richardson, and Wells). Includes "Women Novelists," "Philosophy in Fiction," and "Freudian Fiction." See X28.

A31 VIRGINIA WOOLF: SELECTIONS FROM HER ESSAYS. Ed. Walter James. London: Chatto and Windus, 1966.
    Anthology of twenty-five essays and selections, arranged under three subheadings: Political Writings, Literary and Other Critical Essays, and Biography. Includes "Professions for Women" (in A26), "Mr. Bennett and Mrs. Brown" (A18), "Modern Fiction" (in A19), "The Leaning Tower" (in A27), and "The New Biography" (in A29), five extracts from A ROOM OF ONE'S OWN (A21), and two extracts from THREE GUINEAS (A24). See X36.

A32 COLLECTED ESSAYS, BY VIRGINIA WOOLF. 4 vols. Ed. Leonard Woolf. London: Hogarth, 1966-67. New York: Harcourt, 1967.
    Collects and rearranges (in chronological order and by subject), the contents of VW's first six essay collections (155 titles in all; see A19, A22, A26, A27, A28, A29). Volumes 1-2 are predominantly the critical essays, volumes 3-4 the biographical essays.

A33 STEPHEN VERSUS GLADSTONE. Headington Quarry, Engl.: Rampant Lions Press, 1967.
    Uncollected juvenile essay (c. 1892).
    (Pamphlet--8 pp.)

A34 "Three Characters." ADAM INTERNATIONAL REVIEW, Nos. 364-66 (1972), pp. 24-30.
    Gathers sketches of "The Low Brow, the High Brow, the Broad Brow," a note on Stendhal, and three letters to Angus Davidson (1926-38). See G1.

A35 THE LONDON SCENE: FIVE ESSAYS. New York: Hallman, 1975.
    Five previously uncollected essays on London locales (1931-32).

A36 FRESHWATER: A COMEDY. Ed. Lucio P. Ruotolo. New York: Harcourt; London: Hogarth, 1976.
    First publication of the two versions (1923, 1935) of VW's only play, a comedy concerning the Victorian photographer Julia Cameron. Privately performed in 1935. See Y4.

A37 BOOKS AND PORTRAITS: SOME FURTHER SELECTIONS FROM THE LITERARY AND BIOGRAPHICAL WRITINGS OF VIRGINIA WOOLF. Ed. Mary Lyon. London: Hogarth, 1977. New York: Harcourt, 1978.
> Gathers forty-eight previously uncollected, early essays, many originally reviews (c. 1900-15). Includes thirty-nine articles on literary subjects and figures (e.g., Austen, Brooke, Coleridge, Dostoevsky, Emerson, Kipling, Melville, Sassoon, Thoreau), nine biographical essays, and the editor's brief "Introduction" (pp. vii-x).

A38 "Virginia Woolf's 'Byron and Mr. Briggs.'" Ed. Edward A. Hungerford. YALE REVIEW, 68 (1979), 325-49.
> First publication of VW's unfinished essay (1922) on the "common reader's" response to Byron. (Introductory comment by Hungerford, pp. 321-24).

A39 WOMEN AND WRITING. Ed. Michèle Barrett. New York: Harcourt, 1979.
> Collects twenty-five previously published essays and extracts on the status of women and on women writers (including Austen, Mansfield, Richardson). Includes five previously uncollected articles. See X8.

B. AUTOBIOGRAPHICAL WRITINGS, DIARIES, LETTERS, AND DOCUMENTS

For additional publications containing letters by VW, see "Three Characters" (A34), Collet (F21), Ruas (F84), Smith (F87), Novak (G62), LA QUINZAINE LITTÉRAIRE (G67), and Sackville-West (P29).

B1 THE DIARY OF VIRGINIA WOOLF. Vol. 1: 1915-1919. Ed. Anne Oliver Bell. London: Hogarth; New York: Harcourt, 1977. Vol. 2: 1920-1924; Vol. 3: 1925-1930; Vol. 4: 1931-35. Ed. Anne Oliver Bell and Andrew McNeillie. London: Hogarth; New York: Harcourt, 1978; 1980; 1982.
 Full publication of VW's diaries, 1915-41 (also see B6), to be completed in five volumes. Bibliographical, biographical, and textual annotations provided. Well-indexed. See F12.

B2 THE LETTERS OF VIRGINIA WOOLF. Vol. 1: THE FLIGHT OF THE MIND, 1888-1912 (VIRGINIA STEPHEN); Vol. 2: THE QUESTION OF THINGS HAPPENING, 1912-1922; Vol. 3: A CHANGE OF PERSPECTIVE, 1923-1928; Vol. 4: A REFLECTION OF THE OTHER PERSON, 1929-1931; Vol. 5: THE SICKLE SIDE OF THE MOON, 1932-1935; Vol. 6: LEAVE THE LETTERS TILL WE'RE DEAD, 1936-1941. Ed. Nigel Nicolson and Joanne Trautmann. London: Hogarth; New York: Harcourt, 1975; 1976; 1977; 1978; 1979; 1980.
 Scrupulously edited, generously annotated, and well-indexed publication of VW's correspondence, averaging over 600 letters per volume. Each volume contains an introduction to the biographical backgrounds of the letters. (Note: English edition publishes subtitle first; the American edition omits the subtitle altogether. In the interests of space and clarity, the above entry conflates the American and English titles.) Assimilates B4.

B3 MOMENTS OF BEING: UNPUBLISHED AUTOBIOGRAPHICAL WRITINGS. Ed. Jeanne Schulkind. London: Chatto and Windus, Sussex Univ. Press; New York: Harcourt, 1976.
 Draws together from VW's unpublished papers her various memories and reminiscences, most of which were never intended for publication in their present unrevised state. Useful supplement to the DIARIES and LETTERS. Includes "Reminiscences," "A Sketch of the Past," "The Memoir Club Contributions: 22 Hyde Park Gate," "Old Bloomsbury," and "Am I a Snob?" See U30.

B4 VIRGINIA WOOLF & LYTTON STRACHEY: LETTERS. Ed. Leonard Woolf and James Strachey. London: Hogarth, Chatto and Windus; New York: Harcourt, 1956.
> Both sides of the Woolf-Strachey correspondence: 105 letters and cards (1906-31). Several "trivial" notes and sensitive passages omitted. VW's letters absorbed, with most omissions restored, into THE LETTERS OF VIRGINIA WOOLF (B2).

B5 "The Will of Virginia Woolf." VIRGINIA WOOLF QUARTERLY, 2, Nos. 1-2 (1975), 28-29.
> Photocopy and transcription of VW's will (1930).

B6 A WRITER'S DIARY: BEING EXTRACTS FROM THE DIARY OF VIRGINIA WOOLF. Ed. Leonard Woolf. London: Hogarth, 1953. New York: Harcourt, 1954.
> Considerably abridged version of VW's diaries, 1918-41. Includes a useful glossary of names and an index. Extracts reprinted in F31 and N1. Also see B1.

C. MANUSCRIPT TRANSCRIPTIONS AND SCHOLARLY EDITIONS

C1 "'Anon' and 'The Reader': Virginia Woolf's Last Essays." Ed. Brenda R. Silver. TCL, 25 (1979), 356-441.
   Reconstruction of VW's work in progress at the time of her death, a "Common History" book. Includes several editorial introductions and notes. See C4.

C2 "MELYMBROSIA," BY VIRGINIA WOOLF: AN EARLY VERSION OF *THE VOYAGE OUT*. Ed. Louise A. DeSalvo. New York: New York Public Library, 1982.
   Annotated transcription of the second of four lengthy drafts of VW's first novel, "the earliest nearly complete version which survives (probably in progress from 1909-1912) of the novel which was published as THE VOYAGE OUT in 1915." Also includes DeSalvo's "Introduction" (see J6) and three appendixes: "Later Versions of Missing Passages" (pp. 247-60), edited "Fragments of a Very Early Draft" (1908; pp. 261-70), and a table of "Variants and Editorial Emendations" for the manuscript transcription (pp. 271-99).

C3 "THE PARGITERS": THE NOVEL-ESSAY PORTION OF *THE YEARS*. Ed. Mitchell A. Leaska. New York: New York Public Library, 1977. London: Hogarth, 1978.
   First publication of the feminist essays originally intended to be included in the first chapter of THE YEARS ("1880"), as commentary on and counterpoint to the fictional chapter. Also includes Leaska's "Introduction" (see R9), several deleted fictional "extracts," and a previously unpublished feminist speech (1931--a longer version of "Professions for Women," see A26). Reviewed in H225.

C4 TWENTIETH CENTURY LITERATURE. 25 (1979), i-v, 237-441. "Virginia Woolf Issue."
   Special tribute issue, publishing for the first time edited texts of an early story fragment, three essays, and manuscript extracts, with editorial introductions and notes. Includes C1, C8, C9, and C11.

C5 VIRGINIA WOOLF, "POINTZ HALL": THE EARLIER AND LATER TYPESCRIPTS OF *BETWEEN THE ACTS*. Ed. Mitchell A. Leaska. New York: John Jay Press, 1982.
   Edited transcriptions of the first two (of three) drafts of VW's last novel (1938-40).

Leaska also provides an "Introduction," an "Afterword," and two sections of factual and interpretive annotations for the typescripts (see S18), and seven editorial appendixes. Lola Szladits, curator of the Berg Collection, contributes a brief "Personal Note" (pp. ix-xi) describing her sorting and cataloguing of the severely scrambled typescripts after they were acquired by the New York Public Library in 1958.

C6   VIRGINIA WOOLF, *THE WAVES*: THE TWO HOLOGRAPH DRAFTS. Ed. John W. Graham. Toronto: Univ. of Toronto Press, 1976.
Annotated transcriptions of the surviving holograph material for THE WAVES, comprising two essentially complete drafts (1929-30, 1930-31), with the editor's "Introduction" (see Q25) and four brief appendixes. Reviewed in Q17.

C7   VIRGINIA WOOLF, *TO THE LIGHTHOUSE*: THE ORIGINAL HOLOGRAPH DRAFT. Ed. Susan Dick. Toronto: Univ. of Toronto Press, 1982.
Annotated transcription of the one surviving holograph draft of TL (1925-27), with the editor's "Introduction" (see N28), and four appendixes: transcriptions of VW's working notes (1925), her outline to "Time Passes," four essay fragments contained within the manuscripts, and a chronology for TL's composition.

C8   "Virginia Woolf's 'Friendships Gallery.'" Ed. Ellen Hawkes. TCL, 25 (1979), 270-302.
"Spoof biography" of VW's friend and teacher, Violet Dickinson. Includes editorial "Introduction" (pp. 270-74) and "Notes" (pp. 300-02). See C4.

C9   "Virginia Woolf's ORLANDO: An Edition of the Manuscript." Ed. Madeline Moore. TCL, 25 (1979), 303-55.
Publishes significant variations between a manuscript and the final versions of the novel. Includes editorial "Introduction" (pp. 303-07), "Notes and Commentary" (pp. 340-46), and several appendixes. See C4.

C10   VIRGINIA WOOLF'S READING NOTEBOOKS. Ed. Brenda R. Silver. Princeton, N. J.: Princeton Univ. Press, 1983.
Publishes extracts, with editorial commentaries, and "describes, dates, and identifies the sources of sixty-seven volumes" of VW's reading notes (1905-41), found among her papers in the New York Public and Univ. of Sussex libraries. Also includes Silver's "Introduction" (see X53), textual notes, bibliographical appendixes, and a useful subject index.

C11 "Virginia Woolf's 'The Journal of Mistress Joan Martyn.'" Ed.
Susan M. Squier and Louise A. DeSalvo. TCL, 25 (1979), 237-69.
Unfinished early story (1906) concerning a
woman historian's researches; titled by the
editors. Includes editorial "Introduction"
(pp. 237-39) and "Notes" (pp. 268-69). See C4

D. CONCORDANCES

In addition to the two titles below, Oxford Microforms Ltd. has announced the forthcoming microfiche publication of computer concordances for VW's remaining novels. For a "Glossary" for ORLANDO, see Steele et al. (P32).

D1 Haule, James M., and Philip H. Smith, Jr., eds. A CONCORDANCE TO *BETWEEN THE ACTS* BY VIRGINIA WOOLF. Oxford Engl.: Oxford Microform Publications, 1982.
> Contains the editors' introductory note on "The Condition of the Text" (pp. 1-6), a list of selected variants between the American and English editions (pp. 6-8), a page-number conversion table for the American and English editions (pp. 9-11), and, on six microfiche cards, *complete* "Key Word in Context" concordances for the American edition of both the novel and the play within the novel.

D2 Haule, James M., and Philip H. Smith, Jr., eds. A CONCORDANCE TO *THE WAVES* BY VIRGINIA WOOLF. Oxford, Engl.: Oxford Microform Publications, 1981.
> Contains the editors' introductory comment on the "Editions of THE WAVES" (pp. 1-2), a list of the major variants between the American and English editions of the novel (pp. 2-10), a page-number conversion table for the American and English editions (pp. 11-13), and, on fourteen microfiche cards, a *complete* "Key Word in Context" concordance for the American edition of the novel.

Part 2
Secondary Bibliography

For information on the scope and arrangement of this bibliography
see the introduction.

Note: There are three irregularly-appearing periodicals concerned
with VW and her works: THE VIRGINIA WOOLF NEWSLETTER (1971--),
THE VIRGINIA WOOLF QUARTERLY (1972--), and THE VIRGINIA WOOLF MIS-
CELLANY (1973--). Each of these journals publishes bibliographical,
biographical, and critical material on VW. THE VIRGINIA WOOLF QUAR-
TERLY also contains information and commentary on VW's "friends,
associates, and acquaintances," as well as on contemporary works of
art and literature which reflect the continuing influence of Bloomsbury.

E. BIBLIOGRAPHIES

Also see Gaither (F33), Spater (F88), Blackstone (G8), Gorsky (G28), Guiguet (G30), Freedman (H86), Jackson (H124), Grünewald-Huber (Q3), McLaurin (Q38), Moore (R16), and Steele (X7).

E1 Barrett, Michèle. "Towards a Virginia Woolf Criticism." In THE SOCIOLOGY OF LITERATURE: APPLIED STUDIES. Ed. Diana Laurenson. Keele, Engl.: Univ. of Keele, 1978. Pp. 145-60.
> Describes the "common aspects" of VW criticism and argues that most commentaries on VW are "unsatisfactory" because they underestimate her radical, anti-authoritarian politics and sociology.

E2 Beebe, Maurice, comp. "Criticism of Virginia Woolf: A Selected Checklist with an Index to Studies of Separate Works." MFS, 2 (1956), 36-45.
> Still useful checklist of VW studies, though now very dated. Supplemented by Weiser (E14). Also see G55.

E3 Füger, Wilhelm. EINE "EXTRAVAGANTE ENGLÄNDERIN": UNTERSUCHUNGEN ZUR DEUTSCHEN FRÜHREZEPTION VON VIRGINIA WOOLF. Heidelberg: Winter, 1980.
> A very useful survey and summary of the German critical response to VW, from the first mentions in the early twenties to the obituaries in 1941. Füger opens by discussing the present status of VW in English-speaking countries, noting Majumdar's irresponsible ignorance of German scholarship in her slipshod bibliography (E9) and Majumdar's and McLaurin's total omission of German commentaries in their "Critical Heritage" volume (G49). The body of Füger's book describes the growing continental awareness of VW and German reviews and commentaries from 1923 to the war, chiefly concentrating on the most active years, 1928-35, and devoting several paragraphs to the major critics (e.g., Bernhard Fehr, Reinald Hoops) and the book-length publications (see G5, G23, G29, G46, and G85). His survey concludes with a note on the post-war rediscovery of VW (Erich Auerbach [see N7], and after). [In German; English "Summary," pp. 103-05.]

E4 Henig, Suzanne. "Bibliography of Hogarth Press Publications (1917-1946)." VIRGINIA WOOLF QUARTERLY, 2 (1975), 106-52.
    Annual lists of authors and titles for all Hogarth Press publications, 1917-1946, arranged by subject, and for all "Hogarth Series" publications. Also see F33.

E5 Holleyman, G. A., comp. CATALOGUE OF BOOKS FROM THE LIBRARY OF LEONARD AND VIRGINIA WOOLF: TAKEN FROM MONKS HOUSE, RODMELL, SUSSEX, AND 24 VICTORIA SQUARE, LONDON, AND NOW IN THE POSSESSION OF WASHINGTON STATE UNIVERSITY, PULLMAN, U.S.A. Brighton, Engl.: Holleyman and Treacher, 1975.
    Incomplete and confusingly arranged catalogue of the Woolfs' library (including items from Leslie Stephen's library). Fortunately contains an index of authors represented. Also see F88 and X7.

E6 Inglis, Anthony A. H. "Virginia Woolf et la critique"; "Discussion." Trans. Christine Giudia and Suzanne Lévy. In VIRGINIA WOOLF—COLLOQUE DE CERISY. Ed. Maurice deGandillac and Jean Guiguet. Pp. 219-41; 243-50. See F34.
    Chronicles the weaknesses and limitations of most critical discussion of VW, from the populist philistinism of the Marxists (e.g., Kettle; see N60) and the grotesque distortions of the SCRUTINY critics (e.g., Mellers; see R14), to the well-intentioned yet inadequate studies by the admirers of VW and the radical revaluations of contemporary theoretical critics. [In French.]

E7 Kirkpatrick, Brownlee Jean, ed. A BIBLIOGRAPHY OF VIRGINIA WOOLF. 1957. 3rd ed. Oxford: Clarendon, 1980.
    The standard primary bibliography. Contains full collations and notes for first and all subsequent editions, through 1979, of VW's books and pamphlets (54 titles), and of her translations and contributions to books, excluding anthology selections (18 titles), an annual checklist of VW's contributions to periodicals, 1904-79 (532 titles, including 152 items identified since this bibliography's first edition in 1957), and lists of "doubtful and untraced" periodical contributions (47 titles), of the translations of VW's works, in twenty-five languages, of foreign language editions of her works, of scattered publications of her letters, and of the locations of her manuscripts. Indexed.

E8 McNeillie, Andrew, ed. AN ANNOTATED CRITICAL BIBLIOGRAPHY OF VIRGINIA WOOLF. Totowa, N. J.: Barnes and Noble, 1983.
    "Includes sections on manuscript materials, sources, and editions of her works; biographic information; criticism and commentary. Sections

on the Victorian patriarchal heritage, the philosophic and Apostolic Cambridge background, and the Bloomsbury Group are also provided." (Quoted from publisher's announcement. Published late in 1983 and not seen.)

E9 Majumdar, Robin, ed. VIRGINIA WOOLF: AN ANNOTATED BIBLIOGRAPHY OF CRITICISM, 1915-1974. New York: Garland, 1976.
Incomplete and consistently inaccurate listings of books, articles, chapters, introductions, memoirs, correspondence, and reviews concerning VW and her works. Arranged alphabetically by author, under seven topical headings. 1170 items, with only selected major titles briefly annotated. Slight index. See E3.

E10 Majumdar, Robin, and Allen McLaurin. "Introduction." In VIRGINIA WOOLF: THE CRITICAL HERITAGE. Ed. Majumdar and McLaurin. Pp. 1-46. See G49.
Useful survey of VW's growing critical reputation, 1915-41, in England, France, and America, with a brief overview of later critical studies.

E11 Novak, Jane, ed. "Recent Criticism of Virginia Woolf: January 1970-June 1972. Abstracts of Published Criticism and Unpublished Dissertations." VIRGINIA WOOLF QUARTERLY, 1, No. 1 (1972), 141-55.
Of limited use. For an extensive checklist of dissertations on VW, see section Z of this bibliography.

E12 Rudikoff, Sonya. "Afraid of Virginia Woolf?" AMERICAN SCHOLAR, 47 (1978), 245, 247-49, 251-52, 254, 270-71.
Overview of "the size and scope of the... Woolf revival" between 1970 and 1975.

E13 Toerien, B. J., comp. A BIBLIOGRAPHY OF VIRGINIA WOOLF (STEPHEN), "MRS. LEONARD SIDNEY WOOLF," 1882-1941. Cape Town: Privately printed, 1943.
Annotated list of books, articles, reviews, and bibliographies concerning VW, and of novels, stories, translations, and essays by VW, together with partial lists of translations, portraits, and obituaries of VW. Despite its early date, this bibliography would still be useful were it more generally available.

E14 Weiser, Barbara, comp. "Criticism of Virginia Woolf from 1956 to the Present: A Selected Checklist with an Index to Studies of Separate Works." MFS, 18 (1972), 477-86.
Supplements Beebe's checklist (E2). See G56.

E15 Wiley, Paul L., comp. "Virginia Woolf (1882-1941)." In THE
BRITISH NOVEL: CONRAD TO THE PRESENT. Northbrook, Ill.: AHM,
1973. Pp. 114-18.
   Brief primary and secondary checklist.

F. BIOGRAPHIES, MEMOIRS, REMINISCENCES, INTERVIEWS

Note: A writer as frequently autobiographical as VW, and whose sources of inspiration have been so often traced to her personal experiences, invites criticism which often shades into biography, and biographies and memoirs of critical value. In this bibliography every attempt has been made to locate writings that are primarily biographical in matter, or value, in this subdivision, although discrimination has not always been easy. Similarly, essay collections which devote over half their contents to biographical material have been entered here. Many of the book-length studies and essays entered in subsequent sections, however, do summarize the life of VW, apply the biography to her works, or reflect her personal relationships with a number of her critics.

For a fuller study of the biographical materials concerning VW, consult her diaries, letters, and autobiographical writings (listed in section B above), and the various commentaries on her personal writings (in section U below). Also see Hill (X31).

F1 Alley, Henry M. "A Rediscovered Eulogy: Virginia Woolf's 'Miss Janet Case: Classical Scholar and Teacher.'" TCL, 28 (1982), 290-301.
    Backgrounds to VW's obituary of her teacher Case, "one of the most important and sustained influences in her life." (Here reprinted from the LONDON TIMES, 1937; pp. 298-300.)

F2 Alpers, Antony. "Katherine and Virginia, 1917-1923." In THE LIFE OF KATHERINE MANSFIELD. 1953. 2nd ed. New York: Viking, 1980. Pp. 247-61.
    Account of VW's friendship and competition with Mansfield. (Also see numerous additional references to VW, passim.)

F3 Annan, Noel. "The Intellectual Aristocracy." In STUDIES IN SOCIAL HISTORY. Ed. John H. Plumb. London: Longmans, 1955. Pp. 243-87.
    Traces the labyrinthine familial relationships within the newly emerging intellectual class of the twentieth century, the lineal descendants of the major intellectuals of the nineteenth century (the Stephens, including VW, pp. 274-77).

F4 -----. LESLIE STEPHEN: HIS THOUGHT AND CHARACTER IN RELATION TO HIS TIME. Cambridge, Mass.: Harvard Univ. Press, 1952. Passim.
    Comments on VW's relations with and debts to her parents, Leslie and Julia Stephen. Extracts reprinted in N1.

F5 Back, Kurt W. "Clapham to Bloomsbury: Life Course Analysis of an Intellectual Aristocracy." BIOGRAPHY, 5 (1982), 38-52.
     Considers the possibilities of combining the methods of the individual biographer and the sociological study of the group, for analyzing the evolution of the nineteenth-century Clapham Sect into the Bloomsbury Group.

F6 Bagnold, Enid. "Virginia." ADAM INTERNATIONAL REVIEW, Nos. 364-66 (1972), p. 15.
     Memoir of a few brief meetings with VW in the early forties, in Sussex. See G1.

F7 Beer, John. "Forster, Lawrence, Virginia Woolf, and Bloomsbury." ALIGARH JOURNAL OF ENGLISH STUDIES, 5 (1980), 6-37.
     Not seen.

F8 Bell, Clive. "Virginia Woolf." In OLD FRIENDS: PERSONAL RECOLLECTIONS. New York: Harcourt, 1957. Pp. 92-118.
     Character sketch of VW as a high spirited and "loveable," but not tormented genius, by her brother-in-law. Extract reprinted in F70.

F9 Bell, Millicent. "Portrait of the Artist as a Young Woman." VQR, 52 (1976), 670-86.
     Traces VW's growing sense of her feminine personality through the autobiographical hints in her fiction.

F10 Bell, Quentin. BLOOMSBURY. New York: Basic Books, 1968. Passim.
     VW referred to throughout the discussions of the ideas and personalities of Bloomsbury.

F11 -----. "Bloomsbury and 'the Vulgar Passions.'" CRITICAL INQUIRY, 6 (1979), 239-56.
     Attacks the commonplace view of VW and the Bloomsbury Group as isolated aesthetes, illustrating their concern for "the machinery of government" and the "mobilization of opinion."

F12 -----. "Introduction." In THE DIARY OF VIRGINIA WOOLF. Ed. Anne Oliver Bell. I, xiii-xxviii. See B1.
     Praises VW's DIARIES as a "major work" and provides biographical backgrounds for his wife's edition.

F13 -----. VIRGINIA WOOLF: A BIOGRAPHY. New York: Harcourt, 1972.
     The standard biography, by VW's nephew. Despite the family connection, however, Bell succeeds in presenting a balanced and uncensored portrait of VW's life, her relationships (especially within the Bloomsbury Group),

and her struggles with her mental illness,
inviting controversy in his speculation on
the sources of VW's breakdowns in childhood
and adolescent traumas (early deaths of her
mother and beloved step-sister, overbearing
father, "fondling" affection of step-brother).
Bell's avoidance of critical comment on the
works, however, at times suggests a fundamental lack of sympathy with his subject.
Published in two- and one-volume editions,
Bell's biography unfortunately retains two
separate paginations and indexes in its
single-volume printings. Extracts reprinted
in F83. For reviews and commentaries see
F22, F39, F40, F45, F54, F73, F80, and F99.
Also see F61, F74, F77, F81, F89, F95, F100,
and G67.

F14 Bell, Vanessa. NOTES ON VIRGINIA'S CHILDHOOD: A MEMOIR. Ed.
Richard J. Schaubeck, Jr. New York: Hallman, 1974.
VW's sister's memories of their childhood and
early adolescence, recounting VW's temperament,
interests, and first attempts at writing. Originally written in the early forties. (Pamphlet--
11 pp.)

F15 Bernikow, Louise. AMONG WOMEN. New York: Harmony, 1980. Pp.
92-104, 126-41, 169-76 and passim.
Essentially biographical survey of VW's relations with women, as a sister (of Vanessa
Bell), a friend (of Katherine Mansfield),
and a lover (of Vita Sackville-West).

F16 Blanche, Jacques-Émile. "Entretien avec Virginia Woolf." NOU-
VELLES LITTÉRAIRES, 13 Aug. 1927, pp. 1-2.
The first of an impressively large number of
French studies exclusively concerned with VW.
In an imitative, Woolfian interior monologue,
the painter and early French champion of her
works summarizes the unanswered questions
occasioned by his brief meeting with VW in
1927. [In French.] Reprinted in translation
in G49. Also see F21 and G34.

F17 Brée, Germaine. "Two Vintage Years: France 1913; England 1922."
VIRGINIA WOOLF QUARTERLY, 1, No. 4 (1973), 19-30.
Parallels between the two "anni mirabili"
of French and English literature, and the
literary communities of the NOUVELLE REVUE
FRANÇAISE (Gide et al.) and Bloomsbury.
Also see F29.

F18 Brenan, Gerald. SOUTH FROM GRANADA. London: Hamilton, 1957.
Pp. 139-46.
Memories of VW's literary opinions and conversation, during her visit to Brenan's Spanish
retreat in 1923. Extract reprinted in F83.

Biographical Materials

F19 Chapman, Robert T. "The 'Enemy' versus Bloomsbury." ADAM INTERNATIONAL REVIEW, No. 364-66 (1972), pp. 81-84.
Surveys Wyndham Lewis's published attacks on VW and Bloomsbury (e.g., X42). See G1 and below.

F20 -----. "The Malefic Cabal." In WYNDHAM LEWIS: FICTIONS AND SATIRES. New York: Barnes and Noble, 1973. Pp. 83-98.
Wyndham Lewis the aesthetic "antithesis" of VW. Summarizes Lewis's assaults on Bloomsbury and VW in THE APES OF GOD (1930), MEN WITHOUT ART (1934; see X42), and THE REVENGE FOR LOVE (1937). Expanded version of essay above.

F21 Collet, Georges-Paul. "Jacques-Émile Blanche and Virginia Woolf." COMPARATIVE LITERATURE, 17 (1965), 73-81.
VW's relationship with the critic and painter Blanche, the man most "responsible for the diffusion of her books in France." Prints an incomplete correspondence (seven letters from VW to Blanche, 1927-31). For Blanche's commentaries on VW, see F16 and H18. Also see G34.

F22 Cook, Blanche Wiesen. "'Women Alone Stir My Imagination': Lesbianism and the Cultural Tradition." SIGNS, 4 (1979), 718-39.
Regrets the confusion among VW's biographers, especially Bell (F13), regarding her homosexuality.

F23 DeSalvo, Louise A. "Lighting the Cave: The Relationship between Vita Sackville-West and Virginia Woolf." SIGNS, 8 (1982), 195-214.
Summarizes VW's love relationship with Sackville-West, which coincided with "the most productive period of each of their lives" (1923-33), and speculates on their influences on each other's creativity (e.g., "Sackville-West probably provided the emotional climate that allowed TO THE LIGHTHOUSE to come into being").

F24 Drabble, Margaret. ARNOLD BENNETT: A BIOGRAPHY. New York: Knopf, 1974. Pp. 291-94 and passim.
Overview of VW's attacks on Bennett, noting their several mutually unrecognized similarities as writers. Also see G21.

F25 Edel, Leon. BLOOMSBURY: A HOUSE OF LIONS. London: Hogarth, 1979. Pp. 85-94, 148-57, 175-86, and passim.
Distinguished biographer and literary historian's survey of the ideological and personal relationships among the Bloomsbury circle. Reviewed in F62 and U26.

F26 -----. "The Madness of Virginia Woolf." In STUFF OF SLEEP AND
DREAMS: EXPERIMENTS IN LITERARY PSYCHOLOGY. New York: Harper
and Row, 1982. Pp. 192-203.
> The sources of VW's tragic and heroic struggle
> with madness found in her "confusion of infan-
> tile sexual feeling." Surveys VW's relations
> to her father and step-brothers, her phobias,
> and her attitudes toward death.

F27 Efron, Arthur. "On Learning to Evade Virginia Woolf." PAUNCH,
No. 52 (1978), pp. 103-12.
> Objects to the concentration on VW's personal
> life and psychological development as a blurring
> of her chief "value, both as artist and as
> human being," which is to be found in her art.
> (Reviews Love's biography [F61]).

F28 Fassler, Barbara. "Theories of Homosexuality as Sources of
Bloomsbury's Androgyny." SIGNS, 5 (1979), 237-51.
> The Bloomsbury Group's ideal of androgyny ex-
> plicitly linked to the homosexuality of sev-
> eral of its members (including VW).

F29 Fawcett, Peter. "Bloomsbury et la France"; "Discussion." In
VIRGINIA WOOLF--COLLOQUE DE CERISY. Ed. Maurice de Gandillac
and Jean Guiguet. Pp. 57-72; 73-82. See F34.
> Surveys relations of Bloomsbury with France and
> French literary life, including a comparison
> with distinctions between the Group and French
> artists and writers, more consciously organized
> in association with the NOUVELLE REVUE FRANÇAISE
> (André Gide et al.). [In French.] Also see F17.

F30 Fiedler, Leslie. "Class War in British Literature." ESQUIRE,
49 (Apr. 1958), 79-81.
> Sees the "angry young men" of the fifties re-
> acting explicitly against the social and intel-
> lectual elitism of "Bloomsbury."

F31 Forrester, Viviane. VIRGINIA WOOLF. Paris: Éditions de LA
QUINZAINE LITTÉRAIRE, 1973.
> Transcriptions of seven ORTF broadcasts (Jan-
> uary 1973), combining discussions, interviews,
> and readings from VW's A WRITER'S DIARY and
> various memoirs of VW, and presenting VW as
> one of the greatest writers of her era: a
> novelist, editor, critic, pamphleteer, mili-
> tant socialist, and precursor of the modern
> women's liberation movement. Forrester's
> broadcasts, respectively, describe the Blooms-
> bury Group, the operations of the Hogarth
> Press (VW's interactions with T. S. Eliot,
> Mansfield, and Freud), her feminism (inter-
> views with Monique Wittig and Ann Tomas),
> memories of VW (interviews with Quentin Bell,

John Lehmann, Victoria Ocampo, Stephen
Spender, and Alix Strachey), VW's madness,
the connections between her madness and her
art (emphasizing the symbolism of water in
her work), and her death. Publishes extensive extracts, in translation, from B6,
F70, and F100. [In French.]

F32 Gadd, David. "Virginia and Leonard." In THE LOVING FRIENDS:
A PORTRAIT OF BLOOMSBURY. New York: Harcourt, 1974. Pp. 154-73.
Summarizes VW's life and writing career,
between the wars, in the general context of
the Bloomsbury Group. (Numerous additional
references to VW elsewhere in Gadd's book.)

F33 Gaither, Mary E. "The Hogarth Press: 1917-1938." In A CHECK-
LIST OF THE HOGARTH PRESS, 1917-1938. Ed. J. Howard Woolmer.
Andes, N. Y.: Woolmer & Brotherson, 1976. Pp. 3-24.
Describes the growth and editorial policies of
the press, during the years of Leonard's and
VW's partnership. (Note: the accompanying
bibliography lists and describes VW's Hogarth
publications.) Also see E4.

F34 Gandillac, Maurice de, and Jean Guiguet, eds. VIRGINIA WOOLF--
COLLOQUE DE CERISY: VIRGINIA WOOLF ET LE GROUPE DE BLOOMSBURY.
Paris: Union Générale d'Éditions, 1977.
Gathering of seven papers, and transcriptions
of subsequent discussions, presented during the
Cerisy-la-Salle colloquim on "Virginia Woolf
and the Bloomsbury Group" in August 1974, to-
gether with Guiguet's introductory comments.
Includes E6, F29, F38, F64, H55, H101, H245,
and V3. [In French.]

F35 Garnett, David. "Keynes, Strachey and Virginia Woolf." LONDON
MAGAZINE, 2 (Sept. 1955), 48-55.
Memories of encounters with several Bloomsbury
figures, during the first war, and admiring
character sketch of VW. (Reprinted from his
FLOWERS OF THE FOREST [London: Chatto and
Windus, 1955].) Extract reprinted in F35.

F36 -----. "Virginia Woolf." 1965. In GREAT FRIENDS. London:
Macmillan, 1979. Pp. 114-30.
Biographical summary, character sketch, and
memoir.

F37 Gillespie, Diane F. "Vanessa Bell, Virginia Woolf, and Duncan
Grant: Conversation with Angelica Garnett." MODERNIST STUDIES,
3 (1979), 151-58.
Interview with Vanessa's daughter (by Duncan
Grant), commenting on VW but principally con-
cerned with Vanessa.

F38 Guiguet, Jean. "Introduction"; "Discussion"; "Conclusions"; "Discussion." In VIRGINIA WOOLF--COLLOQUE DE CERISY. Ed. Maurice de Gandillac and Guiguet. Pp. 9-19; 21-31; 251-56; 257-63. See F34.
    Guiguet notes the increasing academic study and recent publications concerning VW, for the 1974 Cerisy-la-Salle colloquium, questions the oversimplified popular conception of a Bloomsbury "Group," and announces the colloquium's preeminent concerns with VW's intellectual relations. Guiguet's conclusion briefly summarizes the conference's accomplishments. [In French.]

F39 Gindin, James. "Method in the Biographical Study of Virginia Woolf." BIOGRAPHY, 4 (1981), 95-107.
    Attempt to formulate "criteria requisite for writing literary biography" (e.g., historical setting, connections between life and writings, treatment of entire career), with comment on four recent biographical studies of VW (see F13, F61, F77, and F81).

F40 -----. "A Precipice Marked V." STUDIES IN THE NOVEL, 11 (1979), 82-98.
    VW's "growing confidence in herself as artist" visible in her recently published personal writings (e.g., the DIARY [B1] and volume three of LETTERS [B2]). Also comments on her relationship with Vita Sackville-West and reviews four principal biographical studies of VW (see F13, F61, F77, and F81).

F41 Halperin, John. "Bloomsbury and Virginia Woolf: Another View." DALHOUSIE REVIEW, 59 (1979), 426-42.
    The multiplicity of attitudes within and varying popular reputation of the Bloomsbury Group epitomized in the "good and bad," "the most interesting and contradictory" qualities of VW.

F42 Harrod, Roy F. "Bloomsbury." In THE LIFE OF JOHN MAYNARD KEYNES. New York: Harcourt, 1951. Pp. 172-94.
    Survey of Keynes' connections to and relationships with the Bloomsbury circle (VW passim).

F43 Hawkes, Ellen. "Woolf's 'Magical Garden of Women.'" In NEW FEMINIST ESSAYS ON VIRGINIA WOOLF. Ed. Jane Marcus. Pp. 31-60. See G51.
    Feminist view of VW's biography.

F44 Hayman, Ronald. LITERATURE AND LIVING: A CONSIDERATION OF KATHERINE MANSFIELD & VIRGINIA WOOLF. London: Covent Garden Press, 1972.
    Superficial biographical similarities between the writers, with, unfortunately, no critical discussion of the two as writers. (Pamphlet--22 pp.)

F45 Henig, Suzanne. "Quentin Bell: VIRGINIA WOOLF: A BIOGRAPHY."
VIRGINIA WOOLF QUARTERLY, 1, No. 2 (1973), 55-69.
> Negative review-essay, listing eighteen specific
> weaknesses or omissions in Bell's biography:
> "the scholarly biography [of VW] is yet to be
> written." See F13.

F46 -----. "ULYSSES in Bloomsbury." JAMES JOYCE QUARTERLY, 10 (1973), 203-08.
> The Woolfs' frustrated willingness to publish
> Joyce's novel (1922), despite some doubts of
> its merit.

F47 Holroyd, Michael. LYTTON STRACHEY AND THE BLOOMSBURY GROUP. HIS WORK, THEIR INFLUENCE. Harmondsworth, Engl.: Penguin, 1971. Pp. 22-32 and passim.
> Unflattering portrait of a "bitter," "malicious,"
> "jealous" VW, a neurotic with a persecution complex.
> See F64 and U20. Condensed version of Holroyd's
> discussion of the VW-Strachey relationship in his
> LYTTON STRACHEY: A CRITICAL BIOGRAPHY (2 vols., New
> York: Holt, 1967), passim.

F48 Hynes, Samuel. "The Whole Contention Between Mr. Bennett and Mrs. Woolf." In EDWARDIAN OCCASIONS: ESSAYS ON ENGLISH WRITING IN THE EARLY TWENTIETH CENTURY. London: Routledge, 1972. Pp. 24-38.
> The public and personal quarrel between Bennett
> and VW reflects the conflict between popular and
> coterie art. Also see H16, X22, and X25.

F49 Isherwood, Christopher. "Virginia Woolf." 1941. In EXHUMATIONS: STORIES, ARTICLES, VERSES. New York: Simon and Schuster, 1966. Pp. 132-35.
> Obituary tribute and brief memoir. Reprinted in
> F70.

F50 Izzo, Carlo. "Testimonianze sul 'Bloomsbury Group.'" In STUDI IN ONORE DI VITTORIO LUGLI E DIEGO VALERI. Ed. Carlo Cordie et al. Venice: Pozza, 1961. Pp. 523-49.
> Intellectual and aesthetic influences on the
> Bloomsbury Group (e.g., G. E. Moore, Roger Fry,
> Clive Bell), and the Group's reputation and
> relations with their contemporaries. [In
> Italian.]

F51 Jardin, Claudine. VIRGINIA WOOLF, TROIS OU QUATRE CHOSES QUE JE SAIS D'ELLE... Paris: Hachette Littérature, 1973.
> Occasionally confused and critically simple-
> minded French biography for the general audi-
> ence, relying extensively on documents not then
> available in France (Bell's biography [F13] and
> Leonard Woolf's autobiography [F100]). Jardin,
> aside from her strong sympathy for VW, "un per-
> sonnage fascinant et insaissable," offers little
> to the reader already familiar with the facts of
> VW's life or the major characteristics of her
> works. [In French.]

Biographical Materials

F52 Kennedy, Richard. A BOY AT THE HOGARTH PRESS. London: Whittington, 1972.
>   Fascinating and unpretentious memoir of the Woolfs, 1928-29. The diary of Leonard's adolescent assistant at the Press.

F53 Kenney, Susan M., and Edwin J. Kenney. "Virginia Woolf and the Art of Madness." MASSACHUSETTS REVIEW, 23 (1982), 161-85.
>   VW's life and art "governed after all by her creative genius and its expression rather than by her mental instability." Solid and convincing, non-reductive view of VW's psychic make-up and mental health.

F54 Kondo, Ineko. "Shin-Woolf-Den no Omoshirosa" ["The Interest of the New Biography of Woolf"]. EIGO SEINEN, 119 (1973), 198-200.
>   Review essay on Bell's biography (F13). [In Japanese.]

F55 Lehmann, John. IN MY OWN TIME: MEMOIRS OF LITERARY LIFE. Boston: Little, Brown, 1969. Pp. 106-14, 119-22, 289-93, and passim.
>   VW's relationship with Lehmann and his literary periodicals (e.g., NEW SIGNATURES and NEW WRITING), in the late thirties and early years of the war. Extract reprinted in F83.

F56 -----. "(A lecture delivered at various times and in various places in the USA.)" In RECOLLECTIONS OF VIRGINIA WOOLF. Ed. Joan Russell Noble. Pp. 23-46. See F70.
>   Recounts his associations with the Woolfs and the Hogarth Press (1930-32, 1938 and after), with several personal sidelights on VW while publishing THE WAVES and in the last two years of her life.

F57 -----. THROWN TO THE WOOLFS. London: Weidenfeld and Nicolson, 1979.
>   Bittersweet memories of Lehmann's associations with the Hogarth Press, the Woolfs together, and Leonard Woolf in the forties, expanded and modified from earlier publication in light of more recent memoirs by others and newly published documents (e.g., VW's DIARIES and LETTERS). Reviewed in U26.

F58 -----. VIRGINIA WOOLF AND HER WORLD. London: Thames and Hudson, 1975.
>   Generously illustrated pictorial biography.

F59 Lehmann, Rosamond. "For Virginia Woolf." PENGUIN NEW WRITING, No. 7 (June 1941), pp. 53-58.
>   Memorial tribute, memoir, and critique. Revised version reprinted in F70.

F60 Lesser, Simon O. "Creativity versus Death: Virginia Woolf (1882-1941)." HARTFORD STUDIES IN LITERATURE, 10 (1978), 49-69.
General overview of VW's despondency and breakdowns, with speculations on her psychology.

F61 Love, Jean O. VIRGINIA WOOLF: SOURCES OF MADNESS AND ART. Berkeley: Univ. of California Press, 1977.
Intensive and specialized study of VW's family backgrounds and first twenty-five years, including extended commentaries on her parents, siblings, and early experiences, but focusing on the continuing enigmas of her biography: i.e., her "so-called madness," her health problems, her "atypical sexuality," her preoccupation with death, and, most important, the relationship between her psychological instability and her art. Reviewed in F27, F39, F40, and H225.

F62 McLaughlin, Thomas M. "Virginia Woolf and Bloomsbury." ConL, 21 (1980), 639-45.
The weaknesses of recent Stracheyan biographical studies of VW and Bloomsbury. Reviews Edel (F25) and Poole (F77).

F63 Mansfield, Katherine. "Fifteen Letters from K.M. to Virginia Woolf." ADAM INTERNATIONAL REVIEW, Nos. 370-75 (1973), pp. 19-24.
Documents the Mansfield-Woolf friendship (c. 1917-20).

F64 Merle, Gabriel. "Virginia Woolf et Lytton Strachey": "Discussion." In VIRGINIA WOOLF--COLLOQUE DE CERISY. Ed. Maurice de Gandillac and Jean Guiguet. Pp. 139-64; 165-78. See F34.
Reviews the close personal bond between VW and Strachey (established 1904-09 and strengthened, rather than otherwise, by their aborted engagement in 1909), and seeks their mutual influences on each other's works (VW's awakened interest in pre-eighteenth century English culture, the parallel structures of MD and QUEEN VICTORIA [1921], VW's biographical methods, characters modeled on Strachey in THE VOYAGE OUT and THE WAVES, etc.). [In French.] Also see F47.

F65 Meyer, Doris. "Virginia Woolf and Gilded Butterflies." In VICTORIA OCAMPO: AGAINST THE WIND AND TIDE. New York: Braziller, 1979. Pp. 120-29.
Account of Ocampo's meetings and correspondence with VW (1934-39), and VW's somewhat condescending response to Ocampo's worshipful admiration. [Ocampo (1890-1979), the aristocratic and strikingly beautiful founder of the literary periodical SUR, established and preserved VW's high critical reputation in Argentina.] See F71, P25, U1, and W21.

F66   Meyerowitz, Selma S. LEONARD WOOLF. Boston: Twayne, 1982. Pp. 12-22, 62-64, 154-57, 160-62, 178-88, 191-93, and passim.
    Competent survey of the facts of the Woolfs' marriage, their shared attitudes and activities, from Leonard's point of view, but avoids discussing either his personal eccentricities or at times peculiar handling of VW's literary remains.

F67   Meyers, Jeffrey. KATHERINE MANSFIELD: A BIOGRAPHY. London: Hamilton, 1978. Pp. 136-48 and passim.
    Compares and distinguishes Mansfield's and VW's temperaments and attitudes, and summarizes their acquaintance.

F68   -----. "Virginia and Leonard Woolf: Madness and Art." In MARRIED TO GENIUS. New York: Barnes and Noble, 1977. Pp. 92-112.
    Competent, brief account of VW's marriage.

F68a Morizot, Carol Ann. JUST THIS SIDE OF MADNESS: CREATIVITY AND THE DRIVE TO CREATE. Houston, Tex.: Harold House, 1978.
    A study of the relationship between creative ability and psychological abnormality, prominently considering VW. Not seen.

F69   Nicolson, Nigel. PORTRAIT OF A MARRIAGE. New York: Atheneum, 1973. Pp. 200-08 and passim.
    The "Sackville-West" side of the VW and Vita Sackville-West affair: they "did no damage to each other." Extract reprinted in G44. Also see F84.

F70   Noble, Joan Russell, ed. RECOLLECTIONS OF VIRGINIA WOOLF BY HER CONTEMPORARIES. London: Owen, 1972.
    Gathers twenty-eight memoirs and character sketches of VW: twelve specially commissioned for this volume, ten previously published items, and the remainder drawn from various unpublished sources (public lecture, BBC broadcasts). Includes F49, F56, F59, F96, and extracts from F8, F35, and G25. One memoir, by the Woolfs' cook Louie Mayer (1934-70), reprinted in F31 and G44.

F70a O'Brien, Edna. VIRGINIA: A PLAY. London: Hogarth, 1981.
    Drama based on VW's life and work. (Monograph--63 pp.) Not seen.

F71   Ocampo, Victoria. "Virginia Woolf in My Memory"; "Women in the Academy." 1941; 1977. In VICTORIA OCAMPO: AGAINST THE WIND AND THE TIDE. Trans. and ed. Doris Meyer. New York: Braziller, 1979. Pp. 235-40; 278-84.
    The distinguished Argentine woman of letters' eloquent obituary reverie on VW, testifying to

VW's influence on her, and her speech upon
being received into the Argentine Academy
of Letters, invoking VW as one of those
most responsible for the contemporary recognition of women intellectuals (with Gabriela
Mistral). Both originally published in
Spanish in SUR, No. 79 (1941), pp. 108-14
(and in Ocampo's TESTIMONIOS II [Buenos Aries:
SUR, 1941]) and in her TESTIMONIOS X (Buenos
Aries: SUR, 1977), pp. 13-23. Also see F65.

F72 Olson, Stanley. "North from Richmond, South from Bloomsbury."
ADAM INTERNATIONAL REVIEW, Nos. 364-66 (1972), pp. 70-74.
Brief note on the early days of the Woolfs'
Hogarth press. See G1.

F73 Ozick, Cynthia. "Mrs. Virginia Woolf." COMMENTARY, 56, No. 2
(1973), 33-44.
Comments and questions about VW's life, occasioned by Bell's biography (see F13).

F74 Pippett, Aileen. THE MOTH AND THE STAR: A BIOGRAPHY OF VIRGINIA
WOOLF. Boston: Little, Brown, 1955.
The first biography of VW, unauthorized, inac-
curate, and fully superseded by Bell (F13).
Includes superficial discussions of VW's
writings.

F75 Plomer, William. AT HOME. London: Cape, 1958. Pp. 43-44, 50-58.
Memories of VW's tastes and conversation, and of
literary evenings in Bloomsbury. Extract reprinted in F83.

F76 -----. "A Note on Virginia Woolf." MEANJIN, 6 (1947), 16-19.
Though an intellectually "exceptional" and
"daunting" presence, VW "was not in the least
aloof from" the political and social concerns
of "her own time."

F77 Poole, Roger. THE UNKNOWN VIRGINIA WOOLF. Cambridge: Cambridge
Univ. Press, 1978.
Remote psychological speculation. Reacting
against Leonard Woolf's and Bell's views of
VW's "madness" (see F13 and F100), Poole
finds VW's own documentation of the reasons
for her "mental distress," and her thera-
peutic "exorcism" of her psychological trauma,
principally in her fiction. Thus MD becomes
an account of her nervous collapse ten years
earlier, TL an exorcism of her childhood
problems, BETWEEN THE ACTS a reflection of
her incompatibility with Leonard, and so on.
Biographical interpretation with a vengeance.
Reviewed in F39, F40, F62, H225, and U26.

F78 Rantavaara, Irma. "Bloomsbury Today." VIRGINIA WOOLF QUARTERLY, 2 (1976), 281-84.
    One of the earliest commentators on "Bloomsbury" (see G68) reflects on the recent surge of studies devoted to the group.

F79 Ridley, Hilda. "Leslie Stephen's Daughter." DALHOUSIE REVIEW, 33 (1953), 65-72.
    Finds Stephen's influence on VW substantial, particularly in her life-long effort to establish an assertive view of femininity counter, yet complementary to his "undiluted" masculine point of view.

F80 Rogat, Ellen H. "The Virgin in the Bell Biography." TCL, 20 (1974), 96-113.
    Attacks the limited insight into the feminine psyche revealed by Bell's portrait of VW as "a neurotic virgin" (see F13).

F81 Rose, Phyllis. WOMAN OF LETTERS: A LIFE OF VIRGINIA WOOLF. New York: Oxford Univ. Press, 1978.
    The Oxford entry in the VW biographical "sweepstakes." Rose retells the life, unnecessarily reduplicating, with marginal differences, the work of Bell (F13). While claiming to find new biographical significance in the works, as "personal treatments of vital and immediate problems of identity," Rose comments, superficially, on just four of the novels (THE VOYAGE OUT, MD, TL, and BETWEEN THE ACTS). Reviewed in F39, F40, H225, and U26.

F82 Rosenbaum, Stanford P. "Preface to a Literary History of the Bloomsbury Group." NEW LITERARY HISTORY, 12 (1981), 329-44.
    The "primary reason" for a literary history of the Bloomsbury Group "found in the interconnectedness" of the writings of its members.

F83 -----, ed. THE BLOOMSBURY GROUP: A COLLECTION OF MEMOIRS, COMMENTARY, AND CRITICISM. Toronto: Univ. of Toronto Press, 1975. Passim.
    Collects numerous commentaries and criticisms concerning the Bloomsbury circle, including considerable memoir material on VW. Includes F90, G25, and extracts from F13, F18, F55, F75, F96, and F100.

F84 Ruas, Charles. "An Interview with Nigel Nicolson." BOOK FORUM, 4 (1979), 618-35.
    Nicolson's memories of VW (1922-39), impressions of her character (as contributing editor for her LETTERS and DIARIES), and portrait of her relationship with his mother, Vita Sackville-West. Also see F69.

F85 Sakamoto, Kiminobu. "V. Woolf no Zahyō" ["The Coordinates of V. Woolf"]. EIGO SEINEN, 122 (1976), 119-21.
> Review article on numerous recent studies of VW and Bloomsbury. [In Japanese.]

F86 Simon, Irène. "Bloomsbury and Its Critics." REVUE DES LANGUES VIVANTES, 23 (1957), 385-414.
> Discusses the chief determining influences on the Bloomsbury Group (Moore's PRINCIPIA ETHICA [1903] and Fry's aesthetics), its members, and its chief adversaries (e.g., D. H. Lawrence and F. R. Leavis).

F87 Smith, Logan Pearsall. "Tavistock Square." ORION: A MISCELLANY, 2 (1945), 73-86.
> Describes his "curious kind of relationship" with VW, a mixture of "friendship and *malice*," and publishes nine letters from VW (1919-32).

F88 Spater, George A. "The Monks House Library." VIRGINIA WOOLF QUARTERLY, 1, No. 3 (1973), 60-65.
> Description of the contents and dispersion of the Woolfs' library. Reprinted from AMERICAN BOOK COLLECTOR, 21, No. 4 (1971), 18-20. Also see E5.

F89 Spater, George A., and Ian Parsons. A MARRIAGE OF TRUE MINDS: AN INTIMATE PORTRAIT OF LEONARD AND VIRGINIA WOOLF. New York: Harcourt, 1977.
> Extended, gossipy account and analysis of the Woolfs' early lives, courtship, and marriage, exploiting several sources of information unavailable to Bell (see F13), but hardly justifying a book-length study. Over 150 illustrations, including numerous fascinating, previously unpublished photographs.

F90 Spender, Stephen. WORLD WITHIN WORLD. London: Hamilton, 1951. Pp. 151-59 and passim.
> Memories of VW, her dinner parties, and her conversation in the thirties. Reprinted in F83.

F91 Stresau, Hermann. "Totentanz." DIE NEUE RUNDSCHAU, 52 (1941), 362-64.
> Generous obituaries of VW and Sherwood Anderson, two last "lights" extinguished in the darkening storm of the world war ("in einen nächtlichen Orkan"). [In German.]

F92 Trautmann, Joanne. THE JESSAMY BRIDES: THE FRIENDSHIP OF VIRGINIA WOOLF AND V. SACKVILLE-WEST. University Park, Pa.: Pennsylvania State Univ. Press, 1973.
> Surveys the strong personal and literary "ties" between the two writers (1922-41), with special emphasis on Sackville-West's role in and impact on ORLANDO. Extract reprinted in G44.

F93 -----. "A Talk with Nigel Nicolson." VIRGINIA WOOLF QUARTERLY, 1, No. 1 (1972), 38-44.
    Nicolson's childhood memories of VW and his mother Vita Sackville-West.

F94 Trivedi, H. K. "Forster and Virginia Woolf: The Critical Friends." In E. M. FORSTER: A HUMAN EXPLORATION: CENTENARY ESSAYS. Ed. G. K. Das and John Beer. New York: New York Univ. Press, 1979. Pp. 216-30.
    Summarizes VW's and Forster's personal relationship and their responses to each other's works. See A26, G25, and H81.

F95 Trombley, Stephen. "ALL THAT SUMMER SHE WAS MAD": VIRGINIA WOOLF AND HER DOCTORS. London: Junction Books, 1981.
    Contending that the VW of THREE GUINEAS "was perfectly sane," Trombley "seeks to uncover some of the presuppositions behind the attribution of madness in the case of Virginia Woolf; briefly in relation to the lay persons who have maintained that she was not sane" (Leonard Woolf [F100] and Quentin Bell [F13] in particular), "and at length where four of her doctors were concerned." Trombley studies VW's relations with her body, food, and doctors, as they are reflected in her works and, extensively, in the writings of Drs. George Henry Savage, Henry Head, Maurice Craig, and T. B. Hyslop, concluding with discussions of her confinements in the Twickenham asylum and of the relevance of "her 'biography' of Elizabeth Barrett Browning's dog, FLUSH, read as autobiography." Much interesting information, put to curious use.

F96 "Virginia Woolf." HORIZON, 3 (1941), 313-27, 402-06.
    Obituary memoirs and tributes by T. S. Eliot, Rose Macaulay, V. Sackville-West, William Plomer, and Duncan Grant. Reprinted in F70. Eliot reprinted in F83 and G49. Grant reprinted in F83.

F97 Walpole, Hugh. "Virginia Woolf." NEW STATESMAN AND NATION, 31 (1941), 602-03.
    Obituary memoir, recalling his first discovery of VW's fiction, in JACOB'S ROOM, and first meeting with her in person. Written very shortly before his own death. Reprinted in G49.

F98 Watt, Donald J. "G. E. Moore and the Bloomsbury Group." ENGLISH LITERATURE IN TRANSITION, 12 (1969), 119-34.
    Summarizes impact of Moore's PRINCIPIA ETHICA (1903) on several members of Bloomsbury, including VW.

F99   Watts, Janet. "Dear Quentin: Janet Watts Interviews Mr. Bell of Bloomsbury." VIRGINIA WOOLF QUARTERLY, 1, No. 1 (1972), 111-16.
      Bell's equivocal feelings about writing his aunt's biography (see F13).

F100 Woolf, Leonard. AUTOBIOGRAPHY. 5 vols. SOWING (1880-1904); GROWING (1904-11); BEGINNING AGAIN (1911-18); DOWNHILL ALL THE WAY (1919-39); THE JOURNEY, NOT THE ARRIVAL MATTERS (1939-69). London: Hogarth, 1960, 1961, 1964, 1967, 1969.
      Volumes one, three, four, and five (beginning), covering his years with VW, are appropriately the most pertinent part of Woolf's memoirs. Extracts reprinted in F31, F83, and N1. Also see F13, F77, F89, and F95.

F101 -----. "Virginia Woolf: Writer and Personality." LISTENER, 73 (1965), 327-28.
      Stresses VW's essentially "normal" interests and attitudes, which were punctuated by moments of imaginative genius.

F102 Yourcenar, Marguerite. "Sur Virginia Woolf." IMPRESSIONS, 5, Nos. 19-20 (1938), 5-6.
      The translator of THE WAVES (LES VAGUES [1937]), recalls a visit and brief conversation with VW, in 1937. [In French.] See G34. Reprinted in G1.

G. BOOK-LENGTH CRITICAL STUDIES AND ESSAY COLLECTIONS

Also see the numerous books, essay collections, monographs, and pamphlets on VW's individual novels and other writings listed in sections J, M, N, P, Q, R, U, W, and X below. All unpublished dissertations are listed in section Z below.

Also see Delattre (H59), Kumar (H133), and Moore (J12).

This section includes critical studies, collections, monographs, and pamphlets concerned with VW generally or with more than *two* of her individual works or principal genres. Thus, studies of VW's stories, autobiographical writings, biographies, feminist tracts, and critical essays are entered in the appropriate generic sections (T through X), though they frequently deal with more than two works and are, one could argue, general in significance. Studies of two works or *genres* (e.g., MD and TL, or THE YEARS and the feminist tracts), are entered and annotated (with cross references), in the *two* appropriate sections on individual works below.

G1 ADAM INTERNATIONAL REVIEW. Nos. 364-66 (1972), pp. 2-84.
Heterogeneous collection of two previously unpublished essays and three letters by VW (see A34), and several original notes and essays about VW, Leonard Woolf, Bloomsbury, and Proust. Includes "Proust," by Clive Bell (pp. 31-65), "Leonard Woolf--The Creative Writer," by Freema Gottlieb (pp. 66-70), "THE VILLAGE IN THE JUNGLE," on one of Leonard's novels, by Stephen Medcalf (pp. 75-79), and the following essays concerning VW: F6, F19, F72, F102, H100, and H186.

G2 Alexander, Jean. THE VENTURE OF FORM IN THE NOVELS OF VIRGINIA WOOLF. Port Washington, N. Y.: Kennikat, 1974.
Competent study of VW's developing ideas and form in her fiction. Alexander extricates VW from her biography and from literary history, seeing within the novels her "radical if unobtrusive" rebellion against inherited systems of thought and her rejection of rational institutions as comparable to, but independent of the responses of the modern existentialist artists. Pursuing this thesis, Alexander studies VW's existential attitudes in her "style, structure, and characters, as well as in [her] explicit statements."

G3 Amoruso, Vito. VIRGINIA WOOLF. Bari: Adriatica Editrice, 1968.
Critical overview of VW's fiction and theory of
fiction, finding her both an equal to Joyce and
Proust and a representative example of the ultimate and "most radical" phase of innovation in
Western literary realism. After an opening
discussion of the Bloomsbury Group, Amoruso reviews the first two, conventionally realistic
novels, the evolving theory of fiction ("Mr.
Bennett and Mrs. Brown" and "Modern Fiction"),
and the successive novel experiments from
JACOB'S ROOM on. Following English rather
than Continental opinion, Amoruso sees TL as
a turning point in VW's career, leading to
the increasingly abstract experiments of
ORLANDO and THE WAVES (a "tour de force").
THE YEARS, in its return to realism, and
BETWEEN THE ACTS are partial recoveries of
the strengths of her unquestionably suc-
cesful TL. [In Italian.]

G4 Apter, T. E. VIRGINIA WOOLF: A STUDY OF HER NOVELS. New York:
New York Univ. Press, 1979.
Unexciting and generally superficial investigation of the psychological and epistemological
bases for VW's sensibility, symbolism, and vision.
Apter sees the first two novels (THE VOYAGE OUT
and NIGHT AND DAY) focusing on VW's central theme,
the "need for consciousness." Her later short
and long fictions explore permutations of this
theme, while THE YEARS and BETWEEN THE ACTS
show "a destruction of...vision."

G5 Badenhausen, Ingeborg. DIE SPRACHE VIRGINIA WOOLFS: EIN BEITRAG
ZUR STILISTIK DES MODERNEN ENGLISCHEN ROMANS. Marburg: Univ. of
Marburg, 1932.
The first major German study of VW's fiction.
Closely analyzing VW's writing style in selected
passages from her mature writings (chiefly JACOB'S
ROOM through ORLANDO), Badenhausen systematically
traces the appropriateness of VW's sentence rhythms
and structures, her syntax, and her parts of speech
(verbs, nouns, adjectives), for her narrative
strategies and themes. The critic also suggests
a larger, less convincing purpose in her analyses,
seeing style as an essential expression of national
and individual spirit and the "inneren Sprachform"
of VW as a key to the essential meaning of her
work (viz. Wilhelm von Humbolt's linguistic
philosophy). Badenhausen's final chapter, expanding on Bernhard Fehr's distinction between
the arts of objective materialism and subjective
consciousness ("Dingkunst" and "Bewusstseinskunst"; see H76), argues VW's central significance for the modern novel. [In German.] Reviewed in E3.

G6 Bazin, Nancy T. VIRGINIA WOOLF AND THE ANDROGYNOUS VISION. New Brunswick, N. J.: Rutgers Univ. Press, 1973.
> VW's ideal of the androgynous artist, as one who synthesizes or reconciles warring opposites within the art work as well as within the personality, applied to her own practice in fiction. Bazin sees VW's extensive use of dualistic symbols (e.g., night and day) and polarized forces (e.g., the timeless feminine and the temporal masculine) as characteristic both of her aesthetic and of her personal need to search for her Jungian, integrated "self," the "point of balance that would stabilize her personality." Good general discussion of VW's idea of androgyny and often fine commentaries on the fiction; however, ORLANDO, the one novel with an androgyne as central character, is strangely omitted from the study. See G38 and G62.

G7 Bennett, Joan. VIRGINIA WOOLF: HER ART AS A NOVELIST. 1945. 2nd ed. Cambridge: Cambridge Univ. Press, 1964.
> Excellent introduction. Bennett argues that VW rejected both objective realism and subjective, autobiographical impressionism, seeking rather to recreate and to elicit imaginative order from experience. She proceeds to distinguish VW's "human beings" from characters, her "sequences" from stories, and her "values" from morals, as determined by VW's intention to recognize and reveal meaning rather than to impose it: "continuity and fluidity" in experience are emphasized "rather than boundary and definition." Bennett concludes with a discussion of form in VW's novels and a study of BETWEEN THE ACTS, as an illustration of VW's vision, structure, and style. The second edition adds short chapters on A WRITER'S DIARY and on VW as a critic. Reviewed in H87. Extracts reprinted in G40.

G8 Blackstone, Bernard. VIRGINIA WOOLF. 1952. 2nd ed. London: Longmans, 1966.
> Brief introduction to VW as a representative modern writer, fully involved with the ideas and issues of her time despite the apparent detachment of her abstract works. Blackstone has added a postscript on VW's recent critical reputation (1962) and a revised bibliography (1966).

G9 -----. VIRGINIA WOOLF: A COMMENTARY. New York: Harcourt, 1949.
> Excellent general view of the works. Arguing the preeminent importance of the "pattern" woven "across the void," both within and among her writings, Blackstone sees in VW's fiction and nonfiction a three-phase pattern: the early works (through JACOB'S ROOM) are primarily concerned with the individual's

42   *General Critical Books*

        need for love and freedom, the middle works
        (through A ROOM OF ONE'S OWN) explore the
        tensions of married life, and the remaining
        works treat the claims of society on the
        individual. Uniformly fine readings. Ex-
        tract reprinted in G40. Reviewed in H21
        and Q3.

G10 Brewster, Dorothy. VIRGINIA WOOLF. New York: New York Univ. Press, 1962.
        Pleasant, conscientious summaries of VW's life,
        critical essays and attitudes, and nine novels,
        showing only occasional flashes of critical
        judgment.

G11 -----. VIRGINIA WOOLF'S LONDON. London: Allen and Unwin, 1959.
        Surveys VW's use of London in her fiction and
        non-fiction both "to suggest how some...general
        impression of London grows in our minds as we
        read the [works] in their chronological order"
        and to trace her shifting use of the city, first
        as background and later as part of her characters'
        consciousnesses. Interesting, though uncritical
        view of VW as a unique, incontestably "urban"
        modern writer.

G12 Chambers, Richard L. THE NOVELS OF VIRGINIA WOOLF. Edinburgh: Oliver and Boyd, 1947.
        Modest introduction to VW as "*par excellence*
        the novelist of the Nineteen-Twenties." Chambers
        summarizes VW's significance, literary milieu,
        and critical reputation, concluding, despite his
        admiration, that VW lacks the scope and "moral
        positiveness" of the "permanently great" writers.

G13 Chastaing, Maxime. LA PHILOSOPHIE DE VIRGINIA WOOLF. Paris: Presses Universitaires de France, 1951.
        Extraordinary essay on the perception of reality,
        stimulated by VW's works, but contributing less
        to the interpretation of VW's ideas than to
        Chastaing's elaboration of his personal phil-
        osophic system. Chastaing initially asserts that
        VW is the twentieth-century's chief exponent of
        "la grande tradition de la pensée anglo-saxonne"
        and that her various technical experiments re-
        flect her assimilation and adaptation of eight-
        eenth-century empiricism (cf. Berkeley and Hume).
        From this direction, he offers several intri-
        guing observations on VW's use of multiple
        perspectives and "cinematographic" techniques,
        her presentation of character, her conceptions
        of art, truth, reality, and the mind, and her
        narrative form, illustrating his points through
        copious references to the long and short fic-
        tion and the essays. Yet Chastaing imposes a

system on VW that does not exist *in* her work,
and relates her to a philosophic tradition that
she has repeatedly and explicitly rejected.
[In French.]

G14 Claro, Maria Elena. ALGO SOBRE VIRGINIA WOOLF. Santiago, Chile: Editorial Universitaria, 1967.
> Two-part study introducing the "common reader" to the world of VW, by stressing her vision of the torment and fragility of existence and her search for an integrating, affirmative reality, and by surveying her fiction to describe how she expresses this vision and quest in her fiction. Concentrates on A WRITER'S DIARY, MD, TL, and THE WAVES. [In Spanish.]

G15 Clements, Patricia, and Isobel Grundy, eds. VIRGINIA WOOLF: NEW CRITICAL ESSAYS. Totowa, N. J.: Barnes and Noble, [1983].
> Eleven essays exploring "patterns of connection in Virginia Woolf's work, demonstrating the integrity of her achievement and viewing it in light of its relation to the work of other eminent Victorians and moderns." (Quoted from publisher's announcement. Announced for publication late in 1983--not seen.)

G16 Daiches, David. VIRGINIA WOOLF. 1942. 2nd ed. New York: New Directions, 1963.
> Balanced introduction to VW's fiction and essays, finding her greatest contribution to English literature in her development of an "intellectually exciting and aesthetically satisfying" formula for the novel of sensibility. Daiches views her achievement, nevertheless, as limited and doubts that she has "permanently expanded the art of fiction." The second edition, which entails no revision, includes a "Preface" acknowledging some slight modifications of opinion. Extracts reprinted in G40, N1, and N5.

G17 Delattre, Floris. LE ROMAN PSYCHOLOGIQUE DE VIRGINIA WOOLF. Paris: Vrin, 1932.
> The first book-length critical study of VW, strongly emphasizing the influence of Henri Bergson's philosophy on her work (see H58). Delattre attempts to "place" VW in terms of her intellectual heritage and contemporary culture. Beginning with a general survey of "le roman féminin en Angleterre," from the Victorian period, through the turn-of-the century feminist period, to the post-war era (Austen, the Brontes, Eliot, Mrs. Ward, Sinclair, Richardson, and Mansfield), Delattre moves to a consideration of VW's "espirit et sa culture"

(reviewing VW's critical views of the Russian
novelists, the English Victorians, and the
contemporary feminist movement). Delattre's
chapter-by-chapter study of VW's novels
through THE WAVES (interspersed with commentaries on psychology in literature, the
influences of Bergson, Joyce, and Proust,
and the relation of realism and "Lyrisme"),
generally reviews VW's technical development
and major themes. He concludes with a summary of VW's objections to Edwardian realism,
compositional techniques (especially "monologue intérieur"), and "magical" style.
[In French.] Extract reprinted in G49.
Also see H59.

G18 DiBattista, Maria. VIRGINIA WOOLF'S MAJOR NOVELS: THE FABLES
OF ANON. New Haven, Conn.: Yale Univ. Press, 1980.
Study of VW's response to modern subjectivity
and perspectivism in fiction, in her creation
of the "non-egotistical," anonymous narrator
"Anon," the semi-comic and "many-sided voice
of...the one in the many" (see VW's discussion of "Anon," C1). DiBattista concentrates
on the problems of narrative "authority,"
"voice," "time and event," and "succession"
in MD, TL, ORLANDO, THE WAVES, and BETWEEN
THE ACTS, with passing reference to the other
fiction and the essays. Reviewed in U26.

G19 Dölle, Erika. EXPERIMENT UND TRADITION IN DER PROSA VIRGINIA
WOOLFS. Munich: Fink, 1971.
An instructive study of VW's individual, mod-
ernistic approach to fiction, assimilating
and expanding the thesis of Brandt's study of
THE WAVES (See Q1). Dölle's introduction
summarizes VW's relationship to her immediate
predecessors and contemporary novelists,
seeing her "Suche nach einer neuen Romanform"
characterizing both her attacks on traditional
conventions for fiction and her practice as
a novelist. She reviews VW's essays on
fiction, stressing her concern for the con-
ditions of and possibilities for a modern
novel in light of the century's new conceptions of consciousness, as well as her
responses to Lubbock's and Forster's theories
of narration. Differentiating VW's two forms
of fictional point of view, the "Er-Perspek-
tiv" (objective and distant) and the "Ich-
Perspektiv" (subjective and personal), with
illustration from the stories, Dölle examines
VW's movement toward increasing subjectivity,
and ironic exposure of the limitations of
traditional realism, in her narrative and

structural techniques in MD and THE WAVES.
Her brief conclusion describes THE YEARS and
BETWEEN THE ACTS as relapses into convention-
ality. [In German.] Reviewed in Q3.

G20 Donahue, Delia. THE NOVELS OF VIRGINIA WOOLF. Rome: Bulzoni, 1977.
> Fresh, though irreverently negative view of
the nine novels. Donahue recapitulates the
biography, stressing the class snobbery,
emotional sterility, and intellectual arro-
gance fostered by VW's upbringing. As a
novelist, VW is a writer with "few ideas"
who represses "effervescence" and shuns
"facility like the plague." THE VOYAGE OUT
could only be published by a step-brother
(as it was); ORLANDO is "a very bad book";
BETWEEN THE ACTS should have been a play
were VW capable of writing theatre; and
most of the other novels betray VW's af-
fectation, her inability to write in a
"more natural, human vein." VW will be
remembered only for those "parts of her
work into which she put whatever passion
she was capable of feeling."

G21 Drabble, Margaret. VIRGINIA WOOLF: A PERSONAL DEBT. AN ESSAY. New York: Aloe Editions, 1973.
> Distinguished novelist's account of her "dis-
covery" of VW. Reprinted from MS.,1(Nov. 1972).
(Pamphlet--12 pp.) Also see F24.

G22 Elert, Kerstin. PORTRAITS OF WOMEN IN SELECTED NOVELS BY VIRGINIA WOOLF AND E. M. FORSTER. Umea, Sweden: Univ. of Umea, 1979.
> Pedestrian discussion of Victorian ideals of
womanhood inherited by Forster and Woolf, and
of the novelists' portraits of various women
(young women, wives, mothers, educators) in
their novels. Considers THE VOYAGE OUT, NIGHT
AND DAY, MD, and TL.

G23 Finke, Ilse. VIRGINIA WOOLFS STELLUNG ZUR WIRKLICHKEIT. Marburg: Bauer, 1933.
> Early examination of VW's theoretical objections
to traditional literary realism, in her critical
essays, and her somewhat different and more il-
luminating presentation of reality in her fiction,
through THE WAVES. Finke describes VW's increasing subjectivism in the early novels, MD,
TL, and THE WAVES, and considers ORLANDO VW's
greatest accomplishment, fulfilling her implicit
ethical ideal by presenting the artist's encounter with reality as the opportunity for self-
development and greatest self-fulfillment.
Finke argues that VW's representation of reality

approaches a classical, rather than impressionistic, attitude and that her affirmative vision of reality tempering the spiritual sensibility of the artist distinguishes her from those writers of the "cultural depression" ("Kulturjammer") with whom she is often associated (e.g., Joyce; see Fehr, H76). Reviewed in E3.

G24 Fleishman, Avrom. VIRGINIA WOOLF: A CRITICAL READING. Baltimore, Md.: Johns Hopkins Univ. Press, 1975.
"Simply a reading" of VW's nine novels. Viewing VW as encyclopedic in her approach to fiction and adopting an appropriately eclectic approach to the discussion of her fiction, Fleishman focuses on one dominant generic characteristic, or fictional element, as a fulcrum for his often insightful critical analyses of each novel. For example, in THE VOYAGE OUT he examines the Jungian "journey within" archetype. MD and TL are considered generally in spatial and symbolic terms. ORLANDO is an adaptation of new biographical techniques to fiction. And BETWEEN THE ACTS is the "*summa* of the thematic concerns and experimental modes with which Woolf had been occupied" throughout her career. Reviewed in Q3 and U15.

G25 Forster, E. M. VIRGINIA WOOLF. Cambridge: Cambridge Univ. Press, 1942.
Sympathetic and insightful lecture on VW, commenting on her intensity, her interests, and her one major weakness: characterization. (Pamphlet--28pp.) Collected in Forster's TWO CHEERS FOR DEMOCRACY (London: Arnold, 1951), pp. 242-58. Reprinted in F70 (extract), F83, and G80 (extract). Reviewed in H21 and V4. Also see F94, H7, X24, and X40.

G26 Freedman, Ralph, ed. VIRGINIA WOOLF: REVALUATION AND CONTINUITY. Berkeley: Univ. of California Press, 1980.
Thirteen original essays: three of general criticism, an interpretive essay on each of the nine novels, and a prefatory commentary on VW's critical reputation. Includes H86, H103, H201, J11, K8, L8, M74, N27, P21, Q43, R17, S13, and T11. Reviewed in U26.

G27 Ginsberg, Elaine, ed. VIRGINIA WOOLF: CENTENNIAL PAPERS. Troy, N. Y.: Whitston, 1983.
Not seen.

G28 Gorsky, Susan. VIRGINIA WOOLF. Boston: Twayne, 1978.
Introductory guide to VW's works. Gorsky reviews VW's life, preparatory to a series of

competent critical discussions of VW's literary
essays, her stories and early novels, her first
mature novels and her biographies (JACOB'S ROOM,
MD, ORLANDO, FLUSH, and ROGER FRY), her experiments in symbolism (TL and THE WAVES) and structure (THE YEARS and BETWEEN THE ACTS), her
feminist tracts, and her critical reputation.

G29 Gruber, Ruth. VIRGINIA WOOLF: A STUDY. Leipzig: Tauchnitz, 1935.
    Early feminist study of VW's values and achieve-
ment as a novelist. Gruber finds the early VW
torn between dominant, "masculine" forces (criticism, realism, the past) and her feminine temperament (poetry, romanticism, the present).
Her career becomes a "struggle" to attain a
feminine style which, under the influence of
less "masculine" writers (poets and rhetoricians
such as Burke, Gibbon, and Shelley), is achieved
in her synthesizing, "completed" style (JACOB'S
ROOM and after). THE WAVES, her most mature
work, is in its rhythmic counterpoint of polari-
ties, "her final solution to her problem of
style." Reviewed in E3.

G30 Guiguet, Jean. VIRGINIA WOOLF AND HER WORKS. 1962. Trans. Jean Stewart. London: Hogarth, 1965.
    An important, thorough, and useful critical
examination of VW's writings, though occasionally doctrinaire in categorizing the works
and critically uninspired in methodically reviewing them. The first several parts of
Guiguet's study examine VW's critical reputation (with particularly good comments on her
reception in France), her inherited ideas
of fiction, her Bloomsbury intellectual milieu,
and her developing idea of the artist ("The
Self, Life and Artistic Creation"). Moving
from VW's views of the artist to her art,
Guiguet discusses her critical essays and
pamphlets and analyzes her novels, stories,
and biographies work-by-work, chiefly focusing
on the basic "problems" created by her formal
and technical experimentation in the "quest
for reality." Many parts of Guiguet's book
have been superseded by specialized full-
length studies, but his work remains valuable
as a compilation of much of the basic biographical, bibliographical, and critical information
on a great many of VW's writings. Originally
published in French as VIRGINIA WOOLF ET SON
OEUVRE: L'ART ET LE QUÊTE DU RÉEL (Paris:
M. Didlier, 1962). Extracts reprinted in
G40, G80, N1, and N5. Also see M48.

G31 Hafley, James. THE GLASS ROOF: VIRGINIA WOOLF AS NOVELIST. Berkeley: Univ. of California Press, 1954.
Admirably lucid analysis of VW's developing ideas and techniques in her novels, as she repudiates "positivistic realism" and consequently searches for an original and unified "vision of experience." VW's philosophic perspective first finds adequate expression in MD, and it and the remaining novels, despite variations in conception and scope, are judged "masterpieces" even by "her own rigorous standard." Includes excellent discussions of VW's adaptations of Bergsonian conceptions of time, in MD and in later works. Extracts reprinted in G40, G44, and N1.

G32 Harper, Howard. BETWEEN LANGUAGE AND SILENCE: THE NOVELS OF VIRGINIA WOOLF. Baton Rouge: Louisiana State Univ. Press, 1982.
The most significant recent critical study of VW's fiction. Harper adopts a phenomenological approach (and the phenomenologist's occasionally opaque terminology) to describe the chief interest in VW's fiction: the manner in which each novel's "narrative consciousness" (the persona of the teller) realizes its own creative potentialities, achieving a coherent perspective, meaning, order, and stability. VW's development through her nine novels becomes a progress from lyric, through epic, to dramatically impersonal perspectives (cf. Joyce's aesthetic). Harper draws interesting parallels to the search for impersonal vision in modern art and stylistic analogies to cinematic techniques, in presenting his interpretations, and insightfully analyzes VW's stylistic and structural patterns in her novels, yet his developmental approach occasionally leads to debatable evaluations (e.g., BETWEEN THE ACTS, VW's last novel, which completes the pattern of development, is therefore her "fullest revelation").

G33 Holtby, Winifred. VIRGINIA WOOLF. London: Wishart, 1932.
First critical book in English (Floris Delattre's LE ROMAN PSYCHOLOGIQUE DE VIRGINIA WOOLF appeared in France, earlier in 1932; see G17). Holtby summarizes VW's biography and her critical essays, preparatory to individual chapters on the novels and stories, through THE WAVES. Her critiques trace VW's developments in theme and form, in general terms, finding her achievements modest, though distinguished. Extract reprinted in G44.

G34 IMPRESSIONS. 5, Nos. 19-20 (1938), 2-20. "Homage à Virginia Woolf."
Scarce collection of six biographical and critical articles on VW: "Avant-propos," by Yves Picart (pp. 2-3), "Sur Virginia Woolf," by Marguerite

Yourcenar (see F102), "Un Roman lyrique de
Virginia Woolf: THE WAVES," by Floris Delattre
(pp. 7-10), "Le dernier roman de Virginia Woolf:
THE WAVES," by Léon Lemonnier (pp. 11-16),
"Virginia Woolf et ses Compagnes," by Louis
Pimienta (pp. 17-18), and "Entretien avec
Jacques-Émile Blanche," by Pierre Stouls
(pp. 19-20). Not seen. [In French.]

G35 Ishii, Koichi. VIRGINIA WOOLF NO SEKAI [THE WORLD OF VIRGINIA
WOOLF]. Tokyo: Nanundo, 1977.
Not seen. [In Japanese.]

G36 Johnson, Manly. VIRGINIA WOOLF. New York: Ungar, 1973.
Good brief introduction. Johnson reviews VW's
life, essays, and biographies, as a preface
to brief, necessarily superficial, but eminently
readable commentaries on the nine novels and
the short stories. Throughout Johnson traces
VW's struggles with both her developing themes
and her evolving ideas of the novel's form.

G36a Juszczak, Wiesław. ZASŁONA W RAJSKIE PTAKI, ALBO, A GRANICACH
"OKRESU POWIEŚCI" [THE VEILED BIRD OF PARADISE, OR, CONCERNING
THE BOUNDARIES OF NOVEL WRITING]. Warsaw: Państwowy Instytut
Wydawniczy, 1981.
Not seen. [In Polish.]

G37 Kapur, Vijay. VIRGINIA WOOLF'S VISION OF LIFE AND HER SEARCH
FOR SIGNIFICANT FORM: A STUDY IN THE SHAPING VISION. Atlantic
Highlands, N. J.: Humanities Press, 1980.
Finds VW's fiction developing toward a dialectical pattern, "formed by a process of change
or interaction...which is continuous, cumula-
tive and consummatory." Kapur disputes the
critical tradition which characterizes VW's
vision as dualistic (the first chapter summarizes the major "approaches to Virginia
Woolf"), traces her "Search for Significant
Form" in the essays, and surveys her evolution
toward a dialectical synthesis of art and life,
mystical vision and primeval instincts, etc.,
in her novels. Interesting and well-supported
thesis, though opaquely written.

G38 Kelley, Alice van Buren. THE NOVELS OF VIRGINIA WOOLF: FACT AND
VISION. Chicago: Univ. of Chicago Press, 1973.
Thematic and technical analyses of eight of the
novels (ORLANDO omitted), exploring VW's consistently dualistic world-view, here identified
primarily as a dichotomy between "fact" and
"vision." Following "the trail of these elusive
terms" through the fiction, Kelly argues that
the first two novels propose balance of the
physical and spiritual worlds as a possible
cure for modern man's sense of isolation; that
the middle novels refine this formula; and

that the last three novels look toward a final
vision which, in the face of growing chaos,
"can offer solace" from fact. Bazin's study
(see G6), however, is a more satisfactory
analysis of VW's dualistic thought.

G39 Kondo, Ineko. JANE AUSTEN AND VIRGINIA WOOLF. Tokyo: Kenkyusha, 1956.
Not seen. [In Japanese.]

G40 Latham, Jacqueline E. M., ed. CRITICS ON VIRGINIA WOOLF. Coral Gables, Fla.: Univ. of Miami Press, 1970.
Twenty-four brief extracts, from nineteen previously published essays and studies, presenting a representative picture of the critical reputation of VW and her works. Includes H96 and extracts from G7, G9, G16, G30, G31, G57, G75, H9, H23, M25, M69, M83, P14, P29, S2, S34, and T4.

G41 Leaska, Mitchell A. THE NOVELS OF VIRGINIA WOOLF: FROM BEGINNING TO END. New York: The John Jay Press of the City Univ. of New York, 1977.
Applies the methods for the analysis of "multiple perspectives" within the omniscient voice, defined and illustrated in his VIRGINIA WOOLF'S LIGHTHOUSE (see N3), to seven of the novels (ORLANDO and BETWEEN THE ACTS omitted, with questionable justifications). Leaska's chapters on JACOB'S ROOM and THE YEARS, which present unique technical problems, differ in approach and methodology from the balance of the study, so we have, by the author's tacit admission, the application of a rhetorical approach to VW which is only partly appropriate, despite the critic's claims otherwise. Still, Leaska offers several refreshing insights. Includes an "Afterword" by John Lehmann (237-41), essentially disputing Leaska's "ethical" argument against including BETWEEN THE ACTS. Extract originally published in R1. Extract reprinted in J1.

G42 Lee, Hermione. THE NOVELS OF VIRGINIA WOOLF. London: Methuen, 1977.
Well-written, sensitive, and sensible readings of the nine novels, useful as an introduction to VW for the neophyte, or as a purgative for those immersed in recent criticism. Lee dismisses the feminists, the Bloomsburyans, and the dichotomists, seeing VW foremost as a "remarkable, though not a major figure" in the Modernist movement. She regards VW's novels as consistent, energetic, self-conscious struggles "for an accurate rendering of life as she perceived it," for "mastery over the intractable and the chaotic, both inside and outside the mind." Refreshing criticism.

G43 LETTRES FRANÇAISES, No. 882 (1961), pp. 1-6.
Special issue, commemorating the twentieth
anniversary of VW's death. Contains translations of two essays and excerpts of MD by
VW, an essay (H143), and an interview (H213).

G44 Lewis, Thomas S. W., ed. VIRGINIA WOOLF: A COLLECTION OF CRITISICM. New York: McGraw-Hill, 1975.
Two original and twelve previously published
essays, including two items by VW (A19 [extract], A20), a brief memoir by her cook
(from F70), and nine critical articles on
her fiction. Includes M13, M72, N22, Q26,
S6, T18, and extracts from F69, F92, G31,
G33, and H111.

G45 Little, Judy. COMEDY AND THE WOMAN WRITER: WOOLF, SPARK, AND
FEMINISM. Lincoln: Univ. of Nebraska Press, 1983.
A redefinition of the comic mode, with extensive
application to the works of VW and Muriel Spark.
Little sees an important feminine subtradition
of "renegade comedy," which mocks "the deepest
possible norms" of male patriarchy, "norms four
thousand years old," characterizing the comedy
and "comic imagery" of VW's fiction. Her works
routinely satirize the archetypal themes (e.g.,
the quest) and "the traditional, most intimately
learned, norms of primary socialization" (e.g.,
institutions, manners), through "motifs of inversion, of blurred or unusual sex identity, of
a classless community, [and] of annulled normality." An excellent, original treatment of
an undervalued dimension of VW's fiction. Assimilates Little's essay on JACOB'S ROOM, previously published in G51. Also see G65.

G46 Lohmüller, Gertrud. DIE FRAU IM WERK VIRGINIA WOOLFS: EIN BEITRAG ZUR PSYCHOLOGISCHEN UND STILISTISCHEN UNTERSUCHUNG DES NEUSTEN ENGLISCHEN FRAUENROMANS. Leipzig: Noske, 1937.
Classification of the varieties of women depicted
by VW in her fiction (through THE WAVES) and selected other works (critical essays, A ROOM OF
ONE'S OWN, and FLUSH), culminating in a general
overview of VW's technical development as a novelist. Lohmüller categorizes and describes, with
copious illustration from the writings, six distinct types of women in VW's work: the romantic
woman detached from reality, the erotic woman,
the intellectual woman, the stoically reflective
woman of late middle-age, the motherly woman, and
the artistic woman. In her overview, Lohmüller
parallels VW's development from relatively conventional psychological realist, to stream-of-consciousness novelist, ultimately to "metaphysical poet" (in THE WAVES), with her growing realization of the isolated woman as a symbol of
universal human alienation. [In German.] Reviewed in E3.

G47 Love, Jean O. WORLDS OF CONSCIOUSNESS: MYTHOPOETIC THOUGHT IN THE NOVELS OF VIRGINIA WOOLF. Berkeley: Univ. of California Press, 1970.

Deplorably jargon-laden and opaque definition of a critical methodology, adapting "developmental cognitive psychology" to literary study, and application of the interpretive method to seven of VW's novels (ORLANDO and THE YEARS omitted). The limited value of this study is to be found in Love's analysis of recurrent "mythopoetic elements" (i.e., patterns) within the novels considered. Reviewed in H225 and Q3.

G48 McLaurin, Allen. VIRGINIA WOOLF: THE ECHOES ENSLAVED. Cambridge: Cambridge Univ. Press, 1973.

Important, two-part study of the provenance and VW's literary explorations of her ideas of form and rhythm in art. McLaurin considers VW's musical use of rhythmic devices, under the influence of Samuel Butler, specifically in MD, THE WAVES, and THE YEARS. The problem of how to represent and contain rhythm within form ("echoes enslaved"), addressed by VW under the influence of Roger Fry, McLaurin studies in the "visual" and structural elements of THE VOYAGE OUT, NIGHT AND DAY, MD, FLUSH, and BETWEEN THE ACTS. McLaurin's final chapter, on TL, draws rhythm and form and their study together, seeing the novel as a commentary on its own composition.

G49 Majumdar, Robin, and Allen McLaurin, eds. VIRGINIA WOOLF: THE CRITICAL HERITAGE. London: Routledge, 1975.

Useful annotated collection of major reviews of VW's works, general commentaries, obituaries, notes, and letters (1915-41), with an editorial introduction (see E10). Includes A18, F16, F97, H14, H16, H23, H28, H115, H157, H174, H175, H234, H251, K7, L1, L19, N6, N30, P2, P22, R14, T6, W17, and extracts from F96, G17, H34, H38, H58, H64, H69, H81, H125, H129, H168, H176, H242, K9, L10, N68, P5, P24, P27, Q39, X38, and X42. Also see E3.

G50 Mancioli Billi, Mirella. VIRGINIA WOOLF. Florence: La Nuova Italia, 1975.

Brief, general introduction to VW's life and works, surveying the WRITER'S DIARY, the feminist and critical essays, the biographies, and, more fully, the themes and techniques of the nine novels: "the first novels" (THE VOYAGE OUT and NIGHT AND DAY), "the epiphanic moment" (JACOB'S ROOM), "the stream-of-consciousness technique" (MD), "In quest of the central moment" (TL), "the experiment in biography" (ORLANDO), "the poetic novel" (THE WAVES), "the attention to facts " (THE YEARS, THREE GUINEAS, and the biographies), and "the final novel" (BETWEEN THE ACTS). [In Italian.]

G51 Marcus, Jane, ed. NEW FEMINIST ESSAYS ON VIRGINIA WOOLF. Lincoln: Univ. of Nebraska Press, 1981.
> Gathering of twelve "feminist" perspectives on VW and her works. Some excellent contributions, and some gratingly polemical and reductive arguments. Includes F43, G45 (extract), H152, J12, L17, M34, N64, P38, R24, S7, T9, and T22. Also see below.

G52 -----, ed. VIRGINIA WOOLF: A FEMINIST SLANT. Lincoln: Univ. of Nebraska Press, 1983.
> Essay collection, presumably a sequel to the above, containing thirteen papers that "develop a feminist critical theory using not only techniques of deconstruction but also the approaches of biography, textual scholarship, and history...and reveal a radical feminist writer who suppressed and repressed thoughts even more dangerous than those she published." Includes studies of VW's unpublished early diaries (by Louise A. DeSalvo), the influence of VW on her aunt Caroline Emilia Stephen, the Quaker mystic (by Marcus), VW's relationship with Mansfield and Richardson (by Diane F. Gillespie and Ann Landis McLaughlin), VW and the women's movement (by Naomi Black), the public responses to THREE GUINEAS (by Brenda R. Silver), the influence of the Elizabethans on VW's imagination (by Alice Fox), VW's Joycean use of myth (by Evelyn Haller), her attitude toward "fathers in general" (by Beverly Ann Schlack), her increasing feminist anger in the thirties (by Carolyn Heilbrun), and close readings of MD (by Emily Jensen), the drafts of THE YEARS (by Susan M. Squier), and BETWEEN THE ACTS (by Sallie Sears). Not seen (quoted from publisher's announcement).

G53 Marder, Herbert. FEMINISM & ART: A STUDY OF VIRGINIA WOOLF. Chicago: Univ. of Chicago Press, 1968.
> One of the few thematic studies of VW, though Marder does devote space to extended commentaries on seven pertinent works (NIGHT AND DAY, MD, TL, ORLANDO, A ROOM OF ONE'S OWN, THE YEARS, and THREE GUINEAS). Asserting the existence of feminism as an implicit social theme in VW's works, a kind of "latent propaganda" in fact uniting the writings, Marder considers both her "ideas in relation to social history and the feminist movement" and the ramifications of her ideas in selected works. Marder's enthusiasm for his theme, however, leads him to overrate its most complete embodiment, THE YEARS, as VW's masterwork.

G54 Miroiu, Mihai. VIRGINIA WOOLF. Bucharest, Rumania: Editura Univers, 1977.
Well-informed and comprehensive introduction to VW's life and works. Miroiu devotes two opening chapters to surveying the social and cultural influences of VW's late-Victorian childhood and of the Bloomsbury Group, and, in ten chapters, examines VW's long and short fiction. Miroiu summarizes the chief literary features of the novels in turn, proposing a developmental pattern of increasing experimentation (through THE WAVES) and return to convention (THE YEARS and BETWEEN THE ACTS), and relates each work to VW's critical theories and contemporary experiences and concerns. Miroiu's Marxist orientation only occasionally distracts from the analyses (e.g., "The Worldly Obsession with Money" in MD, VW's insightful exposure of the complacencies of the "privileged class," etc.). Given the introductory purposes of the book, Miroiu rehearses generally familiar opinions (e.g., the influences of Mansfield and Proust, impressionism, psychological preoccupations, etc.). [In Rumanian.]

G55 MODERN FICTION STUDIES. 2 (1956), 1-45. "Virginia Woolf: A Special Number."
Collects five original critical essays and a checklist of VW criticism. Includes E2, H63, M4, P16, S34, and T14.

G56 MODERN FICTION STUDIES. 18 (1972), 331-486. "Virginia Woolf Number."
Miscellaneous compilation of twelve original essays on VW's fiction and a bibliographical checklist. Includes E14, K2, L13, M3a, M5, M47, M75, N76, N104, Q23, Q54, S11, and T5.

G57 Moody, Anthony D. VIRGINIA WOOLF. New York: Grove Press, 1963.
Balanced introduction and evaluation, concentrated on VW's fiction. Acknowledging his debt to Leavis's criticism of VW's works after TL (see S19), Moody considers VW limited by her lack of experience and by the dearth of "spontaneous natural emotion" in her writing, yet he departs from Leavis in finding both THE WAVES and BETWEEN THE ACTS considerable achievements. Good comments throughout on VW's materials, her maturing techniques, and her critical reputation. Extracts reprinted in G40 and N5.

G58 Morris, Jill. TIME AND TIMELESSNESS IN VIRGINIA WOOLF. Hicksville, N. Y.: Exposition Press, 1977.
Methodical, uninspired, and uninspiring summary of the counterpoint between the perpetually changing

temporal world and the immutable, timeless world of visionary states of mind in VW's fiction. VW's desire to "escape" time and her special visionary "gift" are "discovered" through Morris's amateur and unconvincing speculations on VW's psychology.

G59 Naremore, James. THE WORLD WITHOUT A SELF: VIRGINIA WOOLF AND THE NOVEL. New Haven, Conn.: Yale Univ. Press, 1973.
Frequently intriguing analyses of the recurrent symbolism in six of VW's novels (NIGHT AND DAY, JACOB'S ROOM, and THE YEARS excluded), and an attempt to describe the uncomfortable, unfamiliar, unusual "world" of her fiction. While conceding that VW is reticent about sex, Naremore contends that her symbolism is persistently erotic, that her major themes are sexual, and that her recurrent injection of fear and nervousness into her eroticism is related to her search for some "permanent union," in effect a "death-wish." Similarly, her muffled, indistinct, fluid world is the preeminent English example of "the material imagination of water." Thus, death by water, the method of VW's suicide, is immanent throughout VW's writings. Includes a discriminating discussion of VW's self-transcending stream-of-consciousness technique. Reviewed in Q3.

G60 Nathan, Monique. VIRGINIA WOOLF. 1956. Trans. Herma Briffault. New York: Grove Press, 1961.
General introduction to VW's life and work, in the context of the Bloomsbury Group and against the background of English life and culture (like the painting of the Impressionists, her work cannot be seen "apart from the landscapes that inspired it"), with useful discussion of her chief concerns (e.g., feminism) and techniques (e.g., water symbolism). Nathan includes numerous illustrations and an anthology of five substantial extracts from the fiction and essays (pp. 144-88). Originally published in French as VIRGINIA WOOLF PAR ELLE MÊME (Paris: Éditions du Seuil, 1956), Nathan's study has had a major impact on the revival of VW's reputation in France over the last two decades.

G61 Newton, Deborah. VIRGINIA WOOLF. Melbourne: Melbourne Univ. Press, 1946.
Discursive and admittedly "impressionistic" monograph (79 pp.) on the novels, stories, and essays, with a weak attempt at a critical "summing up" in the last few pages.

G62 Novak, Jane. THE RAZOR EDGE OF BALANCE: A STUDY OF VIRGINIA
WOOLF. Coral Gables, Fla.: Univ. of Miami Press, 1974.
Study of the "controlling idea" of the "oscillation between opposites," as characteristic of VW's "temperament, aesthetics, criticism, and fictional theory." The first part of Novak's book elucidates VW's "search for balance as method and form," drawing illustration from a variety of writings, including then unpublished correspondence, with useful comparison to the techniques of the visual artist. The second part contains formal analyses of four of the first five novels (through TL, NIGHT AND DAY omitted), in terms of the "tentative" theory established in part one. Theoretically interesting, yet a less satisfactory book than Bazin's similar work (see G6). Reviewed in U15.

G63 Osawa, Nimoru. VIRGINIA WOOLF. Tokyo: Nanundo, 1956.
Not seen. [In Japanese.]

G64 Parasuram, Laxmi. VIRGINIA WOOLF: THE EMERGING REALITY. Burdwan, India: Univ. of Burdwan, 1978.
Sees VW's development as a movement from the new modes of subjective perception, which involved a "shrinkage of the range and amplitude of experience in her fiction," toward her recognition of the objective "reality of the 'given' world, and the multitudinous forms of nature" symbolizing "the presence of an order outside and beyond the luminous order captured by consciousness." This unexceptional thesis, which often deteriorates into summaries of VW's use of nature images, is pursued through eight of the nine novels (ORLANDO omitted).

G65 Pasternack, Gerhard. ASPEKTE DES KOMISCHEN BEI VIRGINIA WOOLF.
Cologne: Univ. of Cologne, 1962.
Useful examination of the often overlooked or understressed comic dimension of VW's fiction. Though overly methodical, Pasternack offers a valuable perspective on VW's caricature and wit in THE VOYAGE OUT and NIGHT AND DAY, her satire and humor in MD and TL, and her irony and grotesquerie in ORLANDO, THE YEARS, and BETWEEN THE ACTS. The two predominantly elegiac novels, JACOB'S ROOM and THE WAVES, are understandably omitted. [In German.] Also see G45.

G66 Poresky, Louise A. THE ELUSIVE SELF: PSYCHE AND SPIRIT IN VIRGINIA WOOLF'S NOVELS. Newark: Univ. of Delaware Press, 1981.
Overview of VW's thematic and technical development, finding a highly systematic pattern of relationship among her nine novels. Poresky sees each novel as a quest by the "composite personality" of VW's fiction to discover the core of

selfhood, however momentarily, in spite of the
various forces which impede self-realization:
society (THE VOYAGE OUT and NIGHT AND DAY) and
gender (JACOB'S ROOM and MD). In TL this "composite personality" (embodied in Lily Briscoe)
finds Godhood within the self and Orlando finds
the androgynous nature of the self. THE WAVES
forces a recognition of the inevitable fragmentation of self in a fallen world. THE YEARS
shows the struggle for reintegration achieved
only by the discovery, in BETWEEN THE ACTS,
of the healing power of love. Some perceptive
comments on the works but, overall, an un-
convincingly imposed and occasionally forced
thesis.

G67 LA QUINZAINE LITTÉRAIRE. No. 172 (Oct. 1973), pp. 11-19. "Virginia Woolf."
Special "dossier" concerning VW, containing a
substantial essay by Mayoux (see H156), a
letter from VW to Julian Bell (1935), a review of recent studies of VW by Geneviève
Serreau, and an interview with Quentin Bell
by Viviane Forrester. Guest editor: Forrester. [In French.]

G68 Rantavaara, Irma. VIRGINIA WOOLF AND BLOOMSBURY. Helsinki:
Annales Academiae Fennicae, 1953.
Important first definition of the Bloomsbury
Group, its philosophic underpinnings (via
J. McTaggart, G. E. Moore, and Bertrand
Russell, among others), and its "aesthetic
attitude toward life" (via Clive Bell's
CIVILIZATION [1928]), in relation to VW's
work. Rantavaara examines VW's criticism,
her early fiction ("toleration in human
relationships"), and her emancipation of
herself from fictional and social conventions in her major novels and feminist
tracts (JACOB'S ROOM through THE WAVES,
"the peak of her art"). She concludes with
brief commentaries on THE YEARS, a "de-
bunking" of Galsworthy, and BETWEEN THE ACTS,
which she sees as a fragmentary "summary"
of VW's "lifetime's quest of beauty and
truth."

G69 Richter, Harvena. VIRGINIA WOOLF: THE INWARD VOYAGE. Princeton,
N. J.: Princeton Univ. Press, 1970.
Intensive analysis of VW's subjective methods
as a novelist, inspired by her description of
a book not as a "form which you see," but as an
"emotion which you feel" (in "On Re-reading
Novels"; from A27). Richter argues that VW
aimed to create a "complex synthesis of the

individual's total response to life" through
methods which directly involve the "common"
reader, processes which "tend to make the act
of reading approximate the experience itself."
She examines through the fiction four "modes"
of subjectivity presented by VW: the ways
the character "thinks," "sees the object,"
"experiences time," and "feels." Excellently
written, original, and insightful. Reviewed
in Q3.

G70 Rillo, Lila E. KATHERINE MANSFIELD (1888-1923) AND VIRGINIA
WOOLF (1882-1941). Buenos Aires: Talleres Gráficos Contreras,
1944.
Mansfield's and VW's friendship, and common
themes and concerns in their works. (Pamphlet--12 pp.)

G71 Rosenthal, Michael. VIRGINIA WOOLF. New York: Columbia Univ.
Press, 1979.
Solid and substantial studies of VW's novels,
her biographies, her feminist tracts, and her
literary criticism, prefaced by summary discussions of her life, Bloomsbury, and "the
problem of the fiction." In analyzing the
novels Rosenthal emphasizes no single theme
or "angle" of interpretation, seeing the
individual works holistically as exercises
in form, as VW's orchestrations of parts to
compose wholes of experience. He surveys
the nonfiction as complementary to the
fiction. Useful as a detailed introduction,
yet Guiguet's study serves the same purpose better (see G30).

G72 Sakamoto, Kiminobu. TOZASARETA TAIWA--V. WOOLF NO BUNGAKU TO
SONO SHUHEN [SOLITARY DIALOGUE--V. WOOLF'S LITERATURE AND CIRCLE].
Tokyo: Ofusha, 1970.
Not seen. [In Japanese.]

G73 Sakamoto, Tadanobu. VIRGINIA WOOLF: SHOSETSU NO HIMITSU [VIRGINIA WOOLF: SECRETS OF THE NOVEL]. Tokyo: Kenkyusha, 1978.
Not seen. [In Japanese.]

G74 Sanna, Vittoria. IL ROMANZO DI VIRGINIA WOOLF: ISPIRAZIONE E
MOTIVI FONDAMENTALI. Florence: Marzocco, 1951.
First book-length study of VW in Italian. Sanna
opens with a brief biography of VW and a summary
of her critical essays, prior to a chapter-by-chapter survey of the nine novels. Sanna's
criticism is competent, but undistinguished and
generally derivative (e.g., the often-noted
influence of Joyce and Proust on MD, of
Bergson and Proust on TL, of VW's own biographical essays and of popular literary histories on
ORLANDO, or of the later Joyce on THE WAVES).
[In Italian.]

G75 Schaefer, Josephine O'Brien. THE THREE-FOLD NATURE OF REALITY IN THE NOVELS OF VIRGINIA WOOLF. The Hague: Mouton, 1965.
> Critical readings of eight of the novels (ORLANDO omitted), focusing on VW's "amazingly" unchanging imagery and themes, on her experiments with form, and on her interplay, in each work, of the three "realities": physical nature, social conventions, and inner consciousness. The novels are grouped in terms of VW's gradual recognition of her primary concern with the reality of individual experience (THE VOYAGE OUT through JACOB'S ROOM), her explorations of consciousness (MD through THE WAVES), and her lapse from the vision of "heightened consciousness" (THE YEARS and BETWEEN THE ACTS). Competent. Extracts reprinted in G40, G80, and N5.

G76 Schlack, Beverley Ann. CONTINUING PRESENCES: VIRGINIA WOOLF'S USE OF LITERARY ALLUSION. University Park: Pennsylvania State Univ. Press, 1979.
> Specialized study of VW's idiosyncratic use of literary allusion, to emphasize the "immanence of the past in the present moment," in five novels: THE VOYAGE OUT, JACOB'S ROOM, MD, ORLANDO, and THE WAVES. Schlack examines the allusions for their impact on characterization, setting, structure, theme, and plot. Generally intelligent discussions, but the exclusion of the remaining novels, which is insufficiently justified, weakens the book. Reviewed in U26. Also see J15.

G77 Schwank, Klaus. BILDSTRUKTUR UND ROMANSTRUKTUR BEI VIRGINIA WOOLF: UNTERSUCHUNGEN ZUM PROBLEM DER SYMBOLKONSTITUTION IN *JAKOB'S ROOM, MRS. DALLOWAY*, UND *TO THE LIGHTHOUSE*. Heidelberg: Winter, 1975.
> Description, illustration, and categorization of VW's visual symbols in three novels. Schwank argues that VW's symbols shift within and among her works, suggesting numerous associated meanings in various contexts, for she conceived of the symbol as a visual patterning device (cf. Bell's concept of "significant form"), rather than a concrete representation of fixed, abstract ideas. Schwank's study deteriorates from this promising theoretical premise into a highly fragmented catalogue of associated symbols in JACOB'S ROOM (e.g., clocks, butterflies, bones, the sea, waves, trees), MD (e.g., the city, nature, clothes, leitmotifs, time, waves, trees), and TL (e.g., Lily's painting, the journey, the lighthouse). The lighthouse in TL, for example, he interprets as a structural symbol representing, in various ways, reality, Mrs. Ramsay, androgyny, transience, egoism, timelessness, and the novel itself. Overly systematic, yet diffuse criticism. [In German.]

G78 Segura, Celia. THE TRANSCENDENTAL AND THE TRANSITORY IN VIR-
GINIA WOOLF'S NOVELS. Buenos Aires: Talleres Gráficos Contreras, 1943.
> Monograph, bound with A. Jehin's IMPORTANCE OF
> IMAGINATION IN CHARLES MORGAN'S NOVELS as TWO
> STUDIES IN THE CONTEMPORARY NOVEL. Not seen.

G79 Spilka, Mark. VIRGINIA WOOLF'S QUARREL WITH GRIEVING. Lincoln:
Univ. of Nebraska Press, 1980.
> Provocative, "psycholiterary" study of VW's
> "inhibited response" to death, principally the
> deaths of her mother, stepsister, and father,
> as seen in her novels and memoirs. After
> tracing VW's "compulsive need" and sense of
> her inability "to cope with death," in six of
> VW's novels and in MOMENTS OF BEING, Spilka
> relates both Clarissa's response to death,
> in MD, to VW's mother's "stoic atheism," and
> Lily's "liberating grief on the lawn," in
> TL, to VW's eventual sublimation of her per-
> sonal griefs. Perceptive and persuasive.

G80 Sprague, Claire, ed. VIRGINIA WOOLF: A COLLECTION OF CRITICAL
ESSAYS. Englewood Cliffs, N. J.: Prentice-Hall, 1971.
> Four distinguished general essays and nine
> important commentaries on individual works,
> together with the editor's introduction (H226).
> All but one essay reprinted from earlier pub-
> lication. Includes H7, M10, N100, P14, Q36,
> S32, and extracts from G25, G30, G75, H67,
> H242, N7, and X1.

G81 Sugiyama, Yōko. RAINBOW AND GRANITE: A STUDY OF VIRGINIA WOOLF.
Tokyo: Hokuseido, 1973.
> Plodding, generally superficial commentaries on
> the novels, the "feminist" books, the biographies
> (where Sugiyama places ORLANDO), and the short
> fiction, with routine observations on form,
> imagery, plot, and theme. Well-intentioned, but
> critically naive and literal-minded.

G82 Thakur, N. C. THE SYMBOLISM OF VIRGINIA WOOLF. London: Oxford
Univ. Press, 1965.
> Commentaries on the novels, only partially sub-
> sumed into a general, theoretical context. Ar-
> riving at a definition of the literary symbol
> from VW's own critical writings, as something
> similar to what it represents, as a "suggestion"
> or "insight" rather than a "literal representa-
> tion," as a conscious creation (contra Freud and
> Jung), and as a concretion of the intangible,
> Thakur itemizes and explains the symbols in
> each of VW's nine novels, relating her symbolic
> techniques to the practice of numerous other
> modern novelists. Thakur's discussions, however,
> often stray from the ostensible topic and, in
> their diffuseness, become incoherent. Worthy
> thesis, poorly executed.

G83 Verga, Ines. VIRGINIA WOOLF'S NOVELS AND THEIR ANALOGY TO MUSIC. Buenos Aires: Talleres Gráficos Contreras, 1945.
    VW's structural use of musical elements in her fiction. (Pamphlet--6pp.)

G84 Warsi, Shaheen. THE MIND AND ART OF VIRGINIA WOOLF. Varanasi, India: Chaukhambha Orientalia, 1976.
    Pedestrian study of VW as an originator of the "stream-of-consciousness" novel. Includes useful summaries of VW's reflection of contemporary ideas (Bergson, Jung, Freud, Adler, the Russians, Symbolists, Impressionists, and Expressionists), and of the "meaning, mode, method, scope and value" of the stream-of-consciousness technique. The final third of Warsi's book is an uninspired survey of VW's contribution to modern fiction.

G85 Weidner, Eva F. IMPRESSIONISMUS UND EXPRESSIONISMUS IN DEN ROMANEN VIRGINIA WOOLFS. Greifswald: Hans Adler, 1934.
    Facile application of the terms "impressionism" and "expressionism" to characterize the development of VW's style and fictional techniques, from THE VOYAGE OUT through THE WAVES. Weidner finds VW's transformation into an expressionist beginning in JACOB'S ROOM, as she embarks on her "Neue Romanprogramm" to capture the "semi-transparent envelope" of life and chronicle the inner life of her characters, rather than the outward aspects of living ("das innere Erlebnis über das aüssere Leben"). Her discussions of VW's first seven novels generally survey their contents, form, and merits, noting their impressionistic and expressionistic qualities respectively. Modest and uninspired. [In German.] Reviewed in E3.

G86 Wiget, Erik. VIRGINIA WOOLF UND DIE KONZEPTION DER ZEIT IN IHREN WERKEN. Zürich: Juris-Verlag, 1949.
    First post-war study exclusively concerned with VW which, together with Auerbach's MIMESIS (see N7), initiated the rediscovery and widespread study of VW in German-speaking nations. Adopting Bernhard Fehr's term "Bewusstseinskunst" ("art of consciousness") to describe VW's fictional method (see H76), Wiget examines the three stages of VW's development as a novelist, from JACOB'S ROOM to BETWEEN THE ACTS. The "experiment" of JACOB'S ROOM consists largely of VW's adaptation of Bergsonian ideas, chiefly durational time, in fiction. MD and TL reflect her most "concrete" explorations of consciousness through their bases in her own experience, her allusions to the musical and visual arts, and her association of "eternal moments" with natural symbols (cf. Joyce and Richardson). The highpoint of this, her

second phase, however, is ORLANDO, which finds
a concrete structure for the abstractions of
time, memory, and consciousness in the histori-
cal-biographical form. VW's later novels are
experiments in further abstraction of "Bewusstseinskunst," unified only through her nature
symbolism (the sun in THE WAVES and time in
THE YEARS). BETWEEN THE ACTS, like ORLANDO
which opened her abstractionist phase, achieves
a remarkable synthesis of abstract and concrete
through its historical-dramatic structure for
individual consciousness. An impressive, though
overly systematic thesis. [In German.]

G87 WOMEN'S STUDIES. 4 (1977), 149-300. "Special Issue: Virginia
Woolf."
Collects eight papers, presented at two VW con-
ferences in 1974, "exploring the often-neglected
social and political aspects of Woolf's novels."
Includes a brief introduction by the issue's
guest editor, Madeline Moore ("Another Version
of Virginia Woolf," pp. 149-51), several illustrations, and the following essays: H253, K1,
M73, N83, R16, S26, U19, and W19.

G88 Woodring, Carl. VIRGINIA WOOLF. New York: Columbia Univ. Press,
1966.
Introduction to VW's nonfiction, short stories,
and novels, concentrating on her experiments
with fictional techniques: "she made each novel
after her second find a new form to express the
idea that generated it." Reprinted in SIX
MODERN BRITISH NOVELISTS, ed. George Stade
(New York: Columbia Univ. Press, 1974), pp.
175-217.

G89 Yoshida, Yasuo. VIRGINIA WOOLF RONSHU: SHUDAI TO BUNTAI [ESSAYS
ON VIRGINIA WOOLF: THEME AND STYLE]. Tokyo: Aratake, 1977.
Not seen. [In Japanese.]

G90 Zaccaria, Paola. VIRGINIA WOOLF, TRAMA E ORDITO DI UNA SCRITTURA
[VIRGINIA WOOLF, WARP AND WOOF OF A WRITER]. Bari, Italy:
Dedalo libri, 1980.
Not seen. [In Italian.]

H. GENERAL CRITICAL ARTICLES OR CHAPTERS ON WOOLF

Many "general" studies of VW in reality concentrate on one or two of her novels (usually some combination of MD, TL, and THE WAVES). In most cases such items have been placed, with cross-references if necessary, in the appropriate sections following this (i.e., sections J through S, devoted to studies of her nine novels); however, several articles which are truly "general" in their significance have been placed in the section below though they may draw their illustration from a narrow base in VW's writings. As much as possible, the individual works considered in the following essays have been identified in the annotations. For a full accounting of the significant discussions of individual works, to be found among the general essays included in this section as well as in all other publications entered in this guide, see the concluding index: "Virginia Woolf's Works."

H1 Adams, Robert M. AFTERJOYCE: STUDIES IN FICTION AFTER ULYSSES. New York: Oxford Univ. Press, 1977. Pp. 67-78.
    VW indebted to, frightened by, and jealous of Joyce.

H2 Albright, Daniel. "Virginia Woolf." In PERSONALITY AND IMPERSONALITY: LAWRENCE, WOOLF, AND MANN. Chicago: Univ. of Chicago Press, 1978. Pp. 96-197.
    VW's novels illustrate a characteristically modern imbalance between "the subjective author and the objective world of mimesis," leading ultimately to the "proliferation of ego and suppression of object" (in THE WAVES).

H3 Allen, Walter. THE ENGLISH NOVEL: A SHORT CRITICAL HISTORY. New York: Dutton, 1954. Pp. 413-16, 419-23, and passim.
    Comments on VW's role in fiction, "1914 and after," particularly in the development of stream-of-consciousness techniques.

H4 -----. THE MODERN NOVEL IN BRITAIN AND THE UNITED STATES. New York: Dutton, 1964. Pp. 17-21 and passim.
    VW a "highly original and most accomplished novelist," but "a novelist of very narrow limits" attempting on a smaller scale what Proust and Joyce have done with similar subjects and techniques.

H5 Amorós, Andrés. "Virginia Woolf: El Impresionismo." In INTRODUCCIÓN A LA NOVELA CONTEMPORÁNEA. 1966. 2nd ed. Salamanca, Spain: Ediciones Anaya, 1971. Pp. 315-19.
    VW's novels the fullest modern realization of fictional impressionism, merging psychological themes, intellectual speculation, and exacerbating sensitivity. [In Spanish.]

H6 Badt-Strauss, Bertha. "Das Werk der Virginia Woolf." DIE LIT-
ERATUR, 34 (1931-32), 607-09.
Brief, general appreciation of VW's novels (JACOB'S
ROOM through THE WAVES). [In German.]

H7 Batchelor, J. B. "Feminism in Virginia Woolf." ENGLISH, 17
(1968), 1-17.
Disputes Forster (see G25), finding VW's "passionate concern with the nature of womanhood"
legitimate, "in the context of the thirties,"
and distinguishable from political and social
feminism. Reprinted in G80.

H8 Beach, Joseph Warren. THE TWENTIETH-CENTURY NOVEL: STUDIES IN
TECHNIQUE. New York: Appleton, 1932. Pp. 428-32, 470-73, 490-
93, and passim.
VW's experiments with fictional "breadth" (MD),
composite perspectives (JACOB'S ROOM), and ex-
pressionist techniques (ORLANDO and THE WAVES).

H9 -----. "Virginia Woolf." ENGLISH JOURNAL, 26 (1937), 603-12.
Admires VW's fictional innovations, but notes the
flaws and limitations in her conception of character. Extract reprinted in G40.

H10 Beckson, Karl, and John H. Munro. "Symons, Browning and the
Development of the Modern Aesthetic," STUDIES IN ENGLISH LIT-
ERATURE, 10 (1970), 687-99.
Anticipations of VW's "moment of being," Joyce's
"epiphany," and Pound's "image," in Symons's
aesthetic (derived, in turn, from Browning,
Pater, and the French "symbolistes"). Chiefly
on Symons.

H11 Beede, Margaret. "Virginia Woolf: Romantic." NORTH DAKOTA
QUARTERLY, 27 (1959), 21-29.
Finds antecedents in English Romantics for VW's
"attitude of rebellion against traditional cus-
toms and practices as well as her desire for
experimentation."

H12 Beer, Gillian. "Beyond Determinism: George Eliot and Virginia
Woolf." In WOMEN WRITING AND WRITING ABOUT WOMEN. Ed. Mary
Jacobus. New York: Barnes and Noble, 1979. Pp. 80-99.
Eliot's and VW's reactions to deterministic pat-
terns in experience, thought, and fiction (e.g.,
VW's rejection of plot).

H13 Beja, Morris. "Virginia Woolf: Matches Struck in the Dark."
In EPIPHANY IN THE MODERN NOVEL. Seattle: Univ. of Washington
Press, 1971. Pp. 112-47.
Structural and symbolic significance of "moments
of vision" in VW's novels. Reprinted in N1.

H14 Bell, Clive. "Virginia Woolf." DIAL, 76 (1924), 451-65.
The first major critical essay on VW, by a
renowned art critic (and her brother-in-law),

finding her early works developing toward the
achievement of "significant form" in JACOB'S
ROOM. Reprinted in G49.

H15 Bell, Millicent. "Virginia Woolf Now." MASSACHUSETTS REVIEW,
14 (1973), 655-87.
General critique, noting VW's frequently overlooked social awareness and topical concerns.

H16 Bennett, Arnold. THE AUTHOR'S CRAFT, AND OTHER CRITICAL WRITINGS.
Ed. Samuel Hynes. Lincoln: Univ. of Nebraska Press, 1968. Pp.
87-89, 218-27.
Collects five reviews of and comments on VW
(1923-29), documenting Bennett's side of the
Woolf-Bennett controversy. Hynes adds the
first version of VW's "Mr. Bennett and Mrs.
Brown" as an appendix (pp. 269-73; see A18).
All items also reprinted in G49. Also see
F48 and L1.

H17 Bentley, Phyllis. SOME OBSERVATIONS ON THE ART OF NARRATIVE.
New York: Macmillan, 1947. Pp. 40-45.
Brief description of VW's technical innovations.

H18 Blanche, Jacques-Émile. MORE PORTRAITS OF A LIFETIME: 1918-1938.
Trans. and ed. Walter Clement. London: Dent, 1939. Pp. 45-57,
215-18, 285-90, and passim.
French portrait-painter's enthusiastic admirations of VW's essays and fiction. Includes
Blanche's portrait of VW (1927; frontispiece).
For discussion of Blanche's early championship
of VW in France, see F21. [Never published
in French.]

H19 Blöcker, Günter. "Virginia Woolf." In DIE NEUEN WIRKLICHKEITEN:
LINIEN UND PROFILE DER MODERNEN LITERATUR. Berlin: Argon, 1957.
Pp. 103-11.
VW's view of "reality" as "fleeting, ambiguous,
and inestimable" ("Fliessendes, Vieldeutiges,
Unermessliches"). Groups VW with Joyce, Proust,
and Faulkner. [In German.]

H20 Borinski, Ludwig. "Die Vollendung der radikalen Stilformen und
Virginia Woolf." In MEISTER DES MODERNEN ENGLISCHEN ROMANS.
Heidelberg: Quelle and Meyer, 1963. Pp. 158-201.
VW's innovative conceptions of narrative form and
style (cf. the visual arts), a prominent example
of modern experimentation in fiction.

H21 Bowen, Elizabeth. "Virginia Woolf." 1941, 1942; "The Achievement of Virginia Woolf." 1949. In her COLLECTED IMPRESSIONS.
New York: Knopf, 1950. Pp. 71-75, 76-78; 78-82.
Three review essays on works by and about VW,
a novelist who both "affected" and "recreated"
the "consciousness of the age in which she wrote."
Reviews G9 and G25.

H22 Bradbrook, Frank W. "Virginia Woolf: The Theory and Practice of Fiction." In THE MODERN AGE. 1961. 2nd ed. Ed. Boris Ford. Harmondsworth, Engl.: Penguin, 1963. Pp. 257-69.
VW's genius culminates in TL (her one "lasting" contribution to fiction; the later novels are burnt-out cases), and her reputation as an innovator is largely a misrepresentation: "To pass from [her] theories, ideas, and criticism" to her novels "is to realize how much more conventional she was then she imagined."

H23 Bradbrook, Muriel C. "Notes on the Style of Virginia Woolf." SCRUTINY, 1 (1932), 33-38.
Attack on VW's use of an abstract and indirect style as a refuge from powerful feeling. Reprinted in G40 (extract), G49, and in WOMEN AND LITERATURE, 1779-1982: THE COLLECTED PAPERS OF MURIEL BRADBROOK, VOLUME TWO (Totowa, N. J.: Barnes and Noble, 1982), pp. 152-57.

H24 Bradbury, Malcolm. POSSIBILITIES: ESSAYS ON THE STATE OF THE NOVEL. New York: Oxford Univ. Press, 1973. Pp. 121-36 and passim.
VW's pivotal role in the English modernist movement, developing the "insubstantized," subjective, symbolic novel and influencing the emerging *nouveau roman*.

H25 Breton, Maurice Le. "Problème du moi et technique du roman chez Virginia Woolf." JOURNAL DE PSYCHOLOGIE NORMALE ET PATHOLOGIQUE, 40 (1947), 20-34.
VW's masterful innovations (cf. Joyce's and Faulkner's less convincing experiments), capture the complexity and fluidity of "la vie psychologique profonde." [In French.]

H26 Brewster, Dorothy. "Virginia Woolf." 1930. In her and Angus Burrell's MODERN FICTION. New York: Columbia Univ. Press, 1934. Pp. 218-47.
VW's "pursuit of Mrs. Brown, the spirit we live by, life itself, reality" in her fiction (through THE WAVES).

H27 Briffault, Herma. "Virginia Woolf y la revolución novelística." LA TORRE, 11, No. 43 (1963), 121-40.
VW's technical innovations from JACOB'S ROOM (cf. Joyce and Proust) to BETWEEN THE ACTS substantial contributions to the revolution in modern fiction. [In Spanish.]

H28 Brooks, Benjamin G. "Virginia Woolf." NINETEENTH CENTURY AND AFTER, 130 (1941), 334-40.
VW's "disinterested research into the fundamentals of her art," increasing experimentation through her career, "peculiar sensibility,"

"brilliance in exploration," "intellectual
integrity," and final attempt "to write one
understandable book" (BETWEEN THE ACTS). Reprinted in G49.

H29 Brown, Robert Curtis. "Laurence Sterne and Virginia Woolf: A
Study in Literary Continuity." UNIVERSITY OF KANSAS CITY REVIEW,
26 (1959), 153-59.
Traces of Sterne in "The Mark on the Wall" (the
moment of vision), ORLANDO (time), and TL (Mr.
Ramsay as counterpart to Mr. Shandy).

H30 Bryher, [Winifred]. "A Good Pasture Needs Many Grasses." LIFE
AND LETTERS TODAY, 30 (1941), 195-97.
Reacts against the view that VW writes from an
"ivory tower": "it was never remoteness but
inability to escape the universal suffering
of humanity that is the prevalent feature" in
her writings.

H31 Büchler, Franz. "Fenster zum Transparenten (Virginia Woolf und
Jorge Guillén)" ["Window to Transparency"]. In WASSERSCHEIDE
ZWEIER ZEITALTER: ESSAIS [WATERSHED BETWEEN TWO GENERATIONS:
ESSAYS]. Heidelberg: Stiehm, 1970. Pp. 60-71.
Compares the network of evanescent threads ("das
Netz der geistigen Fäden"), which composes the
world of VW's fiction, with the affirmative,
"geometrical" world view of the Spanish poet
Guillén. [In German.]

H32 Bullett, Gerald. MODERN ENGLISH FICTION: A PERSONAL VIEW.
London: Jenkins, 1926. Pp. 86-93.
The "singular quality" of VW's prose style and
method of narration.

H33 Burgum, Edwin B. "Virginia Woolf and the Empty Room." In THE
NOVEL AND THE WORLD'S DILEMMA. New York: Oxford Univ. Press,
1947. Pp. 120-39.
The loss of the "well-integrated personality" in
the modern world VW's constant theme.

H34 Burra, Peter. "Virginia Woolf." NINETEENTH CENTURY, 115 (1934),
112-25.
Sees mystical tendencies in VW's visionary approach to the everyday. Extracts reprinted in
G49.

H35 Carroll, Bernice A. "'To Crush Him in Our Own Country': The
Political Thought of Virginia Woolf." FEMINIST STUDIES, 4
(1978), 99-131.
Despite her dislike of practical politics and
"deliberate concealment of her political views,"
VW's works permeated by an informed, feminist
political consciousness.

General Critical Articles

H36 Cecil, David. "Virginia Woolf and E. M. Forster"; "Virginia Woolf." In POETS AND STORY-TELLERS. New York: Macmillan, 1949. Pp. 155-59; 160-80.
Brief note on VW's and Forster's similarities, and attack on VW as an "aesthete."

H37 Chapman, Robert T. "'Parties...Parties...Parties': Some Images of the 'Gay Twenties.'" ENGLISH, 21 (1972), 93-97.
While most writers portraying social gatherings in the twenties saw their underlying ennui and spiritual malaise, VW uses the party as a metaphor for "aesthetic achievement" in the momentary shaping of "the flux of life" (cf. Douglas, Huxley, Lawrence, Wyndham Lewis, and Waugh.)

H38 Charques, Richard D. CONTEMPORARY LITERATURE AND SOCIAL REVOLUTION. London: Secker, 1933. Pp. 108-14.
Though social themes work implicitly in VW's fiction and she has commented explicitly on social questions in A ROOM OF ONE'S OWN, her work, in its aesthetic detachment from "ordinary preoccupations," "remains the art of a [decadent] governing class in English society." Extracts reprinted in G49.

H39 Chattopadhyaya, Sisir. "Virginia Woolf and the Capture of the Moment." In THE TECHNIQUE OF THE MODERN ENGLISH NOVEL. Calcutta: Mukhopadhyay, 1959. Pp. 168-216.
Summarizes VW's concern for and experimentation with narrative techniques, concentrating on MD, TL, and BETWEEN THE ACTS.

H40 Chevalley, Abel. THE MODERN ENGLISH NOVEL. Trans. Ben Ray Redman. New York: Knopf, 1927. P. 245.
Brief but perceptive early observation of VW's characterization and influential correlation of her methods to "our great impressionists." Originally published in French as LE ROMAN ANGLAIS DE NOTRE TEMPS (London: H. Milford, 1921).

H41 Church, Margaret. "The Moment and Virginia Woolf." In TIME AND REALITY: STUDIES IN CONTEMPORARY FICTION. Chapel Hill: Univ. of North Carolina Press, 1963. Pp. 67-101.
The moment of permanence in the midst of change the central concept in VW's "theory of time" (cf. Proust). See L4.

H42 Cohn, Dorrit. TRANSPARENT MINDS: NARRATIVE MODES FOR PRESENTING CONSCIOUSNESS IN FICTION. Princeton, N. J.: Princeton Univ. Press, 1978. Passim.
VW's experimentation with narrative techniques (MD, TL, THE WAVES).

H43 Cohn, Ruby. "Nathalie Sarraute et Virginia Woolf: 'Sisters under the Skin.'" REVUE DES LETTRES MODERNES, Nos. 94-99 (1964), pp. 167-80.
    Similarities in the two novelists' style, approach to subjects, atmosphere, narration, characterization, and symbolism. [In French.]

H44 Collins, Arthur S. ENGLISH LITERATURE OF THE TWENTIETH CENTURY. 1951. 4th ed. London: University Tutorial Press, 1961. Pp. 217-30.
    General overview of VW's career (cf. Joyce).

H45 Compton-Rickett, Arthur. "Virginia Woolf." In PORTRAITS AND PERSONALITIES. London: Selwyn and Blount, 1937. Pp. 75-81.
    VW's unconvincing but interesting innovations in fiction, particularly her ghostly, insubstantial characterization.

H46 Conradi, Peter. "The Metaphysical Hostess: The Cult of Personal Relations in the Modern English Novel." ENGLISH LITERARY HISTORY, 48 (1981), 427-53.
    Prototypes for the hostess as "*artist-by-proxy*," in Murdoch's novels, found in the hostess figures in Forster (HOWARDS END [1910]) and VW (e.g., MD, TL).

H47 Cornwell, Ethel F. "Virginia Woolf's Moment of Reality." In THE "STILL POINT": THEME AND VARIATIONS IN THE WRITINGS OF T. S. ELIOT, COLERIDGE, YEATS, HENRY JAMES, VIRGINIA WOOLF, AND D. H. LAWRENCE. New Brunswick, N. J.: Rutgers Univ. Press, 1962. Pp. 159-207.
    The structural, symbolic, and thematic significance of the moment of transcendental insight into "reality" in VW's fiction.

H48 Coveny, Peter. THE IMAGE OF CHILDHOOD: THE INDIVIDUAL AND SOCIETY: A STUDY OF THE THEME IN ENGLISH LITERATURE. 1957. Rev. ed. Baltimore, Md.: Penguin, 1967. Pp. 312-20.
    VW's presentation of the "inward sensibilities of the child" (cf. Joyce and Lawrence).

H49 Cox, C. B. "The Solitude of Virginia Woolf." In THE FREE SPIRIT: A STUDY OF LIBERAL HUMANISM IN THE NOVELS OF GEORGE ELIOT, E. M. FORSTER, VIRGINIA WOOLF, ANGUS WILSON. London: Oxford Univ. Press, 1963. Pp. 103-17.
    VW's novels probing critiques of the humanist's confidence in the possibility of complete, lasting fulfillment.

H50 Crosland, Margaret. BEYOND THE LIGHTHOUSE: ENGLISH WOMEN NOVELISTS IN THE TWENTIETH CENTURY. London: Constable, 1981. Pp. 17-33 and passim.
    VW's principal contributions to modern fiction her "innovation in method" and her "preoccupation with the psychology of women and their position in society."

H51 Cunliffe, J. W. "Georgian Novelists: Virginia Woolf." In ENGLISH LITERATURE IN THE TWENTIETH CENTURY. New York: Macmillan, 1934. Pp. 245-53.
VW's work "new and strange and elusive in its significance."

H52 Dahl, Liisa. "The Attributive Sentence Structure In the Stream-of-Consciousness Technique, with Special Reference to the Interior Monologue Used by Virginia Woolf, James Joyce, and Eugene O'Neill." NEUPHILOLOGISCHE MITTEILUNGEN, 68 (1967), 440-54.
Specialized stylistic analysis of VW's "impressionistic" sentences (pp. 443-49).

H53 -----. LINGUISTIC FEATURES OF THE STREAM-OF-CONSCIOUSNESS TECHNIQUES OF JAMES JOYCE, VIRGINIA WOOLF, AND EUGENE O'NEILL. Turku, Finland: Turun Yliopisto, 1970. Pp. 17-18, 42-53.
Describes VW's varied uses of vocabulary and syntax in her fiction.

H54 Daiches, David. "Virginia Woolf." In THE NOVEL AND THE MODERN WORLD. 1939. Rev. ed. Chicago: Univ. of Chicago Press, 1960. Pp. 187-217.
VW responds to the "breakdown of a public sense of [the] significance" of fiction by evolving a "purely personal," as opposed to traditional, view of the novel. Survey.

H55 -----. "Le Londres de Virginia Woolf"; "Discussion." Trans. Jean Guiguet. In VIRGINIA WOOLF--COLLOQUE DE CERISY. Ed. Maurice de Gandillac and Guiguet. Pp. 83-112; 113-18. See F34.
Stresses the importance of a familiarity with the topography of London for a full understanding of VW's fiction (JACOB'S ROOM, THE YEARS, and particularly MD). Reviews the city's development into distinct social and intellectual quarters, of which VW was acutely aware. [In French.]

H56 Daniel-Rops, Henry. "Une Technique nouvelle: Le monologue intérieur." LE CORRESPONDENT, No. 1664 (1932), pp. 281-305.
Important definition of the interior monologue technique, principally concerned with Joyce but useful for the study of VW's narrative methods. [In French.]

H57 Dash, Irene G. "Virginia Woolf: Fact and Fiction, an Onamastic Study." LITERARY ONAMASTICS STUDIES, 5 (1978), 172-91.
Surveys Albee's allusions to VW's life, aspirations, anguish, weaknesses, and "philosophy and point of view" in WHO'S AFRAID OF VIRGINIA WOOLF? (1962).

H58 Delattre, Floris. "La Durée Bergsonienne dans le roman de Virginia Woolf." REVUE ANGLO-AMÉRICAINE, 9 (1931), 97-108.
Influential early analysis of VW's theories of time as influenced by Bergson's philosophy. A

major thesis of Delattre's book on VW (which assimilates this article; see G17). Extract reprinted, in translation, in G49.

H59 -----. "Virginia Woolf et le monologue intérieur." In his FEUX D'AUTOMNE: ESSAIS CHOISIS. Ed. Maurice Le Breton. Paris: M. Didier, 1950. Pp. 225-47.
Brief summary of the development of "le monologue intérieur," by French authors and Joyce (whose ULYSSES [1922] Delattre considers a direct influence on VW, despite her strong objection in a 1931 letter to Delattre, quoted here), expressing serious reservations concerning VW's nearly total abandonment of surface reality in her experimentation with the technique (e.g., THE WAVES). [In French.] Only completed portion of Delattre's proposed second book on VW: LA CONSCIENCE ET LA VIE DANS LE ROMAN DE VIRGINIA WOOLF, unfinished at the time of his death in 1949. See G17.

H60 Delbaere-Garant, Jeanne. "The Divided Worlds of Emily Bronte, Virginia Woolf and Janet Frame." ENGLISH STUDIES, 60 (1979), 299-711.
Similarities in the fundamental sense of the incompleteness of a "divided world" in the three novelists.

H61 Didier, Béatrice. "Virginia Woolf ou la chambre maternelle." In L'ÉCRITURE-FEMME. Paris: Presses Universitaires de France, 1981. Pp. 223-45.
Surveys VW's obsessive preoccupations with death (suicide, death of the mother) and with enclosure (rooms), and her attempts to resuscitate beauty, lost in her mother's death, through her art. [In French.]

H62 DiGaetani, John Louis. "Mythic Characterization: Richard Wagner and Virginia Woolf." In RICHARD WAGNER AND THE MODERN BRITISH NOVEL. Rutherford, N. J.: Fairleigh Dickinson Univ. Press, 1978. Pp. 109-29.
VW's critical responses to Wagner and Wagnerian elements in THE VOYAGE OUT, JACOB'S ROOM, THE WAVES, and THE YEARS.

H63 Doner, Dean. "Virginia Woolf: The Service of Style." MFS, 2 (1956), 1-12.
VW's development of a poetically heightened style to convey the "essence" of character. See G55.

H64 Dottin, Paul. "Les Sortilèges de Virginia Woolf." REVUE DE FRANCE, 10 (1930), 556-66.
Welcomes the available and forthcoming translations of VW's major fiction into French and surveys her "charms" as a novelist: her seductive though obscure style, her challenging

nihilism, and her avant garde experiments with
form. [In French.] Extracts reprinted, in
translation, in G49.

H65 Drew, Elizabeth A. THE MODERN NOVEL: SOME ASPECTS OF CONTEM-
PORARY FICTION. New York: Harcourt, 1926. Pp. 254-62.
VW's challenge to conventional fiction, in "Mr.
Bennett and Mrs. Brown," not successfully sup-
ported by her own fiction. Extract reprinted
in N5.

H66 Eagleton, Mary, and David Pierce. "Virginia Woolf." In ATTITUDES
TO CLASS IN THE ENGLISH NOVEL, FROM WALTER SCOTT TO DAVID STOREY.
London: Thames and Hudson, 1979. Pp. 118-25.
VW's "upper-middle-class response to the philis-
tinism of twentieth-century bourgeois culture"
(MD, TL, and THE WAVES).

H67 Edel, Leon. THE MODERN PSYCHOLOGICAL NOVEL. 1955. Rev. ed.
New York: Grosset and Dunlap, 1964. Pp. 124-36 and passim.
VW's experiments with the stream of consciousness
and the "novel as poem" (cf. Joyce). Extract reprinted in G80.

H68 Edgar, Pelham. "The Stream of Consciousness: Virginia Woolf."
In THE ART OF THE NOVEL: FROM 1700 TO THE PRESENT TIME. New
York: Macmillan, 1933. Pp. 328-37.
Survey, stressing VW's successful achievement of
poetry, subtlety, and detachment in her best fic-
tion (e.g., MD and TL).

H69 Eliot, T. S. "Le Roman anglais contemporain." NOUVELLE REVUE
FRANÇAISE, 28 (1927), 669-75.
Introduces VW to the French audience, in the ex-
alted company of Joyce (the greater genius) and
Lawrence (whom Eliot characteristically dis-
parages, to VW's benefit). [In French.] Extracts reprinted, in translation, in G49.

H70 Elkan, Lucy. "Virginia Woolf: Ihre Künstlerische Idee und Ihre
Auffassung der Frau." DER KREIS, 8 (1931), 148-52.
VW's maturing conception of woman and evolving
preoccupation with feminism, traced through MD,
TL, ORLANDO, and A ROOM OF ONE'S OWN. [In Ger-
man.]

H71 Ellis, Geoffrey U. TWILIGHT ON PARNASSUS: A SURVEY OF POST-WAR
FICTION AND PRE-WAR CRITICISM. London: Michael Joseph, 1939.
Pp. 330-41 and passim.
VW's emphasis on the "inner consciousness" of
character both her greatest achievement and her
greatest limitation.

H72 Endicott, N. J. "The Novel in England Between the Wars." UTQ, 12 (1942-43), 18-31.
    Identifies VW, Joyce, Lawrence, and Huxley as the English novelists of lasting significance from the period between the wars (rather than Bennett, Wells, Galsworthy, or Maugham).

H73 "Epitaph on Virginia Woolf: Interpreter of the Age Between the Wars: The Vision and the Pursuit." TIMES LITERARY SUPPLEMENT, 12 Apr. 1941, p. 175.
    Obituary praise for VW's clarity, cogency, wit, passion, and "unswerving integrity" in her pursuit of a poetic ideal for fiction.

H74 Evans, B. Ifor. "Virginia Woolf." In ENGLISH LITERATURE BETWEEN THE WARS. London: Methuen, 1948. Pp. 68-74.
    VW's fiction reflects the sense of social fragmentation of the period between the wars.

H75 Faulkner, Peter. HUMANISM IN THE ENGLISH NOVEL. London: Elek, 1976. Pp. 116-33.
    Though reluctant to make a humanistic affirmation and preoccupied with the complexities of human relationships, VW clearly within the tradition of the English humanist novel.

H76 Fehr, Bernhard. "Ernst und Spiel: Virginia Woolf." In DIE ENGLISCHE LITERATUR DER GEGENWART UND DIE KULTURFRAGEN UNSERER ZEIT. Leipzig: Tauchnitz, 1930. Pp. 50-66.
    Reviews VW's serious and playful contributions to the modern stream-of-consciousness novel (among Joyce, Richardson, and Sinclair) in JACOB'S ROOM ("Jacob ist ein Magnet"), MD (a much larger "room" than Jacob's), TL (the symphonic interplay between reality and fantasy), and ORLANDO (a playful "Satire über alles"). Important early commentary on VW by an influential Swiss-German observer of contemporary English literature and culture. [In German.] Reviewed in E3. Also see G5, G23, G86, Q21, and R5.

H77 -----. "Vom englischen Roman der Gegenwart." ARCHIV, 148 (1925), 42-49.
    Assimilated into essay above.

H78 Fischer, Hermann. "Virginia Woolf, 1882-1941." In ENGLISCHE DICHTER DER MODERNE: IHR LEBEN UND WERK. Ed. Rudolf Sühnel and Dieter Riesner. Berlin: Schmidt, 1971. Pp. 299-316.
    Discusses VW's Bloomsbury milieu, her inheritance of intellectual skepticism, and her compensatory movement toward irrational transcendentalism and aestheticism in her fiction. [In German.]

H79 Fleishman, Avrom. "'To Return to St. Ives': Woolf's Autobiographical Writings." In FIGURES OF AUTOBIOGRAPHY: THE LANGUAGE OF SELF-WRITING IN VICTORIAN AND MODERN ENGLAND. Berkeley: Univ. of California Press, 1983. Pp. 454-70.
    Through art VW "anesthesized her response" to childhood wounds, "achieving an esthetic distance" from life and reality. Comments on VW's distancing techniques in TL and THE WAVES, and her views of autobiography in "A Sketch of the Past" (in MOMENTS OF BEING, see B3).

H80 -----. "Virginia Woolf: Tradition and Modernity." In FORMS OF MODERN BRITISH FICTION. Ed. Alan W. Friedman. Austin: Univ. of Texas Press, 1975. Pp. 133-63.
    VW's fiction a fabric of "metaphors, allusions, and quotations" drawn from her reading, a synthesis of intellectual tradition.

H81 Forster, E. M. "The Early Novels of Virginia Woolf." 1925. In ABINGER HARVEST. New York: Harcourt, 1936. Pp. 106-15.
    Praises the "visual sensitiveness," intuitive insight, and "remarkable intellectual powers" found in VW's innovative and influential fiction (through MD). Extract reprinted in G49. Also see F94, X24, and X40.

H82 Francis, Herbert E. "Virginia Woolf and 'The Moment.'" EMORY UNIVERSITY QUARTERLY, 16 (1960), 139-51.
    Superficial general overview of VW's fictional intentions and achievement.

H83 Franks, Gabriel. "Virginia Woolf and the Philosophy of G. E. Moore." PERSONALIST, 50 (1969), 222-40.
    Fine summary of Moore's ethical principles and demonstration of their considerable influence on VW and her fiction.

H84 Fraser, G. S. THE MODERN WRITER AND HIS WORLD: CONTINUITY AND INNOVATION IN TWENTIETH-CENTURY ENGLISH LITERATURE. 1953. Rev. ed. London: Deutsch, 1964. Pp. 115-19 and passim.
    Underlying VW's subtle and exact "feminine" sensibility is "her father's sturdy agnosticism."

H85 Freedman, Ralph. "Awareness and Fact: The Lyrical Vision of Virginia Woolf." In THE LYRICAL NOVEL: STUDIES IN HERMANN HESSE, ANDRÉ GIDE, AND VIRGINIA WOOLF. Princeton, N. J.: Princeton Univ. Press, 1963. Pp. 185-270.
    Describes VW's "ideas of lyricism and narrative" and analyzes the lyric elements of her fiction (chiefly JACOB'S ROOM, MD, TL, and THE WAVES).

H86 -----. "Introduction: Virginia Woolf, the Novel, and a Chorus of Voices." In VIRGINIA WOOLF. Ed. Freedman. Pp. 3-12. See G26.
    Brief commentary and speculation on the varieties of critical responses to VW and her work.

H87 Fremantle, Anne. "And the Bush Was Not Consumed." COMMONWEAL, 43 (1945), 71-74.
> General assessment of VW's career and character: "In her 'experimental humanism' she used the novel as an extension of consciousness as others have used religion or poetry." (Reviews Joan Bennett's study [G7]).

H88 Freund, Philip. THE ART OF READING THE NOVEL. 1947. Rev. ed. New York: Macmillan, 1965. Pp. 181-91 and passim.
> VW and Joyce as popularizers and most accomplished practitioners of the stream-of-consciousness technique.

H89 Fricker, Robert. "Virginia Woolf." In DER MODERNE ENGLISCHE ROMAN. 1958. 2nd ed. Göttingen: Vandenhoeck & Ruprecht, 1966. Pp. 138-54.
> Defines VW's contributions to the "novel of consciousness" ("bewusstseinsroman"), and distinguishes her methods from Joyce's and Richardson's.

H90 Friedman, Melvin J. STREAM OF CONSCIOUSNESS: A STUDY IN LITERARY METHOD. New Haven, Conn.: Yale Univ. Press, 1955. Pp. 187-209.
> Traces the gradual development of the stream of consciousness in VW's fiction, deploring the preoccupation with technique in her later works.

H91 Frierson, William C. THE ENGLISH NOVEL IN TRANSITION, 1885-1940. Norman: Univ. of Oklahoma Press, 1942. Pp. 214-23.
> VW as a representative modern literary "impressionist."

H92 Fromm, Harold. "Virginia Woolf: Art and Sexuality." VQR, 55 (1979), 441-59.
> Attacks, as misleading and narrow, the conventional criticism that VW's fiction is sexless.

H93 Gill, Richard. HAPPY RURAL SEAT: THE ENGLISH COUNTRY HOUSE AND THE LITERARY IMAGINATION. New Haven, Conn.: Yale Univ. Press, 1972. Passim.
> The country house as symbol in VW's fiction.

H94 Gillet, Louis. "L'ORLANDO de Mme Virginia Woolf." REVUE DES DEUX MONDES, 53 (1929), 218-30.
> Sees VW thoroughly indebted to the greater genius, Joyce, for her themes and techniques in MD, TL, and ORLANDO. Reprinted in his ESQUISSES ANGLAISES (Paris: Firmin Didot, 1930), pp. 207-24.

H95 Graham, John W. "A Negative Note on Bergson and Virginia Woolf." ESSAYS IN CRITICISM, 6 (1956), 70-74.
> Fundamental differences between VW's and Bergson's conceptions of memory, consciousness, and reality.

H96   -----. "Time in the Novels of Virginia Woolf." UTQ, 18 (1949), 186-201.
      Important study of VW's use of durational concepts of time. Reprinted in G40.

H97   Greene, Graham. "François Mauriac." In THE LOST CHILDHOOD, AND OTHER ESSAYS. New York: Viking, 1951. Pp. 69-73.
      Contrasts the "great traditional" novelist (e.g., Mauriac) to the modernist VW, who has lost both a "religious sense" of the importance of man and the human act (cf. James), and a concrete sense of visible reality in her post-Romantic subjectivism (cf. Conrad).

H98   Gregor, Ian. "Voices: Reading Virginia Woolf." SEWANEE REVIEW, 88 (1980), 572-90.
      Considers VW's "creation of a voice...in the process of writing itself," and the influence of her voice, or presence, on "shaping the reader's response."

H99   Greig, John Young Thomson [John Carruthers]. SCHEHERAZADE, OR THE FUTURE OF THE ENGLISH NOVEL. New York: Dutton, 1928. Pp. 58-62, 68-74, 79-81.
      Faults VW, and modern "subjective" novelists generally, for her failure to recognize the ultimate reality of "Plan, shape, form, organic pattern, call it what you will...[as] the ultimate fact about life" and art. Calls for a return to "story" in the novel.

H100 Grindea, Miron. "The Stuff of Which Legends Are Made." ADAM INTERNATIONAL REVIEW, Nos. 364-66 (1972), pp. 2-14.
      On Bloomsbury, VW, and the state of VW studies. See G1.

H101 Guiguet, Jean. "Les Vacances et l'engagement"; "Discussion." In VIRGINIA WOOLF--COLLOQUE DE CERISY. Ed. Maurice de Gandillac and Guiguet. Pp. 33-47; 49-55. See F34.
      VW's characters, despite their apparent disengagement from experience, are, precisely because of this detachment, engaged in the more profound, personal, and intimate business of *living*. [In French.]

H102 -----. "Virginia Woolf et James Joyce: Un problème de dates et de tempéraments." In *ULYSSES*: CINQUANTE ANS APRÈS. Ed. Louis Bonnerot. Paris: M. Didier, 1974. Pp. 23-31.
      Argues that the similarities between their works are too general and superficial to suggest that Joyce had any significant influence on VW, or that VW imitated Joyce in any fashion. [In French.]

H103 Hafley, James. "Virginia Woolf's Narrators and the Art of 'Life Itself.'" In VIRGINIA WOOLF. Ed. Ralph Freedman. Pp. 29-43. See G26.
VW's experiments with narration in her short fiction and early novels, in search of the unique narrative voice found in MD and TL.

H104 Hamblen, Abigail Ann. "Edward Albee...and the Fear of Virginia Woolf." TRACE, No. 68 (1969), pp. 198-203.
Albee's play WHO'S AFRAID OF VIRGINIA WOOLF? (1962) dramatizes VW's central themes of the "essential loneliness and suffering of individuals and of the pain of heightened perceptiveness."

H105 Hampshire, Stuart N. "Virginia Woolf." In MODERN WRITERS AND OTHER ESSAYS. New York: Knopf, 1970. Pp. 38-46.
The impression of "a wildness and violence below a hard and beautiful surface which scarcely contains them" in VW's finest writing.

H106 Hanquart, Evelyn. "Humanisme féministe ou humanisme au féminin? Une lecture de l'oeuvre romanesque de Virginia Woolf et E. M. Forster." ÉTUDES ANGLAISES, 26 (1973), 278-89.
VW's feminism, seen as a natural though late development of Renaissance humanism, traced in her essays and fiction, chiefly TL, and related to Forster's similar attitudes (chiefly HOWARDS END [1910]). [In French.]

H107 Hardwick, Elizabeth. "Bloomsbury and Virginia Woolf." In SEDUCTION AND BETRAYAL: WOMEN AND LITERATURE. New York: Random House, 1974. Pp. 125-39.
VW's "great mind" and beautiful novels survive her biographers' and critics' preoccupation with the small "pond" of Bloomsbury.

H108 Hartman, Geoffrey H. "Virginia's Web." 1961. In BEYOND FORMALISM: LITERARY ESSAYS, 1958-1970. New Haven, Conn.: Yale Univ. Press, 1970. Pp. 71-84.
VW's "use of a realistic plot and an expressionistic continuity," through her imaginative knitting of consciousnesses, to achieve structural unity. Reprinted in N5.

H109 Hasler, Jörg. "Virginia Woolf and the Chimes of Big Ben." ENGLISH STUDIES, 63 (1982), 145-58.
While other writers surpass VW in the structural experimentation with time, only Proust parallels her "thematic" preoccupation with time (e.g., her characters' "abnormal sensitivity with regard to the transience of human life").

H110 Havard-Williams, Peter, and Margaret Havard-Williams. "Perceptive Contemplation in the Work of Virginia Woolf." ENGLISH STUDIES, 35 (1954), 97-116.
    VW's "real interest was in the contemplative mind and its apprehensions of the visible universe; and her analysis of sensation is innately bound up with the philosophical question of perception and with the psychology of aesthetic contemplation."

H111 Heilbrun, Carolyn G. TOWARDS ANDROGYNY: ASPECTS OF MALE AND FEMALE IN LITERATURE. London: Gollancz, 1973. Pp. 151-67 and passim.
    The ideals of "fusion," synthesis, and unity in VW's work characterize her androgynous vision. Extract reprinted in G44.

H112 -----. "Virginia Woolf in Her Fifties." TCL, 27 (1981), 16-33.
    The works of VW's fifties (THE YEARS, THREE GUINEAS, ROGER FRY, BETWEEN THE ACTS) characterized by her now fearless expression of feminist anger and her self-transformation as a novelist and writer.

H113 Heine, Elizabeth. "The Significance of Structure in the Novels of E. M. Forster and Virginia Woolf." ENGLISH LITERATURE IN TRANSITION, 16 (1973), 289-306.
    Structure in VW's works implies an order, the unity of which is formed by the mind of the artist, in contrast to the mystical perception of order in Forster.

H114 Heinemann, Jan. "The Revolt against Language: A Critical Note on Twentieth-Century Irrationalism with Special Reference to the Aesthetico-Philosophical Views of Virginia Woolf and Clive Bell." ORBIS LITTERARUM, 32 (1977), 212-28.
    VW's and Bell's philosophic skepticism informs their "logically untenable" distrust in language and ethically questionable faith in intuition.

H115 Henderson, Philip. "Bloomsbury: Virginia Woolf." In THE NOVEL TODAY: STUDIES IN CONTEMPORARY ATTITUDES. London: Lane, 1936. Pp. 87-91.
    VW a combination of Proust and Joyce, ensconced in an ivory tower. Reprinted in G49.

H116 Herrick, Robert. "The Works of Mrs. Woolf." SATURDAY REVIEW, 8 (5 Dec. 1931), 346.
    VW's "progress from concern with the dreary particulars" of life in her early fiction, to the "forlorn universals" of her later novels (through THE WAVES), merely the "rationalization of the intellectual in face of futility." Regrets VW's coterie appeal.

H117 Hidalgo, Pilar. "Virginia Woolf: El contexto inglés." ARBOR, Nos. 417-18 (1980), pp. 85-91.
    Acclaims VW's works, now generally available in Spanish translation, as major contributions to the novel, particularly praising MD, THE WAVES, and BETWEEN THE ACTS. [In Spanish.]

H118 Hintikka, Jaakko. "Virginia Woolf and Our Knowledge of the External World." JOURNAL OF AESTHETICS AND ART CRITICISM, 38 (1979), 5-14.
    Influence of the "epistemology and ontology of Russell, Moore, and Whitehead" on VW's basic philosophical themes.

H119 Hoare, Dorothy M. "Virginia Woolf." In SOME STUDIES IN THE MODERN NOVEL. London: Chatto and Windus, 1938. Pp. 36-67.
    VW's "exceedingly delicate sensibility" controlled and shaped by her "critical intelligence."

H120 Hoffman, Frederick J. THE MORTAL NO: DEATH AND THE MODERN IMAGINATION. Princeton, N. J.: Princeton Univ. Press, 1964. Pp. 386-91.
    Tension between death, or the vision of death, and the "vitality and discrimination" of the sensitive observer in VW's fiction.

H121 Hoffmann, Charles G. "'From Lunch to Dinner': Virginia Woolf's Apprenticeship." TSLL, 10 (1969), 609-27.
    A study of the manuscripts shows VW's sudden maturation in JACOB'S ROOM owes more to her experiments in narration and style in THE VOYAGE OUT and NIGHT AND DAY than the experimental short stories. Important contradiction to a popular view of VW's development.

H122 Hoops, Reinald. "Virginia Woolf." In DER EINFLUSS DER PSYCHOANALYSE AUF DIE ENGLISCHE LITERATUR. Heidelberg: Winter, 1934. Pp. 141-47.
    Sees the general influence of psychoanalysis on VW's fiction, though admitting her avoidance of any "clinical" concern with psychological analysis, and distinguishes her stream-of-consciousness from Joyce's "stream-of-preconsciousness" technique. [In German.]

H123 Humphrey, Robert. STREAM OF CONSCIOUSNESS IN THE MODERN NOVEL. Berkeley: Univ. of California Press, 1954. Pp. 99-104 and passim.
    Fine consideration of the conception, mechanics, and form of VW's stream-of-consciousness novels.

H124 Jackson, Gertrude. "Bemerkungen zur Kritik des Woolfschen Realitätbegriffs." SPRACHKUNST, 4 (1973), 296-313.
    Interesting overview of the continental, as well as American and English, critical ap-

proaches to VW's ideas of reality in fiction.
Cites numerous studies. [In German.]

H125 Jameson, Storm. THE GEORGIAN NOVEL AND MR. ROBINSON. London:
Heinemann, 1929. Pp. 18-23 and passim.
VW as a chief example of the experimentation
with inner dimensions of character in fiction
(MD, TL, and ORLANDO). Extract reprinted in
G49.

H126 Johnstone, J. K. THE BLOOMSBURY GROUP: A STUDY OF E. M. FORSTER,
LYTTON STRACHEY, VIRGINIA WOOLF, AND THEIR CIRCLE. New York:
Noonday, 1954. Pp. 126-56, 320-73, and passim.
VW's conceptions of beauty, reality, and the
intellect (cf. Forster and Strachey), and her
reflection of the Bloomsbury ethos in her long
and short fiction.

H127 Jones, E. B. C. "E. M. Forster and Virginia Woolf." In THE
ENGLISH NOVELISTS: A SURVEY OF THE NOVEL BY TWENTY CONTEMPO-
RARY NOVELISTS. Ed. Derek Verschoyle. London: Chatto and
Windus, 1936. Pp. 261-76.
VW's sentimentality and her transformation
from conventional to innovative novelist.

H128 Josephson, Matthew. "Virginia Woolf and the Modern Novel."
NEW REPUBLIC, 66 (1931), 239-41.
See's VW's first five novels (through TL) as
increasingly "impressionistic," modern attempts "to write a novel *without telling a
story*."

H129 Kelsey, Mary E. "Virginia Woolf and the She-Condition." SE-
WANEE REVIEW, 39 (1931), 425-44.
Incisive attempt to describe the "feminine"
qualities of VW's fiction. Extract reprinted
in G49.

H130 Kiely, Robert. BEYOND EGOTISM: THE FICTION OF JAMES JOYCE,
VIRGINIA WOOLF, AND D. H. LAWRENCE. Cambridge, Mass.: Harvard
Univ. Press, 1980. Pp. 30-34, 40-43, 68-80, 87-91, 119-29,
168-84, 222-35.
Distinguished study of the three novelists who,
despite numerous particular differences, both
share similar backgrounds and basic assumptions,
and reflect comparable thematic and technical
concerns.

H131 Kohler, Dayton. "Time in the Modern Novel." CE, 10 (1948),
15-24.
VW illustrates several recent experimental uses
of time in fiction.

H132 Kondo, Ineko. "Virginia Woolf to E. M. Forster"["Virginia Woolf
and E. M. Forster"]. EIGO SEINEN, 116 (1970), 64-66; 119 (1974),
659-61.
[In Japanese.]

H133 Kumar, Shiv K. "Virginia Woolf." In BERGSON AND THE STREAM OF CONSCIOUSNESS NOVEL. New York: New York Univ. Press, 1963. Pp. 64-102.
    Despite the lack of direct influence, VW's works parallel Bergsonian "theories of flux and intuition." Extended comparison. Portions of Kumar's discussion of VW, which were published in 1957, in the Univ. of Panjab RESEARCH BULLETIN (ARTS), have since been separately republished as pamphlets: VIRGINIA WOOLF AND BERGSON'S DURÉE (Folcroft, Pa.: Folcroft Library Editions, 1977; 17pp.), and VIRGINIA WOOLF AND INTUITION (Norwood, Pa.: Norwood Editions, 1978; 6pp.).

H134 Kushen, Betty. "The Psychogenic Imperative in the Works of Virginia Woolf." L&P, 27 (1977), 52-66.
    Influence of adolescent traumas on VW's "emotions and fantasies, the inner pattern of imagination" revealed in her fiction.

H135 -----. "Virginia Woolf: Metaphor of the Inverted Birth." AMERICAN IMAGO, 38 (1981), 279-304.
    Psychological analysis of VW's images of merger, confluence, or swallowing, "a compensatory defense against separation, loss, deprivation," in her last three novels.

H136 Lakshmi, Vijay. "The Solid and the Intangible: Virginia Woolf's Theory of the Androgynous Mind." LITERARY CRITERION, 10, No. 1 (1971), 28-34.
    The artist's mind reconciles the warring opposites of the universe.

H137 Lehmann, John. "Virginia Woolf." In THE OPEN NIGHT. New York: Harcourt, 1952. Pp. 23-33.
    VW an influential innovator and valuable mentor of younger writers, who was ultimately destroyed by the "strain" of "giving birth to masterpieces." Memoir critique.

H138 Lehmann, Rosamond. "For Virginia Woolf." PENGUIN NEW WRITING, No. 7 (June 1941), pp. 53-58.
    Memorial tribute, memoir, and critique. Finds ROGER FRY her "masterpiece."

H139 Lilienfeld, Jane. "Reentering Paradise: Cather, Colette, Woolf and Their Mothers." In THE LOST TRADITION: MOTHERS AND DAUGHTERS IN LITERATURE. Ed. Cathy N. Davidson and E. M. Broner. New York: Ungar, 1980. Pp. 160-75.
    Discusses the presentation of mother-daughter relations in the novels of three unorthodox women novelists, from orthodox family backgrounds (stressing their homosexuality).

H140 Livi, Grazia. "Disgragazione e fusione in Virginia Woolf" ["Disintegration and Fusion in Virginia Woolf"]. PARAGONE, No. 364 (1980), pp. 15-40.
: General biographical summary and survey of VW's writing career, in light of the recent Italian translations of her major works. [In Italian.]

H141 Lodge, David. "Virginia Woolf." In THE MODES OF MODERN WRITING: METAPHOR, METONYMY, AND THE TYPOLOGY OF MODERN LITERATURE. London: Arnold, 1977. Pp. 177-88.
: VW's movement from realist to lyric symbolist, effectively complete by MD, seen in the general context of modern literary history.

H142 Lorberg, Aileen D. "Virginia Woolf: Benevolent Satirist." PERSONALIST, 33 (1952), 148-58.
: Attends to the unexplored and underestimated qualities of VW's sense of humor.

H143 Lotringer, Sylvère. "La Chambre de Virginia." LETTRES FRANÇAISES, No. 882 (1961), pp. 4-5.
: Character sketch of VW, drawing generously from previously published memoirs and interviews with her surviving acquaintances, but concluding that her fiction remains the best introduction to her personality. [In French.] See G43.

H144 Lovett, Robert M., and Helen S. Hughes. "Virginia Woolf." In THE HISTORY OF THE NOVEL IN ENGLAND. Boston: Houghton Mifflin, 1932. Pp. 449-53.
: VW's neo-romantic anti-realism truly expresses the fictional trend of her time.

H145 MacCarthy, Desmond. "Le Roman anglais d'après-guerre (1919-1929)." REVUE DE PARIS, 39 (May 1932), 129-52.
: VW's unsuccessful search to capture "Mrs. Brown" in fiction (pp. 149-51). Includes his friend VW only in a disappointly brief afterword to his extended discussion of the post-war English novel. [In French.]

H146 McIntyre, Clara F. "Is Virginia Woolf a Feminist?" PERSONALIST, 41 (1960), 176-84.
: Compares the alternating strains of serenity and stridency in several of VW's essays and novels concerned with "the woman question."

H147 McLaughlin, Ann L. "The Same Job: The Shared Writing Aims of Katherine Mansfield and Virginia Woolf." MFS, 24 (1978), 369-82.
: Similarities between Mansfield's and VW's "early visions" of their art.

H148 McLaughlin, Thomas M. "Fiction and Interpretation in Virginia Woolf." ESSAYS IN LITERATURE, 8 (1981), 173-87.
: VW's fiction and criticism both focus on the "difficult effort" of defining the center or

essence of personality (in character or the
literary work), and question the possibilities
of success in this search. Examines the critical essays, short fiction, and TL.

H149 Maes-Jelinek, Hena. "Virginia Woolf." In CRITICISM OF SOCIETY
IN THE ENGLISH NOVEL BETWEEN THE WARS. Paris: Societe d'Éditions "Les Belles Lettres," 1970. Pp. 101-58.
Traces the tension between the sensitive individual and the outside world in VW's novels,
arguing for a greater appreciation of VW's
social awareness. Focuses on her first two
and last two novels.

H150 Magny, Claude-Edmonde. LITTÉRATURE ET CRITIQUE. Paris: Payot,
1971. Pp. 304-07 and passim.
Existentialist critic's view of VW's morbid
fascination with death and pessimistic themes
of isolated human existence as relieved only
by her vision of the cosmic "sea" of human
consciousness "où son oeuvre cherche à nous
replonger." [In French.]

H151 Manning, Hugo. "Virginia Woolf: Amazona entre las sombras"
["Virginia Woolf: Amazon among the shadows"]. SUR, No. 80
(1941), pp. 43-48.
Praises VW's extraordinary creative skills and
her refusal to compromise her art, despite her
growing conviction of the imminent collapse of
western society. Obituary tribute. [In Spanish.]

H152 Marcus, Jane. "Thinking Back through Our Mothers." In NEW
FEMINIST ESSAYS ON VIRGINIA WOOLF. Ed. Marcus. Pp. 1-30.
See G51.
VW a "revolutionary" writer, alienated from
"British patriarchal culture and its capital-
ist and imperialist forms and values." Finds
VW a "Marxist" and a "mystic," deeply influ-
enced by several spiritual "mothers" (e.g.,
Ethel Smyth).

H153 Marill, René [Albérès, René-Marill]. HISTOIRE DU ROMAN MODERNE.
Paris: Albin Michel, 1962. Pp. 188-98 and passim.
Surveys VW's fiction as an extreme example of
literary impressionism (and pointillism) in
its luminous moments of vision (cf. Sarraute).
[In French.]

H154 Maurois, André. "Virginia Woolf." In POINTS OF VIEW: FROM
KIPLING TO GRAHAM GREENE. Trans. Mary Ilford. New York:
Ungar, 1968. Pp. 349-79.
Appreciation, noting the similarity of VW's
technical mastery, without the display of
"erudition," to the style of Proust, Colette,
and the modern French novelists. Original
French publication untraced.

H155 May, Keith M. "Virginia Woolf and her Contemporaries." In CHARACTERS OF WOMEN IN NARRATIVE LITERATURE. New York: St. Martin's Press, 1981. Pp. 128-49.
> Skeptical view of VW's feminism and attempt to "display the feminine mind in fiction" (she has "many admirers...but no disciples"), with commentaries on her "contemporaries" Dorothy Richardson, Katherine Mansfield, and Gertrude Stein.

H156 Mayoux, Jean-Jacques. "Le Pouvoir des images." LA QUINZAINE LITTÉRAIRE, No. 172 (1973), pp. 11-17.
> The variety, consistency, and power of VW's imagery, and the agony at the heart of her fiction. See G67.

H157 -----. "Le Roman de l'Espace et du Temps: Virginia Woolf." REVUE ANGLO-AMÉRICAINE, 7 (1930), 312-26.
> VW's variegated fictions unified by their insistent return to universal ideas (e.g., space and time). Surveys JACOB'S ROOM through ORLANDO. [In French.] Reprinted, in translation, in G49.

H158 -----. "Virginia Woolf au pouvoir des images." In VIVANTS PILIERS II--SOUS DE VASTES PORTIQUES: ÉTUDES DE LITTÉRATURE ET D'ART ANGLAIS. Paris: Maurice Nadeau et Papyrus, 1981. Pp. 243-61.
> The qualities and varieties of VW's imagery in her major fiction (MD, TL, THE WAVES). [In French.]

H159 -----. "Virginia Woolf et l'univers féminin." In VIVANTS PILIERS: LE ROMAN ANGLO-SAXON ET LES SYMBOLES. Paris: Jullimard, 1960. Pp. 201-27.
> Attributes VW's feminism to her polarized relations with her parents and contrasts her feminine (subjective, social) vision with the masculine (objective, metaphysical) vision (e.g., Joyce). [In French.]

H160 Melchiori, Giorgio. THE TIGHTROPE WALKERS: STUDIES OF MANNERISM IN MODERN ENGLISH LITERATURE. London: Routledge, 1956. Pp. 179-82 and passim.
> VW's "novels are a series of efforts to express, and hold, the moment of vision."

H161 Mellers, W. H. "Virginia Woolf: The Last Phase." KENYON REVIEW, 4 (1942), 381-87.
> VW's sentimentality, ineptitude, and limited grasp of experience in her fiction since (and before) her one triumph: TL. Expanded version of R14. Also see S19 and W17.

H162 Mendez, Charlotte Walker. "I Need a Little Language." VIRGINIA WOOLF QUARTERLY, 1, No. 1 (1972), 87-105.
> VW's sense of the inadequacies of language and linguistic experimentation "in her effort to meet deeply felt aesthetic and communicative needs."

H163 -----. "Virginia Woolf and the Voices of Silence." LANGUAGE & STYLE, 13, No. 4 (1980), 94-112.
> VW a "visionary," exploring the "aesthetic and metaphysical dimensions of [the] interrelationships" between language and silence in communication, style, and the "mysteries of life, death, selfhood."

H164 Mendilow, A. A. "The Modern Psychological Novel." In TIME AND THE NOVEL. New York: Humanities, 1952. Pp. 200-33.
> Extensive reference to VW as "a typical representative of the twentieth century 'time school of fiction.'"

H165 Mercier, Michel. LE ROMAN FÉMININ. Paris: Presses Universitaires de France, 1976. Pp. 9-11, 14-17, 96-101, 158-60, and passim.
> Critical overview of VW's search for order in her fiction and her life, her theories for the novel, her criticism, and her fictional portraits of men (cf. Colette, and other women novelists). [In French.]

H166 Meyer, Kurt Robert. "Virginia Woolf (1882-1941)." In ZUR ERLEBTEN REDE IN ENGLISCHEN ROMAN DES ZWANZIGSTEN JAHRHUNDERTS. Bern: Francke, 1957. Pp. 83-104.
> Technical analysis of VW's exemplary use of the free indirect style of narration, in JACOB'S ROOM, TL, and THE WAVES. [In German.]

H167 Miles, Rosalind. THE FICTION OF SEX: THEMES AND FUNCTIONS OF SEX DIFFERENCE IN THE MODERN NOVEL. New York: Barnes and Noble, 1974. Pp. 73-82 and passim.
> VW's creation of a "distinctly feminine style" and the sexual polarization of her critics.

H168 Mirsky, Dmitri. "The Highbrows, 6: Bloomsbury." In THE INTELLIGENTSIA OF GREAT BRITAIN. Trans. Alec Brown. London: Gollancz, 1935. Pp. 111-20.
> Marxist view of the bourgeois liberal humanism of Bloomsbury and its affinities with Russian writers (e.g., VW's and Chekhov's "technical perfection" and "discreet lyricism"). Extract reprinted in G49. Originally published in Russian in INTELLIGENTSIA (Moskow: Sovetskaya Literatura, 1934).

H169 Moers, Ellen. LITERARY WOMEN. Garden City, N. Y.: Doubleday, 1976. Pp. 13-18, 232-40, and passim.
   VW the "most brilliant of all critics of women's literature" and, with Cather, Colette, and Stein, significant for her development of the modern female *Bildungsroman*.

H170 Moloney, Michael F. "The Enigma of Time: Proust, Virginia Woolf and Faulkner." THOUGHT, 32 (1957), 69-85.
   Comparative consideration of VW's use of fluid time.

H171 Monroe, Nellie Elizabeth. "Experimental Humanism in Virginia Woolf." In THE NOVEL AND SOCIETY: A CRITICAL STUDY OF THE MODERN NOVEL. Chapel Hill: Univ. of North Carolina Press, 1941. Pp. 188-224.
   VW a "great" and "serious" artist, an influential innovator in form, style, and psychology.

H172 -----. "The Inception of Mrs. Woolf's Art." CE, 2 (1940), 217-30.
   Finds VW's fiction indebted to Bergsonian theories of time and, chiefly, to Proust's exhaustive studies of the "flux of emotion and sensation" in character.

H173 Morra, Umberto. "Il nuova romanzo inglese: Virginia Woolf." LA CULTURA, 10 (1931), 34-51.
   Prominent, early Italian recognition of VW's experimentation and contributions to contemporary fiction. Reviews the novels, through ORLANDO. [In Italian.]

H174 Muir, Edwin. "Virginia Woolf." BOOKMAN (New York), 74 (1931), 362-67.
   Traces the evolution of VW's fiction from THE VOYAGE OUT to her "authentic and unique masterpiece," THE WAVES, a novel most remarkable for its unsentimentally "pessimistic" conception of life, "lightened only by the supersensual pleasures of the contemplating self." Reprinted in G49.

H175 -----. "Virginia Woolf." In TRANSITION: ESSAYS ON CONTEMPORARY LITERATURE. New York: Viking, 1926. Pp. 67-82.
   VW firmly within the English prose tradition in her "eminently practical, tolerant, appreciative, intelligent" attitude toward her characters. Reprinted in G49.

H176 Muller, Herbert J. "Virginia Woolf, and Feminine Fiction." In MODERN FICTION: A STUDY OF VALUES. New York: Funk and Wagnalls, 1937. Pp. 317-28.
   Surveys VW's technical and thematic strengths, praising MD in particular, but registering disappointment with her frequent "insubstantiality." Extract reprinted in G49.

H177 Nashashibi, Pauline R. "Alive and There: Virginia Woolf's Presentation of Reality." DUTCH QUARTERLY REVIEW, 7 (1977), 184-99.
    Particularly in the visual qualities of her work, VW "constantly examining the relationship of the human mind to the rest of nature."

H178 Neill, S. Diana. A SHORT HISTORY OF THE ENGLISH NOVEL. 1951. Rev. ed. New York: Collier, 1964. Pp. 284-93 and passim.
    VW's painstaking search of the "faintly illumined recesses of consciousness," in quest of the ultimate secrets of life.

H179 Neubert, Albrecht. DIE STILFORMEN DER "ERLEBTEN REDE" IM NEUEREN ENGLISCHEN ROMAN. Halle: Saale, 1957. Pp. 92-98, 124-30, 137-40, and passim.
    Distinguishes among "erlebten Rede" (free narration, *style indirect libre*, or indirect free discourse), "erlebten Eindrucks" (free impressions), and the interior monologue in VW, with comparisons to Joyce and Richardson. [In German.]

H180 Neuschäffer, Walter. "Virginia Woolf." In DOSTOJEWSKIJS EINFLUSS AUF DEN ENGLISCHEN ROMAN. Heidelberg: Winter, 1935. Pp. 81-88.
    Discusses VW's familiarity with Dostoevsky's works (viz. "The Russian Point of View" in A19 and her translation of STAVROGIN'S CONFESSION), discovers allusions to Dostoevsky in her fiction, and sees her technical innovations as conscious adaptations and extensions of the Russian's psychological realism. [In German.]

H181 Noël, Roger. "Nathalie Sarraute's Criticism of Virginia Woolf." REVUE DES LANGUES VIVANTES, 36 (1970), 266-71.
    Surveys Sarraute's "harsh, hasty, and undeserved" criticism of VW in THE AGE OF SUSPICION (see H212), defines the French "new novelist's" theories of fiction, and compares the two novelists' achievements. [In English and French.]

H182 Oates, Joyce Carol. "The Art of Relationships: Henry James and Virginia Woolf." 1964. In NEW HEAVEN, NEW EARTH: THE VISIONARY EXPERIENCE IN LITERATURE. New York: Vanguard, 1974. Pp. 11-35.
    James and VW, two considerably different novelists, both unjustifiably condemned for creating a "dehumanized" art.

H183 O'Faolain, Sean. "Virginia Woolf and James Joyce, or 'Narcissa and Lucifer.'" In THE VANISHING HERO: STUDIES IN NOVELISTS OF THE TWENTIES. London: Eyre and Spottiswoode, 1956. Pp. 193-222.
    VW's failures to feel life or to control her novels, the frailties of a "narcissist locked up in [her] own ego" (cf. Joyce).

H184 Ogoshi, Tetsuya. "Mizu no Tosa: Virginia Woolf no Motif a Megutte" ["An Exploration of Water: Concerning Virginia Woolf's Motif"]. In SUGA YASUO, OGOSHI KAZUGO: RYOKYOJU TAIKAN KINEN RONBUNSHU. Kyoto: Apollonsha, 1980. Pp. 552-63.
Not seen. [In Japanese.]

H185 Pachmuss, Temira. "Dostoevsky, Werfel, and Virginia Woolf: Influences and Confluences." COMPARATIVE LITERATURE STUDIES, 9 (1972), 416-28.
Thematic and metaphysical parallels between VW and two continental novelists.

H186 Painter, George. "Proust and Virginia Woolf." ADAM INTERNATIONAL REVIEW, Nos. 364-66 (1972), pp. 17-23.
Brief comparison, by the distinguished biographer of Proust. See G1.

H187 Paterson, John. "Virginia Woolf: Fire in the Mist." In THE NOVEL AS FAITH: THE GOSPEL ACCORDING TO JAMES, HARDY, CONRAD, JOYCE, LAWRENCE, AND VIRGINIA WOOLF. Boston: Gambit, 1973. Pp. 184-229.
The epistemological and methodological assumptions underlying both VW's "impatience" with the novel's limitations and her experimental "reform" of representational fiction.

H188 Peel, Robert. "Virginia Woolf." CRITERION, 13 (1933), 78-96.
Surveys VW's fiction through THE WAVES equivocally, seeing her extreme developments of the novel of "sensibility" in the tradition of Meredith, James, and Proust.

H189 Pendry, E. D. "Feminism, Fiction and Virginia Woolf." In THE NEW FEMINISM OF ENGLISH FICTION: A STUDY IN CONTEMPORARY WOMEN-NOVELISTS. Tokyo: Kenkyusha, 1956. Pp. 19-45.
VW's break-up of the world of the masculine novel marks the third stage in the emergence of feminine fiction, from "subordination" and "feminism" to "femininity."

H190 Phelps, Gilbert. THE RUSSIAN NOVEL IN ENGLISH FICTION. London: Hutchinson, 1956. Pp. 132-37 and passim.
Influence of Russians, especially Turgenev, on VW's work.

H191 Pillat, Monica. "Virginia Woolf şi Timpul Oglindă" ["Virginia Woolf and the Mirror of Time"]. VIAŢA ROMÂNEASCĂ, 26, No. 5 (1973), 150-56.
General introductory survey of VW's attempts to capture the flow of consciousness ("fluxului de conştiinţă") in her fiction. [In Rumanian.]

H192 Pomeroy, Elizabeth W. "Garden and Wilderness: Virginia Woolf Reads the Elizabethans." MFS, 24 (1978), 497-508.
VW's views of Elizabethan life and literature traced in seven essays, A ROOM OF ONE'S OWN, ORLANDO, and BETWEEN THE ACTS.

H193   Porter, Katherine Anne. "Virginia Woolf." 1950. In THE DAYS
       BEFORE. New York: Harcourt, 1952. Pp. 111-15.
              General commentary on VW, "one of the writers
              who touched the real life of my mind and feeling
              very deeply."

H194   Priestley, J. B. "Some Reflections of a Popular Novelist."
       ESSAYS AND STUDIES, 18 (1932), 149-59.
              Middle-brow novelist's reaction to a "high-brow"
              VW: she is, "very wisely, more admired than
              imitated" (cf. Joyce, among others).

H195   Pritchard, William H. WYNDHAM LEWIS. New York: Twayne, 1968.
       Pp. 101-03, 126-28.
              Lewis's ridicule of VW, "a feminine talent for
              whose works he had little respect." See X42.

H196   Rahme, Mary. "Coleridge's Concept of Symbolism." STUDIES IN
       ENGLISH LITERATURE, 9 (1969), 619-32.
              Notes parallels between VW's and Coleridge's
              "conception of the universe" and use of "trans-
              lucent symbols." Chiefly on Coleridge.

H197   Rahv, Philip. "Mrs. Woolf and Mrs. Brown." In IMAGE AND IDEA.
       Norfolk, Conn.: New Directions, 1949. Pp. 139-43.
              VW's ultimate failure to realize her praise-
              worthy ideals for fiction (see A18), despite
              her "minor successes" in MD and TL.

H198   Ramløv, Preben. "Bloomsbury og Virginia Woolf." In FREMMEDE
       DIGTERE I DET 20 ÅHRHUNDREDE. Ed. Sven M. Kristensen. Copen-
       hagen: G.E.C. Gads, 1968. II, 213-30.
              General introductory survey of VW's life,
              works, and Bloomsbury milieu. [In Danish.]

H199   Ramsay, Warren. "The Claims of Language: Virginia Woolf as
       Symbolist." ENGLISH FICTION IN TRANSITION, 4, No. 1 (1961),
       12-17.
              Affinities between VW's use of language and
              the French Symbolistes'.

H200   Reade, Arthur R. "Experiment and Virginia Woolf." In MAIN
       CURRENTS IN MODERN LITERATURE. London: Nicholson and Watson,
       1935. Pp. 165-78.
              VW's fictional experimentation a "highly self-
              conscious" result of her wide understanding of
              literary and intellectual traditions (as the
              child of Leslie Stephen). Finds her psycho-
              logical and social insight superior to Joyce's
              or Bennett's, and her sensitivity akin to
              Whitman's.

H201 Richter, Harvena. "Hunting the Moth: Virginia Woolf and the Creative Imagination." In VIRGINIA WOOLF. Ed. Ralph Freedman. Pp. 13-28. See G26.
>VW's use of the moth as a symbol both for herself and for the act of imagination, from JACOB'S ROOM through THE WAVES.

H202 Roberts, John H. "Toward Virginia Woolf." VQR, 10 (1934), 587-602.
>Early commentary on VW's original "conception of character in fiction" in her essays (e.g., "Mr. Bennett and Mrs. Brown") and novels. Extract reprinted in N5.

H203 Robson, W. W. MODERN ENGLISH LITERATURE. London: Oxford Univ. Press, 1970. Pp. 98-102 and passim.
>VW's failure as novelist found in her extravagant attempts to "spiritualize" character and experience.

H204 Rogat, Ellen H. "A Form of One's Own." MOSAIC, 8, No. 1 (1974), 77-90.
>VW's search for new literary forms a reaction against "masculine" styles and conventions in fiction.

H205 Rohde, Peter P. "Fra Realisme til Virkelighed" ["From Realism to Reality"]. EDDA, 31 (1931), 369-85.
>On the experimentations with conventions of fictional realism in Joyce (pp. 369-78) and VW (pp. 378-85). [In Danish.]

H206 Rosati, Salvatore. "Virginia Woolf." ENGLISH MISCELLANY, 1 (1950), 145-59.
>Not seen. [In Italian.]

H207 Rosenbaum, Stanford P. "The Philosophical Realism of Virginia Woolf." In ENGLISH LITERATURE AND BRITISH PHILOSOPHY. Ed. Rosenbaum. Chicago: Univ. of Chicago Press, 1971. Pp. 316-56.
>Full discussion of the impact of G. E. Moore's epistemology and ethics on VW's works.

H208 Rubenstein, Roberta. "The Evolution of an Image: Virginia Woolf and the 'Globe of Life.'" ANTIGONISH REVIEW, No. 15 (1973), pp. 43-50.
>Recurrent image in VW's fiction traced to its source in Tolstoy's WAR AND PEACE (1869).

H209 -----. "Virginia Woolf and the Russian Point of View." COMPARATIVE LITERATURE STUDIES, 9 (1972), 196-206.
>VW's critical dissatisfaction with literary realism and her fictional innovations influenced by her reading in Russian literature.

H210 Sakamoto, Koen. "Virginia Woolf no Buntai: 'Shiten' no Shiten kara" ["The Style of Virginia Woolf: From the Viewpoint of Point of View"]. EIGO SEINEN, 126 (1980), 13-14.
>Not seen. [In Japanese.]

H211 Samuelson, Ralph. "More Than One Room of Her Own: Virginia Woolf's Critical Dilemmas." WESTERN HUMANITIES REVIEW, 19 (1965), 249-56.
VW's attempts to reconcile sexual equality and difference get her into "some rather serious contradictions and inconsistencies" (cf. Lawrence).

H212 Sarraute, Nathalie. "The Age of Suspicion"; "Conversation and Sub-Conversation." 1950; 1956. In THE AGE OF SUSPICION: ESSAYS ON THE NOVEL. Trans. Maria Jolas. New York: Braziller, 1963. Pp. 53-74; 77-117.
Two reprinted essays (from TEMPS MODERNES and NOUVELLE REVUE FRANÇAISE) on the art of the novel, by a "new novelist" much influenced by VW. "The Age of Suspicion" acclaims the modern writer's rejection of conventional notions of fictional character and structure (cf. Impressionism) and "Conversation and Sub-Conversation," with explicit reference to VW, qualifies her earlier enthusiasm for modernist fiction, arguing that the contemporary novelist must revitalize the traditional novel through skillful and suggestive dialogue (viz. Henry Green). Originally published in French in L'ERE DU SOUPÇON: ESSAIS SUR LE ROMAN (Paris: Gallimard, 1956). See H181 and X15.

H213 -----. "Virginia Woolf ou la visionnaire du 'Maintenant.'" LETTRES FRANÇAISES, No. 882 (1961), pp. 1, 3.
Interview. Sarraute discusses her personal and critical responses to VW (e.g., above), but rejects the assumption that she was directly influenced by VW. [In French.] See G43.

H214 Savage, Derek S. "Virginia Woolf." In THE WITHERED BRANCH: SIX STUDIES IN THE MODERN NOVEL. London: Eyre and Spottiswoode, 1950. Pp. 70-105.
Distinguished attack on and "drastic revaluation" of VW's overrated, "tenuous, amorphous and vague" novels. See M76.

H215 Schneider, Daniel J. "'Orts, Scraps, Fragments' and the Circle of Wholeness: The Symbolism of Virginia Woolf." In SYMBOLISM: THE MANICHEAN VISION. A STUDY IN THE ART OF JAMES, CONRAD, WOOLF, AND STEVENS. Lincoln: Univ. of Nebraska Press, 1975. Pp. 118-53.
Dualistic tensions and symbolic oppositions in VW's fiction.

H216 Schorer, Mark. "The Chronicle of Doubt." VQR, 18 (1942), 200-15.
The modern writers' exaltation of individuality (VW passim; cf. Joyce and Lawrence).

H217 Scott, Nathan A. "The Bias of Comedy and the Narrow Escape into Faith." CHRISTIAN SCHOLAR, 44 (1961), 9-39.
Revealing a lack of "deep faith or confidence," VW's fiction an attempt to flee coarse reality into "bloodless" and exquisite consciousness, falsely "removed from the elemental things of human life."

H218 Scott-James, Rolfe A. FIFTY YEARS OF ENGLISH LITERATURE, 1900-1950; WITH A POSTSCRIPT 1951-1955. London: Longmans, 1956. Pp. 142-49.
Survey of VW's reaction to literary realism in her fiction of "interior vision" (cf. Joyce, Lawrence, and Dorothy Richardson).

H219 Serafini, Guglielmo. "Su David Herbert Lawrence." IL SAGGIATORE, Oct. 1932, pp. 297-304.
Considers Lawrence's relationships to Huxley, Joyce, and VW.

H220 Seward, Barbara. THE SYMBOLIC ROSE. New York: Columbia Univ. Press, 1960. Pp. 127-31.
VW's use of rose symbolism in MD, TL, and other works.

H221 Showalter, Elaine. "Virginia Woolf and the Flight Into Androgyny." In A LITERATURE OF THEIR OWN: BRITISH WOMEN NOVELISTS FROM BRONTE TO LESSING. Princeton, N. J.: Princeton Univ. Press, 1977. Pp. 263-97.
Biographical and critical discussion of VW's feminism and of feminist issues and themes in her writing.

H222 Simon, Irène. "Virginia Woolf." In FORMES DU ROMAN ANGLAIS DE DICKENS À JOYCE. Liège, Belg.: Bibliothèque de la Faculté de Philosophie et Lettres de l'Université de Liège, 1949. Pp. 341-87.
Historical and critical survey of VW's pursuit of the "mysterious spirit" of life, in reaction against the Edwardian materialists, in her most successful novels (JACOB'S ROOM, MD, TL, and THE WAVES). [In French.]

H223 Smart, J. A. E. "Virginia Woolf." DALHOUSIE REVIEW, 21 (1941), 37-50.
VW "a supreme writer when judged by her own standards," but when she ventures beyond her characteristic subject matter, as in her later work (THREE GUINEAS and THE YEARS), "her touch is less deft, her direction less sure."

H224 Spender, Stephen. "The Novel and Narrative Poetry." PENGUIN NEW WRITING, No. 14 (1942), pp. 123-32.
The narrative poem assimilated by the emerging modern poetic novels of Joyce, Lawrence, and VW:

"the experiments of the romantic poets in
verse narrative" correspond "to such achievements as the novels of Virginia Woolf to-day."

H225 Spilka, Mark. "New Life in the Works: Some Recent Woolf Studies." NOVEL, 12 (1979), 169-84.
Sees the recent publications offering new insight into VW's personal life (e.g., MOMENTS
OF BEING [B3], the DIARY [B1], and the LETTERS
[B2]), providing exciting possibilities for
studies of the interactions between her life
and works. Reviews C3, F61, F77, F81, G47,
and R1.

H226 Sprague, Claire. "Introduction." In VIRGINIA WOOLF. Ed.
Sprague. Pp. 1-13. See G80.
VW "less frail" in her life and art, in her
arduous quest to "write about Silence," than
her popular "legend" would suggest.

H227 Squier, Susan. "Mirroring and Mothering: Reflections on the
Mirror Encounter Metaphor in Virginia Woolf's Works." TCL,
27 (1981), 272-88.
The "psychological and feminist significance"
of the mirror encounter in VW's essays and
fiction.

H228 Stanzel, Franz K. "Die Erzählsituation in Virginia Woolfs
JACOB'S ROOM, MRS. DALLOWAY und TO THE LIGHTHOUSE." GERMAN-
ISCHROMANISCHE MONATSSCHRIFT, 4 (1954), 196-213.
The developing relationships among the reader's,
the author's, and the character's points of
view in VW's three novels. [In German.]

H229 Starkie, Enid. FROM GAUTIER TO ELIOT: THE INFLUENCE OF FRANCE
ON ENGLISH LITERATURE, 1851-1939. London: Hutchinson, 1960.
Pp. 186-97.
Influence of Proust and the *monologue intérieur*
on Joyce and VW.

H230 Steinberg, Günter. ERLEBTE REDE: IHRE EIGENART UND IHRE FORMEN
IN NEUERER DEUTSCHER, FRANZÖSISCHER UND ENGLISCHER ERZÄHLLITERATUR
[FREE INDIRECT DISCOURSE: ITS CHARACTERISTICS AND FORMS IN IN-
NOVATIVE GERMAN, FRENCH AND ENGLISH FICTION]. Göppingen, Ger-
many: Kümmerle, 1971. Passim.
Remarks on MD, TL, and THE WAVES, in the con-
text of highly schematic and technical discus-
sions of narrative techniques in modern fiction.
[In German.]

H231 Stevenson, Lionel. THE HISTORY OF THE ENGLISH NOVEL Vol. 11.
YESTERDAY AND AFTER. New York: Barnes and Noble, 1967. Pp.
230-47 and passim.
Historical survey of VW's introspective, "solip-
sistic" fiction.

H232 Stewart, Jack F. "Impressionism in the Early Novels of Virginia Woolf." JOURNAL OF MODERN LITERATURE, 9 (1982), 237-66.
"Interrelations" between VW's "early style" in her first three novels and Impressionist paintings (cf. Renoir, Monet, Sisley, Whistler, Pissaro and Seurat). Twenty painting reproduced. Also see P35 and Q55.

H233 Stubbs, Patricia. "Mr. Lawrence and Mrs. Woolf." In WOMEN AND FICTION: FEMINISM AND THE NOVEL, 1880-1920. New York: Barnes and Noble, 1979. Pp. 225-35.
VW's "failure to carry her feminism through into her novels" (cf. Lawrence's essential "anti-feminism").

H234 Swinnerton, Frank. "Virginia Woolf." In THE GEORGIAN LITERARY SCENE, 1910-1935. 1935. 2nd ed. London: Hutchinson, 1969. Pp. 290-94.
VW's fiction "very clever, very ingenious, but creatively unimportant." Reprinted in G49.

H235 Tajima, Yoko. "Vriginia Woolf." EIGO SEINEN, 127 (1981), 318-19.
[In Japanese.]

H236 -----. "Virginia Woolf Shoron: 'Halo' to 'Door'" ["An Introduction to Virginia Woolf: 'Halo' and 'Door'"]. OBERON, 15, No. 2 (1974), 77-88.
Not seen. [In Japanese.]

H237 Talamantes, Florence. "Virginia Woolf and Alfonsina Storni: Kindred Spirits." VIRGINIA WOOLF QUARTERLY, 1, No. 3 (1973), 4-21.
Comparison of VW and the Argentine poet who "mirrors in her life and art many of the same problems and concerns." Publishes, with facing translations, ten poems by Storni.

H238 Tindall, William York. FORCES IN MODERN BRITISH LITERATURE, 1885-1956. New York: Knopf, 1956. Pp. 199-205 and passim.
VW's fictional achievements, particularly her adaptations of the stream-of-consciousness technique, in the context of modern literary movements.

H239 -----. THE LITERARY SYMBOL. New York: Columbia Univ. Press, 1955. Pp. 158-63, 203-05, and passim.
VW's views of symbolism in fiction and her practice in MD and TL, among other works.

H240 -----. "Many-Leveled Fiction: Virginia Woolf to Ross Lockridge." CE, 10 (1948), 65-71.
Notes the resurgence of "many-leveled" novels, largely influenced by VW's success, culminating in Lockridge's RAINTREE COUNTY (1948).

H241 Toynbee, Philip. "Virginia Woolf: A Study of Three Experimental Novels." HORIZON, 14 (1946), 290-304.
VW's experiments with new forms to express modern man's "new complexity of vision." Discusses MD, TL, and THE WAVES.

H242 Troy, William. "Virginia Woolf and the Novel of Sensibility." 1932. In his SELECTED ESSAYS. Ed. Stanley E. Hyman. New Brunswick, N. J.: Rutgers Univ. Press, 1967. Pp. 65-88.
Analysis of the limitations of VW's fictional techniques, despite their contemporaneity, and distinguished rejection of her work: "its charm seems false, its authority invalid, and its beauty sterile." Extracts reprinted in G49, G80, and N1.

H243 Turnell, Martin. MODERN LITERATURE AND CHRISTIAN FAITH. London: Darton, Longman and Todd, 1961. Pp. 39-45.
VW's attempts "to find a way out of the materialist prison" in her works weakened by her fundamental lack of faith.

H244 -----. "Virginia Woolf." HORIZON, 4 (1942), 44-56.
VW "essentially a literary critic who wrote novels...more at home in interpreting the work of other writers than in the direct interpretation of experience." Surveys major fiction and essays.

H245 Vigne, Marie-Paule. "Réflexions autour d'un theme: Virginia Woolf et l'eau"; "Discussion." In VIRGINIA WOOLF--COLLOQUE DE CERISY. Ed. Maurice de Gandillac and Jean Guiguet. Pp. 179-209; 211-17. See F34.
Emphasizes the symbolic significance of water in VW's life and work, seeing both negative (in light of her suicide) and dynamically positive meanings in her water references. [In French.]

H246 Vowinckel, Ernst R. DER ENGLISCHE ROMAN ZWISCHEN DEN JAHRZEHNTEN, 1927-1935. Berlin: F. A. Herbig, 1936. Pp. 36-38 and passim.
VW's novels of consciousness explore new aesthetic possibilities for the story-within-a-story technique, sublimating the external framework of reality (space and time) and emphasizing the internal lives of her characters. [In German.]

H247 Wagenknecht, Edward. "The Stream and the World: Virginia Woolf."
In CAVALCADE OF THE ENGLISH NOVEL. New York: Holt, 1954. Pp.
522-32.
> VW, living in a dynamic world, could not "establish an absolute style." Each of her major novels is a "fresh experiment."

H248 Ward, Alfred C. THE NINETEEN-TWENTIES: LITERATURE AND IDEAS
IN THE POST-WAR DECADE. London: Methuen, 1930. Pp. 60-63.
> VW's "discontinuous method" and limitations in characterization.

H249 Wicht, Wolfgang. VIRGINIA WOOLF, JAMES JOYCE, UND T. S. ELIOT:
KUNSTKONZEPTIONEN UND KÜNSTLERGESTALTEN. Berlin: Akademie-Verlag, 1981. Pp. 16-102 and passim.
> Marxist study of three major modern examples of aestheticism. Wicht finds VW's reaction against realistic conventions paralleling contemporary political reactions against bourgeois capitalism and, despite the "dead-end" ("Sackgasse") of aestheticism in THE WAVES, her humanistic social vision implicitly echoing socialist ideals.
> [In German.]

H250 Wild, Friedrich. DIE ENGLISCHE LITERATUR DER GEGENWART SEIT
1870. Vol. 1: DRAMA UND ROMAN. Wiesbaden: Im Dioskuren-Verlag, 1928. Pp. 336-38.
> Places VW with Joyce and Richardson as a principal exponent of the modern English stream-of-consciousness novel. [In German.]

H251 Williams, Orlo. "TO THE LIGHTHOUSE." MONTHLY CRITERION, 6,
No. 1 (1927), 74-78.
> Praises VW's increasing mastery of her "uniquely reflective impressionism" through her first five novels, but questions whether her poetic ideal of "making of the moment something permanent" can ever be realized in fiction. Reprinted in G49.

H252 Wilson, Angus. "The Always-Changing Impact of Virginia Woolf."
STUDIES IN THE LITERARY IMAGINATION, 11, No. 2 (1978), 1-9.
> Wilson describes his contemporary responses to VW's fiction and her impact on his novels.

H253 Wilson, J. J. "A Comparison of Parties, with Discussion of
their Function in Woolf's Fiction." WOMEN'S STUDIES, 4 (1977),
201-17.
> The parties in VW's fiction celebrate the moment of unified, communal vision, "joining outer and inner experience, the individual with humanity, the instant with the constant, all goals of Virginia Woolf's art." See G87.

H254 Wilson, James Southall. "Time and Virginia Woolf." VQR, 18 (1942), 267-76.
> General summary of VW's thematic and structural uses of time in her attempt to capture the "solid, living flesh-and-blood Mrs. Brown."

H255 Zeman, Anthea. PRESUMPTIOUS GIRLS: WOMEN AND THEIR WORLD IN THE SERIOUS WOMEN'S NOVEL. London: Weidenfeld and Nicolson, 1977. Passim.
> Notes VW's "temperate" and "observant" reflection of pre-liberated woman's "accommodation to difficulties" in her fiction.

H256 Zéraffa, Michel. PERSONNE ET PERSONNAGE: LE ROMANESQUE DES ANNÉES 1920 AUX ANNÉES 1950. Paris: Klincksieck, 1969. Pp. 77-85 and passim.
> The distinguished French critic's survey of VW's achievement of a higher realism through experimentation with form and character in fiction. Also includes numerous comments (passim) on VW's affinities with other major modern novelists (1920-1950). [In French.]

H257 -----. ROMAN ET SOCIÉTÉ. Paris: Presses Universitaires de France, 1971. Passim.
> Comments on the problems posed for sociological criticism, by the subjective fiction of Joyce, Proust, and Woolf (whose novels are composed essentially of characters, yet characters in social relationships). [In French.]

J. STUDIES OF *THE VOYAGE OUT* (1915)

The following section is subdivided into two parts: i. Books and Essay Collections on THE VOYAGE OUT; and ii. Critical Articles or Chapters on THE VOYAGE OUT.

For transcriptions of the holograph manuscript of THE VOYAGE OUT and the surviving manuscript fragments of the novel's early version, "Melymbrosia," see C2. For the forthcoming concordance to the novel, see section D.

For bibliographical information on THE VOYAGE OUT, see Kirkpatrick (E7), and, for biographical backgrounds to the novel, see Bell (F13), Poole (F77), Rose (F81), Trombley (F95), and Woolf (F100).

For the most significant additional critical commentaries and information on THE VOYAGE OUT, see the following books, in section G above: Alexander (G2), Bazin (G6), Blackstone (G9), Daiches (G16), Delattre (G17), Donahue (G20), Finke (G23), Fleishman (G24), Gorsky (G28), Gruber (G29), Guiguet (G30), Hafley (G31), Harper (G32), Johnson (G36), Kapur (G37), Kelley (G38), Leaska (G41), Lee (G42), Little (G45), Lohmüller (G46), Love (G47), McLaurin (G48), Marder (G53), Moody (G57), Naremore (G59), Novak (G62), Pasternack (G65), Poresky (G66), Rantavaara (G68), Richter (G69), Rosenthal (G71), Schaefer (G75), Schlack (G76), Spilka (G79), Thakur (G82), Woodring (G88); the following critical articles, in section H above: Albright (H2), Bell (H14), Borinski (H20), Bradbrook (H22), Crosland (H50), Daiches (H54), Fleishman (H81), Forster (H81), Hafley (H103), Hoffmann (H121), Johnstone (H126), Kiely (H130), Kumar (H133), Muir (H174), Savage (H214), Scott (H217), Stewart (H232), Troy (H242), Wicht (H249), Williams (H251); and the following studies, entered in other sections of this bibliography: Howarth (K4) and Meisel (X3). For a complete listing of substantial commentaries on THE VOYAGE OUT, see the concluding index: "Virginia Woolf's Works."

J, i. Books and Essay Collections on THE VOYAGE OUT

J1 BULLETIN OF RESEARCH IN THE HUMANITIES [formerly BNYPL]. 82 (1979), 271-366. "Virginia Woolf Issue II."
    Five essays on VW's first novel, including studies of the early drafts and the 1920 revised editions by Louise A. DeSalvo, largely assimilated into her VIRGINIA WOOLF'S FIRST VOYAGE (below), and the following: G41 (extract), J9, and J15. Also see R1.

J2 DeSalvo, Louise A. VIRGINIA WOOLF'S FIRST VOYAGE: A NOVEL IN THE MAKING. Totowa, N. J.: Rowman and Littlefield, 1980.
    Reconstruction of the "four distinct earlier versions of the novel within the manuscripts at the Berg Collection" of the New York Public Library, including two "virtually complete" versions, with accurate dating of VW's composition of her most personally revealing novel. DeSalvo summarizes the book's development from "Melymbrosia" (1908-09; see C2), through the revisions of the second English edition (1920), connecting VW's varying treatments of the death of Rachel with her contemporary emotional crises and showing her evolving "use of fiction as a device for masquerading and structuring her own feelings." Extracts previously published above.

J, ii. Critical Articles or Chapters on THE VOYAGE OUT

J3 Bishop, Edward L. "Toward the Far Side of Language: Virginia Woolf's THE VOYAGE OUT." TCL, 27 (1981), 343-61.
    VW's mature concern for the limitations of language, for "how words can encompass and communicate human experience," a significant theme in her first novel.

J4 Brown, Carole O. "The Art of the Novel: Virginia Woolf's THE VOYAGE OUT." VIRGINIA WOOLF QUARTERLY, 3 (1977), 67-84.
    VW's "overriding conception of her first novel in visual, painterly terms," influenced by Roger Fry.

J5 Cláudio, Mário. "Virginia Woolf e Portugal: Lisboa, Porto, THE VOYAGE OUT." COLÓQUIO LETRAS, No. 41 (1978), pp. 19-25.
    The influence of VW's sea voyage to Spain and Portugal, in 1905, on her conception of her first novel. [In Portugese.]

J6 DeSalvo, Louise A. "Introduction." In "MELYMBROSIA," BY VIRGINIA WOOLF. Ed. DeSalvo. Pp. xiii-xliv. See C2.
    Describes the monumental task of recovering the 390 pages of VW's "earliest nearly complete version" of

her first novel, scattered among "nine drafts
or fragments of drafts" in the Berg Collection
(New York Public Library), and reconstructs
the history and biographical backgrounds of
the novel's composition.

J7 Fox, Alice. "Virginia Woolf at Work: The Elizabethan VOYAGE
OUT." BULLETIN OF RESEARCH IN THE HUMANITIES, 84 (1981), 65-84.
VW's increasing use of Elizabethan allusions and
motifs, and their appropriateness, traced through
the successive drafts of the novel.

J8 Frye, Joanne S. "THE VOYAGE OUT: Thematic Tensions and Narrative Techniques." TCL, 26 (1980), 402-23.
VW's struggle with "form as the arrangement of
potent emotions into a pattern" in THE VOYAGE
OUT. Her "blending of metaphysical concerns
into its structure lays the foundation for the
formal originality of her later fiction."

J9 Heine, Elizabeth. "The Earlier VOYAGE OUT: Virginia Woolf's
First Novel." BULLETIN OF RESEARCH IN THE HUMANITIES, 82 (1979),
294-316.
Discusses the substantial changes in VW's conception of the novel through its several revisions. See J1.

J10 Johnson, Reginald Brimley. "Virginia Woolf." In SOME CONTEMPORARY NOVELISTS (WOMEN). London: Parsons, 1920. Pp. 149-60.
Laments VW's capitulation to the "prevailing
taste for tragedy," in her first two novels.

J11 McDowell, Frederick P. W. "'Surely Order Did Prevail': Virginia
Woolf and THE VOYAGE OUT." In VIRGINIA WOOLF. Ed. Ralph Freedman. Pp. 73-96. See G26.
While formally traditional, THE VOYAGE OUT
anticipates VW's chief themes and preoccupations in her later, experimental works (e.g.,
THE WAVES).

J12 Moore, Madeline. "Some Female Versions of Pastoral: THE VOYAGE
OUT and Matriarchal Mythologies." In NEW FEMINIST ESSAYS ON
VIRGINIA WOOLF. Ed. Jane Marcus. Pp. 82-104. See G51.
Biographical models and mythological archetypes in the novel. From a yet unpublished
study: THE SHORT SEASON BETWEEN TWO SILENCES:
THE POLITICAL AND THE MYSTICAL IN THE WORKS OF
VIRGINIA WOOLF.

J13 Pitt, Rosemary. "The Exploration of Self in Conrad's 'Heart of
Darkness' and Woolf's THE VOYAGE OUT." CONRADIANA, 10 (1978),
141-54.
Largely self-evident comparisons and contrasts
with Conrad's story (1899).

J14 Rousseaux, André. "Virginia Woolf dans son premier livre." 1952. In LITTÉRATURE DU VINGTIÈME SIÈCLE. Vol. VI. Paris: Albin Michel, 1958. Pp. 244-52.
> THE VOYAGE OUT prefigures the chief themes and techniques (e.g., the moment of vision) of VW's mature fiction. Review of the 1952 French translation. [In French.]

J15 Schlack, Beverly Ann. "The Novelist's Voyage from Manuscripts to Text: Revisions of Literary Allusions in THE VOYAGE OUT." BULLETIN OF RESEARCH IN THE HUMANITIES, 82 (1979), 317-27.
> Schlack extends her earlier study of VW's allusive method (see G76) to consider the early drafts of THE VOYAGE OUT. See J1.

J16 Snow, Lotus. "Clarissa Dalloway Revisited." RS, 46 (1978), 197-202.
> Speculates on VW's motives for resurrecting Clarissa, from THE VOYAGE OUT, to become the focal character in MD.

J17 Walker, Cynthia. "Virginia Woolf's THE VOYAGE OUT: A Prelude of Images." VIRGINIA WOOLF QUARTERLY, 3 (1978), 222-29.
> VW's characteristic use of recurrent images and motifs, fully developed in her first novel.

K. STUDIES OF *NIGHT AND DAY* (1919)

Since there are no books, essay collections, monographs, or pamphlets on NIGHT AND DAY, this section consists entirely of critical articles or chapters on the novel.

For the forthcoming concordance to the novel, see section D.

For bibliographical information on NIGHT AND DAY, see Kirkpatrick (E7), and, for biographical backgrounds to the novel, see Bell (F13), Poole (F77), Rose (F81), Trombley (F95), and Woolf (F100).

For the most significant additional critical commentaries and information on NIGHT AND DAY, see the following books, in section G above: Alexander (G2), Bazin (G6), Blackstone (G9), Daiches (G16), Delattre (G17), Donahue (G20), Finke (G23), Fleishman (G24), Gorsky (G28), Gruber (G29), Guiguet (G30), Hafley (H31), Harper (G32), Johnson (G36), Kapur (G37), Kelley (G38), Leaska (G41), Lee (G42), Little (G45), Lohmüller (G46), Love (G47), McLaurin (G48), Marder (G53), Moody (G57), Pasternack (G65), Poresky (G66), Rantavaara (G68), Richter (G69), Rosenthal (G71), Schaefer (G75), Thakur (G82), Woodring (G88); the following critical articles, in section H above: Albright (H2), Bell (H14), Borinski (H20), Bradbrook (H22), Daiches (H54), Faulkner (H75), Franks (H83), Hoffman (H121), Johnstone (H126), Kumar (H133), Savage (H214); and the following study, entered elsewhere in this bibliography: Meisel (X3). For a complete listing of substantial commentaries on NIGHT AND DAY, see the concluding index: "Virginia Woolf's Works."

K1 Comstock, Margaret. "'The Current Answers Don't Do': The Comic Form of NIGHT AND DAY." WOMEN'S STUDIES, 4 (1977), 153-71.
    NIGHT AND DAY classically comic in form, but "the comic renewal of society is not left to depend... on the marriage of a single couple." The comic-romantic heroine, Katherine Hilbery, is paralleled by the political heroine, Mary Datchet. See G87.

K2 Cumings, Melinda Feldt. "NIGHT AND DAY: Virginia Woolf's Visionary Synthesis of Reality." MFS, 18 (1972), 339-49.
    Attempted synthesis of polarities (the mundane and the visionary, reality and dream, day and night), the subject and method of the novel. See G56.

K3 George, W. L. "A Painter's Literature." ENGLISH REVIEW, 30 (1920), 223-34.
    The "Neo-Georgians" (Joyce, Wyndham Lewis, Richardson, Sinclair, and VW, among others) seen "as painters rather than writers...slaves of impression." Includes NIGHT AND DAY in his discussion. Extract reprinted in G49.

K4 Howarth, R. G. "Dayspring of Virginia Woolf." SOUTHERLY, 3, No. 1 (1942), 18-21.
> Erroneously speculates that NIGHT AND DAY, "obviously less mature, less *experienced* than THE VOYAGE OUT," was written earlier. See Leonard Woolf's correction, SOUTHERLY, 3, No. 3 (1942), 10-11.

K5 Johnson, Reginald Brimley. "Virginia Woolf." In SOME CONTEMPORARY NOVELISTS (WOMEN). London: Parsons, 1920. Pp. 149-60.
> On THE VOYAGE OUT and NIGHT AND DAY. For annotation see J10.

K6 Mais, Stuart P. B. "NIGHT AND DAY." In WHY WE SHOULD READ. London: Richards, 1921. Pp. 105-11.
> VW's novel "a real treat, both emotional and intellectual," despite its claustrophobic atmosphere and passionlessness.

K7 Mansfield, Katherine. "NIGHT AND DAY." 1919. In NOVELS AND NOVELISTS. Ed. John Middleton Murry. New York: Knopf, 1930. Pp. 107-11.
> Novel a "fresh, new, and exquisite" work in the tradition of Austen. Specious praise. Reprinted in G49.

K8 Marcus, Jane. "Enchanted Organs, Magic Bells: NIGHT AND DAY as Comic Opera." In VIRGINIA WOOLF. Ed. Ralph Freedman. Pp. 97-122. See G26.
> VW's conscious use of the "initiation, quest, and journey myths of [Mozart's] THE MAGIC FLUTE [1791]" for structure (with asides on her debts to Austen for style and Ibsen for theme).

K9 Sharma, O. P. "Virginia Woolf's NIGHT AND DAY: A Study in Feminist Assertion." INDIAN JOURNAL OF ENGLISH STUDIES, 12 (1971), 55-66.
> VW's psychological and artistic feminism, emerging in NIGHT AND DAY, not to be confused with contemporary social and political feminist agitation.

K10 Zuckerman, Joanne P. "Anne Thackeray Ritchie as the Model for Mrs. Hilbery in Virginia Woolf's NIGHT AND DAY." VIRGINIA WOOLF QUARTERLY, 1, No. 3 (1973), 32-46.
> Influences of W. M. Thackeray and his daughter on VW's novel.

L. STUDIES OF *JACOB'S ROOM* (1922)

Since there are no books, essay collections, monographs, or pamphlets on JACOB'S ROOM, this section consists entirely of critical articles or chapters on the novel.

For the forthcoming concordance to the novel, see section D.

For bibliographical information on JACOB'S ROOM, see Kirkpatrick (E7), and, for biographical backgrounds to the novel, see Bell (F13), Rose (F81), and Woolf (F100).

For the most significant additional critical commentaries and information on JACOB'S ROOM, see the following books, in section G above: Alexander (G2), Badenhausen (G5), Bazin (G6), Blackstone (G9), Daiches (G16), Delattre (G17), Donahue (G20), Finke (G23), Fleishman (G24), Gorsky (G28), Gruber (G29), Guiguet (G30), Hafley (G31), Harper (G32), Johnson (G36), Kapur (G37), Kelley (G38), Leaska (G41), Lee (G42), Little (G45), Lohmüller (G46), Love (G47), McLaurin (G48), Marder (G53), Moody (G57), Novak (G62), Poresky (G66), Rantavaara (G68), Richter (G69), Rosenthal (G71), Schaefer (G75), Schlack (G76), Schwank (G77), Spilka (G79), Thakur (G82), Wiget (G86), Woodring (G88); the following critical articles, in section H above: Albright (H2), Beach (H8), Bell (H14), Borinski (H20), Bradbrook (H22), Brooks (H28), Cornwell (H47), Daiches (H54), Delattre (H59), Fehr (H76), Forster (H81), Freedman (H85), Friedman (H90), Hafley (H103), Hoffmann (H121), Johnstone (H126), Kiely (H130), Kumar (H133), Mayoux (H157, H159), Muir (H174), Neuschäffer (H180), Richter (H201), Rosenbaum (H207), Savage (H214), Simon (H222), Stanzel (H228), Stewart (H232), Troy (H242), Williams (H251), Wilson (H253), Zéraffa (H256); and the following study, entered elsewhere in this bibliography: Meisel (X3). For a complete listing of substantial commentaries on JACOB'S ROOM, see the concluding index: "Virginia Woolf's Works."

L1 Bennett, Arnold. "Is the Novel Decaying?" 1923. In THE AUTHOR'S CRAFT, AND OTHER CRITICAL WRITINGS. Ed. Samuel Hynes. Lincoln: Univ. of Nebraska Press, 1968. Pp. 87-89.
    Review of VW's "clever" novel, faulting its characterization. Reprinted in G49. Bennett's review provoked VW's "Mr. Bennett and Mrs. Brown" and the ensuing Woolf-Bennett controversy (see A18, F48, and H16).

L2 Borgal, Clément. "Virginia Woolf ou le point de vue de Sirius." CRITIQUE (Paris), 16 (1960), 609-14.
    Sees VW's innovative techniques in JACOB'S ROOM fully matured in THE WAVES. Reviews recent French translations of both novels (1958, 1957). [In French.]

L3 Buckley, Jerome H. SEASON OF YOUTH: THE BILDUNGSROMAN FROM DICKENS TO GOLDING. Cambridge, Mass.: Harvard Univ. Press, 1974. Pp. 262-67.
    Bildungsroman elements in the novel.

L4 Church, Margaret. "Concepts of Time in the Novels of Virginia Woolf and Aldous Huxley." MFS, 1, No. 2 (1955), 19-24.
    VW's acceptance of Bergsonian durational time (JACOB'S ROOM and THE WAVES) contrasted with Huxley's rejection of Bergson (THOSE BARREN LEAVES [1925] and TIME MUST HAVE A STOP [1944]). Also see H41.

L5 -----. "Joycean Structure in JACOB'S ROOM and MRS. DALLOWAY." INTERNATIONAL FICTION REVIEW, 4 (1977), 101-09.
    VW employs Joyce's structural concept of "the hours" in her two novels, though "in different contexts and with different tone and emphasis." Reprinted in her STRUCTURE AND THEME: *DON QUIXOTE* TO JAMES JOYCE (Columbus: Ohio State Univ. Press, 1983), pp. 169-84.

L6 Dalgarno, Emily. "SOLDIERS' PAY and Virginia Woolf." MISSISSIPPI QUARTERLY, 29 (1976), 339-46.
    Superficial comparison of Faulkner's narrative technique in his early novel (1926), and VW's in JACOB'S ROOM.

L7 Dowling, David. "Virginia Woolf's Own JACOB'S ROOM." SOUTHERN REVIEW (Adelaide, Australia), 15 (1982), 60-72.
    The novel a "collage which possesses, ultimately, an extremely significant form," rather than a work structured upon any sculptural sense of Jacob's character.

L8 Freedman, Ralph. "The Form of Fact and Fiction: JACOB'S ROOM as Paradigm." In VIRGINIA WOOLF. Ed. Freedman. Pp. 123-40. See G26.
    VW's evolution of a fictional form which "resolves the tensions between person and life," between vision and reality.

L9 Grabo, Carl. THE TECHNIQUE OF THE NOVEL. New York: Scribner's, 1928. Pp. 297-306.
    Novel a failed experiment in impressionism.

L10 Hawkins, E. W. "The Stream of Consciousness Novel." ATLANTIC, 138 (1926), 356-60.
    The subtlety and impressionistic effects of the stream-of-consciousness technique in Mansfield, Richardson, and VW (chiefly JACOB'S ROOM and MD). Extract reprinted in G49.

L11 Koutsoudaki, Mary. "The 'Greek' Jacob: Greece in Virginia Woolf's JACOB'S ROOM." PAPERS IN ROMANCE, 2 (1980), supp. 1, 67-75.
    Not seen.

L12 Maack, Annegret. "Das Simultanerlebnis der Wirklickkeit: Zur Struktur von Virginia Woolfs Roman JACOB'S ROOM." LITERATUR IN WISSENSCHAFT UND UNTERRICHT, 10 (1977), 88-103.
    Not seen. [In German.]

L13 Morgenstern, Barry. "The Self-Conscious Narrator in JACOB'S ROOM." MFS, 18 (1972), 351-61.
    VW's characteristic "mask" of the omniscient narrator-as-recorder. See G56.

L14 Moss, Roger. "JACOB'S ROOM and the Eighteenth Century: From Elegy to Essay." CRITICAL QUARTERLY, 23, No. 3 (1981), 39-54.
    Finds the "intellectual, as well as the artistic, roots of the way [Jacob] is created firmly in the eighteenth century" and explores VW's "sense of the relationship between Victorianism and the eighteenth century" in the novel.

L15 Murry, John Middleton. "The 'Classical' Revival." ADELPHI, 3 (1926), 585-95.
    VW and T. S. Eliot both "serious" modern classicists, yet their finest achievements to date, JACOB'S ROOM and THE WASTE LAND (1922), both unspontaneous and "over-intellectualized" failures.

L16 Ohmann, Carol. "Culture and Anarchy in JACOB'S ROOM." ConL, 18 (1977), 160-72.
    Novel displays VW's "iconoclastic attitudes... toward education and politics, toward culture and the state."

L17 Ruddick, Sara. "Private Brother, Public World." In NEW FEMINIST ESSAYS ON VIRGINIA WOOLF. Ed. Jane Marcus. Pp. 185-215. See G51.
    Symbolic and emotional significance for VW of the older-brother figure, chiefly in JACOB'S ROOM and THE WAVES.

L18 Schaefer, Josephine O'Brien. "Sterne's A SENTIMENTAL JOURNEY and Woolf's JACOB'S ROOM." MFS, 23 (1977), 189-97.
    Technical resemblances between the works, especially in the authors' humor and tone of voice.

L19 West, Rebecca. "JACOB'S ROOM." NEW STATESMAN, 4 Nov. 1922, p. 142.
    VW "at once a negligible novelist and a supremely important writer." Praises VW's descriptive power, but faults her characterization. Reprinted in G49.

L20 Zwerdling, Alex. "JACOB'S ROOM: Woolf's Satiric Elegy." ENGLISH LITERARY HISTORY, 48 (1981), 894-913.
    VW's "fragmented narrative creates a kaleidoscopic picture of the range of Jacob's opportunities," while her "narrative reticence," creating an inscrutable central character, avoids the sentimental insincerity inherent in the elegaic mode.

M. STUDIES OF *MRS. DALLOWAY* (1925)

The following section is subdivided into two parts: i. Books and Essay Collections on MD; and ii. Critical Articles or Chapters on MD.

For backgrounds to MD's composition, see MRS. DALLOWAY'S PARTY (A16) and VW's "Introduction" (A20). For the forthcoming concordance to MD, see section D.

For bibliographical information on MD, see Kirkpatrick (E7), and, for biographical backgrounds to the novel, see Bell (F13), Forrester (F31), Love (F61), Poole (F77), Rose (F81), Trombley (F95), and Woolf (F100).

For the most significant additional critical commentaries and information on MD, see the following books, in section G above: Alexander (G2), Badenhausen (G5), Bazin (G6), Blackstone (G9), Daiches (G16), Delattre (G17), DiBattista (G18), Dölle (G19), Donahue (G20), Finke (G23), Fleishman (G24), Gorsky (G28), Gruber (G29), Guiguet (G30), Hafley (G31), Harper (G32), Johnson (G36), Kapur (G37), Kelley (G38), Leaska (G41), Lee (G42), Little (G45), Lohmüller (G46), Love (G47), McLaurin (G48), Marder (G53), Moody (G57), Naremore (G59), Novak (G62), Pasternack (G65), Poresky (G66), Rantavaara (G68), Richter (G69), Rosenthal (G71), Schaefer (G75), Schlack (G76), Schwank (G77), Spilka (G79), Thakur (G82), Wiget (G86), Woodring (G88); the following critical articles, in section H above: Albright (H2), Beach (H8), Beja (H13), Borinski (H20), F. Bradbrook (H22), M. Bradbrook (H23), Burgum (H33), Carroll (H35), Cornwell (H47), Crosland (H50), Daiches (H54), Delattre (H59), Edel (H67), Faulkner (H75), Fehr (H76), Forster (H81), Franks (H83), Freedman (H85), Friedman (H90), Graham (H96), Greig (H99), Hartman (H108), Humphrey (H123), Johnstone (H126), Kiely (H130), Kumar (H133), Mayoux (H157-H159), Muir (H174), Neuschäffer (H180), Richter (H201), Rosenbaum (H207), Savage (H214), Showalter (H221), Simon (H222), Stanzel (H228), Williams (H251), Zéraffa (H256); and the following study, entered elsewhere in this bibliography: Meisel (X3). For a complete listing of substantial commentaries on MD, see the concluding index: "Virginia Woolf's Works."

M, i. Books and Essay Collections on MRS. DALLOWAY

M1 Carey, Gary. *MRS. DALLOWAY*: NOTES. Lincoln, Neb.: Cliff's Notes, 1969.
> Uninspired undergraduate student "outline" for the study of MD, consisting of a brief biographical summary, a list of the novel's characters, a "critical commentary" on MD (divided into twelve sections), character analyses (limited to Clarissa and Septimus), and questions for review and study. This publication, which is of no merit whatsoever, is included in this guide solely to make the list of books and pamphlets on VW more nearly complete. (Monograph--59 pp.)

M1a Gilbert, Sandra M. MONARCH NOTES ON WOOLF'S *MRS. DALLOWAY* AND *TO THE LIGHTHOUSE*. New York: Monarch, 1966.
> Pedestrian student "outline" for the study of VW's two novels, consisting of plot summaries, with interspersed "commentaries," character analyses, questions for study, paper topics, etc. This publication, unlike Carey's above, is included here not only to make the listing of books and pamphlets on VW more nearly complete, but also because Gilbert is a critic of some ability. Her commentaries are intelligent and, presumably, are useful and informative for the lower-level undergraduate audience for which her outline is intended. (Monograph--64 pp.)

M2 Hawthorn, Jeremy. VIRGINIA WOOLF'S *MRS. DALLOWAY*: A STUDY IN ALIENATION. Sussex, Engl.: Sussex Univ. Press, 1975.
> Extended analysis of MD as a profoundly dualistic novel, exploring and juxtaposing the characters' paradoxical senses of togetherness and apartness, their public and private selves, their isolation within the urban scene, their material and spiritual needs, their self-transcendence and self-fulfillment through love, and their escape into a society (the "party") which ironically confirms their alienation.

M2a Tilak, Raghukul. *MRS. DALLOWAY* (A CRITICAL STUDY). New Delhi: Rama Brothers, 1971.
> An introduction to VW's novel, "in an easy popular form" for students in Indian Universities. Tilak's discussion is "comprehensive and elaborate," but painfully elementary and devoid of critical interest.

M, ii. Critical Articles or Chapters on MRS. DALLOWAY

M3 Abel, Elizabeth. "Narrative Structure(s) and Female Development: The Case of MRS. DALLOWAY." In THE VOYAGE IN: FICTIONS OF FEMALE DEVELOPMENT. Ed. Abel, Marianne Hirsch, and Elizabeth Langland. Hanover, N. H.: Univ. Press of New England, 1983. Pp. 161-85.
> MD's submerged plot depicts Clarissa's arrested maturation in her "unresolved attachment to an adolescent female world." The editors' "Introduction" to this essay collection (pp. 3-19) also briefly comments on VW's THE VOYAGE OUT as a paradigm for the frustration of development found in the female *bildungsroman*.

M3a Ames, Kenneth J. "Elements of Mock-Heroic in Virginia Woolf's MRS. DALLOWAY." MFS, 18 (1972), 363-74.
> VW's use of neo-classic devices of ironic detachment in her characterization and themes (cf. Pope). See G56.

M4 Baldanza, Frank. "Clarissa Dalloway's 'Party Consciousness.'" MFS, 2 (1956), 24-30.
> In her several appearances in VW's fiction, Clarissa an embodiment of the "average traits" of people on VW's "social, cultural, and economic level." See G55.

M5 Beker, Miroslav. "London as a Principle of Structure in MRS. DALLOWAY." MFS, 18 (1972), 375-85.
> The city used to define character in MD, VW's most "spatial" novel (as opposed to TL, her most "temporal" work). See G56.

M6 Benjamin, Anna. "Towards an Understanding of the Meaning of Virginia Woolf's MRS. DALLOWAY." WISCONSIN STUDIES IN COMTEMPORARY LITERATURE, 6 (1965), 214-27.
> MD's "circular" imagery, plot, and time VW's method for presenting an "organic reality" in the novel.

M7 Blanchard, Margaret. "Socialization in MRS. DALLOWAY." CE, 34 (1972), 287-305.
> Feminist study of VW's insight into woman's social dilemma, despite her weak conception of Clarissa and her novel's lack of social commitment.

M8 Blunt, Katherine K. "Jay and Hawk: Their Song, and Echoes in MRS. DALLOWAY." VIRGINIA WOOLF QUARTERLY, 2 (1976), 313-37.
> Free-associative survey of VW's conscious and unconscious name symbolism and literary allusion.

M9   Bonnot, René. "Le Roman du Temps (A propos de Virginia Woolf et de James Joyce)." JOURNAL DE PSYCHOLOGIE NORMALE ET PATHOLOGIQUE, 53 (1956), 454-72.
     Explores the technical parallels between ULYSSES (1922) and MD. [In French.]

M10 Brower, Reuben A. "Something Central Which Permeated: Virginia Woolf and MRS. DALLOWAY." In THE FIELDS OF LIGHT: AN EXPERIMENT IN CRITICAL READING. New York: Oxford Univ. Press, 1951. Pp. 123-37.
     MD's symbolic unity and "single metaphorical nucleus" illustrate VW's "Shakespearian imagination." Reprinted in G80.

M11 Brownstein, Rachel M. "MRS. DALLOWAY." In BECOMING A HEROINE: READING ABOUT WOMEN IN NOVELS. New York: Viking, 1982. Pp. 271-91.
     Finds Clarissa an "utterly" new conception in the tradition of the "heroine-centered" novel, yet says little that is original or valuable about MD.

M12 Brumm, Anne-Marie. "The World as Madhouse: Motifs of Absurdity in Virginia Woolf's MRS. DALLOWAY, William Faulkner's AS I LAY DYING, and Jean-Paul Sartre's LE MUR." NEOHELICON, 4, Nos. 3-4 (1976), 295-330.
     "Analyzing the emotional milieu and response of the insane characters in the novels [i.e., Septimus]...gives us greater insight and understanding of the individuals who become lost in the world's madhouse."

M13 Carlson, Julia. "The Solitary Traveller in MRS. DALLOWAY." In VIRGINIA WOOLF. Ed. Thomas S. W. Lewis. Pp. 56-62. See G44.
     Relation of "solitary traveller" section to the themes and structure of MD.

M14 Church, Margaret. "Joycean Structure in JACOB'S ROOM and MRS. DALLOWAY." INTERNATIONAL FICTION REVIEW, 4 (1977), 101-09.
     For annotation see L5.

M15 Cohan, Steven. "Narrative Form and Death: THE MILL ON THE FLOSS and MRS. DALLOWAY." GENRE, 11 (1978), 109-29.
     VW's novel's obsession with death related to its "formal impulse to be finished" (cf. Eliot's novel, 1860).

M16 Davis, Edward. "MRS. DALLOWAY." In READINGS IN MODERN FICTION. Capetown: Simondium, 1964. Pp. 282-301.
     Extremely negative view of VW's work, particularly MD, as this "century's most conscienceless exhibition of preciousness and narcissism."

M17 Deurbergue, Jean. "Pour une rhétorique du recit romanesque: l'exemple de MRS. DALLOWAY." RECHERCHES ANGLAISES ET AMÉRICAINES, 4 (1971), 157-71.
     Theories for the structural analysis of narration applied to MD. [In French.]

M18 Eagleton, Terry. EXILES AND ÉMIGRÉS: STUDIES IN MODERN LITERA-
TURE. New York: Schocken, 1970. Pp. 33-38.
Despite her thrusts of social criticism, VW en-
dorses the upper-class world that her fiction
depicts (chiefly on MD).

M19 Edwards, Lee R. "War and Roses: The Politics of MRS. DALLOWAY."
In THE AUTHORITY OF EXPERIENCE: ESSAYS IN FEMINIST CRITICISM.
Ed. Arlyn Diamond and Edwards. Amherst: Univ. of Massachusetts
Press, 1977. Pp. 160-77.
VW's recognition of the world's division of
"politics and feelings or values" in MD marks
the beginning of her "feminist and social"
analysis of "limitation and liberation" in
her works.

M20 Erzgräber, Willi. "Virginia Woolf: MRS. DALLOWAY." In DER
MODERNE ENGLISCHE ROMAN: INTERPRETATIONEN. Ed. Horst Oppel.
Berlin: Schmidt, 1965. Pp. 160-200.
Extended analysis of VW's use of nuance, nar-
rative technique, adaptation of realism, struc-
ture, and chief themes in MD. [In German.]

M21 Fortin, René. "Sacramental Imagery in MRS. DALLOWAY." RENASCENCE,
18 (1965), 23-31.
MD's "traditional religious symbols and values."

M22 Frazer, June M. "MRS. DALLOWAY: Virginia Woolf's Greek Novel."
RS, 47 (1979), 221-28.
Elements of Greek culture, language, and litera-
ture inform the "classical spirit" of MD.

M23 Friedman, Norman. FORM AND MEANING IN FICTION. Athens: Univ.
of Georgia Press, 1975. Pp. 331-35.
Examines the Septimus sections of MD as an
example of a significant, "static" plot line.

M24 Frye, Joanne S. "MRS. DALLOWAY as Lyrical Paradox." BALL STATE
UNIVERSITY FORUM, 22 (1982), 42-56.
The undecipherable plot and unknowable characters of MD, VW's "deliberate rejection not only
of narrative convention but also of the reader's
anticipation of determinate meaning."

M25 Gamble, Isabel. "The Secret Sharer in MRS. DALLOWAY." ACCENT,
16 (1956), 235-51.
The theme of self-discovery in MD analogous to
Conrad's theme in his "The Secret Sharer" (1910).
Extract reprinted in G40.

M26 Gelfant, Blanche H. "Love and Conversion in MRS. DALLOWAY."
CRITICISM, 8 (1966), 229-45.
MD's thematic conflict between creative and
coercive forces and its optimistic ending,
implying triumph over destructive instincts.

M27 Ghiselin, Brewster. "Virginia Woolf's Party." SEWANEE REVIEW, 80 (1972), 47-50.
> VW's novel a "lonely communion transcending loneliness itself" in its theme of love, the "sympathetic imagination" which enables one to "see truly."

M28 Gillen, Francis. "'I Am This, I Am That': Shifting Distance and Movement in MRS. DALLOWAY." STUDIES IN THE NOVEL, 4 (1972), 484-93.
> VW's use of narrational shifts balances the reader between acceptance and rejection of her characters and their visions.

M29 Graves, Nora C. "The Case of Mrs. Dalloway." VIRGINIA WOOLF QUARTERLY, 1, No. 3 (1973), 51-59.
> The relative sanity and insanity of Clarissa and Septimus.

M30 Hamburger, Käte. "Mrs. Dalloway." In WISSEN AUS ERFAHRUNGEN. WERKEBEGRIFF UND INTERPRETATION HEUTE. FESTSCHRIFT FÜR HERMAN MEYER ZUM 65. GEBURTSTAG. Ed. Alexander von Bormann, Karl Robert Mandelkow, and Anthonius H. Touber. Tübingen: Niemeyer, 1976. Pp. 712-23.
> Analysis of MD's structure (space, time, and juxtaposition of character). [In German.]

M31 Harper, Howard M. "Mrs. Woolf and Mrs. Dalloway." In THE CLASSIC BRITISH NOVEL. Ed. Harper and Charles Edge. Athens: Univ. of Georgia Press, 1972. Pp. 220-39.
> Clarissa's recognition and acceptance of the nature of life parallels VW's own attainment of psychic stability.

M32 Hawkins, E. W. "The Stream of Consciousness Novel." ATLANTIC, 138 (1926), 356-60.
> On JACOB'S ROOM and MD. For annotation see L10.

M33 Hayashi, Toshitaka. "'Time and the Sea': Background in MRS. DALLOWAY and THE WAVES." STUDIES IN ENGLISH LITERATURE (Tokyo), 53, Nos. 1-2 (1976), 43-57.
> [In Japanese.]

M34 Henke, Suzette A. "MRS. DALLOWAY: The Communion of Saints." In NEW FEMINIST ESSAYS ON VIRGINIA WOOLF. Ed. Jane Marcus. Pp. 125-47. See G51.
> MD a "scathing indictment of the British class system and a strong critique of patriarchy." The novel's social satire achieved largely by "ironic patterns of mythic reference" fusing "models from Greek Tragedy and from the Christian liturgy."

M35 Hessler, John G. "Moral Accountability in MRS. DALLOWAY." RENASCENCE, 30 (1978), 126-36.
Clarissa, in her "struggle for self-definition," no existential heroine but "an all too pathetic product of social forces she has not recognized."

M36 Hildick, Wallace. "In That Solitary Room." KENYON REVIEW, 27 (1965), 302-17.
Casual description of the manuscript of MD.

M37 Hochman, Baruch. "Virginia Woolf: The Self in Spite of Itself." In THE TEST OF CHARACTER: FROM THE VICTORIAN NOVEL TO THE MODERN. East Brunswick, N. J.: Associated University Presses, 1983. Pp. 157-76.
Although VW appears to reject character as a principal element of fiction, her novels are preeminently concerned with generating the "palpable thereness" of characters by dramatizing "their own sense of their evanescence" and the "possibility of vital contact with the objective world." Chiefly discusses MD.

M38 Hoffmann, Charles G. "From Short Story to Novel: The Manuscript Revisions of Virginia Woolf's MRS. DALLOWAY." MFS, 14 (1968), 171-86.
MD's textual evolution seen in a study of its holograph version ("complete in all its major elements"). See M47.

M39 -----. "The 'Real' Mrs. Dalloway." UNIVERSITY OF KANSAS CITY REVIEW, 22 (1956), 204-08.
VW's concept of the momentary integration and realization of character determines the "interaction of time and character" in MD.

M40 Hollingsworth, Keith. "Freud and the Riddle of MRS. DALLOWAY." In STUDIES IN HONOR OF JOHN WILCOX. Ed. A. Dayle Wallace and Woodburn O. Ross. Detroit: Wayne State Univ. Press, 1958. Pp. 239-50.
MD intended by VW as a study of both the double personality and the death wish.

M41 Hungerford, Edward A. "'My Tunnelling Process': The Method of MRS. DALLOWAY." MFS, 3 (1957), 164-67.
Defines VW's conception of "tunnelling," as distinguished from the stream-of-consciousness technique.

M42 Jaloux, Edmond. "MRS. DALLOWAY, par Virginia Woolf." In AU PAYS DU ROMAN. Paris: Éditions R.-A. Corrêa, 1931. Pp. 185-98.
Praises VW's capture of "toute notre vie intérieure...ce flux et ce reflux de nos émotions; ces parcours d'idées sensitives" in a story "la plus banale du monde." [In French.]

M43 Kaplan, Sydney Janet. "Virginia Woolf." In FEMININE CONSCIOUSNESS IN THE MODERN BRITISH NOVEL. Urbana: Univ. of Illinois Press, 1975. Pp. 76-109.
    Achievement of "feminine consciousness" for VW's characters in MD and TL, a preliminary stage in the attainment of an essentially androgynous, aesthetic consciousness.

M44 Kreutz, Irving. "Mr. Bennett and Mrs. Woolf." MFS, 8 (1962), 103-15.
    Comparison of the authors' techniques and intentions for HILDA LESSWAYS (1911) and MD suggest Bennett and VW had more in common that either was willing to admit.

M45 Lanoire, Maurice. "Le Témoignage de MRS. DALLOWAY." LES LETTRES, N.S. 1 (1930), 81-91.
    Sees VW's uses of time and stream of consciousness in MD directly indebted to Joyce's, in ULYSSES (1922). [In French.]

M46 Latham, Jacqueline E. M. "Archetypal Figures in MRS. DALLOWAY." NEUPHILOLOGISCHE MITTEILUNGEN, 71 (1970), 480-88.
    Prometheus and Adonis (the "drowned sailor") archetypes in Septimus's visions.

M47 -----. "The Manuscript Revisions of Virginia Woolf's MRS. DALLOWAY: A Postscript." MFS, 18 (1972), 475-76.
    Comments on Hoffmann's textual study (M38). See G56.

M48 -----. "The Model for Clarissa Dalloway--Kitty Maxse." NOTES AND QUERIES, 214 (1969), 262-63.
    Clarissa clearly modeled on the "conservative hostess Kitty Maxse" (not Lady Ottoline Morrell, as Guiguet guesses [see G30]).

M49 -----. "The Origin of MRS. DALLOWAY." NOTES AND QUERIES, 211 (1966), 98-99.
    Notes the role of the earlier story, "Mrs. Dalloway in Bond Street," in MD's composition.

M50 -----. "Thessaly and the 'Colossal Figure' in MRS. DALLOWAY." NOTES AND QUERIES, 214 (1969), 263-65.
    VW's confused use of classical allusion and archaeological information.

M51 Lewis, A. J. "From 'The Hours' to MRS. DALLOWAY." BRITISH MUSEUM QUARTERLY, 28 (1964), 15-18.
    Describes the three-volume autograph manuscript of MD, acquired by the British Museum.

M52 Marcel, Gabriel. "MRS. DALLOWAY, par Virginia Woolf." NOUVELLE REVUE FRANÇAISE, 33 (1929), 129-31.
    Finds VW's original adaptations of the interior monologue technique in MD (via Bergson) an ad-

vance upon Proust's achievement. Review of
French translation (1929). [In French.]

M53 Markovic, Vida E. "Clarissa Dalloway." In THE CHANGING FACE:
DISINTEGRATION OF PERSONALITY IN THE TWENTIETH-CENTURY BRITISH
NOVEL, 1900-1950. Carbondale: Southern Illinois Univ. Press,
1970. Pp. 54-69.
    Clarissa a disintegrating character whose whole
attitude to life leads "to its denial."

M54 Miller, David N. "Authorial Point of View in Virginia Woolf's
MRS. DALLOWAY." JOURNAL OF NARRATIVE TECHNIQUE, 2 (1972), 125-32.
    VW's complex narrative technique in MD integrates
the novel's various consciousnesses, "despite the
near-absence of an omniscient voice."

M55 Miller, J. Hillis. "MRS. DALLOWAY: Repetition as the Raising
of the Dead." 1970. In FICTION AND REPETITION: SEVEN ENGLISH
NOVELS. Cambridge, Mass.: Harvard Univ. Press, 1982. Pp. 176-
202.
    Patterns of narrative repetition in MD, sug-
gesting the continuities of past and present
(in the character's memory), and of tradition
and innovation (in VW's narrative technique).
Earlier version published as "Virginia Woolf's
All Souls' Day: The Omniscient Narrator in
MRS. DALLOWAY." Also see S22.

M56 Moody, A. D. "The Unmasking of Clarissa Dalloway." REVIEW OF
ENGLISH LITERATURE, 3, No. 1 (1962), 67-79.
    Too much like Clarissa herself, VW unable to
criticize successfully the life and world of
her central character.

M57 Moon, Kenneth. "Where is Clarissa? Doris Kilman and Recoil
from the Flesh in Virginia Woolf's MRS. DALLOWAY." COLLEGE
LANGUAGE ASSOCIATION JOURNAL, 23 (1980), 273-86.
    The correspondences between Miss Kilman and
Mrs. Dalloway suggest a major dimension of
Clarissa's "unseen" character: her "sup-
pressed" and "unrealized" passionate nature.

M58 Mueller, William R. "Virginia Woolf: The Soul's Sad Delight."
In CELEBRATION OF LIFE: STUDIES IN MODERN FICTION. New York:
Sheed and Ward, 1972. Pp. 188-206.
    MD, an "anatomy of an entire culture," centered
on Clarissa's "soul" as it reflects on "itself,
other souls, and the physical world in which
she rejoices."

M59 Muir, Edwin. THE STRUCTURE OF THE NOVEL. London: Hogarth,
1928. Pp. 132-33.
    Praises MD as "the most skilful spatial picture
of life in comtemporary literature," in elabor-
ating his formula for distinguishing novels of
action (temporal) and character (spatial).

M60 Oltean, Ştefan. "Textual Functions of Free Indirect Discourse in the Novel MRS. DALLOWAY by Virginia Woolf." REVUE ROUMAINE DE LINGUISTIQUE, 26 (1981), 533-47.
> Technical and theoretical linguistic analysis of the polyvocal functions of VW's narrative technique (e.g., irony, distance, empathy).

M61 Page, Alex. "A Dangerous Day: Mrs. Dalloway Discovers Her Double." MFS, 7 (1961), 115-24.
> Clarissa's final vision a recognition that Septimus is "the id to her ego."

M62 Payne, Michael. "Beyond Gender: The Example of MRS. DALLOWAY." COLLEGE LITERATURE, 5 (1978), 1-11.
> MD transcends the ideology of feminism in advocating "a transcendence of sexual roles."

M63 Perazzini, Randolph. "MRS. DALLOWAY: 'Buds on the Tree of Life.'" MIDWEST QUARTERLY, 18 (1977), 406-17.
> VW's subtle unification of diverse points of view in MD.

M64 Philipson, Morris. "MRS. DALLOWAY, 'What's the Sense of Your Parties?'" CRITICAL INQUIRY, 1 (1974), 123-48.
> Analyzes MD as a "conversion fable," in Jungian terms.

M65 Quick, Jonathan R. "The Shattered Moment: Form and Crisis in MRS. DALLOWAY and BETWEEN THE ACTS." MOSAIC, 7, No. 3 (1974), 127-36.
> VW's successful integration of form and meaning in the novels.

M66 Rachman, Shalom. "Clarissa's Attic: Virginia Woolf's MRS. DALLOWAY Reconsidered." TCL, 18 (1972), 3-19.
> Finds VW's antagonism toward Dr. Bradshaw a flaw in MD.

M67 Richter, Harvena. "The Canonical Hours in MRS. DALLOWAY." MFS, 28 (1982), 236-40.
> The pattern of the seven canonical hours (from "matins" to "complin"), give MD a "personal," "psychological," and "symbolic" order.

M68 Rigney, Barbara H. "'The Sane and the Insane': Psychosis and Mysticism in MRS. DALLOWAY." In MADNESS AND SEXUAL POLITICS IN THE FEMINIST NOVEL: STUDIES IN BRONTE, WOOLF, LESSING, AND ATWOOD. Madison: Univ. of Wisconsin Press, 1978. Pp. 41-63.
> VW's significant counterpoint of the clinically insane Septimus and the "'normally' alienated" Clarissa an implied commentary on their victimization by "male-supremacist" society.

M69 Roberts, John H. "'Vision and Design' in Virginia Woolf." PMLA, 61 (1946), 835-47.
    Study of Roger Fry's theories of art demonstrates his influence on VW's conceptions of MD and TL. Extract reprinted in G40.

M70 Rosenberg, Stuart. "The Match in the Crocus: Obtrusive Art in Virginia Woolf's MRS. DALLOWAY." MFS, 13 (1967), 211-20.
    VW's authorial intrusions in MD a calculated attempt to make art out of the traditional, experientially realistic matter of the novel.

M71 Rowe, Margaret Moan. "Balancing Two Worlds: Setting and Characterization in MRS. DALLOWAY." VIRGINIA WOOLF QUARTERLY, 3 (1978), 268-75.
    Dichotomy between MD's physical, urban setting and its characters' spiritual concerns.

M72 Ruotolo, Lucio P. "Clarissa Dalloway." In SIX EXISTENTIAL HEROES: THE POLITICS OF FAITH. Cambridge, Mass.: Harvard Univ. Press, 1973. Pp. 13-35.
    Clarissa's resistance to the "temptation to withdraw" an "existential triumph." Reprinted in G44.

M73 -----. "MRS. DALLOWAY: The Journey Out of Subjectivity." WOMEN'S STUDIES, 4 (1977), 173-78.
    Clarissa's "posture of disengagement...an act of resistance that has political implications," leading her to an objectively "expanded vision of the external as well as of the internal world." See G87.

M74 -----. "MRS. DALLOWAY: The Unguarded Moment." In VIRGINIA WOOLF. Ed. Ralph Freedman. Pp. 141-60. See G26.
    Clarissa's depth as a character measured in her "willingness to question the given" and in her acceptance of the unstabilizing, but revelatory moment of insight.

M75 Samuels, Marilyn Schauer. "The Symbolic Function of the Sun in MRS. DALLOWAY." MFS, 18 (1972), 387-99.
    Symbolism of light and enlightenment. See G56.

M76 Samuelson, Ralph. "The Theme of MRS. DALLOWAY." CHICAGO REVIEW, 11, No. 4 (1958), 57-76.
    Asserts, in reaction to Savage's attack on VW (see H214), that MD possesses a significant theme (individual worth), not just a distinguished technique.

M77 Schlack, Beverly Ann. "A Freudian Look at MRS. DALLOWAY." L&P, 23 (1973), 49-58.
    Psychoanalytic study of character, motivation, and imagery in MD.

M78 Schug, Charles. "Virginia Woolf: MRS. DALLOWAY, TO THE LIGHTHOUSE." In THE ROMANTIC GENESIS OF THE MODERN NOVEL. Pittsburgh: Univ. of Pittsburgh Press, 1979. Pp. 189-225.
   VW's debts to the romantic literary tradition in MD and TL (especially in her "lyric" conception of fiction and concern for point of view).

M79 Sharma, O. P. "Feminism as Aesthetic Vision: A Study of Virginia Woolf's MRS. DALLOWAY." PUNJAB UNIVERSITY RESEARCH BULLETIN (Arts), 2, No. 2 (1971), 1-10.
   VW's feminist concerns of the late twenties and thirties immanent in the presentation of the women characters of MD. Reprinted in WOMEN'S STUDIES, 3 (1975), 61-73. Also see N89.

M80 Shibata, Tetsushi. "MRS. DALLOWAY no Kakushie" ["MRS. DALLOWAY's Picture Puzzle"]. EIGO SEINEN, 121 (1975-76), 340-41, 388-89, 474-75, 522-23.
   [In Japanese.]

M81 Shields, E. F. "The American Edition of MRS. DALLOWAY." STUDIES IN BIBLIOGRAPHY, 27 (1974), 157-75.
   Significant textual variation between the first American and British editions.

M82 -----. "Death and Individual Values in MRS. DALLOWAY." QUEEN'S QUARTERLY, 80 (1973), 79-89.
   Septimus's suicide and the novel's final scene show death as a "positive affirmation" of man's need for "meaningful values by which to live."

M83 Simon, Irène. "Some Aspects of Virginia Woolf's Imagery." ENGLISH STUDIES, 41 (1960), 180-96.
   VW's structural and symbolic use of "lyric" imagery to suggest both stability and flux. Extracts reprinted in G40.

M84 Snow, Lotus. "Clarissa Dalloway Revisited." RS, 46 (1978), 197-202.
   On MD and THE VOYAGE OUT. For annotation see J16.

M85 -----. "The Heat of the Sun: The Double in MRS. DALLOWAY." RS, 41 (1973), 75-83.
   Clarissa and Septimus both *Doppelgängers* and halves of one, integrated personality.

M86 Stamirowska, Krystyna. "Virginia Woolf's Concept of Reality and Some Theories of Her Time." KWARTALNIK NEOFILOLOGICZNY, 22 (1975), 207-17.
   Relates VW's "concept of reality," in MD and TL, to the psychological theories of William James and the philosophical ideas of Henri Bergson.

M87 Steinberg, Erwin R. "Freudian Symbolism and Communication."
L&P, 3, No. 2 (1953), 2-5.
> VW's obvious and superficial phallic symbolism
> in MD, in contrast to her more successful Freud-
> ian symbols in TL. See M95. Also see subse-
> quent comments by Steinberg in L&P, 4, No. 2
> (1954), 23-26.

M88 -----. "MRS. DALLOWAY and T. S. Eliot's Personal Waste Land."
JOURNAL OF MODERN LITERATURE, 10 (1983), 3-25.
> Reviews Eliot's "growing intimacy with the
> Woolfs" (1918-25) and traces echoes of
> Eliot's life and THE WASTE LAND (1922) in
> VW's novel.

M89 Tada, Minoru. "DALLOWAY FUJIN Oboegaki" ["A Note on MRS. DAL-
LOWAY"]. In SUGA YASUO, OGOSHI KAZUGO: RYOKYOJU TAIKAN KINEN
RONBUNSHU. Kyoto: Apollonsha, 1980. Pp. 515-27.
> Not seen. [In Japanese.]

M90 Takahashi, Kazuhisa. "Shinya no Vision: Dalloway Fujin No Eta
Mono" ["Vision of Midnight: What Mrs. Dalloway Learns"]. In
SUGA YASUO, OGOSHI KAZUGO: RYOKYOJU TAIKAN KINEN RONBUNSHU.
Kyoto: Apollonsha, 1980. Pp. 541-51.
> Not seen. [In Japanese.]

M91 Villanueva, Darío. "Virginia Woolf." In ESTRUCTURA Y TIEMPO
REDUCIDO EN LA NOVELA. Valencia, Spain: Editorial Bello, 1977.
Pp. 98-101.
> VW's structural use of time and contrapuntal
> "streams of consciousness" in MD and TL. [In
> Spanish.]

M92 Wade, Michael. "Mrs. Dalloway's Affirmation of Value." HEBREW
UNIVERSITY STUDIES IN LITERATURE, 7 (1979), 245-70.
> VW's complex presentation, through structure and
> symbol, of the "idea of hierarchy" in contemporary
> society.

M93 Weber, Robert W. "Die Glocken von Big Ben: Zur Strukturfunktion
der Uhrzeit in MRS. DALLOWAY." DEUTSCHE VIERTELJAHRSSCHRIFT FUR
LITERATURWISSENSCHAFT UND GEISTESGESCHICHTE, 39 (1965), 246-58.
> The thematic as well as technical functions of
> time in MD emphasized by the striking of Big
> Ben, which mediates between the historical
> and durational uses of time in the novel.
> [In German.]

M94 Wright, Nathalie. "MRS. DALLOWAY: A Study in Composition."
CE, 5 (1944), 351-58.
> VW's structural juxtaposition of "characters,
> psychological states, sounds, and colors."

M95 Wyatt, Frederick. "Some Comments on the Use of Symbols in the Novel." L&P, 4 (1954), 15-23.
    VW's perceptive use of Freudian imagery and psychoanalytic themes in MD. Reply to Steinberg (M87).

M96 Wyatt, Jean M. "MRS. DALLOWAY: Literary Allusion as Structural Metaphor." PMLA, 88 (1973), 440-51.
    VW's uses of Shakespearian allusions to construct character and to define theme and structure. Also see David Leon Higdon's and Joyce Carol Oates' subsequent attacks on this article, PMLA, 89 (1974), 178-79 and 580-81, and Wyatt's reply, pp. 179-80.

M97 Zwerdling, Alex. "MRS. DALLOWAY and the Social System." PMLA, 92 (1977), 69-82.
    In MD, VW analyzes the "ideal of stoical fortitude" dominant in the governing class in postwar English society.

N. STUDIES OF *TO THE LIGHTHOUSE* (1927)

The following section is subdivided into two parts: i. Books and Essay Collections on TL; and ii. Critical Articles or Chapters on TL.

For a transcription of the holograph manuscript of TL and related textual materials, see C7. For the forthcoming concordance to TL, see section D.

For bibliographical information on TL, see Kirkpatrick (E7), and, for biographical backgrounds to the novel, see Bell (F13), DeSalvo (F23), Forrester (F31), Love (F61), Poole (F77), Rose (F81), and Woolf (F100).

For the most significant additional critical commentaries and information on TL, see the following books, in section G above: Alexander (G2), Badenhausen (G5), Bazin (G6), Blackstone (G9), Daiches (G16), Delattre (G17), DiBattista (G18), Donahue (G20), Finke (G23), Fleishman (G24), Gorsky (G28), Gruber (G29), Guiguet (G30), Hafley (G31), Harper (G32), Johnson (G36), Kapur (G37), Kelley (G38), Leaska (G41), Lee, (G42), Little (G45), Lohmüller (G46), Love (G47), McLaurin (G48), Marder (G53), Moody (G57), Naremore (G59), Novak (G62), Pasternack (G65), Poresky (G66), Rantavaara (G68), Richter (G69), Rosenthal (G71), Schaefer (G75), Schwank (G77), Spilka (G79), Thakur (G82), Wiget (G86), Woodring (G88); the following critical articles, in section H above: Albright (H2), Beja (H13), Borinski (H20), F. Bradbrook (H22), M. Bradbrook (H23), Bradbury (H24), Brooks (H28), Burgum (H33), Carroll (H35), Cornwell (H47), Crosland (H50), Daiches (H54), Delattre (H59), Faulkner (H75), Fehr (H76), Fleishman (H79), Franks (H83), Freedman (H85), Friedman (H90), Graham (H96), Greig (H99), Hanquart (H106), Hartman (H108), Heilbrun (H111), Humphrey (H123), Johnstone (H126), Kiely (H130), Kumar (H133), McLaughlin (H148), Mayoux (H157-H159), Mellers (H161), Muir (H174), Neuschäffer (H180), Richter (H201), Rosenbaum (H207), Showalter (H221), Simon (H222), Stanzel (H228), Troy (H242), Wicht (H249), Williams (H251), Wilson (H253), Zéraffa (H256); and the following study, entered elsewhere in this bibliography: Meisel (X3). For a complete listing of substantial commentaries on TL, see the concluding index: "Virginia Woolf's Works."

N, i. Books and Essay Collections on TO THE LIGHTHOUSE

N1 Beja, Morris, ed. VIRGINIA WOOLF: *TO THE LIGHTHOUSE*: A CASE-
BOOK. London: Macmillan, 1970.
> Fine anthology of background materials, reviews, and studies concerning TL. Includes Beja's "Introduction" (N9), generous selections from VW's A WRITER'S DIARY (B6), extracts from A19, A28, F4, F100, G16, G30, G31, H242, and the following essays: H13, N6, N7, N10, N38, and N56.

N2 Davenport, William A. *TO THE LIGHTHOUSE*. Oxford: Blackwell, 1969.
> Good monograph-introduction to VW's ideas of fiction and narrative technique, discussion of subject, structure, character, and imagery in TL, and model analysis of a brief segment of the novel's text.

N2a Gilbert, Sandra M. MONARCH NOTES ON WOOLF'S *MRS. DALLOWAY* AND *TO THE LIGHTHOUSE*. New York: Monarch, 1966.
> For annotation see M1a.

N3 Leaska, Mitchell A. VIRGINIA WOOLF'S LIGHTHOUSE: A STUDY IN CRITICAL METHOD. New York: Columbia Univ. Press, 1970.
> Formalist study of VW's complex technical strategies in TL. Leaska defines VW's use of "multiple viewpoints," as distinguished from omniscient narration, examines in detail "the rhetorical effects of shifting point of view" and "the stylistics associated with each of those points of view," and relates VW's method both to her novel's meaning and to her place among the "disappearing" modern novelists. Fine chapters on the critical theory underlying his analyses and on the rhetoric and style of TL (including computer analysis). Portions absorbed into G41.

N3a McNichol, Stella. VIRGINIA WOOLF: *TO THE LIGHTHOUSE*. London: Arnold, 1971.
> Introductory critical survey of TL, emphasizing "clarification and evaluation" of VW's subject matter and techniques as well as "biographical and historical backgrounds" to the study of the novel. McNichol aims her introduction toward undergraduate students, but attains a higher degree of critical sophistication than that found in most student "outlines" (e.g., see Gilbert, N2a).

N4 Ruddick, Lisa. THE SEEN AND THE UNSEEN: VIRGINIA WOOLF'S *TO THE LIGHTHOUSE*. Cambridge, Mass.: Harvard Univ. Press, 1977.
   Monograph on the visual, spatial, temporal, and emotional perspectives in TL, and on the coherence among these perspectives provided by VW's "thematic and technical" exploration of the "infinite reality" within and behind the "visible human world."

N5 Vogler, Thomas A., ed. TWENTIETH CENTURY INTERPRETATIONS OF *TO THE LIGHTHOUSE*. Englewood Cliffs, N. J.: Prentice-Hall, 1970.
   Reprints one essay complete, substantial portions of four commentaries, and nine brief "view points" on VW and her novel, together with the editor's extended "Introduction" (N102). Includes H108 and extracts from G16, G30, G57, G75, H65, H202, N7, N60, R6, and S19.

N, ii. Critical Articles or Chapters on TO THE LIGHTHOUSE

N6 Aiken, Conrad. "Virginia Woolf." 1927. In A REVIEWER'S ABC. New York: Meridian, 1958. Pp. 389-92.
   TL makes VW's readers think both of Austen (her material) and of Dorothy Richardson and Joyce (her method). Reprinted in G49 and N1.

N7 Auerbach, Erich. "The Brown Stocking." In MIMESIS: THE REPRESENTATION OF REALITY IN WESTERN LITERATURE. Trans. Willard R. Trask. Princeton, N. J.: Princeton Univ. Press, 1953. Pp. 525-53.
   Model analysis of a passage from TL demonstrates VW's experimentation with external and internal realism (cf. Proust and Joyce). Reprinted in N1. Extracts reprinted in G60 and N5. Originally published in German in MIMESIS: DARGESTELLTE WIRKLICHKEIT IN DER ABENDLÄNDISCHEN LITERATUR (Berne: Franke, 1946). Reviewed in E3.

N8 Baldanza, Frank. "TO THE LIGHTHOUSE Again." PMLA, 70 (1955), 548-52.
   TL seen as VW's fictional "revolt against her parents."

N9 Beja, Morris. "Introduction." In VIRGINIA WOOLF: *TO THE LIGHTHOUSE*. Ed. Beja. Pp. 11-31. See N1.
   Good summaries of TL's critical reception and the central problems in its interpretation.

N10 Blotner, Joseph I. "Mythic Patterns in TO THE LIGHTHOUSE." PMLA, 71 (1956), 547-62.
   VW's use of the "Primordial Goddess" archetype (Rhea-Demeter-Persephone), and the Oedipus myth. Reprinted in N1.

N11 Boyd, Elizabeth F. "Luriana, Lurilee." NOTES AND QUERIES, 208 (1963), 380-81.
    Locates the source of the poem quoted in TL.

N12 Bradbrook, Muriel C. "TO THE LIGHTHOUSE." 1978. In WOMEN AND LITERATURE, 1779-1982: THE COLLECTED PAPERS OF MURIEL BRADBROOK, VOLUME 2. Totowa, N. J.: Barnes and Noble, 1982. Pp. 158-64.
    The autobiographical backgrounds, precarious structural balance, and comic dimension of TL ("comedy of affectation").

N13 Brett, Sally Alexander. "'No, Mrs. Ramsay': Feminist Dilemma in TO THE LIGHTHOUSE." BALL STATE UNIVERSITY FORUM, 19, No. 1 (1978), 48-56.
    VW's feminist theme evident in the liberated Lily Briscoe's, or the artist's "triumph" over Mrs. Ramsay, or convention.

N14 Brogan, Howard O. "Science and Narrative Structure in Austen, Hardy, and Woolf." NINETEENTH-CENTURY FICTION, 11 (1957), 276-87.
    TL (pp. 281-86) reflects the modern concept of space and time as relative.

N15 Brower, Reuben A. "The Novel as Poem: Virginia Woolf: Exploring a Critical Metaphor." In THE INTERPRETATION OF NARRATIVE: THEORY AND PRACTICE. Ed. Morton W. Bloomfield. Cambridge, Mass.: Harvard Univ. Press, 1970. Pp. 229-47.
    VW, unlike recent formalist critics, recognized the impossibility of a pure poem-novel. Examines TL (pp. 236-47) as a test case.

N16 Brown, Edward K. RHYTHM IN THE NOVEL. Toronto: Univ. of Toronto Press, 1950. Pp. 64-70.
    Rhythmic qualities in TL, "a novel in sonata form."

N17 Burt, John. "Irreconcilable Habits of Thought in A ROOM OF ONE'S OWN and TO THE LIGHTHOUSE." ENGLISH LITERARY HISTORY, 49 (1982), 889-907.
    Unresolved conflicts in VW's novel (form and content, nostalgia and realism, etc.), and essay (progressivism and nostalgia), skillfully balanced in both works.

N18 Caserio, Robert L. PLOT, STORY, AND THE NOVEL. Princeton, N. J.: Princeton Univ. Press, 1979. Pp. 248-54 and passim.
    TL departs from the "family plot" novel in its "chillingly impassive" distinction between creation and "reproduction."

N19 Cecchi, Emilio. "LA GITA AL FARO de V. Woolf"; "LA GITA AL FARO tradotta." 1946; 1934. In SCRITTORI INGLESI E AMERICANI. Milan: Mondadori, 1947. Pp. 321-29; 330-35.
    Finds a Sophoclean fatality in TL; "la vita appare piú bella, piú dolce, e piú desolata." Second, earlier essay, reviews the Italian trans-

lation of TL (1934), noting VW's balance of
fresh expression and lyrical subject matter.
[In Italian.]

N20 Cohan, Steven. "Why Mr. Ramsay Reads THE ANTIQUARY." WOMEN &
LITERATURE, 7, No. 2 (1979), 14-24.
Appropriateness of Mr. Ramsay's reading of
Scott's "manly" and misogynistic novel.

N21 Cohen, Keith. FILM AND FICTION: THE DYNAMICS OF EXCHANGE. New
Haven, Conn.: Yale Univ. Press, 1979. Pp. 127-32 and passim.
Theoretical comparison of cinematic and narrative
techniques (e.g., time and montage in TL).

N22 Cohn, Ruby. "Art in TO THE LIGHTHOUSE." MFS, 8 (1962), 127-36.
Interrelated themes of life, death, and art
in TL. Reprinted in G44.

N23 Corsa, Helen S. "TO THE LIGHTHOUSE: Death, Mourning, and Transfiguration." L&P, 21 (1971), 115-31.
In its "pattern and movement" TL "evokes, recreates, and delineates the mourning process."

N24 Cox, C. B. "Mental Images and the Style of Virginia Woolf."
CRITICAL SURVEY, 3 (1968), 205-08.
Describes VW's presentation of "freely floating"
mental images in TL (cf. Imagist techniques).

N25 Dash, Irene G., Deena Dash Kushner, and Deborah Dash Moore.
"How Light a LIGHTHOUSE for Today's Women?" In THE LOST TRADITION: MOTHERS AND DAUGHTERS IN LITERATURE. Ed. Cathy N.
Davidson and E. M. Broner. New York: Ungar, 1980. Pp. 176-88.
A mother's and her daughters' reactions to VW's
presentation of Mrs. Ramsay's relations with her
children, and, as mother-surrogate, with Lily.

N26 Derbyshire, S. E. "An Analysis of Mrs. Woolf's TO THE LIGHTHOUSE." CE, 3 (1942), 353-60.
The three sections of TL concerned with time,
death, and personality respectively.

N27 DiBattista, Maria. "TO THE LIGHTHOUSE: Virginia Woolf's Winter's
Tale." In VIRGINIA WOOLF. Ed. Ralph Freedman. Pp. 161-88.
See G26.
TL's Freudian psychology, archetypal myths, and
literary antecedents.

N28 Dick, Susan. "Introduction." In VIRGINIA WOOLF, *TO THE LIGHTHOUSE*. Ed. Dick. Pp. 11-35. See C7.
Describes the surviving manuscript of TL, speculates on "the intermediate stages of the book,"
and reviews "some stylistic and biographical
implications" in the comparative study of the
manuscript and published versions.

N29   -----. "The Restless Searcher: A Discussion of the Evolution
       of 'Time Passes' in TO THE LIGHTHOUSE." ENGLISH STUDIES IN
       CANADA, 5 (1979), 311-29.
            VW's integration of the "restless searcher" figure
            into her composition of TL's middle section.

N30   Empson, William. "Virginia Woolf." In SCRUTINIES. Comp. Edgell
       Rickword. London: Wishart, 1931. II, 204-16.
            VW's delicate use of form, image association,
            detail, and style to enlarge the significance
            of the moment. Reprinted in G49.

N31   Enright, D. J. "To the Lighthouse or to India?" In THE APOTHE-
       CARY'S SHOP: ESSAYS ON LITERATURE. London: Secker and Warburg,
       1957. Pp. 168-86.
            Compares Forster's and VW's "scrupulous concern
            for sincerity in personal relationships" in A
            PASSAGE TO INDIA (1924) and TL.

N32   Erzgräber, Willi. "Nachimpressionistische Anschauungen über
       Kompositionstechnik und Farbsymbolik in Virginia Woolfs Roman
       TO THE LIGHTHOUSE" ["A Post-Impressionist Interpretation of
       the Technique of Composition and Color Symbolism of Virginia
       Woolf's Novel TO THE LIGHTHOUSE"]. In MISCELLANEA ANGLOAMERICANA:
       FESTSCHRIFT FÜR HELMUT VIEBROCK. Ed. Kuno Schuhmann, Wilhelm
       Hortmann, and Armin P. Frank. Munich: Pressler, 1974. Pp. 148-
       83.
            Important discussion of VW's adaptation of the
            visual techniques of the Post-Impressionist
            painters in TL, with an extended analysis of
            her use of color symbolism. [In German.]

N33   Espinola, Judith. "Narrative Discourse in Virginia Woolf's TO
       THE LIGHTHOUSE." In STUDIES IN INTERPRETATION. Vol. 2. Ed.
       Esther M. Doyle and Virginia H. Floyd. Amsterdam: Rodopi, 1977.
       Pp. 29-43.
            Analysis of the kinds of speech within TL
            demonstrates the "speaking presence" of the
            central, undramatized narrator.

N34   Ferguson, Suzanne. "The Face in the Mirror: Authorial Presence
       in the Multiple Vision of Third-Person Impressionist Narrative."
       CRITICISM, 21 (1979), 230-50.
            "Ubiquitous interplay of irony and ambiguity
            created by the narrative method" of TL, among
            other works (e.g., MADAME BOVARY [1857] and
            THE AMBASSADORS [1903]).

N35   Fischer, Gretl Kraus. "Edward Albee and Virginia Woolf." DAL-
       HOUSIE REVIEW, 49 (1969), 196-207.
            Albee directly influenced by VW's story "Lappin
            and Lapinova" and TL in the situation and themes
            of WHO'S AFRAID OF VIRGINIA WOOLF? (1962).

N36 Fleishman, Avrom. "Woolf and McTaggart: An Interrogation of the Metaphysics in TO THE LIGHTHOUSE." 1969. In FICTION AND THE WAYS OF KNOWING. Austin: Univ. of Texas Press, 1978. Pp. 163-78.
: Reveals the significant influence on VW's views of time and collective consciousness of the thought of the Cambridge philosopher J. McT. E. McTaggart (d. 1925).

N37 Fokkema, Douwe W. "An Interpretation of TO THE LIGHTHOUSE: With Reference to the Code of Modernism." PTL: A JOURNAL FOR DESCRIPTIVE POETICS AND THEORY OF LITERATURE, 4 (1979), 475-500.
: Jargon-laden attempt to specify the "modernist" features of TL: contingency, metalanguage, self-reflexivity, etc.

N38 Friedman, Norman. "The Waters of Annihilation: Symbols and Double Vision in TO THE LIGHTHOUSE." 1955. In FORM AND MEANING IN FICTION. Athens: Univ. of Georgia Press, 1975. Pp. 340-58.
: Traces the "intricate web of image, attitude and idea" which holds the novel together. Earlier version (1955) reprinted in N1.

N39 Fromm, Harold. "TO THE LIGHTHOUSE: Music and Sympathy." ENGLISH MISCELLANY, 19 (1968), 181-95.
: VW's evocation of sympathetic, emotional responses in the reader, comparable to the audience response to music.

N40 Gillespie, Diane F. "Virginia Woolf and the 'Reign of Error.'" RS, 43 (1975), 222-34.
: Traces the literary depiction of the suppressed woman-artist, in VW and others (TL and ORLANDO, pp. 230-32).

N41 Gillie, Christopher. MOVEMENTS IN ENGLISH LITERATURE, 1900-1940. Cambridge: Cambridge Univ. Press, 1975. Pp. 101-07.
: Balanced "unity of outer stimulus and inner event" successfully achieved by VW only in TL.

N42 Gregor, Ian. "Spaces: TO THE LIGHTHOUSE." In THE AUTHOR IN HIS WORK: ESSAYS ON A PROBLEM IN CRITICISM. Ed. Louis L. Martz and Aubrey Williams. New Haven, Conn.: Yale Univ. Press, 1978. Pp. 375-89.
: VW's reach exceeds her grasp in her "triumphant" novel, as her "constantly shifting involvement" raises "troubling interpretive questions."

N43 Gunsteren-Viersen, Julia van. "De vrije indirecte rede: Theorie en ontwikkeling." FORUM DER LETTERN, 21 (1980), 266-82.
: Theoretical definition and history of the free-indirect-style of narration, using TL as the primary text for illustration. [In Dutch.]

N44 Hamada, Koichi. "Virginia Woolf's Artistry in TO THE LIGHTHOUSE."
DOSHISHA STUDIES IN ENGLISH, No. 26 (1981), pp. 4-22.
    Awkwardly-written analysis of VW's "intricate
weaving of words or phrases" in four passages
from TL, finding this decipherment of meaning
in complexity a primary theme in the novel.

N45 Hardy, John Edward. "TO THE LIGHTHOUSE: Vision Without Promise."
In MAN IN THE MODERN NOVEL. Seattle: Univ. of Washington Press,
1964. Pp. 96-122.
    VW's triumph in TL, her non-dramatic vision of
personality as a "purely aesthetic mechanism...
whose life has no purposeful, moral continuity,"
the source of the drastic decline in her static
later fiction.

N46 Harrington, Henry R. "The Central Line Down the Middle of TO THE
LIGHTHOUSE." ConL, 21 (1980), 363-82.
    Relates VW's pictorial conception of TL to post-
impressionist theories and practice.

N47 Henke, Suzette. "Virginia Woolf's TO THE LIGHTHOUSE: In Defense of the Woman Artist." VIRGINIA WOOLF QUARTERLY, 2 (1975),
39-47.
    Mrs. Ramsay's and Lily's attainment of the ob-
jective detachment necessary for the artistic
ordering of chaotic experience.

N48 Himmelfarb, Gertrude. "Mr. Stephen and Mr. Ramsay: The Victorian
as Intellectual." TWENTIETH CENTURY, 152 (1952), 513-25.
    Contrasts the "narrow, mean, vitriolic Mr.
Ramsay" with his model, "the broadminded,
enlightened, good-humored Mr. Stephen."

N49 Hoare, Dorothy M. "Introduction." In Woolf's TO THE LIGHTHOUSE.
London: Dent, 1955. Pp. v-x.
    Achieving a "solution" to the technical problem
of her earlier fiction, VW successfully unites
art and life in "the perfection of the moment"
in TL.

N50 Hoffmann, A. C. "Subject and Object and the Nature of Reality:
The Dialectic of TO THE LIGHTHOUSE." TSLL, 13 (1972), 691-703.
    Correlates TL's "philosophic theme" with its
"formal construction."

N51 Hoffmann, Charles G. "TO THE LIGHTHOUSE." EXPLICATOR, 10 (1951),
item 13.
    Structural symbolism of the bowl of fruit, the
lighthouse, and Lily's final brushstroke.

N52 Holliday, Terence. "Introduction." In Woolf's TO THE LIGHTHOUSE.
New York: Modern Library, 1937. Pp. v-xiii.
    Praises VW's presentation of character, her
grasp of psychology, and her novel's "organic"
unity.

N53 Humma, John B. "'Time Passes' in TO THE LIGHTHOUSE; 'Governor Pyncheon' in THE HOUSE OF THE SEVEN GABLES." BALL STATE UNIVERSITY FORUM, 20, No. 3 (1979), 54-59.
Sees the direct influence of Hawthorne's novel (1851) on the artistic design of TL.

N54 Hyman, Virginia R. "The Metamorphosis of Leslie Stephen: 'Those are pearls that were his eyes.'" VIRGINIA WOOLF QUARTERLY, 2 (1975), 48-65.
Mr. Ramsay's philosophic concerns indebted to Leslie Stephen's THE SCIENCE OF ETHICS (1882).

N55 Joyner, Nancy. "The Underside of the Butterfly: Lessing's Debt to Woolf." JOURNAL OF NARRATIVE TECHNIQUE, 4 (1974), 204-11.
Influence of VW, principally TL, on Lessing's THE GOLDEN NOTEBOOK (1962).

N56 Kaehele, Sharon, and Howard German. "TO THE LIGHTHOUSE: Symbol and Vision." BUCKNELL REVIEW, 10 (1962), 328-46.
The structural, symbolic, and thematic unity of TL's three parts. Reprinted in N1.

N57 Kahane, Claire. "The Nuptials of Metaphor: Self and Other in Virginia Woolf." L&P, 30 (1980), 72-82.
VW's mother "seems to have represented precisely that unifying centrality," that completed self achieved by integrating "the fragments of both inner and outer worlds," VW "tries to capture in her fiction."

N58 Kaplan, Sydney Janet. "Virginia Woolf." In FEMININE CONSCIOUSNESS IN THE MODERN BRITISH NOVEL. Urbana: Univ. of Illinois Press, 1975. Pp. 76-109.
On MD and TL. For annotation see M43.

N59 Kendzora, Kathleen. "'Life stands still here': The Frame Metaphor in TO THE LIGHTHOUSE." VIRGINIA WOOLF QUARTERLY, 3 (1978), 252, 254-67.
VW's attempt to make TL a self-enclosed, aesthetic whole through spatial metaphors and imagery.

N60 Kettle, Arnold. "Virginia Woolf: TO THE LIGHTHOUSE." In AN INTRODUCTION TO THE ENGLISH NOVEL. Vol. 2. HENRY JAMES TO THE PRESENT. London: Hutchinson, 1951. Pp. 100-05.
TL's fundamental problem is that "it is, when all is said, not about anything very interesting or important." Extract reprinted in N5. Also see E6.

N61 Kreyling, Michael. "Life with People: Virginia Woolf, Eudora Welty, and THE OPTIMIST'S DAUGHTER." SOUTHERN REVIEW, 13 (1977), 250-71.
Substantial influence of TL on Welty's story (1969--later expanded into the novel inaccurately referred to in this essay's title, 1972).

N62 Lavin, J. A. "The First Editions of Virginia Woolf's TO THE LIGHTHOUSE." PROOF, 2 (1972), 185-211.
> First American edition contains, and subsequent American printings still contain, final revisions not incorporated into the English edition(s). Lists variants.

N63 Lilienfeld, Jane. "'The Deceptiveness of Beauty': Mother Love and Mother Hate in TO THE LIGHTHOUSE." TCL, 23 (1977), 345-76.
> Lily and Mrs. Ramsay VW's psychological surrogates for herself and her mother.

N64 -----. "Where the Spear Plants Grew: The Ramsays' Marriage in TO THE LIGHTHOUSE." In NEW FEMINIST ESSAYS ON VIRGINIA WOOLF. Ed. Jane Marcus. Pp. 148-69. See G51.
> VW's vision of the Ramsays' marriage not the idealized union of the male and female principles, but a "mature, sharp critical examination" of her own parents' relations as well as of destructive Victorian "roles and values" for marriage.

N65 Little, Judith. "Heroism in TO THE LIGHTHOUSE." In IMAGES OF WOMEN IN FICTION: FEMINIST PERSPECTIVES. Ed. Susan K. Cornillon. Bowling Green, Ohio: Bowling Green Univ. Press, 1972. Pp. 237-42.
> Mrs. Ramsay's heroic deference to Mr. Ramsay's "postured heroism," VW's subtle commentary on the fictional convention that the hero must be male.

N66 Masui, Jacques. "Virginia Woolf." LE FLAMBEAU, 15 (1932), 78-90.
> VW's exquisite style (cf. Impressionism), intuitive brilliance, and psychological penetration best seen in TL, her "long poème psychologique." [In French.]

N67 May, Keith M. "The Symbol of 'Painting' in Virginia Woolf's TO THE LIGHTHOUSE." REVIEW OF ENGLISH LITERATURE, 8, No. 2 (1967), 91-98.
> Lily's painting a symbol for TL itself; painting, as object and act, a symbol both for all works of art and for the "proper mode of artistic creation."

N68 Mayoux, Jean-Jacques. "Sur un livre de Virginia Woolf." REVUE ANGLO-AMÉRICAINE, 5 (1928), 424-38.
> Impressively thorough, early critical analysis of TL, focusing on VW's patterning imagery, lyrical rhythms in style and structure, and thematic counterpoint of separate, yet continuous inner and outer worlds (cf. music and painting--Cézanne). [In French.] Extracts reprinted in translation in G49.

N69 Mepham, John. "Figures of Desire: Narration and Fiction in TO THE LIGHTHOUSE." In THE MODERN ENGLISH NOVEL: THE READER, THE WRITER AND THE WORK. Ed. Gabriel Josipovici. New York: Barnes and Noble, 1976. Pp. 149-85.
    Close analysis of VW's narrative techniques in TL, distinguishing VW's creation of order from the traditional novelist's representation of order.

N70 Ottavi, Anne. "La Figure maternelle chez Colette et Virginia Woolf." In ÉTUDES ET RECHERCHES DE LITTÉRATURE GÉNÉRALE ET COMPARÉE. Paris: Les Belles Lettres, 1974. Pp. 181-91.
    Remarkable similarities between VW's presentation of Mrs. Ramsay and Colette's Sido in LA MAISON DE CLAUDINE (1922) and SIDO (1929). [In French.]

N71 Overcarsh, F. L. "The Lighthouse, Face to Face." ACCENT, 10 (1950), 107-23.
    Conscious inversion of Christian symbolism makes TL VW's atheistic "allegory."

N72 Ōya, Fukiyo. "TO THE LIGHTHOUSE." In MAEKAWA SHUNICHI KYŌJU KANREKI KINEN-RONBUNSHŪ [ESSAYS AND STUDIES IN COMMEMORATION OF PROFESSOR SHUNICHI MAEKAWA'S SIXTY-FIRST BIRTHDAY]. Tokyo: Eihōsha, 1968. Pp. 53-64.
    Not seen. [In Japanese.]

N73 Parkes, Graham. "Imagination and Reality in TO THE LIGHTHOUSE." PHILOSOPHY AND LITERATURE, 6 (1982), 33-44.
    Examines VW as a philosophical novelist, rather than a novelist influenced by philosophers, who explores man's "*participation* in phenomena" and the ways in which "it is mediated by the *images* of the novel and by the operations of the *imagination* in our experience of the world" in TL. See response by S. P. Rosenbaum, PHILOSOPHY AND LITERATURE, 7 (1983), 89-91.

N74 Pedersen, Glenn. "Vision in TO THE LIGHTHOUSE." PMLA, 73 (1958), 585-600.
    Lily's final vision resolves TL's conflicts, revealing Mrs. Ramsay as a "negative force" who has prevented the "integration of the family."

N75 Pérez Gállego, Cándido. "TO THE LIGHTHOUSE y la estructura de las novelas de Virginia Woolf." FILOLOGÍA MODERNA, 6, Nos. 25-26 (1966-67), 115-31.
    Analysis of the formal relations of the three parts of TL. [In Spanish.]

N76 Pratt, Annis. "Sexual Imagery in TO THE LIGHTHOUSE: A New Feminist Approach." MFS, 18 (1972), 417-31.
    Examines critical responses to Mr. and Mrs. Ramsay, finding in TL's sexual symbolism Mrs. Ramsay alone approaching Jungian "psychic integration." See G56.

N77 Pratt, Annis, et al. "Mrs. Ramsay and the Androgynous Elixir." In ARCHETYPAL PATTERNS IN WOMEN'S FICTION. Bloomington: Indiana Univ. Press, 1981. Pp. 143-53.
    Structural patterns, erotic symbolism, and archetypal dimensions in TL (e.g., androgynous creativity).

N78 Price, Martin. FORMS OF LIFE: CHARACTER AND MORAL IMAGINATION IN THE NOVEL. New Haven, Conn.: Yale Univ. Press, 1983. Pp. 320-34 and passim.
    TL "traces the emergence of the artist and of the work of art from the circumstances of the artist's life." Lily Briscoe, Mrs. Ramsay, and VW herself, the artists considered.

N79 Pritchard, William H. "Virginia Woolf and TO THE LIGHTHOUSE." In SEEING THROUGH EVERYTHING: ENGLISH WRITERS, 1918-1940. New York: Oxford Univ. Press, 1977. Pp. 106-13 and passim.
    TL, alone among VW's works, presents "human life in neither materialistic nor purely spiritual, ideal terms."

N80 Proudfit, Sharon L. "Lily Briscoe's Painting: A Key to Personal Relations in TO THE LIGHTHOUSE." CRITICISM, 13 (1971), 26-39.
    Structural, symbolic, and thematic significance of Lily's painting.

N81 Roberts, John H. "'Vision and Design' in Virginia Woolf." PMLA, 61 (1946), 835-47.
    On MD and TL. For annotation see M69.

N82 Rose, Phyllis. "Mrs. Ramsay and Mrs. Woolf." WOMEN'S STUDIES, 1 (1973), 199-216.
    VW's need to "kill" in her work the phantom of the selfless, "pelican woman," a figure based on her own mother.

N83 Ruddick, Sara. "Learning to Live with the Angel in the House." WOMEN'S STUDIES, 4 (1977), 181-200.
    Lily's struggle with the "invisible presence" of Mrs. Ramsay paralleled with VW's exploration of her own relations with her mother: "Learning to think back through her mother was an early step in Woolf's feminism." See G87.

N84 Russell, H. K. "Woolf's TO THE LIGHTHOUSE." EXPLICATOR, 8 (1950), item 38.
    The lighthouse, "Mrs. Ramsay's personal symbol," represents her moments of "saving illumination... in the stream of experience."

N85 Sagiyama, Yoko. "A Study of TO THE LIGHTHOUSE." KWANSEI GAKUIN UNIVERSITY ANNUAL STUDIES, 17 (1968), 21-37.
    TL's appeal ranges from the concrete details of its autobiographical foundations to the metaphysical abstraction of VW's "concept of Life" (here explored).

N86 Schug, Charles. "Virginia Woolf: MRS. DALLOWAY, TO THE LIGHTHOUSE." In THE ROMANTIC GENESIS OF THE MODERN NOVEL. Pittsburgh: Univ. of Pittsburgh Press, 1979. Pp. 189-225.
    For annotation see M78.

N87 Schulz, Muriel R. "A Style of One's Own." In WOMEN'S LANGUAGE AND STYLE. Ed. Douglas Butturff and Edmund L. Epstein. Akron, Ohio: L&S Books, 1978. Pp. 75-83.
    Examines VW's representation of "male and female speaking styles" in Mr. and Mrs. Ramsay, and her exploration of "the possibility of an androgynous middle" style of discourse through Lily Briscoe.

N88 Seltzer, Alvin J. "The Tension of Stalemate: Art and Chaos in Virginia Woolf's TO THE LIGHTHOUSE." In CHAOS IN THE NOVEL/THE NOVEL IN CHAOS. New York: Schocken, 1974. Pp. 120-40.
    In TL, VW successfully depicts the threat of chaos and, with no illusion of possible triumph, affirms the value of art as a momentary stay against darkness.

N89 Sharma, O. P. "Feminism as Aesthetic Vision and Transcendence: A Study of Virginia Woolf's TO THE LIGHTHOUSE." PUNJAB UNIVERSITY RESEARCH BULLETIN (ARTS), 3, No. 1 (1972), 1-8.
    Sees TL as a landmark publication for the history of feminism: the novel "created the immortal sublimity of the soul of a woman, as conceived by a woman novelist." Also see M79.

N90 Simon, Irène. "Some Aspects of Virginia Woolf's Imagery." ENGLISH STUDIES, 41 (1960), 180-96.
    On MD and TL. For annotation see M83.

N91 Snow, Lotus. "Visions of Design: Virginia Woolf's 'Time Passes' and BETWEEN THE ACTS." RS, 44 (1976), 24-34.
    Germ of VW's "comprehensive presentation of time" in BETWEEN THE ACTS found in the middle section of TL.

N92 Spivak, Gayatri C. "Unmaking and Making in TO THE LIGHTHOUSE." In WOMEN AND LANGUAGE IN LITERATURE AND SOCIETY. Ed. Sally McConnell-Ginet, Ruth Borker, and Nelly Furman. New York: Praeger, 1980. Pp. 310-27.
    Study of the language of TL, as determined by the novel's grammatical and sexual structural allegories: parts I-III as subject-copula-predicate.

N93 Stamirowska, Krystyna. "Virginia Woolf's Concept of Reality and Some Theories of Her Time." KWARTALNIK NEOFILOLOGICZNY, 22 (1975), 207-17.
    On MD and TL. For annotation see M86.

N94   Steiger, Klaus P. "Der Romananfang von Virginia Woolfs TO THE LIGHTHOUSE." GERMANISCH-ROMANISCH MONATSSCHRIFT, 23 (1973), 105-15.
      Close examination of the opening passages of TL as an embodiment of the chief themes and conflicts of the entire novel. [In German.]

N95   Steinberg, Erwin R. "Freudian Symbolism and Communication." L&P, 3, No. 2 (1953), 2-5.
      On MD and TL. For annotation see M87.

N96   Steinmann, Theo. "Virginia Woolf: TO THE LIGHTHOUSE; Die doppelte Funktion der Malerin." DIE NEUEREN SPRACHEN, 19 (1970), 537-47.
      Lily's dual functions as objective observer (painter) and subjective participant (as character) in the novel confirms the parallel between her painting and the novel itself. [In German.]

N97   Stewart, Grace. "TO THE LIGHTHOUSE." In A NEW MYTHOS: THE NOVEL OF THE ARTIST AS HEROINE. St. Albans, Vt.: Eden Press, 1979. Pp. 69-76.
      VW's use of the Demeter and Persephone myth in TL.

N98   Stewart, Jack F. "Light in TO THE LIGHTHOUSE." TCL, 23 (1977), 377-89.
      Negation and reanimation of consciousness suggested in TL's light symbolism.

N99   Strouse, Louise F. "Virginia Woolf--Her Voyage Back." AMERICAN IMAGO, 38 (1981), 185-202.
      VW's search for a mother-figure attributed to infantile fears of separation, rather than to the death of VW's mother in her adolescence.

N100 Temple, Ruth Z. "Never Say 'I': TO THE LIGHTHOUSE as Vision and Confession." In VIRGINIA WOOLF. Ed. Claire Sprague. Pp. 90-100. See G80.
      The making of TL, VW's "most Proustian" and "most confessional work," "has illuminated or even created" the truth of her memory of and relations with her parents.

N101 Villanueva, Darío. "Virginia Woolf." An ESTRUCTURA Y TIEMPO REDUCIDO EN LA NOVELA. Valencia, Spain: Editorial Bello, 1977. Pp. 98-101.
      On MD and TL. For annotation see M91.

N102 Vogler, Thomas A. "Introduction." In TWENTIETH CENTURY INTERPRETATIONS OF TO THE LIGHTHOUSE. Ed. Vogler. Pp. 1-13. See N5.
      Good general survey of TL's biographical backgrounds and literary themes and techniques (e.g., characterization, men and women, literary allusion, structure and form).

N103 Warner, John M. "Symbolic Patterns of Retreat and Reconciliation in TO THE LIGHTHOUSE." DISCOURSE, 12 (1969), 376-92.
    Thematic and symbolic tensions between isolation and union in the novel.

N104 Whitehead, Lee M. "The Shawl and the Skull: Virginia Woolf's 'Magic Mountain.'" MFS, 18 (1972), 401-15.
    TL's thematic and symbolic counterpoint between the "veil of civilization and beauty" and the horrors beneath the surface. See G56.

N105 Wirth-Nesher, Hana. "Form as Fate: Everyman as Artist in Virginia Woolf's TO THE LIGHTHOUSE." BUCKNELL REVIEW, 22, No. 2 (1976), 71-80.
    VW asserts in TL that the search for form and meaning is a central human activity, not limited to the artist alone.

N106 Wyatt, Jean. "The Celebrations of Eros: Greek Concepts of Love and Beauty in TO THE LIGHTHOUSE." PHILOSOPHY AND LITERATURE, 2 (1978), 160-75.
    Parallels between the central concerns of TL and Plato's SYMPOSIUM: "striving for knowledge through love; the desire to create that beauty arouses; the paradox of the eternal in the midst of the transitory."

N107 Yoshida, Yasuo. "TO THE LIGHTHOUSE to [and] THE PORTRAIT OF A LADY." In GENGO TO BUNTAI: HIGASHIDA CHIAKI KYOJU KANREKI KINEN RONBUNSHU [LANGUAGE AND STYLE: COLLECTED ESSAYS COMMEMORATING THE 60TH BIRTHDAY OF PROF. CHIAKI HIGASHIDA]. Ed. Chiaki Higashida. Osaka: Osaka Kyoiku Tosho, 1975. Pp. 218-28.
    Not seen. [In Japanese.]

P. STUDIES OF *ORLANDO* (1928)

The following section is subdivided into two parts: i. Books and Essay Collections on ORLANDO; and ii. Critical Articles or Chapters on ORLANDO.

For a comparison of the manuscript and published texts of ORLANDO, see C9. For the forthcoming concordance to the novel, see section D.

For bibliographical information on ORLANDO, see Kirkpatrick (E7), and, for biographical backgrounds to the novel, see Bell (F13), DeSalvo (F23), Nicolson (F69), Rose (F81), Trautmann (F92, F93), and Woolf (F100).

For the most significant additional critical commentaries and information on ORLANDO, see the following books, in section G above: Alexander (G2), Badenhausen (G5), Bazin (G6), Blackstone (G9), Daiches (G16), Delattre (G17), DiBattista (G18), Donahue (G20), Finke (G23), Fleishman (G24), Gorsky (G28), Gruber (G29), Guiguet (G30), Hafley (G31), Harper (G32), Johnson (G36), Kapur (G37), Lee (G42), Little (G45), Lohmüller (G46), McLaurin (G48), Marder (G53), Naremore (G59), Pasternack (G65), Poresky (G66), Rantavaara (G68), Richter (G69), Rosenthal (G71), Schlack (G76), Spilka (G79), Thakur (G82), Wiget (G86), Woodring (G88); and the following critical articles, in section H above: Albright (H2), Batchelor (H7), Beach (H8), Borinsky (H20), Cornwell (H47), Daiches (H54), Fehr (H76), Fleishman (H80), Johnstone (H126), Kumar (H133), Mayoux (H157), Muir (H174), Neuschäffer (H180), Pomeroy (H192), Richter (H201), Rosenbaum (H207), and Wicht (H249). For a complete listing of substantial commentaries on ORLANDO, see the concluding index: "Virginia Woolf's Works."

P. i. Books and Essay Collections on ORLANDO

P1 Madsen, Henriette. VIRGINIA WOOLF: *ORLANDO*: ET VENSTREHÅNDSVAERK [VIRGINIA WOOLF: *ORLANDO*: A LEFT-HANDED WORK]. Odense, Denmark: Udgivelsesudvalget ved Odense, 1976.
> Methodical study of ORLANDO's chief themes and techniques, based on the assumption that VW's achievement in her most unusual novel offers significant insights for the study of her more characteristic fiction. Madsen defines ORLANDO as a "left-handed" work: a "literary product that is exceptional with regard to method and subject matter for a certain author's works and that ranks lower in quality than the same author's best works." Reviewing VW's major themes (time and reality, discovery of identity, androgyny

and feminism, English literary history), and
techniques (parody, symbolism, narrative style,
biographical method), Madsen finds ORLANDO both
typical (in themes) and atypical (in techniques)
for VW, and a significant anticipation of both
THE YEARS (narration) and BETWEEN THE ACTS (the
theme of national culture). Useful, but often
superficial criticism. [In Danish.] Includes
a reprint of P29, in Danish translation, as an
appendix.

P, ii. Critical Articles or Chapters on ORLANDO

P2 Aiken, Conrad. "Virginia Woolf." 1929. In A REVIEWER'S ABC.
New York: Meridian, 1958. Pp. 392-94.
  VW carries "ingenuity too far." Reprinted in G49.

P3 Baldanza, Frank. "ORLANDO and the Sackvilles." PMLA, 70 (1955),
274-79.
  Vita Sackville-West and the Sackville family as
  models for the novel. Also see David Bonnell
  Green's comment, PMLA, 71 (1956), 268-69.

P4 Bisanz, Adam J. "Virginia Woolfs Literaturkritiker Nicholas
Greene auf dem Hintergrund der geschichtsphilosophischen
Kulturzyklen-Theorie." In GESCHICHTLICHKEIT UND NEUANFANG
IM SPRACHLICHEN KUNSTWERK: STUDIEN ZUR ENGLISCHEN PHILOLOGIE
ZU EHREN VON FRITZ W. SCHULZE. Ed. Peter Erlebach, Wolfgang
G. Müller, and Klaus Reuter. Tübingen: Narr, 1981. Pp. 239-
46.
  VW's reduction of the theory of cultural cycles
  to absurdity, in 1928, anticipates much more
  recent trends in historiography. [In German.]

P5 Bodkin, Maud. ARCHETYPAL PATTERNS IN POETRY: PSYCHOLOGICAL
STUDIES OF IMAGINATION. London: Oxford Univ. Press, 1934.
Pp. 299-307.
  Examines the archetypes of the father-imago and
  husband-lover, as perceived by woman, in ORLANDO
  (cf. WUTHERING HEIGHTS [1847]). Extracts reprinted in G49.

P6 Bowen, Elizabeth. "Afterword." In Woolf's ORLANDO. New York:
New American Library, 1960. Pp. 216-22.
  The fantasy ORLANDO, shattering the world of actuality, made VW's next novel (THE WAVES) more
  possible. Includes account of the initially
  negative response to ORLANDO.

P7 Castagnino, Raúl Héctor. EXPERIMENTOS NARRATIVOS. Buenos Aires: Juan Goyanarte, 1971. Pp. 111-51 and passim.
> Extended discussion of the mixture of social history, biography, essay, and experimental fiction in ORLANDO. Sees VW, Kafka, and Charles Morgan as three transitional fantasists leading to the full emergence of science fiction as a dominant genre in recent fiction.

P8 DeSalvo, Louise A. "A Note on the Orlando Tapestries at Knole House." VIRGINIA WOOLF MISCELLANY, No. 13 (1979), pp. 3-4.
> Not seen.

P9 Edel, Leon. LITERARY BIOGRAPHY: THE ALEXANDER LECTURES 1955-1956. Toronto: Univ. of Toronto Press, 1957. Pp. 89-98.
> The serious fun of VW's "fantasy in the form of a biography," which suggests that biographers could deal more imaginatively with fact, and VW's debt to several eminent biographers (e.g., Leslie Stephen and Lytton Strachey). VW's scholarly biography of ROGER FRY lifeless and less successful.

P10 Fleishman, Avrom. "Woolf." In THE ENGLISH HISTORICAL NOVEL: WALTER SCOTT TO VIRGINIA WOOLF. Baltimore, Md.: Johns Hopkins Univ. Press, 1971. Pp. 233-55.
> ORLANDO and BETWEEN THE ACTS (pp. 246-55) examined as historical novels which "bring the tradition of the English historical novel to a self-conscious close."

P11 German, Howard, and Sharon Kaehele. "The Dialectic of Time in ORLANDO." CE, 24 (1962), 35-41.
> Novel explores the conflict between "the ephemeral and the enduring."

P12 Gilbert, Sandra M. "Costumes of the Mind: Transvestism as Metaphor in Modern Literature." CRITICAL INQUIRY, 7 (1980), 391-417.
> Counterpoints the "profoundly conservative" clothing imagery of male modernists with the "radically revisionary" costume imagery of modern women writers (Joyce, Lawrence, Eliot; VW, Barnes, and H. D.).

P13 Gillespie, Diane F. "Virginia Woolf and the 'Reign of Error.'" RS, 43 (1975), 222-34.
> On ORLANDO and TL. For annotation see N40.

P14 Graham, John W. "The 'Caricature Value' of Parody and Fantasy in ORLANDO." UTQ, 30 (1961), 345-66.
> Novel's relation to her "more serious works" found in VW's perfection of her caricature method, her isolation of relevant features for sharper "focus of attention." Reprinted in G40 (extract) and G80.

P15 Hoffmann, Charles G. "Fact and Fantasy in ORLANDO: Virginia Woolf's Manuscript Revisions." TSLL, 10 (1968), 435-44.
Traces "significant differences" between manuscript and unpublished versions of novel, as clues to VW's intentions.

P16 Hunting, Constance. "The Technique of Persuasion in ORLANDO." MFS, 2 (1956), 17-23.
Though described by VW as an "escapade," the novel shows considerable technical ingenuity. See G55.

P17 Kellermann, Frederick. "A New Key to Virginia Woolf's ORLANDO." ENGLISH STUDIES, 59 (1978), 138-50.
Furthers the identification of the novel's roman-a-clef elements.

P18 Kushen, Betty. "'Dreams of Golden Domes': Manic Fusion in Virginia Woolf's ORLANDO." L&P, 29 (1979), 25-33.
The forced and unconvincing "manic" tone of ORLANDO VW's response to her "predominantly depressive position" in TL.

P19 Lawrence, Margaret. THE SCHOOL OF FEMININITY. New York: Stokes, 1936. Pp. 373-81.
VW's "profound and weary skepticism" over the role of woman in ORLANDO and A ROOM OF ONE'S OWN.

P20 Longhi Lopresti, Lucia [Anna Banti]. "Umanità della Woolf." 1952. In OPINIONI. Milan: Il Saggiatore, 1961. Pp. 66-74.
High praise for ORLANDO, VW's spiritual autobiography and finest achievement, incorporating several of her principal themes (e.g., the role of woman, as treated in MD, TL, A ROOM OF ONE'S OWN, and THREE GUINEAS). [In Italian.]

P21 Love, Jean O. "ORLANDO and Its Genesis: Venturing and Experimenting in Art, Love, and Sex." In VIRGINIA WOOLF. Ed. Ralph Freedman. Pp. 189-218. See G26.
Parallels VW's "experimental" affair with Vita Sackville-West and her literary experiment in ORLANDO.

P22 MacCarthy, Desmond. "Phantasmagoria." TIMES (London), 14 Oct. 1928, p. 10.
Finds ORLANDO VW's most successful novel and the fantasy as her most congenial mode: her method always has been "a way of escape from the heaviness of actuality." Reprinted in G49.

P23 Mayoux, Jean-Jacques. "A Propos d'ORLANDO de Virginia Woolf." EUROPE, 22 (1930), 117-22.
Sees ORLANDO as a sublime mixture of comedy and seriousness, laughter and tears: "There

is in this liberation from the chains of our
terrestrial condition a cause for joy and
frivolousness." [In French.]

P24 Mortimer, Raymond. "Mrs. Woolf and Mr. Strachey." BOOKMAN
(New York), 68 (1929), 625-29.
The "quality of inherited culture," the unpre-
tentiousness of tact and taste, characterize
the genius of Strachey and VW. Review essay,
on ELIZABETH AND ESSEX (1928) and ORLANDO
(appreciatively described). Extracts reprinted in G49.

P25 Ocampo, Victoria. "Virginia Woolf, ORLANDO y Cia" ["Virginia
Woolf, ORLANDO and Co."]. SUR, No. 35 (1937), pp. 10-67.
Overview of VW's technical development, chief
themes, and significance for modern culture,
focusing on ORLANDO. [In Spanish.] Reprinted
in Ocampo's TESTIMONIOS II (Buenos Aires: SUR,
1941), pp. 415-28. Also see F65.

P26 Philipson, Morris. "Virginia Woolf's ORLANDO: Biography as a
Work of Fiction." In FROM PARNASSUS: ESSAYS IN HONOR OF JACQUES
BARZUN. Ed. Dora B. Weiner and William R. Keylor. New York:
Harper, 1976. Pp. 237-48.
Biography, or fictional biography, an excellent
form for VW's recurrent questions: "what is
life?" and "what constitutes truth?"

P27 Rosati, Salvatore. "Letteratura Inglese: Virginia Woolf--Aldous
Huxley." NUOVA ANTOLOGIA, 370 (1933), 636-45.
VW's novels increasingly internal in their vision
and lyrical in their style, culminating in the
near poetry of ORLANDO (cf. Sterne's and Huxley's
fiction). [In Italian.] Extract reprinted in
translation in G49.

P28 Rubenstein, Roberta. "ORLANDO: Virginia Woolf's Improvisations
on a Russian Theme." FORUM FOR MODERN LANGUAGE STUDIES, 9 (1973),
166-69.
Russian elements and influences in the novel.

P29 Sackville-West, Victoria. "Virginia Woolf and ORLANDO." LISTENER,
53 (1955), 157-58.
Acknowledges that ORLANDO was based on herself,
her family, and her family home. Quotes several
letters from VW and an unpublished passage from
the novel's manuscript. Reprinted in G40 (extract) and P1.

P30 Samuelson, Ralph. "Virginia Woolf, ORLANDO, and the Feminist
Spirit." WESTERN HUMANITIES REVIEW, 15 (1961), 51-58.
Asserts that VW's "feminine spirit" is an essential characteristic, but by no means a weakness
in her work.

P31 Snider, Clifton. "'A Single Self': A Jungian Interpretation of Virginia Woolf's ORLANDO." MFS, 25 (1979), 263-68.
Jung's theories of the creative individual and the collective unconscious reflected in the novel.

P32 Steele, Elizabeth, Karen Reynders, and Judith Lange, eds. "Glossary--Index to Virginia Woolf's ORLANDO." VIRGINIA WOOLF QUARTERLY, 3 (1977), 38-64.
Annotations for the novel, in the form of an alphabetical subject index.

P33 Steele, Philip L. "Virginia Woolf's Spiritual Autobiography." TOPIC, No. 18 (1969), pp. 64-74.
Parallels Orlando's and VW's "internal" histories, sensibilities, and attitudes toward life.

P34 Stewart, Grace. "ORLANDO." In A NEW MYTHOS: THE NOVEL OF THE ARTIST AS HEROINE. St. Albans, Vt.: Eden Press, 1979. Pp. 28-31, 129-32.
VW's use of the Faust myth and the archetypal "journey to the interior."

P35 Stewart, Jack F. "Historical Impressionism in ORLANDO." STUDIES IN THE NOVEL, 5 (1973), 71-85.
Examines VW's application of impressionistic techniques to a historical subject. See H232 and Q55.

P36 Wagenseil, Hans B. "Virginia Woolf." DIE NEUE RUNDSCHAU, 40 (1929), part 1, 717-18.
Early summary of VW's enormously influential experimentation with literary realism, leading to the synthesis of reality and fantasy in ORLANDO (here reviewed). [In German.]

P37 West, Paul. "Enigmas of Imagination: Woolf's ORLANDO through the Looking Glass." SOUTHERN REVIEW, 13 (1977), 438-55.
Ecstatic and pretentious appreciation of VW as a modernist, concentrating on ORLANDO.

P38 Wilson, J. J. "Why is ORLANDO Difficult?" In NEW FEMINIST ESSAYS ON VIRGINIA WOOLF. Ed. Jane Marcus. Pp. 170-84. See G51.
ORLANDO a distinguished contribution to a traditional novelistic sub-genre, the "anti-novel" (from Chaucer's "Tale of Sir Thopas" to the present).

Q. STUDIES OF *THE WAVES* (1931)

The following section is subdivided into two parts: i. Books and Essay Collections on THE WAVES; and ii. Critical Articles or Chapters on THE WAVES.

For transcriptions of the holograph manuscripts of THE WAVES, see C6. For a concordance to THE WAVES, see D2.

For bibliographical information on THE WAVES, see Kirkpatrick (E7), and, for biographical backgrounds to the novel, see Bell (F13), DeSalvo (F23), Forrester (F31), Poole (F77), Rose (F81), Trombley (F95), and Woolf (F100).

For the most significant additional critical commentaries and information on THE WAVES, see the following books, in section G above: Alexander (G2), Bazin (G6), Blackstone (G9), Daiches (G16), Delattre (G17), DiBattista (G18), Dölle (G19), Donahue (G20), Finke (G23), Fleishman (G24), Gorsky (G28), Gruber (G29), Guiguet (G30), Hafley (G31), Harper (G32), Delattre (in G34), Johnson (G36), Kapur (G37), Kelley (G38), Leaska (G41), Lee (G42), Little (G45), Lohmüller (G46), Love (G47), McLaurin (G48), Marder (G53), Moody (G57), Naremore (G59), Poresky (G66), Rantavaara (G68), Richter (G69), Rosenthal (G71), Schaefer (G75), Schlack (G76), Spilka (G79), Thakur (G82), Wiget (G86), Woodring (G88); the following critical articles, in section H above: Albright (H2), Beach (H8), Bradbrook (H23), Brooks (H28), Burgum (H33), Cornwell (H47), Crosland (H50), Daiches (H54), Delattre (H59), Fleishman (H79), Freedman (H85), Friedman (H90), Graham (H96), Hartman (H108), Hoops (H122), Humphrey (H123), Johnstone (H126), Kiely (H130), Kumar (H133), Kushen (H135), Mayoux (H158), Mellers (H161), Muir (H174), Neuschäffer (H180), Richter (H201), Rosenbaum (H207), Savage (H214), Schorer (H216), Simon (H222), Troy (H242), Wicht (H249), Wilson (H253), Zéraffa (H256); and the following study, entered elsewhere in this bibliography: Meisel (X3). For a complete listing of substantial commentaries on THE WAVES, see the concluding index: "Virginia Woolf's Works."

Q, i. Books and Essay Collections on THE WAVES

Q1 Brandt, Magdalene. REALISMUS UND REALITÄT IM MODERNEN ROMAN: METHODOLOGISCHE UNTERSUCHUNGEN ZU VIRGINIA WOOLFS *THE WAVES*. Bad Homberg: Gehlen, 1968.
A "methodological investigation" of VW's THE WAVES, which approaches the novel in terms of its challenges both to traditional and to modern conceptions of fiction and fiction criticism. The first half of Brandt's study examines the opposing tendencies of internal (formalist) and various external approaches to criticism in the twentieth century (viz. James, Lubbock, Forster), the chief issues of critical debate (e.g., the validity and immediacy of stream-of-consciousness techniques), and the connections between the evolution of the novel and the idea of "formal realism" (viz. Ian Watt's THE RISE OF THE NOVEL [1957]). She views VW's criticism and practice of fiction as an attempted synthesis of divergent tendencies, through the decisive ("massgebliche") conception of multiple perspectives, and explores THE WAVES "als Höhepunkt...der Erzählkunst von" VW. Her interpretation stresses, through close analysis of the text, VW's synthesis of reality through the use of time, sharply visualized description, structural counterpoint of character, interludes, and epilogue, and unifying themes (the manner, essence, and uncertainty of life). An imposing defense of THE WAVES as a central work of modern fiction. [In German.] See G19.

Q2 Collins, Robert G. VIRGINIA WOOLF'S BLACK ARROWS OF SENSATION: *THE WAVES*. Ilfracombe, Engl.: Stockwell, 1962.
Monograph-discussion of VW's experimental intentions for THE WAVES and analysis of the interpenetrating motifs, symbolic structure, and characters (such as they are) in the novel: VW's "attempt to present not simply the 'textures' but the substance of life," her "most elemental" and, paradoxically, her most technically complex novel.

Q3 Grünewald-Huber, Elisabeth. VIRGINIA WOOLF: *THE WAVES*: EINE TEXTORIENTIERTE PSYCHOANALYTISCHE INTERPRETATION. Bern: Francke, 1979.
A psychoanalytic interpretation of THE WAVES combined with a review of methodologies in recent Woolf studies. Grünewald-Huber opens with a defense of the Freudian approach to VW's fiction (legitimately citing her "Freudian

Fiction" in support; see A30). The largest
part of her study "outlines the psychic personality structures of the six soliloquizing
characters," by analyzing their language,
fantasies, actions, and relationships, and
the "psychoanalytical connotations" of the
interludes (symbolic interplay of id=sea and
ego=sun), Percival's role ("Super-Ego";
father figure in Oedipal conflicts), the reunions in London and Hampton Court (regressions into "narcissism"; dominance of the
"Id"), and Bernard's epilogue ("Ego").
Grünewald-Huber's interpretations are plausible, though somewhat too systematic and
predictable. She expands her concerns in
her concluding review, governed by psychoanalytic theories of reading, of several
"readings" of VW (by Blackstone [G9],
Dölle [G19], Fleishman [G24], Love [G47],
Naremore [G59], Richter [G69], and Weber-Brandies [Q5]). [In German; English
"Summary," pp. 7-9.]

Q4 Rantavaara, Irma. VIRGINIA WOOLF'S *THE WAVES*. Helsinki: Annales Academiae Fennicae, 1960.
Stylistic study of the novel, commenting on
structure and symbolism, but concentrating on
the qualities of VW's language: rhetorical
devices, "impressionistic" vocabulary and
syntax, "expressionistic" features, and sentence rhythms. Rantavaara concludes that THE
WAVES is a *tour de force* of stylistic, thematic,
and formal unity, though its vision is too
limited.

Q5 Weber-Brandies, Ingeborg. VIRGINIA WOOLF: *THE WAVES*: EMANZIPATION ALS MÖGLICHKEIT DES BEWUSSTSEINSROMANS. Bern: Lang, 1974.
Sociological approach to VW's theory and practice of fiction, vigorously disputing those who
would see her as an aesthete, estranged from
social concerns. Weber-Brandies discusses the
multiple layers of social relevance to be found
in art and, reviewing VW's essays and fiction
generally, finds her "Romantheorie" best understood as an affirmative "gesellschaftstheoretische
Vision" (theoretical social vision) in its ideal
of "Kosmische Solidarität." Her anti-conventional fiction corresponds to her vision of a
"classless and towerless world" (quotes from
"The Leaning Tower," in A27). Most of VW's
experiments correspond with this egalitarian
ideal (impersonal narration, androgyny, moments
of visionary communion), and THE WAVES, by no
means an ultimate product of "aestheticism" or
"decadence," illustrates a major social function

of art, emancipation from isolated self-hood, by showing its six characters' searches for their identities in relation to their ideal communal identity, Percival. Weber-Brandies, finally, correlates these searches to the novel's quest for its own individual form and social identity in its integration of individual monologues and cosmic interludes. Persuasive and well-written study. [In German.] Reviewed in Q3.

Q, ii. Critical Articles or Chapters on THE WAVES

Q6 Arakelian, Paul G. "Feature Analysis of Metaphor in THE WAVES and MANHATTAN TRANSFER." STYLE, 12 (1978), 274-85.
    Linguistic analysis of DosPassos's "adjectival" and VW's "reiterative" styles in MANHATTAN TRANSFER (1925) and THE WAVES.

Q7 Barzilai, Shulamith. "The Knot of Consciousness: THE WAVES." HEBREW UNIVERSITY STUDIES IN LITERATURE, 7 (1979), 214-44.
    Novel a "full-length study of the expressiveness of silence."

Q8 Bell, Carolyn Wilkerson. "Parallelism and Contrast in Virginia Woolf's THE WAVES." PHILOLOGICAL QUARTERLY, 58 (1979), 348-59.
    Parallels and contrasts between moments of vision make THE WAVES VW's "most serious and coherent attempt" to affirm the value of the "moment" and "to capture it in some convincing aesthetic structure."

Q9 Bevis, Dorothy. "THE WAVES: A Fusion of Symbol, Style, and Thought in Virginia Woolf." TCL, 2 (1956), 5-20.
    Each element of the novel leads to the central, inscrutable "shadow" of the book: the "incomprehensible nature of this our life."

Q10 Blanchot, Maurice. "Le Temps et le roman." In FAUX PAS. Paris: Gallimard, 1943. Pp. 282-86.
    Sees the six consciousnesses of THE WAVES representing six distinct images of "time," from Bernard (historical, or conventional fictional time) to Rhoda (pure, unconscious time). [In French.]

Q11 Boone, Joseph Allen. "The Meaning of Elvedon in THE WAVES: A Key to Bernard's Experience and Woolf's Vision." MFS, 27 (1981-82), 629-37.
    Symbolic significance of Bernard's fantasy kingdom of Elvedon found in his and VW's shared desire "to articulate a meaning beyond words" (i.e., Elvedon=THE WAVES).

Q12 Borgal, Clément. "Virginia Woolf ou le point de vue de Sirius."
     CRITIQUE (Paris), 16 (1960), 609-14.
         On JACOB'S ROOM and THE WAVES. For annotation
         see L2.

Q13 Boyd, Michael. "Virginia Woolf's THE WAVES: A Voice in Search
     of Six Speakers." In THE REFLEXIVE NOVEL: FICTION AS CRITIQUE.
     Lewisburg, Pa.: Bucknell Univ. Press, 1983. Pp. 92-117.
         VW's dissolution of plot, setting, and character
         in THE WAVES, one of the most "reflexive" of
         modern novels, "should be viewed as a dramati-
         zation of the author's acts of composition."

Q14 Cazamian, Louis. "Le Temps dans le roman anglais contemporain."
     ÉTUDES ANGLAISES, 3 (1939), 338-42.
         Compares VW's use of time (e.g., in THE WAVES)
         to Huxley's in EYELESS IN GAZA (1936) and
         Joyce's in ULYSSES (1922). [In French.]

Q15 Chastaing, Maxime. "Virginia Woolf et la Conscience Réfléchis-
     sante." JOURNAL DE PSYCHOLOGIE NORMALE ET PATHOLOGIQUE, 35
     (1938), 617-23.
         VW's THE WAVES a pure example of psychological
         analysis in fiction. [In French.]

Q16 Church, Margaret. "Concepts of Time in the Novels of Virginia
     Woolf and Aldous Huxley." MFS, 1, No. 2 (1955), 19-24.
         On JACOB'S ROOM and THE WAVES. For annotation
         see L4.

Q17 Dick, Susan. "The Writings Cast Away: Some Virginia Woolf Man-
     uscripts." HUMANITIES ASSOCIATION REVIEW, 28 (1977), 345-53.
         The value of VW's unpublished manuscripts for
         enlarging our understanding of VW and her work.
         Reviews Graham's edition of THE WAVES man-
         uscripts (C6) and MOMENTS OF BEING (B3).

Q18 Dobrée, Bonamy. MODERN PROSE STYLE. 1935. 2nd ed. Oxford:
     Clarendon Press, 1964. Pp. 51-55.
         VW's instantly recognizable "voice" as a
         prose stylist and "most perfectly" achieved
         novel of pure character (rather than plot):
         THE WAVES.

Q19 Durand, Régis. "Langage et texte du roman: THE WAVES (V. Woolf)
     et la recherche de la 'véritable histoire.'" RECHERCHES ANGLAISES
     ET AMÉRICAINES, 7 (1974), 132-40.
         Theoretical overview of VW's invention of a new
         fictional language and syntax for THE WAVES.
         [In French.]

Q20 Eder, Doris L. "Louis Unmasked: T. S. Eliot in THE WAVES."
     VIRGINIA WOOLF QUARTERLY, 2 (1975), 13-27.
         Eliot as a prototype for the character of
         Louis.

Q21 Fehr, Bernhard. "Bewusstseinskunst bei Virginia Woolf." In
DIE ENGLISCHE LITERATUR DER HEUTIGEN STUNDE ALS AUSDRUCK DER
ZEITWENDE UND DER ENGLISCHEN KULTURGEMEINSCHAFT. Leipzig:
Tauchnitz, 1934. Pp. 75-79.
    Sees THE WAVES as modifying VW's earlier ideas
of consciousness in its emphases on the counterpoint between the flux of humanity and the individual soul, cosmic fragmentation and identity
("sternenscharähnlicher Zerschlagenheit und
Identität"). [In German.] See H76.

Q22 Friedman, Melvin J. "The Symbolist Novel: Huysmans to Malraux."
In MODERNISM, 1890-1930. Ed. Malcolm Bradbury and James McFarlane. Harmondsworth, Engl.: Penguin Books, 1976. Pp. 453-66.
    Faulkner's AS I LAY DYING (1930), Malraux' LA
CONDITION HUMAINE (1933), and THE WAVES ("a
kind of *Bildungsroman* in six voices"), three
examples of "further evolution of Symbolist
fiction" in the wake of Joyce's ULYSSES (1922).

Q23 Gorsky, Susan. "'The Central Shadow': Characterization in THE
WAVES." MFS, 18 (1972), 449-66.
    VW's experimentation with characters "who are at
once individual, representative, and a unity."
See G56.

Q24 Graham, John W. "Editing a Manuscript: Virginia Woolf's THE
WAVES." In EDITING TWENTIETH CENTURY TEXTS. Ed. Francess G.
Halpenny. Toronto: Univ. of Toronto Press, 1972. Pp. 77-92.
    Lecture, outlining his principles for editing
VW's manuscript (see C6 and below).

Q25 -----. "Introduction." In VIRGINIA WOOLF: *THE WAVES*. Ed.
Graham. Pp. 13-48. See C6.
    Account of VW's composition of the novel and
description of its manuscript drafts.

Q26 -----. "Point of View in THE WAVES: Some Services of the Style."
UTQ, 39 (1970), 193-211.
    Examines the gradual development of point of view
in VW's drafts of the "narrative" (distinguished
from traditional point of view in the "novel").
Reprinted in G44.

Q27 Havard-Williams, Peter, and Margaret Havard-Williams. "*Bateau
Ivre*: The Symbol of the Sea in Virginia Woolf's THE WAVES."
ENGLISH STUDIES, 34 (1953), 9-17.
    Appropriateness of sea symbolism as associated
with Rhoda, "the most real" of all VW's characters.

Q28 -----. "Mystical Experience in Virginia Woolf's THE WAVES."
ESSAYS IN CRITICISM, 4 (1954), 71-84.
    Rhoda's and Louis's mysticism crucial to VW's
themes of personality integration and perception of reality.

Q29 Hayashi, Toshitaka. "'Time and the Sea': Background in MRS. DALLOWAY and THE WAVES." STUDIES IN ENGLISH LITERATURE (Tokyo), 53 (1976), 43-57.
    [In Japanese.]

Q30 Heine, Elizabeth. "The Evolution of the Interludes in THE WAVES." VIRGINIA WOOLF QUARTERLY, 1, No. 1 (1972), 60-80.
    Examines textual evolution of the novel's interludes, as well as their structural and thematic purposes.

Q31 Jardine, Alice. "Pre-Texts for the Transatlantic Feminist." YALE FRENCH STUDIES, No. 62 (1981), pp. 220-36.
    Includes a jargon-laden comparison of the stylistic strategies of two "international feminists," VW (in THE WAVES) and Monique Wittig (in LES GUÉRILLÈRES [1969]).

Q32 King, Merton P. "THE WAVES and the Androgynous Mind." UNIVERSITY REVIEW, 30 (1963), 128-34.
    Novel "completes" in fiction VW's developing theories of androgyny in her nonfiction and earlier novels.

Q33 Lalou, René. "Le Sentiment de l'unité humaine chez Virginia Woolf et Aldous Huxley." EUROPE, 45 (1937), 266-72.
    Comparative review of the recent French translations of THE WAVES and Huxley's EYELESS IN GAZA (1936). [In French.]

Q34 Lorsch, Susan E. "Structure and Rhythm in THE WAVES: The Ebb and Flow of Meaning." ESSAYS IN LITERATURE, 6 (1979), 195-206.
    Structural and stylistic analysis of the "prose poems" in the novel.

Q35 Lund, Mary Graham. "The Androgynous Moment: Woolf and Eliot." RENASCENCE, 12 (1960), 74-78.
    The self-transcending, "timeless moment" in THE WAVES and in T. S. Eliot's poetry.

Q36 McConnell, Frank D. "'Death Among the Apple Trees': THE WAVES and the World of Things." BUCKNELL REVIEW, 16 (1968), 23-39.
    VW's totally subjective vision "finally becomes a radical criticism of 'mysticism'... in the face of sheer phenomenalism." Reprinted in G80.

Q37 McGavran, James Holt, Jr. "'Alone Seeking the Visible World': The Wordsworths, Virginia Woolf, and THE WAVES." MODERN LANGUAGE QUARTERLY, 42 (1981), 265-91.
    Thematic, structural, symbolic, and "visionary" parallels between THE WAVES and writings by Dorothy and William Wordsworth.

Q38 McLaurin, Allen. "Virginia Woolf and Unanimism." JOURNAL OF MODERN LITERATURE, 9 (1982), 115-22.
Influence of Jules Romains' notion of group consciousness, the "group mind," in THE WAVES. (Attributes a TIMES LITERARY SUPPLEMENT review of Romains' LES COPAINS [1913] to VW, as does Kirkpatrick [see E7]).

Q39 Marcel, Gabriel. "LES VAGUES, par Virginia Woolf." NOUVELLE REVUE FRANÇAISE, 38 (1932), 303-08.
Despite VW's failure to differentiate her characters' monologues and her perhaps unjustified experimentation, THE WAVES is the culmination of all her previous works: it is a "marvelous basket ['corbeille'] of phrases and verbal melodies, each expressing a privileged moment of feeling" (cf. orchestral composition). Review essay. [In French.] Extracts reprinted in translation in G49.

Q40 Marill, René [Albérès, René-Marill]. "La Parole intérieure: De Virginia Woolf à Nathalie Sarraute." In MÉTAMORPHOSES DU ROMAN. Paris: Albin Michel, 1966. Pp. 199-209.
Compares VW's intensely personal and lyrical stream-of-consciousness technique, in THE WAVES, with Sarraute's methods in several of her novels. [In French.]

Q41 May, Keith M. OUT OF THE MAELSTROM: PSYCHOLOGY AND THE NOVEL IN THE TWENTIETH CENTURY. London: Elek, 1977. Pp. 67-71.
THE WAVES "the consummate" VW novel, exploring "clearly and without distractions" her chief preoccupation, the search for identity.

Q42 Mendez, Charlotte Walker. "Creative Breakthrough: Sequence and the Blade of Consciousness in Virginia Woolf's THE WAVES." In WOMEN'S LANGUAGE AND STYLE. Ed. Douglas Butturff and Edmund L. Epstein. Akron, Ohio: L&S Books, 1978. Pp. 84-98A.
THE WAVES marks a "creative breakthrough" for VW as she explores "the disparity between linearity in language and the nonlinear complexity of consciousness" (cf. her experimentation with linear vs. durational time).

Q43 Moore, Madeline. "Nature and Community: A Study of Cyclical Reality in THE WAVES." In VIRGINIA WOOLF. Ed. Ralph Freedman. Pp. 219-40. See G26.
Identifies social concerns in VW's purportedly "asocial" novel, implicit in her attitudes toward nature.

Q44 Okunishi, Akira. "NAMI Sobyo" ["A Sketch of THE WAVES"]. In SUGA YASUO, OGOSHI KAZUGO: RYOKYOJU TAIKAN KINEN RONBUNSHU. Kyoto: Apollonsha, 1980. Pp. 528-40.
Not seen. [In Japanese.]

Q45 Payne, Michael. "The Eclipse of Order: The Ironic Structure of THE WAVES." MFS, 15 (1969), 209-18.
    Novel's cohesive structure an ironic foil to its characters' multiple failures to perceive order.

Q46 Richardson, Robert O. "Point of View in Virginia Woolf's THE WAVES." TSLL, 14 (1973), 691-709.
    VW's "multiplication and involution of fictive worlds" through her experimental narrative techniques.

Q47 Rigo, Giorgio de. "THE WAVES (LE ONDE) di Virginia Woolf." LETTERATURE MODERNE, 12 (1962), 167-81.
    VW's attainment of a poetic unity through style in THE WAVES (e.g., the use of leit-motif).
    [In Spanish.]

Q48 Rousseaux, André. "Plongeurs dans le temps perdu (Virginia Woolf, Aldous Huxley). In LITTÉRATURE DU VINGTIÈME SIÈCLE. Vol. I. Paris: Albin Michel, 1938. Pp. 221-29.
    Compares the spatial and temporal fragmentation of THE WAVES and Huxley's EYELESS IN GAZA (1936). [In French.]

Q49 Ruddick, Sara. "Private Brother, Public World." In NEW FEMINIST ESSAYS ON VIRGINIA WOOLF. Ed. Jane Marcus. Pp. 185-215. See G51.
    On JACOB'S ROOM and THE WAVES. For annotation see L17.

Q50 Shanahan, Mary S. "The Artist and the Resolution of THE WAVES." MODERN LANGUAGE QUARTERLY, 36 (1975), 54-74.
    Novel a therapeutic projection of VW's psychological anguish.

Q51 Shoukri, Doris E. C. "Nature of Being in Woolf and Duras." ConL, 12 (1971), 317-28.
    THE WAVES and Marguerite Duras's THE RAVISHING OF LOL STEIN (1966) compared as "first-and second-generation ontological" novels.

Q52 Sitter, Deborah A. "The Debate of THE WAVES." DURHAM UNIVERSITY JOURNAL, 37 (1976), 118-25.
    Finds a unifying structure beneath the "surface" of the novel which sustains its superficial, wave-like flow of evanescent impressions.

Q53 Snow, Lotus. "The Wreckful Siege: Disorder in THE WAVES." RS, 42 (1974), 71-80.
    VW's perception both of the fixed stages of life and of the "absoluteness of pattern in human personality" itself, demonstrated in the parallels among the six figures in the novel.

Q54 Stewart, Jack F. "Existence and Symbol in THE WAVES." MFS, 18 (1972), 433-47.
    Systole-diastole rhythms in the novel's techniques and meaning. See G56.

Q55 -----. "Spatial Form and Color in THE WAVES." TCL, 28 (1982), 86-107.
    Adapts spatial theories of fiction to the analysis of space and color in THE WAVES (cf. Monet and Cézanne). Also see H232 and P35.

Q56 Stewart, J. I. M. "Notes for a Study of THE WAVES." In ON THE NOVEL. Ed. B. S. Benedikz. London: Dent, 1971. Pp. 93-112.
    Describes novel's composition and notes VW's effort to "transcend human isolation" by seeing her characters as a group rather than as individuals.

Q57 Swartz, Mary Ann. "Making the Waves Heard." VIRGINIA WOOLF QUARTERLY, 2 (1976), 304-12.
    VW could write her novel "only when she consciously adopted water as a structural principle."

Q58 Tanger, Marilyn. "Looking at THE WAVES through the Symbol of the Ring." VIRGINIA WOOLF QUARTERLY, 3 (1978), 241-51.
    Ring symbolism in character, structure, and theme.

Q59 Torgovnick, Marianna. "Virginia Woolf, the Vision of THE WAVES, and the Novel's Double Ending." In CLOSURE IN THE NOVEL. Princeton, N. J.: Princeton Univ. Press, 1981. Pp. 176-97.
    VW's struggle to achieve "closure" (i.e., an appropriate ending rather than a resolution or conclusion), accomplished in Bernard's final soliloquy, his final words, and the novel's brief epilogue, affirming "the essential unity and continuity of things."

Q60 Wasserman, Jerry. "Mimetic Form in THE WAVES." JOURNAL OF NARRATIVE TECHNIQUE, 9 (1979), 41-52.
    Structural analysis of VW's "ultimate use of the moment as basic narrative unit" in the novel.

Q61 Webb, Igor. "'Things in Themselves': Virginia Woolf's THE WAVES." MFS, 17 (1971), 570-73.
    Influence of Walter Pater's aesthetics on VW's (and Bernard's) conceptions of art.

Q62 Yourcenar, Marguerite. "Virginia Woolf et son oeuvre." In Woolf's LES VAGUES [THE WAVES]. Trans. Yourcenar. 1937. Paris: Le Club Français du Livre, 1953. Pp. 276-82.
    Early, somewhat impressionistic appreciation of VW's innovative novel of sensibility, by her French translator. Originally published as "Préface" in Yourcenar's 1937 translation (Paris: Stock).
    [In French.]

R. STUDIES OF *THE YEARS* (1937)

The following section is subdivided into two parts: i. Books and Essay Collections on THE YEARS; and ii. Critical Articles or Chapters on THE YEARS.

For portions of the holograph manuscript eventually deleted from the published text of THE YEARS, see C3 and R3. For the forthcoming concordance to the novel, see section D.

For bibliographical information on THE YEARS, see Kirkpatrick (E7), and, for biographical backgrounds to the novel, see Bell (F13), Poole (F77), Rose (F81), and Woolf (F100).

For the most significant additional critical commentaries and information on THE YEARS, see the following books, in section G above: Alexander (G2), Bazin (G6), Blackstone (G9), Daiches (G16), Dölle (G19), Donahue (G20), Fleishman (G24), Gorsky (G28), Guiguet (G30), Hafley (G31), Harper (G32), Johnson (G36), Kapur (G37), Kelley (G38), Leaska (G41), Lee (G42), Little (G45), McLaurin (G48), Marder (G53), Moody (G57), Pasternack (G65), Poresky (G66), Rantavaara (G68), Richter (G69), Rosenthal (G71), Schaefer (G75), Spilka (G79), Thakur (G82), Wiget (G86), Woodring (G88); the following critical articles, in section H above: Albright (H2), Carroll (H35), Cornwell (H47), Daiches (H54), Heilbrun (H112), Johnstone (H126), Kiely (H130), Kushen (H135), Mellers (H161), Savage (H214); and the following study, entered elsewhere in this bibliography: Meisel (X3). For a complete listing of substantial commentaries on THE YEARS, see the concluding index: "Virginia Woolf's Works."

R, i. Books and Essay Collections on THE YEARS

R1 BULLETIN OF THE NEW YORK PUBLIC LIBRARY. 80 (1977), 136-301. "Virginia Woolf Issue."
> Contains four brief introductory notes on VW and THE YEARS, nine critical essays on the novel and related works, a photographic reproduction of "two enormous chunks" deleted from the novel's galley proofs (with commentary), and several illustrations. Includes G41 (extract), R4, R10, R12, R15, R20, R22, R23, and W13. Reviewed in H225. Also see J1.

R2 Kamerbeek, Jan Coenraad. ANTIGONE BIJ VIRGINIA WOOLF. Amsterdam: Noord-Hollandsche Uitgevers Maatschappij, 1974.
VW's familiarity with and comments on the Antigone figure (in her essays), and assimilation of various motifs from Sophoclean tragedy into her works (particularly THREE GUINEAS and THE YEARS). (Pamphlet-- 18 pp.) [In Dutch.]

R3 Radin, Grace. VIRGINIA WOOLF'S *THE YEARS*: THE EVOLUTION OF A NOVEL. Knoxville: Univ. of Tennessee Press, 1981.
Careful textual study of VW's evolving conception and composition of THE YEARS, based on the surviving holograph manuscripts (partially published, in edited form, as THE PARGITERS; see C3), galley proofs (1936), page proofs (1936), published text (1937), and satellite publications related to THE YEARS: "Professions for Women," THREE GUINEAS, and VW's DIARY and LETTERS. Radin selectively emphasizes VW's altering treatment of "sexual and ideological material" and "changes in the depiction of one character, Elvira (Sara in THE YEARS)," rather than her "stylistic variations," finding the novel's composition history most significant as an index to VW's evolving conception of what the novel, as a literary form, could and should be. Includes "Galley Proofs of Episodes Excluded During Final Revisions of THE YEARS" as an appendix. Incorporates R20.

R, ii. Critical Articles or Chapters on THE YEARS

R4 Comstock, Margaret. "The Loudspeaker and the Human Voice: Politics and the Form of THE YEARS." BNYPL, 80 (1977), 252-75.
Novel's political themes and open-ended structure related to VW's alarmed reactions to Hitlerism and the unresolved political crises of the thirties. See R1.

R5 Fehr, Bernhard. "Virginia Woolfs Roman der JAHRE: Das Ringen mit der Zeit" ["Virginia Woolf's Novel THE YEARS: The Struggle with Time"]. 1937. In VON ENGLANDS GEISTIGEN BESTÄNDEN: AUSGEWÄHLTE AUFSÄTZE VON BERNHARD FEHR. Ed. Max Wildi. Frauenfeld: Huber, 1944. Pp. 187-92.
VW's themes of simultaneity and temporal flux in her novel lead her to her great, unanswered question: "Was ist das Leben und was bin ich?" Review essay. [In German.] See H76.

R6 Hartley, Lodwick. "Of Time and Mrs. Woolf." SEWANEE REVIEW, 47 (1939), 235-41.
Time the "real protagonist" in VW's perhaps "too exquisite and self-contained" fiction. Reviews THE YEARS. Extract reprinted in N5.

R7 Hoffman, Charles G. "Virginia Woolf's Manuscript Revisions of THE YEARS." PMLA, 84 (1969), 79-89.
    Traces novel's evolution and attributes its final failure to balance "fact and vision" to VW's revisions.

R8 Kuhn, Reinhard. CORRUPTION IN PARADISE: THE CHILD IN WESTERN LITERATURE. Hanover, N. H.: Univ. Press of New England, 1982. Pp. 21-24.
    The universal motif of the "enigmatic" and "inscrutable" child recurs throughout THE YEARS as an emphatic illustration of the gaps of knowledge that exist among all men.

R9 Leaska, Mitchell A. "Introduction." In Woolf's "THE PARGITERS." Ed. Leaska. Pp. vii-xxiv. See C3.
    Describes VW's alterations in her conception of the novel and her manuscript deletions.

R10 Lipking, Joanna. "Looking at the Monuments: Woolf's Satiric Eye." BNYPL, 80 (1977), 141-45.
    Novel "a book full of symmetries" that are "at war with shape." See R1.

R11 Marcus, Jane. "Pargeting 'The Pargiters': Notes of an Apprentice Plasterer." BNYPL, 80 (1977), 416-35.
    Notes on VW's symbolism, structural techniques, language, revision, and character models in the novel. Continuation of essay below.

R12 -----. "THE YEARS as Greek Drama, Domestic Novel, and *Götterdämmerung*." BNYPL, 80 (1977), 276-301.
    Three critical perspectives on the novel. See R1. Also see essay above.

R13 Marder, Herbert. "Beyond the Lighthouse: THE YEARS." BUCKNELL REVIEW, 15, No. 1 (1967), 61-70.
    Symbolic reading, arguing atypically that the novel is, if not an advance, at least a "lineal descendant" of TL and THE WAVES.

R14 Mellers, W. H. "Mrs. Woolf and Life." SCRUTINY, 6 (1937), 71-75.
    VW's decline from TL reaches "dismal finality" in the sentimental and inept THE YEARS. Reprinted in G49. Also see E6, H161, S19, and W17.

R15 Middleton, Victoria S. "THE YEARS: 'A Deliberate Failure.'" BNYPL, 80 (1977), 158-71.
    Considers the alleged stylistic "flaws" of novel purposeful. See R1.

R16 Moore, Madeline. "Virginia Woolf's THE YEARS and Years of Adverse Male Reviewers." WOMEN'S STUDIES, 4 (1977), 247-63.
    The basic misunderstanding of VW's feminist intention in THE YEARS, seen in the novel's first re-

views, all written by male critics, persist to
this day in criticism of the novel. See G87.

R17 Naremore, James. "Nature and History in THE YEARS." In VIRGINIA
WOOLF. Ed. Ralph Freedman. Pp. 241-62. See G26.
As an historical novel, THE YEARS illustrates VW's
characteristic sense of the "split between public
and private worlds, the conflict between a timeless transpersonal human nature and a divisive,
changing social structure."

R18 Proudfit, Sharon L. "Virginia Woolf: Reluctant Feminist in THE
YEARS." CRITICISM, 17 (1975), 59-73.
Parallels between novel and VW's "factual des-
cription of the status of women in THREE GUINEAS."

R19 Radin, Grace. "'I Am Not a Hero': Virginia Woolf and the First
Version of THE YEARS." MASSACHUSETTS REVIEW, 16 (1975), 195-208.
VW's original version far more experimental than
her final, comparatively conventional, and "much
diminished" revision.

R20 -----. "'Two enormous chunks': Episodes Excluded During the
Final Revisions of THE YEARS." BNYPL, 80 (1977), 221-51.
Description and evaluation of VW's most drastic
alterations of the novel, her deletion of two
substantial portions of the galley text (published in photographic reproduction, pp. 228-
33, 237-49). Incorporated into R2. See R1.

R21 Roberts, John H. "The End of the English Novel?" VQR, 13 (1937),
437-39.
VW's "almost perverse" demonstration "that there
is no chance of understanding ourselves or our
neighbors," while subtly celebrating "the mystery of our existence," is "cutting off the
flow of fiction at its source." Review essay.

R22 Schlack, Beverly Ann. "Virginia Woolf's Strategy of Scorn in
THE YEARS and THREE GUINEAS." BNYPL, 80 (1977), 146-50.
Motivated by "ethical anger," VW both "mocks
and defies" social institutions and attitudes
in her novel and its related feminist pamphlet.
See R1.

R23 Sears, Sallie. "Notes on Sexuality: THE YEARS and THREE GUINEAS."
BNYPL, 80 (1977), 211-20.
Novel explores the "principles and practices" of
sexuality, language and consciousness, and mascu-
line and feminine "politics," attacked in THREE
GUINEAS. See R1.

R24 Squier, Susan. "The Politics of City Space in THE YEARS: Street Love, Pillar Boxes and Bridges." In NEW FEMINIST ESSAYS ON VIRGINIA WOOLF. Ed. Jane Marcus. Pp. 216-37. See G51.
> The "examination of the image and experience of the city in THE YEARS reveals both the process and the product of Woolf's vision of woman's experience." Pursues the investigation through VW's successive revisions of the novel's manuscripts.

R25 Warner, Eric. "Re-considering THE YEARS." NORTH DAKOTA QUARTERLY, 48, No. 2 (1980), 16-30.
> Disputes the recent enthusiastic revaluations of the novel, finding it her "critical and creative nadir."

S. STUDIES OF *BETWEEN THE ACTS* (1941)

Since there are no books, essay collections, monographs, or pamphlets on BETWEEN THE ACTS, this section consists entirely of critical articles or chapters on the novel.

For transcriptions of the holograph manuscripts of BETWEEN THE ACTS, see C5. For a concordance to BETWEEN THE ACTS, see D1.

For bibliographical information on BETWEEN THE ACTS, see Kirkpatrick (E7), and, for biographical backgrounds to the novel, see Bell (F13), Forrester (F31), Poole (F77), Rose (F81), and Woolf (F100).

For the most significant additional critical commentaries and information on BETWEEN THE ACTS, see the following books, in section G above: Alexander (G2), Bazin (G6), Blackstone (G9), Daiches (G16), DiBattista (G18), Dölle (G19), Donohue (G20), Fleishman (G24), Gorsky (G28), Guiguet (G30), Hafley (G31), Harper (G32), Johnson (G36), Kapur (G37), Kelley (G38), Leaska (G41), Lee (G42), Little (G45), Love (G47), McLaurin (G48), Marder (G53), Moody (G57), Naremore (G59), Pasternack (G65), Poresky (G66), Rantavaara (G68), Richter (G69), Rosenthal (G71), Schaefer (G75), Thakur (G82), Wiget (G86), Woodring (G88); the following critical articles, in section H above: Albright (H2), Brooks (H28), Crosland (H50), Daiches (H54), Fleishman (H80), Friedman (H90), Graham (H96), Heilbrun (H112), Johnstone (H126), Kiely (H130), Kushen (H135), Mellers (H161), Pomeroy (H192), Savage (H214), Wicht (H249), Zéraffa (H256); and the following study, entered elsewhere in this bibliography: Meisel (X3). For a complete listing of substantial commentaries on BETWEEN THE ACTS, see the concluding index: "Virginia Woolf's Works."

S1 Allen, Walter. "BETWEEN THE ACTS by Virginia Woolf." In READING A NOVEL. 1949. Rev. ed. New York: Hilary House, 1963. Pp. 39-43.
BETWEEN THE ACTS briefly treated as an example of the lyrical, poetic novel.

S2 Basham, C. "BETWEEN THE ACTS." DURHAM UNIVERSITY JOURNAL, 52 (1959), 87-94.
Theme of disintegration unifies the three levels of the novel. Extract reprinted in G40.

S3 Beck, Warren. "For Virginia Woolf." 1942. In FORMS OF MODERN FICTION: ESSAYS COLLECTED IN HONOR OF JOSEPH WARREN BEACH. Ed. William Van O'Connor. Minneapolis: Univ. of Minnesota Press, 1948. Pp. 229-39.
Novel illustrates VW's significant concern for the external world in its successful relationship of "subjective individualism and the social order."

S4 Bell, Quentin. "Introduction." In Woolf's BETWEEN THE ACTS. London: Folio Society, 1974. Pp. 3-9.
   Biographical backgrounds to the novel's composition.

S5 Blöcker, Günter. "Virginia Woolf: ZWISCHEN DEN AKTEN." In LITERATUR ALS TEILHABE: KRITISCHEN ORIENTIERUNGEN ZUR LITERARISCHEN GEGENWART. Berlin: Argon, 1966. Pp. 327-30.
   VW's last novel also the most accessible example of her new novel of sensibility. [In German.]

S6 Deiman, Werner J. "History, Pattern, and Continuity in Virginia Woolf." ConL, 15 (1974), 49-66.
   Pattern of historical continuity in the novel both an affirmation of unity and a "redemption from [fragmenting] time." Reprinted in G44.

S7 Eisenberg, Nora. "Virginia Woolf's Last Words on Words: BETWEEN THE ACTS and 'Anon.'" In NEW FEMINIST ESSAYS ON VIRGINIA WOOLF. Ed. Jane Marcus. Pp. 253-66. See G51.
   In BETWEEN THE ACTS and the related essay "Anon" (C1), which share a "single hero" (Miss LaTrobe and Anon) and theme, VW "imagines an old world in which a communal life flourished free from conventional language, which she thought a male dominion, ruling and often ruining her world."

S8 Fleishman, Avrom. "Woolf." In THE ENGLISH HISTORICAL NOVEL: WALTER SCOTT TO VIRGINIA WOOLF. Baltimore, Md.: Johns Hopkins Univ. Press, 1971. Pp. 233-55.
   On BETWEEN THE ACTS and ORLANDO. For annotation see P10.

S9 Fouchet, Max-Pol. "Un Champ de neige sans empreinte" ["An Unmarked field of snow"]. 1947. In LES APPELS. Paris: MERCURE DE FRANCE, 1967. Pp. 25-44.
   VW's life and works, culminating in BETWEEN THE ACTS and her suicide, unified by a pessimistic sense of human isolation and an unceasing quest for communion and communication. Originally a preface to the French translation of BETWEEN THE ACTS (1947). [In French.]

S10 Fourtina, Hervé. "BETWEEN THE ACTS: L'Impossible entre-pris." ÉTUDES ANGLAISES, 35 (1982), 139-51.
   Dominance of speech and the ambiguous function of language ("instrument ambivalent de cohésion et de division") in the novel. [In French.]

S11 Fox, Stephen D. "The Fish Pond as Symbolic Center in BETWEEN THE ACTS." MFS, 18 (1972), 467-73.
   The pond a symbolic and thematic microcosm of the novel. See G56.

S12 Fromm, Harold. "BETWEEN THE ACTS: The Demiurge Made Flesh."
SOUTHERN HUMANITIES REVIEW, 15 (1981), 209-17.
> VW's final novel "remarkably" accomplishes what she attempted in THE WAVES and THE YEARS: "to 'explain' the intensity of the moment in terms of time and eternity."

S13 Fussell, B. H. "Woolf's Peculiar Comic World: BETWEEN THE ACTS." In VIRGINIA WOOLF. Ed. Ralph Freedman. Pp. 263-83. See G26.
> Elements of burlesque, irony, and satire in the novel too often unrecognized because of VW's impersonal narration.

S14 Gillespie, Diane F. "Virginia Woolf's Miss LaTrobe: The Artist's Last Struggle against Masculine Values." WOMEN AND LITERATURE, 5, No. 1 (1977), 38-46.
> As a writer Miss LaTrobe "both parodies and reflects the values of male dominated society and art."

S15 Higdon, David L. "Virginia Woolf's BETWEEN THE ACTS: 'Increasing the Bounds of the Moment.'" In TIME AND ENGLISH FICTION. Totowa, N. J.: Rowman and Littlefield, 1977. Pp. 124-30.
> The paradoxical dual terrors of isolation and entrapment reinforced by the novel's temporal conflation of all time and one day.

S16 Kenney, Susan M. "Two Endings: Virginia Woolf's Suicide and BETWEEN THE ACTS." UTQ, 44 (1975), 265-89.
> The novel's affirmative ending a key to a possible, affirmative view of VW's suicide.

S17 Lawson, Richard H. "Technique and Function of Time in Virginia Woolf's BETWEEN THE ACTS." MODERN BRITISH LITERATURE, 3 (1978), 19-34.
> Relation between objective and subjective time in the novel.

S18 Leaska, Mitchell A. "Introduction"; "Notes and References"; and "Afterword." In VIRGINIA WOOLF: "POINTZ HALL." Ed. Leaska. Pp. 3-16; 190-246; 441-50; 451-65. See C5.
> Describes the history and methods of VW's composition of BETWEEN THE ACTS, as an escape from the laborious writing of ROGER FRY, provides extremely useful factual and interpretive annotations to each of the typescripts of "Pointz Hall," and summarizes the biographical backgrounds to VW's writing of the novel in the late thirties.

S19 Leavis, F. R. "After TO THE LIGHTHOUSE." SCRUTINY, 10 (1942), 295-98.
> VW's "extraordinary vacancy and pointlessness" in the novel marks her final deterioration as a serious novelist (since TL). Extract reprinted in N5. Also see H161, R14, and W17.

S20 Lyons, Richard S. "The Intellectual Structure of Virginia Woolf's BETWEEN THE ACTS." MODERN LANGUAGE QUARTERLY, 38 (1977), 149-66.
Novel's underlying dialectical structure a "virtually desperate" attempt by VW to integrate history, religion, and art in the midst of despair.

S21 Marcus, Jane. "Some Sources for BETWEEN THE ACTS." VIRGINIA WOOLF MISCELLANY, No. 6 (1977), pp. 1-3.
Not seen.

S22 Miller, J. Hillis. "BETWEEN THE ACTS: Repetition as Extrapolation." In FICTION AND REPETITION: SEVEN ENGLISH NOVELS. Cambridge, Mass.: Harvard Univ. Press, 1982. Pp. 203-31.
Explores the tension between patterns of repetition and patternless fragmentation, both in history (the play) and fiction (the novel itself), and the strategies by which the "creative" human mind embraces similarity within difference, as well as difference within similarity. Also see M55.

S23 Quick, Jonathan R. "The Shattered Moment: Form and Crisis in MRS. DALLOWAY and BETWEEN THE ACTS." MOSAIC, 7, No. 3 (1974), 127-36.
For annotation see M65.

S24 Rantavaara, Irma. "Virginia Woolf, diarist, novelist, critic: A study of some stylistic aspects." In STYLE AND TEXT: STUDIES PRESENTED TO NILS ERIK ENKVIST. Ed. Håkan Ringbom et al. Stockholm: Språkförlaget Skriptor and Åbo Akademi, 1975. Pp. 134-45.
Sees BETWEEN THE ACTS as a "finished piece of art" and examines, in numerous passages, VW's achievement of a "fluid" style, suggesting "more than the words themselves convey."

S25 Shanahan, Mary S. "BETWEEN THE ACTS: Virginia Woolf's Final Endeavor in Art." TSLL, 14 (1972), 123-38.
VW's dialectical counterpoint of civilization and savagery, love and sex, order and violence, art and nature.

S26 Silver, Brenda R. "Virginia Woolf and the Concept of Community: The Elizabethan Playhouse." WOMEN'S STUDIES, 4 (1977), 291-98.
VW's last novel raises the fundamental question of the artist's role in the community: "she retains a sense of the power of art if not to create social unity and social reality, to overcome or survive." See G87.

S27 Snow, Lotus. "Visions of Design: Virginia Woolf's 'Time Passes' and BETWEEN THE ACTS." RS, 44 (1976), 24-34.
On TL and BETWEEN THE ACTS. For annotation see N91.

S28 Stadtfeld, Frieder. "Virginia Woolfs letzter Roman: More
    Quintessential than the Others." ANGLIA, 91 (1973), 56-76.
        Novel's unity found in the parallel historical
        consciousness seen in the pageant and in the
        systematic literary allusions of the narrative
        (several allusions identified here). [In German.]

S29 Summerhayes, Don. "Society, Morality, Analogy: Virginia Woolf's
    World BETWEEN THE ACTS." MFS, 9 (1963), 329-37.
        BETWEEN THE ACTS, VW's last testament, communi-
        cates by analogy, ultimately expressing VW's
        view of the world.

S30 Swingle, L. J. "Virginia Woolf and Romantic Prometheanism."
    BUCKNELL REVIEW, 25, No. 2 (1980), 88-106.
        VW's Romantic heritage evident in her "commit-
        ment to the Promethean ideal of gaining freedom
        through creativity." Chiefly discusses the
        essays and BETWEEN THE ACTS.

S31 Watkins, Renée. "Survival in Discontinuity--Virginia Woolf's
    BETWEEN THE ACTS." MASSACHUSETTS REVIEW, 10 (1969), 356-76.
        General reading of the novel, noting its implicit
        psychology, philosophy of history, and "ethic."

S32 Wilkinson, Ann Y. "A Principle of Unity in BETWEEN THE ACTS."
    CRITICISM, 8 (1966), 53-63.
        Novel's dramatic form its central statement
        (i.e., achievement of form) and symbol. Re-
        printed in G80.

S33 Wyatt, Jean. "Art and Allusion in BETWEEN THE ACTS." MOSAIC,
    11, No. 4 (1978), 91-100.
        VW's use of literary allusion to amplify her
        central theme: "the relation between art and
        life."

S34 Zorn, Marilyn. "The Pageant in BETWEEN THE ACTS." MFS, 2 (1956),
    31-35.
        Pageant and novel affirm the artist's "vision,"
        despite its evanescence. See G55. Extract re-
        printed in G40.

S35 Zwerdling, Alex. "BETWEEN THE ACTS and the Coming of War."
    NOVEL, 10 (1977), 220-36.
        VW shows us a "society and a cultural tradition
        breaking down into its component parts," on the
        eve of war.

T. STUDIES OF THE SHORT STORIES

Since there are no books, essay collections, monographs, or pamphlets on VW's short stories, this section consists entirely of general critical articles on her short fiction and studies of individual stories.

For an edited transcription of the manuscript of VW's early story, "The Journal of Mistress Joan Martyn," see C11.

For bibliographical information on the periodical and collected publication of VW's short stories, see Kirkpatrick (E7), and for biographical backgrounds to her short fiction, see Bell (F13), Rose (F81), and Woolf (F100).

For the most significant additional critical commentaries and information on VW's short fiction, see the following books, in section G above: Alexander (G2), Bazin (G6), Daiches (G16), DiBattista (G18), Dölle (G19), Fleishman (G24), Gorsky (G28), Guiguet (G30), Hafley (G31), Johnson (G36), Lee (G42), Marder (G53), Novak (G62), Richter (G69), Rosenthal (G71); and the following critical articles, in section H above: Albright (H2), Beja (H13), Bell (H14), Forster (H81), Hafley (H103), Johnstone (H126), Kiely (H130), McLaughlin (H148), and Rosenbaum (H207). For a complete listing of substantial commentaries on individual short stories, by title, see the concluding index: "Virginia Woolf's Works."

T1 Araujo, Victor de. "'A Haunted House'--The Shattered Glass." STUDIES IN SHORT FICTION, 3 (1966), 157-64.
      The implied narrative, range of imagery, and embodied "comment on life" in "A Haunted House," make it more than a "study in impressionism."

T2 Baldeshwiler, Eileen. "The Lyric Short Story: The Sketch of a History." STUDIES IN SHORT FICTION, 6 (1969), 443-53.
      Sees "Kew Gardens," among other stories, as an important example of the "lyric" tendency in modern short fiction (moving "the focus of narrative from autonomous external action to interior life").

T3 Bishop, Edward L. "Pursuing 'It' Through 'Kew Gardens.'" STUDIES IN SHORT FICTION, 19 (1982), 269-75.
      VW's "narrative strategies" for creating and engaging "the reader with something as nebulous as an 'atmosphere.'"

T4 Brace, Marjorie. "Worshiping Solid Objects: The Pagan World of Virginia Woolf." In ACCENT ANTHOLOGY. Ed. Kerker Quinn and Charles Shattuck. New York: Harcourt, 1946. Pp. 489-95.
     VW's spectatorial stance, her detached recognition of the "unknowableness of character," gives her stories (e.g., A HAUNTED HOUSE) a "unity the novels...never achieved." Extract reprinted in G40.

T5 Chapman, Robert T. "'The Lady in the Looking Glass': Modes of Perception in a Short Story by Virginia Woolf." MFS, 18 (1972), 331-37.
     VW's concern with the psychology of perception in "The Lady in the Looking Glass," rather than with perception as a vehicle for characterization. See G56.

T6 [Child, Harold.] "KEW GARDENS." TIMES LITERARY SUPPLEMENT, 29 May 1919, p. 293.
     Welcomes VW's rejection of "subject-matter" in favor of color, rhythm, atmosphere, and observation (cf. visual arts). Review of "Kew Gardens." Reprinted in G49.

T7 Collins, Joseph. "Two Lesser Literary Ladies of London: Stella Benson and Virginia Woolf." In THE DOCTOR LOOKS AT LITERATURE. London: Allen and Unwin, 1923. Pp. 181-90.
     Notes the "mysticism" and "spirituality" in the promising early works of VW, principally her short stories in MONDAY OR TUESDAY.

T8 Delbaere-Garant, Jeanne. "'The Mark on the Wall': Virginia Woolf's World in a Snailshell." REVUE DES LANGUES VIVANTES, 40 (1974), 457-65.
     Though superficially loose, the "network of interconnected meanings" in "The Mark on the Wall" shows a preconceived "pattern as rigorous as" in VW's "best novels."

T9 DeSalvo, Louise A. "Shakespeare's *Other* Sister." In NEW FEMINIST ESSAYS ON VIRGINIA WOOLF. Ed. Jane Marcus. Pp. 61-81. See G51.
     Extended commentary on VW's "quest for a female past" as seen in her early fiction fragment, the "Journal of Mistress Joan Martyn" (see C11).

T10 Fischer, Gretl Kraus. "Edward Albee and Virginia Woolf." DALHOUSIE REVIEW, 49 (1969), 196-207.
     On "Lappin and Lapinova" and TL. For annotation see N35.

T11 Fleishman, Avrom. "Forms of the Woolfian Short Story." In VIRGINIA WOOLF. Ed. Ralph Freedman. Pp. 44-70. See G26.
     VW's stories as examples of and contributions to the development of the modernist short story. Surveys VW's various formal experiments in several of the stories.

T12 Fox, Stephen D. "'An Unwritten Novel' and a Hidden Protagonist."
     VIRGINIA WOOLF QUARTERLY, 1, No. 4 (1973), 69-77.
     Central significance of the narrator in "An
     Unwritten Novel," a "dramatic monologue in
     prose."

T13 Graham, John W. "The Drafts of Virginia Woolf's 'The Search-
     light.'" TCL, 22 (1976), 379-93.
     Comparisons of the thirteen drafts and several
     additional fragments of the posthumously pub-
     lished story.

T14 Hafley, James. "On One of Virginia Woolf's Short Stories." MFS,
     2 (1956), 13-16.
     "Moments of Being" studied as a "microcosmic
     illustration" of VW's fictional techniques.
     See G55.

T15 Henig, Suzanne. "Introduction." In Woolf's A COCKNEY'S FARMING
     EXPERIENCES. Pp. i-viii. See A15.
     Early signs of VW's promise in her juvenile
     stories.

T16 Jackson, Gertrude. "Virginia Woolf's A HAUNTED HOUSE: Reality
     and 'moment of being' in her 'Kew Gardens.'" In FESTSCHRIFT
     PROF. DR. HERBERT KOZOIL. Ed. Gero Bauer, Franz K. Stanzel,
     and Franz Zaic. Vienna: Braumuller, 1973. Pp. 116-23.
     VW's sense of the distance and the interplay
     between "common reality of objects and everyday
     life and meaningful reality, representative of
     man's existence," in "Kew Gardens."

T17 Latham, Jacqueline E. M. "The Origin of MRS. DALLOWAY." NOTES
     AND QUERIES, 211 (1966), 98-99.
     On "Mrs. Dalloway in Bond Street" and MD. For
     annotation see M49.

T18 Lewis, Thomas S. W. "Vision in Time: Virginia Woolf's 'An Un-
     written Novel.'" In VIRGINIA WOOLF. Ed. Lewis. Pp. 15-22.
     See G44.
     "An Unwritten Novel" a model for VW's fiction in
     its playfulness and characterization.

T19 Lotringer, Sylvère. "Préface: La Dame au miroir." In Woolf's
     LA MORT DE LA PHALÈNE: NOUVELLES [THE DEATH OF THE MOTH: STORIES].
     Trans. Hélène Bokanowski, et al. Paris: Éditions du Seuil, 1968.
     Pp. 9-26.
     Argues against the rigid distinction between VW's
     "essays" and "stories" (several "essays" are in-
     cluded in Lotringer's selection of "nouvelles")
     and sees VW's development in her longer fiction
     reflected in her stories and sketches. [In
     French.]

Studies of the Short Stories

T20 McNichol, Stella. "Introduction." In Woolf's MRS. DALLOWAY'S
PARTY. Ed. McNichol. Pp. 9-17. See A16.
> VW's seven "party" stories "form a kind of mosaic"
> whole, though they lack the organic wholeness of
> MD, to which they are related.

T21 Mansfield, Katherine. "A Short Story: 'Kew Gardens.'" 1919.
In NOVELS AND NOVELISTS. Ed. John Middleton Murry. New York:
Knopf, 1930. Pp. 36-38.
> VW's exquisite description and her theme of the
> world "on tiptoe," waiting for whatever might
> happen, in "Kew Gardens."

T22 Meyerowitz, Selma S. "What Is to Console Us?: The Politics of
Deception in Woolf's Short Stories." In NEW FEMINIST ESSAYS ON
VIRGINIA WOOLF. Ed. Jane Marcus. Pp. 238-52. See G51.
> VW's "social criticism" and "political vision"
> as central to her stories as to her novels and
> essays. Illustrates from several of the stories.

T23 Olsen, F. Bruce. "'The Duchess and the Jeweller.'" In INSIGHT
II: ANALYSES OF MODERN ENGLISH LITERATURE. Ed. John V. Hagopian
and Martin Dolch. Frankfurt am M.: Hirschgraben, 1964. Pp. 363-67.
> Brief summary, critique, and questions for the
> study of "The Duchess and the Jeweller."

T24 Sakamoto, Kiminobo. "'Mrs. Dalloway in Bond Street.'" EIGO SEINEN,
116 (1970), 524-26.
> [In Japanese.]

T25 Sakamoto, Tadanobu. "Virginia Woolf: 'Mrs. Dalloway in Bond
Street' and MRS. DALLOWAY." STUDIES IN ENGLISH LITERATURE
(Tokyo), 50, English No. (1974), 75-88.
> Appreciation of VW's story, with some discussion
> of its relationship to the novel.

T26 Saunders, Judith P. "Mortal Stain: Literary Allusion and Female
Sexuality in 'Mrs. Dalloway in Bond Street.'" STUDIES IN SHORT
FICTION, 15 (1978), 139-44.
> VW's allusion to Shelley's "Adonais" (1821) the
> "central structuring metaphor" in "Mrs. Dalloway
> in Bond Street."

T27 Tallentire, D. R. "Confirming Intuitions About Style Using Concordances." In THE COMPUTER IN LITERARY AND LINGUISTIC STUDIES.
Ed. Alan Jones and R. F. Churchhouse. Cardiff: Univ. of Wales
Press, 1976. Pp. 309-28.
> Compares results of computer analysis of a number
> of the stories of similar stylists, Katherine
> Mansfield and VW.

T28 Villgradter, Rudolf. "Die Konzeption der Wirklichkeit als Strukturelement der Erzählungen Virginia Woolfs." GERMANISH-ROMANISCH MONATSSCHRIFT, 16 (1966), 283-97.
> Distinguishes three conceptions of reality and corresponding fictional structures in VW's short fiction (e.g., "The Legacy," "Moments of Being," and "Monday or Tuesday"), arguing the significance of VW's stories for a fuller understanding of her longer fiction. [In German.]

T29 Watson, Robert A. "'Solid Objects' as Allegory." VIRGINIA WOOLF MISCELLANY, No. 16 (1981), pp. 3-4.
> Not seen.

T30 Worrell, Elizabeth. "The Unspoken Word." In STUDIES IN INTERPRETATION. Ed. Esther M. Doyle and Virginia H. Floyd. Amsterdam: Rodopi, 1972. Pp. 191-203.
> VW's central concern with the failures in and obstacles to communication, seen in four of her party-stories: "The New Dress," "The Man Who Loved His Kind," "Together and Apart," and "A Summing Up."

U. STUDIES OF THE AUTOBIOGRAPHICAL WRITINGS

The following section is subdivided into two parts: i. Books and Essay Collections on the Autobiographical Writings; and ii. Critical Articles or Chapters on the Autobiographical Writings.

For bibliographical information on the periodical and collected publication of VW's diaries, letters, and autobiographical essays, see Kirkpatrick (E7), and for biographical studies incorporating substantial commentary on VW's autobiographical writings, see Bell (F13), Forrester (F31), Gindin (F40), Love (F61), Poole (F77), Rose (F81), Trombley (F95), and Woolf (F100).

A number of the book-length critical studies of VW, in section G above, rely extensively on VW's autobiographical writings in their discussions of her writing career. See particularly Alexander (G2), Gorsky (G28), Guiguet (G30), Lee (G42), Naremore (G59), Richter (G69), and Spilka (G79). Among the critical articles, in section H above, also see Spilka (H225). For a complete listing of substantial commentaries on individual autobiographical writings, by title, see the concluding index: "Virginia Woolf's Works."

U, i. Books and Essay Collections on the Autobiographical Writings

U1 Ocampo, Victoria. VIRGINIA WOOLF EN SU DIARIO. Buenos Aires: SUR, 1954.
    Exasperated response to Leonard Woolf's extensive editing of VW's A WRITER'S DIARY (B6), seen as an ironically appropriate act of masculine suppression illustrating precisely the kind of oppression against which VW inveighed. To fill some of the gaps left by Leonard's editing, Ocampo summarizes VW's relationship with her father (and the Victorian paterfamilias figure generally), her feminist rejection of the father ("La rebelión de James y Cam"), her views of Gide, her sexual attitudes, her social views (e.g., "The Leaning Tower"), and her nearly mystical visions of reality, the incommunicable, time, and death, which occasionally shade into fantasy (cf. Huxley's THE DOORS OF PERCEPTION [1954]; note: Huxley first introduced Ocampo to VW, in 1934). Ocampo also republishes her first essay on VW as an appendix (see W21). [In Spanish.] Also see F65.

U, ii. Critical Articles or Chapters on the Autobiographical Writings

U2 Auden, W. H. "A Consciousness of Reality." 1954. In his FORE-
    WORDS AND AFTERWORDS. Ed. Edward Mendelson. New York: Random
    House, 1973. Pp. 411-18.
        Appreciative memoir and review of A WRITER'S DIARY
        (B6), seen as a necessary part of the "definitive
        history of Bloomsbury."

U3 Aury, Dominique. "Le Journal de Virginia Woolf." NOUVELLE REVUE
    FRANÇAISE, No. 67 (July 1958), 112-16.
        Marvels at the incessant activity and consider-
        able energy VW reveals in A WRITER'S DIARY (B6),
        yet regrets the incompleteness of the writer's
        portrait created by Leonard Woolf's extensive
        editing and abridgement. Review of the French
        translation (1958). [In French.]

U4 Beaumont, Germaine. "Salut, cher fantôme." NOUVELLES LITTÉRAIRES,
    No. 1602 (15 May 1958), pp. 1-2.
        Impressions of a "pre-Raphaelite" VW, by the
        French translator of her A WRITER'S DIARY (B6).
        [In French.]

U5 Bell, Quentin. "Introduction." In THE DIARY OF VIRGINIA WOOLF.
    Ed. Anne Oliver Bell. I, xiii-xxviii. See B1.
        For annotation see F12.

U6 Bennett, Joan. "Le Journal inédit de Virginia Woolf." ROMAN,
    No. 1 (1951), pp. 6-8.
        Introduction (chiefly biographical summary) for
        first French publication of extracts from VW's
        A WRITER'S DIARY (B6; trans. Rose Celli, pp.
        9-13). Significant lead publication in first
        issue of this short-lived French literary jour-
        nal (ed. Célia Bertin). [In French.]

U7 Blanchot, Maurice. "L'Échec du démon: la vocation." 1958. In
    LE LIVRE À VENIR. Paris: Gallimard, 1959. Pp. 144-54.
        VW's struggle with the "demon" of her idealized
        conceptions of art, her repeated encounters with
        "nothingness" in her writings, and her escape,
        through suicide, from the failure she sensed in
        BETWEEN THE ACTS. Review of A WRITER'S DIARY
        (B6; French trans., 1958). Also see "Le journal
        intime et le récit," pp. 271-79. [In French.]
        Recently reprinted as "Outwitting the Demon--
        A Vocation," trans. Sacha Rabinovich, in THE
        SIREN'S SONG: SELECTED ESSAYS OF MAURICE BLAN-
        CHOT, ed. Gabriel Josipovici (Bloomington:
        Indiana Univ. Press, 1982), pp. 87-93.

U8 Bourniquel, Camille. "Le 'Journal Littéraire' de Virginia Woolf."
ESPRIT, 27 (1959), 201-06.
    VW's exceptional sensibility and fragile meta-
physics both revealed by her unfortunately
abridged A WRITER'S DIARY (B6). Review of
Germaine Beaumont's French translation (1958).
[In French.]

U9 Dahl, Christopher C. "Virginia Woolf's MOMENTS OF BEING and
Autobiographical Tradition in the Stephen Family." JOURNAL OF
MODERN LITERATURE, 10 (1983), 175-96.
    Traces the "rich literary tradition" of auto-
biography in the Stephen family as background
to VW's transition from Victorian to modern
autobiographer in MOMENTS OF BEING (B3).
Complements Schulkind's discussion of the
relation between VW's autobiographical essays
and her later development as a novelist (see
U30).

U10 Daiches, David. "A WRITER'S DIARY." TWENTIETH CENTURY, 154
(1953), 482-83, 485.
    A WRITER'S DIARY (B6) documents VW's serious
and brilliant concern for "one of the great
modern problems," the "possibility of significant human contacts" (cf. her fiction),
a concern which should guarantee her lasting
significance. Review essay.

U11 DeSalvo, Louise A. "The Importance of MOMENTS OF BEING." VIR-
GINIA WOOLF MISCELLANY, No. 5 (1976), pp. 1-3.
    Review of MOMENTS OF BEING (B3). Not seen.

U12 Dick, Susan. "The Writings Cast Away: Some Virginia Woolf
Manuscripts." HUMANITIES ASSOCIATION REVIEW, 28 (1977), 345-53.
    On THE WAVES and MOMENTS OF BEING (B3). For
annotation see Q17.

U13 Eder, Doris L. "Portrait of the Artist as a Young Woman: Virginia Woolf." BOOK FORUM, 3 (1977), 336-44.
    The "profoundly disturbing, haunting vision of
the woman and the writer...as stranger than
her work," found in VW's LETTERS (B2). Reviews volumes I-II.

U14 Fleishman, Avrom. "'To Return to St. Ives': Woolf's Autobio-
graphical Writings." In FIGURES OF AUTOBIOGRAPHY: THE LANGUAGE
OF SELF-WRITING IN VICTORIAN AND MODERN ENGLAND. Berkeley:
Univ. of California Press, 1983. Pp. 454-70.
    On TL, THE WAVES, and "A Sketch of the Past" (in
MOMENTS OF BEING; see B3). For annotation see
H79.

U15 Gindin, James. "Bolts of Iron." STUDIES IN THE NOVEL, 8 (1976), 336-50.
    Traces VW's "struggle for coherence and control" through the first volume of her LETTERS (B2), and reviews, with less enthusiasm, two critical studies that underestimate VW's "controlling point of view" in her fiction (see G24 and G62).

U16 -----. "Lots of Cotton Wool." STUDIES IN THE NOVEL, 9 (1977), 312-25.
    Like her best fiction, VW's autobiographical writings and letters "comb the 'cotton wool'" of experience to find, in the "moment," the hidden "pattern" of meaning. Reviews MOMENTS OF BEING (B3) and volume two of the LETTERS (B2).

U17 -----. "A Precipice Marked V." STUDIES IN THE NOVEL, 11 (1979), 82-98.
    Reviews the third volume of the LETTERS (B2) and recent biographical studies of VW. For annotation see F40.

U18 Griffin, Gail B. "Braving the Mirror: Virginia Woolf as Autobiographer." BIOGRAPHY, 4 (1981), 108-18.
    Dominated by VW's consciousness and serving "the larger aims of the autobiographical enterprise," the study of "the process of memory" and "the discovery of meaning from the vantage point of time," MOMENTS OF BEING (B3) "belongs among the great literary autobiographies of the early twentieth century."

U19 Hulcoop, John. "'The Only Way I Keep Afloat': Work as Virginia Woolf's *Raison d'Être*." WOMEN'S STUDIES, 4 (1977), 223-45.
    The therapeutic value of the discipline of writing, for VW, "helped transform the futility of existence into something she could reconcile to herself." Surveys VW's attitudes toward her writing in A WRITER'S DIARY (B6) and other biographical documents. See G87.

U20 -----. "Virginia Woolf's Diaries: Some Reflections After Reading Them and a Censure of Mr. Holroyd." BNYPL, 75 (1971), 301-10.
    VW's diaries (only partially published as of 1971; see B1 and B6), considered of greater interest and value for the literary historian than the critic. Also a response to Holroyd's attack on VW (see F47). Reprinted in VIRGINIA WOOLF NEWSLETTER, 2 (Nov. 1971), 1-8.

U21 Hyman, Virginia R. "Reflections in the Looking-Glass: Leslie Stephen and Virginia Woolf." JOURNAL OF MODERN LITERATURE, 10 (1983), 197-216.
    Numerous parallels between the experiences and the autobiographies of VW and her father (par-

ticularly their shared vision of the Stephen
heritage of early promise and later decline),
shed light on VW's identification with and
ambivalence toward her father, throughout her
life.

U22 L'Enfant, Julie. "'A Lady Writing': Virginia Woolf Chronicle."
SOUTHERN REVIEW, 13 (1977), 456-67.
Reviews the variable qualities of writing and
personality revealed in VW's recently published
autobiographical writings (MOMENTS OF BEING
[B3] and LETTERS [B2]), among other works.

U23 Lombardo, Agostino. "Il diario di Virginia Woolf." CONVIVIUM,
23 (1955), 175-91.
Summarizes the new viewpoints on VW's creative
intentions provided by A WRITER'S DIARY (B6).
[In Italian.]

U24 López García, Dámaso. "Las novelas de Virginia Woolf desde su
DIARIO." ARBOR, No. 409 (1980), pp. 77-86.
Stresses the importance of VW's A WRITER'S DIARY
(B6) for tracing the aesthetic evolution of her
fiction. [In Spanish.]

U25 Megata, Morikimi. "Stephen Jo no Tegami: V. Woolf Shinkanshū
Dai Ikkan" ["The Letters of Stephen: The First Volume of the
New Edition of V. Woolf's Letters"]. EIGO SEINEN, 121 (1976),
568-69.
Review essay. [In Japanese.]

U26 Richter, Harvena. "Virginia Woolf and the Creative Critic."
REVIEW, 3 (1981), 265-83.
Reviews eight biographical and critical studies
of VW (1978-80), a reissue of Leonard Woolf's
THE WISE VIRGINS (1914), and recent volumes of
VW's DIARY (B1) and LETTERS (B2), her "finest
and most enduring works." Reviews F25, F57,
F77, F81, G18, G26, G76, and X3.

U27 Rousseaux, André. "Virginia Woolf dans l'onde de la vie." 1958.
In LITTÉRATURE DU VINGTIÈME SIÈCLE. Vol. VII. Paris: Albin
Michel, 1961. Pp. 208-19.
VW's pursuit of truth in her A WRITER'S DIARY
(B6) and her fiction. [In French.]

U28 Sackville-West, Victoria. "The Landscape of a Mind." ENCOUNTER,
2, No. 1 (1954), 70-72, 74.
Surveys the elements of VW's genius, the difficulties of her aims for writing, the "sense
of tragedy which underlay her high spirits,"
and the discernment of her self-criticism in
A WRITER'S DIARY (B6).

U29 Schlack, Beverly Ann. "Portrait of the Artist as Young Woman: The Letters of Virginia Woolf." L&P, 26 (1976), 118-23.
    Admiring review of volume one of VW's LETTERS (B2), observing a variety of psychologically interesting details revealed in her correspondence.

U30 Schulkind, Jean. "Introduction." In Woolf's MOMENTS OF BEING. Ed. Schulkind. Pp. 11-24. See B3.
    VW's previously unpublished memoir writings, chiefly concerned with her childhood and adolescence, reveal "the remarkable unity" of her "art, thought and sensibility." Also see U9.

U31 Scott, George. "Virginia Woolf." ADELPHI, 30 (1954), 169-76.
    The "dominant impression" of VW from her A WRITER'S DIARY (B6), "one of arrogance: an arrogance big-boned and belligerent."

U32 Shaw, Valerie. "The Secret Companion." CRITICAL QUARTERLY, 20, No. 1 (1978), 70-77.
    VW's "vigorous sense of the ordinary, so evident in the diary, is paradoxically the source of her fiction's specialness." Reviews the DIARY (vol. I; see B1) and BOOKS AND PORTRAITS (A37).

U33 Shibazaki, Yuko. "Virginia Woolf no Sketch ni Miru Ishiki no Hyogen" ["The Presentation of Consciousness in Virginia Woolf's 'Sketch'"]. In SUGA YASUO, OGOSHI KAZUGO: RYOKYOJU TAIKAN KINEN RONBUNSHU. Kyoto: Appollonsha, 1980. Pp. 564-75.
    Presumably on VW's "A Sketch of the Past," in MOMENTS OF BEING (B3). Not seen. [In Japanese.]

U34 Stürzl, Erwin. "Virginia Woolfs Romankunst im Lichte ihres Tagebuchs." DIE NEUEREN SPRACHEN, 5 (1956), 201-11.
    Usefulness of VW's A WRITER'S DIARY (B6) for charting her Werther-ish emotional shifts, as well as her views of fiction and intentions for her writings. [In German.]

U35 Zéraffa, Michel. "Conscience et fiction: Virginia Woolf." JOURNAL DE PSYCHOLOGIE NORMALE ET PATHOLOGIQUE, 75 (1978), 115-31.
    VW's autobiographical writings, A WRITER'S DIARY (B6) and MOMENTS OF BEING (B3), not particularly useful for investigating the sources or genesis of her fiction, but extremely interesting for their reflection of her ideas, in their earliest states, and her overriding concern for the self in relation to others. [In French.]

V. STUDIES OF THE BIOGRAPHIES: *FLUSH* (1933) AND *ROGER FRY* (1940)

Since there are no books, essay collections, monographs, or pamphlets on VW's biographies, this section consists entirely of general critical essays on the two biographical works.

For edited transcriptions of VW's manuscript of a biographical essay, "Friendships Gallery," see C8, and of VW's reading notes, made partially in preparation for her biographies, see C10.

For bibliographical information on FLUSH and ROGER FRY, see Kirkpatrick (E7), and for biographical backgrounds to the biographies, see Bell (F13), Trombley (F95), and Woolf (F100).

For the most significant additional critical commentaries and information on FLUSH and ROGER FRY, see the following books, in section G above: Alexander (G2), Daiches (G16), Forster (G25), Gorsky (G28), Guiguet (G30), Johnson (G36), Lee (G42), Lohmüller (G46), McLaurin (G48), Naremore (G59), Rosenthal (G71), Woodring (G88); and the following essays, in section H above: Albright (H2), Brooks (H28), and Heilbrun (H112).

Since a number of VW's brief biographies and sketches of personalities have been collected in her various essay collections, several of the discussions of VW's essays, in section X below, comment generally on her biographical interests. See particularly Goldman (X1), Steele (X7), Silver (X53), and Sloman (X54). For a complete listing of substantial commentaries on FLUSH, ROGER FRY, or the biographical essays and sketches, by title, see the concluding index: "Virginia Woolf's Works."

V1   Bishop, Morchard. "Towards a Biography of FLUSH." TIMES LITERARY SUPPLEMENT, 15 Dec. 1966, p. 1180.
    Corrects several inaccuracies in VW's "little masterpiece" (A23), in light of recent publications concerning Elizabeth Browning.

V2   Edel, Leon. LITERARY BIOGRAPHY: THE ALEXANDER LECTURES 1955-1956. Toronto: Univ. of Toronto Press, 1957. Pp. 89-98.
    On ROGER FRY (A25) and ORLANDO. For annotation see P9.

V3   Garnett, David. "John Maynard Keynes, Biographe"; "Discussion." Trans. Laure Villiermet. In VIRGINIA WOOLF--COLLOQUE DE CERISY. Ed. Maurice de Gandillac and Jean Guiguet. Pp. 119-28; 129-38. See F34.
    Similarities among the biographical writings of Strachey, VW, and Keynes (whose biographies have

received scant attention). Notes VW's sparkling love of life, sympathy with her subjects, humor and intelligence, and love of the grotesque in her best biographical work, her character sketches and brief lives. [In French.]

V4 Roberts, R. Ellis. "A Biographer Manquée." SATURDAY REVIEW, 25 (3 Oct. 1942), 9.
   VW's true genius was for biography, a genre she unfortunately disdained. Reviews THE DEATH OF THE MOTH (A26) and Forster's study of VW (G25).

V5 Schaefer, Josephine O'Brien. "Moments of Vision in Virginia Woolf's Biographies." VIRGINIA WOOLF QUARTERLY, 2 (1976), 294-303.
   VW's use of her fictional technique of the visionary moment in her biographies and biographical essays.

V6 Szladits, Lola L. "'The Life, Character and Opinions of Flush the Spaniel.'" BNYPL, 74 (1970), 211-18.
   FLUSH (A23) an "entertainment" with a serious underlying concern for presenting a unique perspective on the subjection of woman.

V7 Vukobrat, Slobodan. "Prekretnica u engleskoj biografiji" ["Turning Point in English Biography"]. STVARANJE, 36 (1981), 377-82.
   On the Bloomsbury Group's views of society and approaches to biography (e.g., Strachey's EMINENT VICTORIANS [1918] and VW's ROGER FRY [A25]). [In Serbo-Croatian.]

V8 Yu, Sau-ling Cynthia. "The Fable of Flush." VIRGINIA WOOLF MISCELLANY, No. 3 (1975), pp. 7-8.
   Compares FLUSH (A23) to Chinese fables. Not seen.

W. STUDIES OF THE FEMINIST TRACTS:
A ROOM OF ONE'S OWN (1929) AND *THREE GUINEAS* (1938)

The following section is subdivided into two parts: i. Books and Essay Collections on the Feminist Tracts; and ii. Critical Articles or Chapters on the Feminist Tracts.

For edited transcriptions of VW's feminist essays, originally intended as part of her novel THE YEARS and partially assimilated into THREE GUINEAS, see C3, and of VW's reading notes, made partly in preparation for her feminist tracts, see C10.

For bibliographical information on A ROOM OF ONE'S OWN and THREE GUINEAS, see Kirkpatrick (E7), and for biographical backgrounds to these writings, see Bell (F13), DeSalvo (F23), Forrester (F31), Poole (F77), Rose (F81), Trombley (F95), and Woolf (F100).

For the most significant additional critical commentaries and information on A ROOM OF ONE'S OWN and THREE GUINEAS, see the following books, in section G above: Bazin (G6), Blackstone (G9), Daiches (G16), Delattre (G17), DiBattista (G18), Forster (G25), Gorsky (G28), Gruber (G29), Guiguet (G30), Johnson (G36), Leaska (G41), Lee (G42), Little (G45), Lohmüller (G46), Marder (G53), Naremore (G59), Poresky (G66), Rantavaara (G68), Richter (G69), Rosenthal (G71), Schlack (G76); and the following critical articles, in section H above: Batchelor (H7), Bradbrook (H23), Carroll (H35), Hartman (H108), Heilbrun (H111, H112), Johnstone (H126), Kiely (H130), Pomeroy (H192), Showalter (H221), and Wicht (H249).

Since a number of VW's feminist essays and speeches have been collected in her various essay collections, several of the discussions of VW's essays, in section X below, comment on the feminist tracts directly, or their relation to the feminist themes in VW's nonfiction generally. See particularly Goldman (X1), Barrett (X8), Bell (X11), Silver (X53), and Sloman (X54). For a complete listing of substantial commentaries on A ROOM OF ONE'S OWN, THREE GUINEAS, or the feminist essays and speeches, by title, see the concluding index: "Virginia Woolf's Works."

W, i. Books and Essay Collections on the Feminist Tracts

W1 Kamerbeek, Jan Coenraad. ANTIGONE BIJ VIRGINIA WOOLF. Amsterdam: Noord-Hollandsche Uitgevers Meatschappij, 1974.
    On THREE GUINEAS (A24) and THE YEARS. For annotation see R2.

W, ii. Critical Articles or Chapters on the Feminist Tracts

W2 Bogan, Louise. "The Ladies and Gentlemen." 1938. In her SELECTED CRITICISM: PROSE, POETRY. New York: Noonday, 1955. Pp. 36-39.
    Finds THREE GUINEAS (A24) unpersuasive feminism. Review essay.

W3 Burt, John. "Irreconcilable Habits of Thought in A ROOM OF ONE'S OWN and TO THE LIGHTHOUSE." ENGLISH LITERARY HISTORY, 49 (1982), 889-907.
    For annotation see N17.

W4 Ćwiąkała-Piątkowska, Jadwiga. "The Feminist Pamphlets of Virginia Woolf." KWARTALNIK NEOFILOLOGICZNY, 19 (1972), 271-79.
    VW more closely related to traditional English feminism than often realized, particularly in her politically and economically insightful feminist pamphlets (see A21 and A24).

W5 Farwell, Marilyn R. "Virginia Woolf and Androgyny." ConL, 16 (1975), 433-51.
    VW's ambivalent conception of androgyny, as a critical and aesthetic principle, analyzed in A ROOM OF ONE'S OWN (A21).

W6 Folsom, Marcia McClintock. "Gallant Red Brick and Plain China: Teaching A ROOM OF ONE'S OWN." CE, 45 (1983), 254-62.
    The difficulties and value of using VW's essay (A21) as a basic text for a "Women in Literature" course.

W7 Forrester, Viviane. "L'Autre Corps." In Woolf's TROIS GUINÉES. Trans. Forrester. Paris: Éditions des Femmes, 1977. Pp. 11-31.
    VW's insights into the causes and consequences of the oppression of women still valid and timely (cf. ORLANDO and BETWEEN THE ACTS). [In French.]

W8 Furman, Nelly. "A ROOM OF ONE'S OWN: Reading Absence." In WOMEN'S LANGUAGE AND STYLE. Ed. Douglas Butturff and Edmund L. Epstein. Akron, Ohio: L&S Books, 1978. Pp. 99-105.
    Using an apparently discursive, "tightly woven" form of "political discourse," VW's revolutionary A ROOM OF ONE'S OWN (A21) "explodes...all the rules of argumentation and literary convention," thus achieving an excellent balance of form and content.

W9   -----. "Textual Feminism." In WOMEN AND LANGUAGE IN LITERATURE
      AND SOCIETY. Ed. Sally McConnell-Ginet, Ruth Borker, and Nelly
      Furman. New York: Praeger, 1980. Pp. 45-54.
         In "The Art of Fiction" (in A27) and A ROOM OF
         ONE'S OWN (A21), VW's early recognition of the
         dynamic qualities of language (words) in litera-
         ture (cf. DeSassure's linguistic theories) and
         of the "creativity of reading" suggest possi-
         bilities for a more essential, feminist textual
         analysis of literature (cf. Barthes' semiotic
         theories).

W10   Gilbert, Sandra M. "Soldier's Heart: Literary Men, Literary
      Women, and the Great War." SIGNS, 8 (1983), 422-50.
         Relates VW's "hostility to men" and "violent
         antipatriarchal fantasies" in THREE GUINEAS
         (A24), "the post war era's great text of
         pacifist feminism," to the impressive vari-
         ety of feminine responses to "the wound of
         the war."

W11   Gunsteren-Viersen, Julia van. "The Marriage of 'He' and "She':
      Virginia Woolf's Androgynous Theory." DUTCH QUARTERLY REVIEW,
      6 (1976), 233-46.
         VW attempts to speak man's language, using "man's
         weapon" to attack "a man's world" in her feminist
         tracts (A21 and A24), illustrating her own union
         of the "masculine and feminine principles."

W12   Hill, James S. "Faulkner's Allusion to Virginia Woolf's A ROOM
      OF ONE'S OWN in THE WILD PALMS." NMAL: NOTES ON MODERN AMERI-
      CAN LITERATURE, 4 (1980), item 10.
         Faulkner uses VW's "thesis in A ROOM OF ONE'S OWN
         [A21] to achieve a feminine perspective in THE
         WILD PALMS" (1939).

W13   Hummel, Madeline M. "From the Common Reader to the Uncommon
      Critic: THREE GUINEAS and the Epistolary Form." BNYPL, 80
      (1977), 151-57.
         VW's adaptations of the conventions of epistolary
         fiction for THREE GUINEAS (A24--originally con-
         ceived as part of THE YEARS). See R1.

W14   Kamuf, Peggy. "Penelope at Work: Interruptions in A ROOM OF
      ONE'S OWN." NOVEL, 16 (1982), 5-18.
         VW's rhetorical strategy in "weaving" the text
         of her essay (A21; e.g., "the double hinging
         effect of interruption").

W15   Lakshmi, Vijay. "The Unviewed Room: An Interpretation of the
      Room Analogy in Virginia Woolf's Critical Writings." RAJASTHAN
      UNIVERSITY STUDIES IN ENGLISH, 6 (1972), 64-69.
         The room, in VW's feminist and critical essays
         (e.g., A21 and A24), a symbol for "the creative
         mind."

W16 Lawrence, Margaret. THE SCHOOL OF FEMININITY. New York: Stokes, 1936. Pp. 373-81.
> On ORLANDO and A ROOM OF ONE'S OWN (A21). For annotation see P19.

W17 Leavis, Q. D. "Caterpillars of the Commonwealth Unite!" SCRUTINY, 7 (1938), 203-14.
> VW's embarrassing intellectual vacuity and emotional excess in her self-indulgent, peevish, and incoherent THREE GUINEAS (A24). Savage, yet substantial critique, representative of the SCRUTINY critics' hostility toward VW's later work. Reprinted in G49. Also see H161, R14, and S19.

W18 Marcus, Jane. "Art and Anger." FEMINIST STUDIES, 4 (1978), 69-98.
> Both Elizabeth Robins, in ANCILLA'S SHARE (1924), and Virginia Woolf, in A ROOM OF ONE'S OWN (A21) and THREE GUINEAS (A24), as artists, "analyzed their own anger, tried to capture its energy for their art, and yet were in certain ways victims of the need to sublimate some of that anger in order to survive."

W19 -----. "'No More Horses': Virginia Woolf on Art and Propaganda." WOMEN'S STUDIES, 4 (1977), 265-90.
> Realizing VW's successful fusion of art and propaganda in THREE GUINEAS (A24) provides a new perspective for regarding the political dimensions of her last novels and essays. See G87.

W20 Middleton, Victoria. "THREE GUINEAS: Subversion and Survival in the Professions." TCL, 28 (1982), 405-17.
> Rhetorical analysis, finding VW's essay (A24) not only an attack on patriarchal authority but also a "subversion of such authority" through its rhetorical strategies (VW's views of ideology and language, her reaction against "masculine argumentation," etc.).

W21 Ocampo, Victoria. "Carta a Virginia Woolf." In TESTIMONIOS I. Madrid: Revista de Occidente, 1935. Pp. 9-17.
> Open letter to VW, praising her appeal for a balance of the masculine and feminine, the rational and the intuitive, in intellectual life generally and in literature particularly. [In Spanish.] Reprinted in U1. Also see F65.

W22 Schlack, Beverley Ann. "Virginia Woolf's Strategy of Scorn in THE YEARS and THREE GUINEAS." BNYPL, 80 (1977), 146-50.
> For annotation see R22.

W23 Sears, Sallie. "Notes on Sexuality: THE YEARS and THREE GUINEAS."
BNYPL, 80 (1977), 211-20.
For annotation see R23.

W24 Starkey, Penelope Schott. "THE YOUNG VISITERS Revisited in
Light of Virginia Woolf." RS, 42 (1974), 161-66.
Daisy Ashford's novel of late-Victorian girl-
hood (1919) aptly illustrates VW's observations
of woman's situation in A ROOM OF ONE'S OWN
(A21).

W25 West, Rebecca. "Autumn and Virginia Woolf." In ENDING IN EAR-
NEST: A LITERARY LOG. Garden City, N. Y.: Doubleday, Doran,
1931. Pp. 208-13.
The vibrancy and honesty of the autumnally frail
VW's feminist polemic, A ROOM OF ONE'S OWN (A21).

X. STUDIES OF THE ESSAYS

The following section is subdivided into two parts: i. Books and Essay Collections on the Essays; and ii. Critical Articles or Chapters on the Essays.

For an edited transcription of VW's reading notes, made partially in preparation for her essays, see C10.

For bibliographical information on the periodical and collected publication of VW's essays, see Kirkpatrick (E7), and for biographical backgrounds to the essays, see Bell (F13), Poole (F77), Rose (F81), Trombley (F95), and Woolf (F100).

For the most significant additional critical commentaries and information on the essays, see the following books, in section G above: Alexander (G2), Bazin (G6), Daiches (G16), Delattre (G17), DiBattista (G18), Dölle (G19), Fleishman (G24), Forster (G25), Gorsky (G28), Gruber (G29), Guiguet (G30), Hafley (G31), Johnson (G36), Kapur (G37), Lee (G42), Little (G45), Lohmüller (G46), Marder (G53), Naremore (G59), Novak (G62), Rantavaara (G69), Richter (G69), Schlack (G76), Spilka (G79), Woodring (G88); the following critical articles, in section H above: Albright (H2), Bradbury (H24), Cornwell (H47), Daiches (H54), Johnstone (H126), Kiely (H130), McLaughlin (H148), Pomeroy (H192), Rosenbaum (H207); and the following studies, entered in other sections of this bibliography: Brandt (Q1), Weber-Brandies (Q5), and Ocampo (U1). For a complete listing of substantial commentaries on individual essays, by title, see the concluding index: "Virginia Woolf's Works."

X, i. Books and Essay Collections on the Essays

X1 Goldman, Mark. THE READER'S ART: VIRGINIA WOOLF AS LITERARY CRITIC. The Hague: Mouton, 1976.
> Impressive examination of VW's critical theories, arrived at through discussion of a generous number of her critical essays and through comparisons with her contemporaries (e.g., Eliot and Forster). Goldman places VW as an "artist-critic" within a distinguished English literary tradition, extracts a theory of fiction from her many comments on the genre, and similarly derives VW's ideas of and ideals for literary criticism itself. He finds VW no merely "occasional essayist," but an important proponent of the "*via media* between the extremes" of impersonal analysis and emotional impressionism in modern literary criticism. Extract reprinted (from original periodical publication in 1965), in G80.

X2 Hoag, Gerald. HENRY JAMES AND THE CRITICISM OF VIRGINIA WOOLF. Wichita, Kan.: Wichita State Univ. Press, 1972.
VW's criticism of and kinship with James (see A26). (Pamphlet--11 pp.) Reprinted from the WICHITA STATE UNIVERSITY BULLETIN, 48, No. 3 (1972), 3-11.

X3 Meisel, Perry. THE ABSENT FATHER: VIRGINIA WOOLF AND WALTER PATER. New Haven, Conn.: Yale Univ. Press, 1980.
Study of VW's debt to Walter Pater, for key "vocabulary" (rather than style), figures of speech, and critical "stance," chiefly in her essays, but with passing reference to her fiction. Meisel overcomes the immediate objections that VW hardly mentions Pater in her writings and that she characteristically attacks the authoritarian Victorianism that Pater represents, by arguing that her silence is a significant "repression" and that her relationship with Pater resembles her ambivalent response to her autocratic father. Good comparison of the writers' aesthetic "vision and sensibility as a whole," despite tendentious theses. Reviewed in U26.

X4 Quennell, Peter. A LETTER TO MRS. VIRGINIA WOOLF. London: Hogarth, 1932.
Response to VW's A LETTER TO A YOUNG POET (in A26), defending modern poetry. (Pamphlet--24 pp.)

X5 Sharma, Kaushal Kishore. MODERN FICTIONAL THEORISTS: VIRGINIA WOOLF AND D. H. LAWRENCE. Atlantic Highlands, N. J.: Humanities Press, 1982.
Companion study of VW and Lawrence as novelist-theorists, which unfortunately avoids any direct comparison between the two writers. Sharma opens with a brief survey of novelists who have expressed their views on the art of fiction, from Defoe to Conrad, and, in his discussion of VW, offers a pedestrian summary of VW's statements on the "nature" and "scope" of fiction, the poetic novel, the novelist's "integrity and values," the "novel and life," and the elements of narration, form, symbolism, time, plot, character, style, and morality in the novel. Draws widely from VW's essays, but ultimately fails to generalize a very satisfactory theory of fiction.

X6 Sharma, Vijay L. VIRGINIA WOOLF AS LITERARY CRITIC: A REVALUATION. New Delhi: Arnold-Heinemann, 1977.
Fine analysis of the intellectual backgrounds of VW's criticism and exploration of the basic principles articulated in her critical essays. Sharma finds an ideological consistency in her "casual seeming" essays and argues effectively against those who charge her with a lack of theory. Individual chapters survey VW's intellectual heritage,

her conception of the androgynous artist, her
fictional theory ("organic form" and perspectivism), her humanistic ideal of the "common
reader," and her practical criticism (reviews).
Sharma concludes with effusive, but not un-
reasonable comparisons of VW, as critic, with
Aristotle, Coleridge, Arnold, Henry James,
Forster, T. S. Eliot, and others.

X7 Steele, Elizabeth. VIRGINIA WOOLF'S LITERARY SOURCES AND ALLU-
SIONS: A GUIDE TO THE ESSAYS. New York: Garland, 1983.
A very useful bibliographical guide to the poorly
edited COLLECTED ESSAYS (A32), identifying for
each of the essays (save nine excluded titles,
that need no identification), VW's "main source"
(such as specific titles reviewed in her book
reviews, which are not given in the collection),
her "supportive source(s)" (related works VW
used in researching her topics), her "important
allusions," and her "passing allusions."
Steele's own sources for this information are
the internal evidence of the essays, the surviving reading notes for several of the pieces
(see C10), the implications of original publication dates (rarely noted in the collection),
and some ingenious literary detection. Steele
includes, as an appendix, a valuable addendum
to the Holleyman sale catalog of Leonard and
Virginia Woolf's library (see E5), listing
numerous additional books owned by the Woolfs.

X, ii. Critical Articles or Chapters on the Essays

X8 Barrett, Michèle. "Introduction." In Woolf's WOMEN AND WRITING.
Ed. Barrett. Pp. 1-39. See A39.
Traces VW's critical attitudes and her views of
the "female literary tradition."

X9 Beaumont, Germaine. "Virginia Woolf: Mrs. Brown ou l'art du
roman." NOUVELLES LITTÉRAIRES, No. 1851 (21 Feb. 1963), pp. 1, 7.
The fundamental importance of "Mr. Bennett and
Mrs. Brown" (A18) for understanding VW's theory
of fiction and conviction that only the novel
could capture the complexity and difficulty of
modern life. Review of Rose Celli's translation
of VW's critical essays, L'ART DU ROMAN (Paris:
Le Seuil, 1963). [In French.]

X10 Beker, Miroslav. "Virginia Woolf's Appraisal of Joseph Conrad."
STUDIA ROMANICA ET ANGLICA ZAGRABIENSIA, 12 (Dec. 1961), 17-22.
Despite several excellent insights, VW's critical
responses to Conrad in several essays and reviews

(e.g., see A19 and A28), chiefly valuable as
expressions of her own fictional preoccupations.

X11 Bell, Barbara Currier, and Carol Ohmann. "Virginia Woolf's
Criticism: A Polemical Preface." 1974. In FEMINIST LITERARY
CRITICISM: EXPLORATIONS IN THEORY. Ed. Josephine Donovan.
Lexington: Univ. Press of Kentucky, 1975. Pp. 48-60.
Celebrates VW's "defiantly feminine" criticism,
her "brilliant and graceful protest" against narrow,
abstract, "or merely professional critical
purpose." Originally published in CRITICAL INQUIRY, 1 (1974).

X12 Blanchard, Lydia. "Women Look at Lady Chatterley: Feminine
Views of the Novel." D. H. LAWRENCE REVIEW, 11 (1978), 246-59.
Surveys the disfavor with LADY CHATTERLEY'S LOVER
(1928) among women critics (e.g., VW, Katherine
Anne Porter, Anais Nin, Joyce Carol Oates, and
others).

X13 Bogan, Louise. "The Skirting of Passion." 1950. In her SELECTED
CRITICISM: PROSE, POETRY. New York: Noonday, 1955. Pp. 365-69.
Reviews VW's "impressionist criticism" in THE CAPTAIN'S DEATH BED essays (A28).

X14 Cecchi, Emilio. "LA MORTE DELLA TIGNUOLA." 1945. In SCRITTORI
INGLESI E AMERICANI. Milan: Mondadori, 1947. Pp. 336-42.
The variety and quality of VW's informal essays
and criticism in THE DEATH OF THE MOTH (A26).
Review essay. [In Italian.]

X15 Cornwell, Ethel F. "Virginia Woolf, Natalie Sarraute, and Mary
McCarthy: Three Approaches to Character in Modern Fiction."
INTERNATIONAL FICTION REVIEW, 4 (1977), 3-10.
Comparative discussion of the writers' theories
and practice in their works (e.g., VW's "Mrs.
Bennett and Mrs. Brown" [A18], and Sarraute's
"Conversation and Sub-Conversation" [H212],
"The Fact in Fiction" [1961], and "Characters
in Fiction" [1961]).

X16 Delord, J. "Virginia Woolf's Critical Essays." REVUE DES LANGUES
VIVANTES, 29 (1963), 126-31.
VW's critical technique calculated to arouse the
reader's "creative response," recreating the
"whole experience of reading." Her method is
not unsystematic, or "impressionistic," though
it is unconventional.

X17 Donaldson, Scott. "Woolf vs. Hemingway." JOURNAL OF MODERN LITERATURE, 10 (1983), 338-42.
Summarizes VW's adverse opinions of Hemingway's
work (e.g., "An Essay in Criticism" [in A29]).

X18 Drescher, Horst W. "James Joyce and Virginia Woolf: Ästhetik, Funktion und Form des Modernen Romans." In ENGLISCHE UND AMERI-KANISCHE LITERATURTHEORIE: STUDIEN ZU IHRER HISTORISCHEN ENTWICKLUNG. Ed. Rüdiger Ahrens and Erwin Wolff. Heidelberg: Winter, 1979. II, 344-61.
    Surveys Joyce's aesthetic (superficially) and VW's views of the novel (e.g., "Mr. Bennett and Mrs. Brown" [A18] and "Modern Fiction" [in A19]), but draws few comparisons between the writers. [In German.]

X19 Eaglestone, Arthur A. [Roger Dataller]. "Mr. Lawrence and Mrs. Woolf." ESSAYS IN CRITICISM, 8 (1958), 48-59.
    Disputes VW's criticism of Lawrence's "inadequate technique" in "Notes on D. H. Lawrence" (in A27).

X20 Eisenberg, Nora. "Virginia Woolf's Last Words on Words: BETWEEN THE ACTS and 'Anon.'" In NEW FEMINIST ESSAYS ON VIRGINIA WOOLF. Ed. Jane Marcus. Pp. 253-66. See G51.
    For annotation see S7.

X21 Fishman, Solomon. "Virginia Woolf on the Novel." SEWANEE REVIEW, 51 (1943), 321-40.
    Surveys VW's "effort to resolve the polar tensions of philosophic and aesthetic criteria" for evaluation in her essays on literature.

X22 Fromm, Gloria G. "Remythologizing Arnold Bennett." NOVEL, 16 (1982), 19-34.
    VW's refusal to grasp Bennett's insightful characterization, irony, coherent imagery and symbolism, compassion, and "distrust of the material world" perhaps attributable to VW's recognition that "they were too similar." See F48.

X23 Furman, Nelly. "Textual Feminism." In WOMEN AND LANGUAGE IN LITERATURE AND SOCIETY. Ed. Sally McConnell-Ginet, Ruth Borker, and Nelly Furman. New York: Praeger, 1980. Pp. 45-54.
    On "The Art of Fiction" [in A27] and A ROOM OF ONE'S OWN. For annotation see W9.

X24 Gish, Robert. "Mr. Forster and Mrs. Woolf: Aspects of the Novelist as Critic." VIRGINIA WOOLF QUARTERLY, 2 (1976), 255-69.
    The two novelists as critics and their critical views of one another. See A26, G25, and H81.

X25 Goetsch, Paul. "A Source of Virginia Woolf's 'Mr. Bennett and Mrs. Brown.'" ENGLISH LITERATURE IN TRANSITION, 7 (1964), 188-89.
    Arnold Bennett's anticipation of VW's essay (A18) in his "Neo-Impressionism and Literature" (1910; reprinted in his BOOKS AND PERSONS [London: Chatto and Windus, 1917], reviewed by VW in 1917). See F48. VW's review reprinted in A30.

X26 Gregory, Horace. "Virginia Woolf: The Spirit of Time and Place."
1942. In SPIRIT OF TIME AND PLACE: COLLECTED ESSAYS. New York:
Norton, 1973. Pp. 175-79.
VW a "mistress" of the form of the "familiar essay."
Review of THE DEATH OF THE MOTH (A26).

X27 Guiguet, Jean. "A Novelist's Essay: 'The Moment: Summer's
Night' by Virginia Woolf." In DER ENGLISCHE ESSAY: ANALYSEN.
Ed. Horst Weber. Darmstadt, Ger.: Wissenschaftliche Buchgesel-
lschaft, 1975. Pp. 291-303.
A close analysis of one representative work from
THE MOMENT (see A27), shows VW's essays embodying
the same interplay between intellect (life) and
imagination (art) as her novels.

X28 -----. "Preface." In Woolf's CONTEMPORARY WRITERS. Comp.
Guiguet. Pp. 7-12. See A30.
Describes VW's methods of reviewing and major
themes in her critical essays.

X29 Henig, Suzanne. "D. H. Lawrence and Virginia Woolf." D. H.
LAWRENCE REVIEW, 2 (1969), 265-71.
Traces VW's ultimately admiring critical opinions
of Lawrence (e.g., in A27).

X30 -----. "Virginia Woolf and Lady Murasaki." LITERATURE EAST AND
WEST, 11 (1967), 421-23.
VW's reading of Arthur Waley's translation of
TALE OF GENJI (in an uncollected review [1925]),
and intimate understanding of "the problem of
being an intelligent and sensitive woman in
tenth-century Japan."

X31 Hill, Katherine C. "Virginia Woolf and Leslie Stephen: History
and Literary Revolution." PMLA, 96 (1981), 351-62.
Describes VW's assimilation of her father's
views of the function of literature in the
processes of history (derived from Saint-
Beuve) in her critical essays (particularly
"The Leaning Tower" [in A27]), and asserts
the positive influences of Stephen on her
development: "He was determined that she
should become his literary and intellectual
heir."

X32 Hungerford, Edward A. "Mrs. Woolf, Freud, and J. D. Beresford."
L&P, 5 (1955), 49-51.
Demonstrates VW's early awareness of the possibilities for Freudian psychoanalysis in
fiction, from her review of J. D. Beresford's
AN IMPERFECT MOTHER (1920), in "Freudian Fiction" (in A30).

X33 Hunting, Robert. "Laurence Sterne and Virginia Woolf." ÉTUDES ANGLAISES, 32 (1979), 283-93.
    Reviews VW's three "brilliant" critical commentaries on Sterne (e.g., see A22), while discounting any debts to Sterne in her fiction.

X34 Hyman, Virginia R. "Late Victorian and Early Modern: Continuities in the Criticism of Leslie Stephen and Virginia Woolf." ENGLISH LITERATURE IN TRANSITION, 23 (1980), 144-54.
    Essentially "conservative" values in VW's criticism, derived from her father's rational moralism.

X35 Hynes, Samuel. "The Whole Contention Between Mr. Bennett and Mrs. Woolf." In EDWARDIAN OCCASIONS: ESSAYS ON ENGLISH WRITING IN THE EARLY TWENTIETH CENTURY. London: Routledge, 1972. Pp. 24-38.
    On VW's and Bennett's exchange of critical essays. For annotation see F48.

X36 James, Walter. "Introduction." In VIRGINIA WOOLF: SELECTIONS FROM HER ESSAYS. Ed. James. Pp. 7-20. See A31.
    VW's essays chronicle her open-minded study of life and literature to enlarge her experience and to defend against "prejudice and falsehood."

X37 Kenney, Edwin J. "The Moment, 1910: Virginia Woolf, Arnold Bennett, and Turn of the Century Consciousness." COLBY LIBRARY QUARTERLY, 13 (1977), 42-66.
    VW's statement that "human character changed" in 1910, in "Mr. Bennett and Mrs. Brown" (A18), related to both national and personal events (death of King Edward; emotional breakdown and meeting Leonard Woolf).

X38 Kronenberger, Louis. "Virginia Woolf as Critic." 1942. In THE REPUBLIC OF LETTERS: ESSAYS ON VARIOUS WRITERS. New York: Knopf, 1955. Pp. 244-49.
    Despite the decline seen in THE DEATH OF THE MOTH collection (A26), the best of VW's criticism is "as distinctive as her finest novels" (i.e., MD and TL). Extract reprinted in G49.

X39 Lakshmi, Vijay. "The Unviewed Room: An Interpretation of the Room Analogy in Virginia Woolf's Critical Writings." RAJASTHAN UNIVERSITY STUDIES IN ENGLISH, 6 (1972), 64-69.
    On the feminist tracts and the critical essays. For annotation see W15.

X40 -----. "Virginia Woolf and E. M. Forster: A Study of Their Critical Relations." LITERARY HALF-YEARLY, 12, No. 2 (1971), 39-49.
    Forster's and VW's critical views of each other. Also published in BANASTHALI PATRIKA, 16 (1971), 8-18. Also see A26, G25, and H81.

X41 "'The Leaning Tower': Replies." FOLIOS OF NEW WRITING, 3 (1941), 24-46.
Four replies to VW's indictment of the embittered younger writers (1925-39) in "The Leaning Tower" (published in FOLIOS OF NEW WRITING, 3 [1940], 11-33; reprinted in THE MOMENT [A27]), by Edward Upward ("The Falling Tower," pp. 24-29), B. L. Coombes ("Below the Tower," pp. 30-36), Louis MacNiece ("The Tower that Once," pp. 37-41), and John Lehmann ("A Postscript," pp. 42-46).

X42 Lewis, Wyndham. "Virginia Woolf ('Mind' and 'Matter' on the Plane of a Literary Controversy)." In MEN WITHOUT ART. London: Cassell, 1934. Pp. 158-71.
Attacks the dimly-argued, unoriginal aestheticism of VW's "Mr. Bennett and Mrs. Brown" (A18). Extract reprinted, with supplementary materials in G49. Also see F19, F20, and H195.

X43 Leyburn, Ellen Douglass. "Virginia Woolf's Judgment of Henry James." MFS, 5 (1959), 166-69.
Surveys and explains VW's critical rejection of James (see A26), despite the similarities in their ideas of fiction.

X44 Majumdar, Robin. "Virginia Woolf and Thoreau." THOREAU SOCIETY BULLETIN, No. 109 (1969), pp. 4-5.
VW's interest in Thoreau and shared "preoccupation with 'the moment'" (viz. "Thoreau" [1917]; reprinted in A37).

X45 Manuel, M. "Virginia Woolf as the Common Reader." LITERARY CRITERION, 7, No. 2 (1966), 28-32.
Notes the connection between the chief themes of VW's two "common reader" collections (A19, A22), and "the problems she was facing in her own work as a novelist."

X46 Maurois, André. "La Jeune Littérature Anglaise." In QUATRE ÉTUDES ANGLAISES. Paris: L'Artisan du Livre 1927. Pp. 187-243.
Sees VW's "Mr. Bennett and Mrs. Brown" (A18) as a key to understanding what the "nouveaux romanciers anglais" were attempting in their fiction (cf. Forster's A PASSAGE TO INDIA [1924]). [In French.]

X47 Mercier, Michel. LE ROMAN FÉMININ. Paris: Presses Universitaires de France, 1976. Pp. 9-11, 14-17, 96-101, 158-60, and passim.
On VW's critical theories and practice in fiction. For annotation see H165.

X48 Novak, Jane. "Virginia Woolf--'A Fickle Jacobean.'" VIRGINIA WOOLF NEWSLETTER, 3 (Apr. 1972), 1-8.
Surveys VW's ambivalent respect for Henry James (and publishes an excerpt from her uncollected

review of THE GOLDEN BOWL--"Mr. Henry James's Last Novel" [1905]). Also see A26.

X49 Pacey, Desmond. "Virginia Woolf as a Literary Critic." UTQ, 17 (1948), 234-44.
  Isolates the principal standards of judgment in VW's criticism: wholeness of vision and effect in the artwork, and impersonality, a sense of values, and a respect for tradition in the artist. Praises VW as well for her contagious enjoyment of literature.

X50 Rest, Jaime. "Virginia Woolf y la función crítica." SUR, No. 238 (1956), 45-59.
  VW's conception of the critic's function is to move the reader toward an active involvement in the dynamics of literary creation, rather than an inert contemplation of the created work. [In Spanish.]

X51 Sakamoto, Tadanobu. "'Modern Novels' and 'Modern Fiction': A Study of Some Discrepancies." STUDIES IN ENGLISH LITERATURE (Tokyo), 43 (1967), 215-28.
  Sorts out the bibliographic confusion concerning two versions of VW's essay on modern fiction (in A19).

X52 Shaw, Valerie. "The Secret Companion." CRITICAL QUARTERLY, 20, No. 1 (1978), 70-77.
  Review of THE DIARY (A1) and BOOKS AND PORTRAITS (A37). For annotation see U32.

X53 Silver, Brenda R. "Introduction: The Uncommon Reader." In VIRGINIA WOOLF'S READING NOTEBOOKS. Ed. Silver. Pp. 3-31. See C10.
  Describes the formation of VW's literary views and the nature, scope, and purpose of her reading notebooks, from which her biographical, critical, and feminist writings were derived.

X54 Sloman, Judith. "Virginia Woolf's Literary History: Integrating the Obscure." VIRGINIA WOOLF QUARTERLY, 3 (1978), 230-40.
  VW's essays on neglected and obscure figures seek their relationship to major cultural figures and traditions.

X55 Swingle, L. J. "Virginia Woolf and Romantic Prometheanism." BUCKNELL REVIEW, 25, No. 2 (1980), 88-106.
  On BETWEEN THE ACTS and the essays. For annotation see S30.

X56 Wagenseil, Hans B. "Virginia Woolf und die künstlerische Aufgabe" ["Virginia Woolf and the aesthetic Problem"], DAS INSEL-SCHIFF, 11 (1930), 145-50.
    Questions whether VW's ideals for fiction (in "Mr. Bennett and Mrs. Brown" [A18]), make her the "torch-bearer" ("Fackelträger") for a great new movement in English literature. [In German.]

X57 Wellek, René. "Virginia Woolf as Critic." SOUTHERN REVIEW, 13 (1977), 419-37.
    Survey of VW's frequently acute, sometimes whimsical, but in no way "impressionistic" critical essays.

X58 Wilson, Edmund. "Virginia Woolf and Logan Pearsall Smith." NEW YORKER, 27 May 1950, pp. 99-100, 103-05.
    Unlike her more impressive fiction, VW's essays, though "beautifully written," are "a little on the surface," "monotonous," and "rather smug" (cf. Smith). Reviews THE CAPTAIN'S DEATH BED (A28).

X59 -----. "Virginia Woolf and the American Language." In THE SHORES OF LIGHT: A LITERARY CHRONICLE OF THE TWENTIES AND THIRTIES. New York: Farrar, Straus, and Giroux, 1952. Pp. 421-28.
    Describes and reprints a controversial exchange of letters on VW's distinction of English and American English in "On Not Knowing French," NEW REPUBLIC, 57 (1929), 348-49 [uncollected].

Y. STUDIES OF THE MISCELLANEOUS WRITINGS

Since there are no books, essay collections, monographs, or pamphlets on VW's miscellaneous writings (chiefly her play FRESHWATER [first published in 1976] and her translations), this section consists entirely of critical essays on these works.

For bibliographical information on FRESHWATER and the translations, see Kirkpatrick (E7), and for biographical backgrounds to the miscellaneous writings see Bell (F13) and Woolf (F100).

For the most significant additional critical commentary on VW's FRESHWATER and her translations, see Gorsky (G28) and Neuschäffer (H180). For a complete listing of commentaries on the miscellaneous writings, by title, see the concluding index: "Virginia Woolf's Works."

Y1 Lewis, Thomas S. W. "Virginia Woolf, FRESHWATER." VIRGINIA WOOLF MISCELLANY, No. 7 (1977), pp. 5-6.
    Review essay. Not seen.

Y2 Muchnic, Helen. "The Latest Phase--1922-1936." In DOSTOEVSKY'S ENGLISH REPUTATION, 1881-1936. Northhampton, Mass.: Smith College, 1939. Pp. 111-55 passim.
    VW's translation of Dostoevsky (with Koleliansky [see A17]), criticism of his work in "The Russian Point of View" (in A19), and assimilation of the "Dostoevskian tradition" in her fiction.

Y3 Richman, David. "Directing FRESHWATER." VIRGINIA WOOLF MISCELLANY, No. 2 (1974), pp. 1-2.
    Comments on the performability of VW's play. Not seen.

Y4 Ruotolo, Lucio P. "Editor's Preface." In Woolf's FRESHWATER. Ed. Ruotolo. Pp. vii-xi. See A36.
    Describes the writing and what little is known of the 1935 private performance of VW's play.

Z. DISSERTATIONS ON VIRGINIA WOOLF

The following section is a slightly annotated, international checklist of unpublished dissertations, wholly or largely concerned with VW and her works, compiled from a variety of reference sources (chiefly DISSERTATION ABSTRACTS INTERNATIONAL), through 1983. In each case, the fullest version of the dissertation title, the institution presenting the degree, and the degree date are provided. Despite the lack of any comprehensive subject index for dissertations, every attempt has been made to identify those dissertations containing significant discussions of VW, or of one or more of her works, which fail to name her or her works in their titles. Master's theses are not included here; however, a number of European theses, the academic equivalents of doctoral dissertations, have been listed. The annotations refer the user to the published dissertation abstracts and/or to any revised or unrevised publication of the dissertation, entered elsewhere in this bibliography.

Z1 Alexander, Jean. "Outsiders and Educated Men's Daughters: The Feminist as Heroine in Six Novels of Virginia Woolf." Florida State Univ., 1975.
  For abstract see DAI, 36 (1975-76), 3723A. Also see G2.

Z2 Alldredge, Betty Jean Edwards. "Levels of Consciousness: Women in the Stream of Consciousness Novels of Joyce, Woolf, and Faulkner." Univ. of Oregon, 1976.
  For abstract see DAI, 37 (1976-77), 3610A.

Z3 Apelt, Walter. "Das romantische Element in den Werken Virginia Woolfs." Univ. of Halle, 1952. [In German.]

Z4 Arkin, Stephen E. "Reluctant Moderns: A Study of E. M. Forster and Virginia Woolf." Yale Univ., 1973.
  For abstract see DAI, 34 (1973-74), 2603A.

Z5 Baillargeon, Gerald Victor. "The Logical Imagination: The Novels of Virginia Woolf." Univ. of British Columbia, 1980.
  For abstract see DAI, 42 (1981-82), 2680A.

Z6 Bain, Patricia Halligan. "Poetry into Prose: The Meaning of Writing for Virginia Woolf." Univ. of Chicago, 1972.

Z7 Baisch, Dorothy R. "London Literary Circles, 1910-1920, With Special Reference to Ford Madox Ford, Ezra Pound, D. H. Lawrence and Virginia Woolf." Cornell Univ., 1950.

Z8   Baldanza, Frank. "The Novels of Virginia Woolf." Cornell Univ., 1954.
     For abstract see DA, 14 (1953-54), 2061.

Z9   Barnett, Alan Wayne. "Who is Jacob?: The Quest for Identity in the Writings of Virginia Woolf." Columbia Univ., 1962.
     For abstract see DA, 26 (1965-66), 2742.

Z10 Barrett, Michèle. "A Theory of Modernism and English Society between the Wars, With Particular Reference to Virginia Woolf." Univ. of Sussex, 1976.

Z11 Barrette, Craig Richard. "Three Modern Novelists as Biographers: E. M. Forster, Virginia Woolf, and Evelyn Waugh." Southern Illinois Univ., Carbondale, 1977.
     For abstract see DAI, 38 (1977-78), 6137A.

Z12 Barzilai, Shulamith. "The Knot of Consciousness: The Development of the Narrative Technique of Virginia Woolf." Hebrew Univ. of Jerusalem, 1979.

Z13 Bazin, Nancy T. "The Aesthetics of Virginia Woolf." Stanford Univ., 1969.
     For abstract see DAI, 30 (1969-70), 1551A. Also see G6.

Z14 Bell, Carolyn Wilkerson. "A Study of Virginia Woolf's 'Moment of Vision.'" Univ. of Texas, 1972.
     For abstract see DAI, 34 (1973-74), 761A.

Z15 Benford, Judith Lynne. "The Evolution of the Theme and Structure of THE WAVES by Virginia Woolf." Bryn Mawr College, 1969.
     For abstract see DAI, 31 (1970-71), 381A.

Z16 Ben-Merre, Diana Arbin. "The English Moderns: A Study of the Romantic Tradition in the Novels of Virginia Woolf and E. M. Forster." City Univ. of New York, 1975.
     For abstract see DAI, 36 (1975-76), 5310A.

Z17 Berets, Ralph Adolph. "The Irrational Narrator in Virginia Woolf's THE WAVES, William Faulkner's THE SOUND AND THE FURY, and Günter Grass's THE TIN DRUM." Univ. of Michigan, 1969.
     For abstract see DAI, 31 (1970-71), 751A.

Z18 Bishop, Edward L. "Toward the Far Side of Language: A Study of Virginia Woolf's Fiction." Queen's Univ., Kingston, Ont., 1979.

Z19 Bizé, Paul. "Virginia Woolf as a Literary Artist." Univ. of Lille, 1930.

Z20 Blumenthal, Helene. "Collaboration and Contact: City Life in ULYSSES and MRS. DALLOWAY." Univ. of Pennsylvania, 1982.
     For abstract see DAI, 43 (1982-83), 2352A.

Z21 Bollas, Sara Flanders. "The Narrow Bridge of Art: A Psychoanalytic Study of Virginia Woolf's First Four Novels." State Univ. of New York, Buffalo, 1976.
For abstract see DAI, 37 (1976-77), 979A.

Z22 Bonne, Rena Barbara. "The Female Presence in the Novels of Virginia Woolf and Colette." Case Western Reserve Univ., 1979.
For abstract see DAI, 39 (1978-79), 6747A.

Z23 Boorda, Timothy F. "Virginia's People: The Vision Behind Woolf's Characters." Univ. of California, Berkeley, 1976.
For abstract see DAI, 37 (1976-77), 5814A.

Z24 Borgers, Wilhelm. "THE WAVES von Virginia Woolf: Die Untersuchung eines literarischen Experiments." Univ. of Hamburg, 1953. [In German.]

Z25 Boshoff, Philip Peter. "Virginia Woolf's Verbal Alchemy: Feeling in Form." Purdue Univ., 1980.
For abstract see DAI, 41 (1980-81), 3571A.

Z26 Bowers, Susan Rae Belle. "The Child as Mother of the Woman: Virginia Woolf's Female *Bildungsromane*." Univ. of Oregon, 1981.
For abstract see DAI, 42 (1981-81), 3607A.

Z27 Brady, E. T. "Rhythm in the Fiction of Virginia Woolf." Univ. of London, Univ. College, 1972.

Z28 Brewer, Wanda M. "Virginia Woolf and the Painter's Vision." Univ. of Northern Colorado, 1968.
For abstract see DAI, 30 (1969-70), 716A.

Z29 Brochard, Lucien. "Henry Davray, LE MERCURE DE FRANCE, et l'Angleterre." Univ. of Paris, 1953. [In French.]

Z30 Brown, Dorothy Ann Duff. "The Aesthetics of Feminism in Virginia Woolf's Fiction." Univ. of California, Berkeley, 1976.
For abstract see DAI, 38 (1977-78), 800A.

Z31 Brown, Robert Curtis. "The World of Virginia Woolf: A Study of Her View of Reality." Rutgers Univ., 1959.
For abstract see DA, 20 (1959-60), 296.

Z32 Buckley, William Kermit. "Contextualist Criticism for the Novel." Miami Univ., 1980.
Discusses BETWEEN THE ACTS. For abstract see DAI, 41 (1980-81), 2102A.

Z33 Buczek, Diane. "Stasis and Progression in the Novels of Virginia Woolf." Univ. of Chicago, 1976.

Z34 Bullock, Rebecca Roberts. "Language into Myth: The Major Fiction of Virginia Woolf." Univ. of North Carolina, 1981.
For abstract see DAI, 42 (1981-82), 3607A.

Z35 Butler, Susan Kirst. "Interior Landscapes: The Symbolist Tradition of Imagery in Selected Fiction and Poetry." Univ. of Massachusetts, 1981.
    Discusses THE WAVES. For abstract see DAI, 41 (1980-81), 5089A.

Z36 Caplan, Brina. "Radical Sensibilities: Reality and Character in Novels of Virginia Woolf, D. H. Lawrence, and Aldous Huxley." Brandeis Univ., 1980.
    For abstract see DAI, 40 (1979-80), 6287A.

Z37 Carson, Sydney. "Indefiniteness in the Novel: Jane Austen, Virginia Woolf, Gertrude Stein." Univ. of California, Berkeley, 1979.
    For abstract see DAI, 40 (1979-80), 4011A.

Z38 Chalfant, Thomas Haight. "The Marriage of Granite and Rainbow: Virginia Woolf as Biographer." Univ. of Wisconsin, 1971.
    For abstract see DAI, 32 (1971-72), 3298A. Also see Novak (E11).

Z39 Chapman, Marjorie Dunn. "Virginia Woolf's Recurrent Imagery: An Approach to the World of Her Imagination." Univ. of New Brunswick, 1970.
    For abstract see DAI, 31 (1970-71), 5391A. Also see Novak (E11).

Z40 Chau, Nguyen van. "Virginia Woolf et le temps." Univ. of Paris, 1964. [In French.]

Z41 Chessman, Harriet Scott. "Talk and Silence in the Novels of Virginia Woolf, Elizabeth Bowen, and Ivy Compton-Burnett." Yale Univ., 1979.
    For abstract see DAI, 40 (1979-80), 5872A.

Z42 Chesson, Diane Marie. "The Intellectual and Emotional Complex as an Expression of the Consciousness in Joyce, Lawrence, and Woolf." Univ. of Illinois, 1975.
    For abstract see DAI, 36 (1975-76), 6081A.

Z43 Collins, Robert G. "Four Critical Interpretations in the Modern Novel." Univ. of Denver, 1961.
    Discusses THE WAVES. For abstract see DA, 22 (1961-62), 3642.

Z44 Commenge, Béatrice. "La 'Mort' de Virginia Woolf." Univ. of Toulouse, 1974. [In French.]

Z45 Comstock, Margaret Von Szeliski. "George Meredith, Virginia Woolf, and Their Feminist Comedy." Stanford Univ., 1975.
    For abstract see DAI, 36 (1975-76), 6111A.

Z46 Condon, Thomas James. "Image as Vision: A Study of the Experimental Nature of Virginia Woolf's Early Fiction." Univ. of Rhode Island, 1978.
    For abstract see DAI, 39 (1978-79), 276A.

Z47 Conklin, Anna Marie. "Historical and Sociocultural Elements in the Novels of Virginia Woolf." Univ. of North Carolina, 1974.
   For abstract see DAI, 35 (1974-75), 3730A.

Z48 Constein, Carl Frey. "Relativity in the Novels of Virginia Woolf." Temple Univ., 1957.
   For abstract see DA, 17 (1956-57), 851.

Z49 Cordish, Penelope Sales. "The View from on High: A Study of a Metaphor of Perspective in the Work of Virginia Woolf." Johns Hopkins Univ., 1973.
   For abstract see DAI, 36 (1975-76), 7433A.

Z50 Core, Deborah Lynn. "'The Atmosphere of the Unasked Question': Women's Relationships in Modern British Fiction." Kent State Univ., 1981.
   Discusses MD. For abstract see DAI, 42 (1981-82), 2127A.

Z51 Couch, F. A. "Methods and Principles in the Literary Criticism of Virginia Woolf." Univ. of London, Birkbeck College, 1970.

Z52 Cousineau, Diane Levine. "Henry James and Virginia Woolf: A Comparative Study." Univ. of California, Davis, 1975.
   For abstract see DAI, 36 (1975-76), 8044A.

Z53 Culver, Sara Elizabeth. "Nature and Human Nature in the Major Novels of Virginia Woolf." Michigan State Univ., 1980.
   For abstract see DAI, 41 (1980-81), 5106A.

Z54 Cumings, Melinda Feldt. "Visionary Ritual in the Novels of Virginia Woolf." Univ. of Wisconsin, 1972.
   For abstract see DAI, 33 (1972-73), 3638A.

Z55 Currier, Susan. "Virginia Woolf: A Whole Vision and a Whole Aesthetic." Univ. of Massachusetts, 1979.
   For abstract see DAI, 40 (1979-80), 1480A.

Z56 Curtin, Jeremy Francis. "'Colour Burning on a Framework of Steel': Form and Identity in the Novels of Virginia Woolf." Univ. of Virginia, 1975.
   For abstract see DAI, 36 (1975-76), 2215A.

Z57 Daugherty, Beth Rigel. "Virginia Woolf's Use of Distance against Patriarchal Control of Women, Death, and Character." Rice Univ., 1982.
   For abstract see DAI, 43 (1982-83), 451A.

Z58 Davidson, Virginia Spencer. "Endowed Renderings--Biography as Literary Artifact." Harvard Univ., 1982.
   Discusses TL, ORLANDO, and ROGER FRY. For abstract see DAI, 43 (1982-83), 2353A.

Z59 Daziel, Bradford Dudley. "'The Sentence in Itself Beautiful': A Study of Virginia Woolf's Mannerist Fiction." Boston Univ., 1975.
For abstract see DAI, 36 (1975-76), 1520A.

Z60 Dean, Michael P. "The British Novel in 1914." Univ. of South Carolina, 1977.
Discusses THE VOYAGE OUT. For abstract see DAI, 38 (1977-78), 5443A.

Z61 Deiman, Werner J. "Virginia Woolf's BETWEEN THE ACTS: The Culmination of a Career and the Resolution of a Vision." Yale Univ., 1967.
For abstract see DA, 27 (1966-67), 4245A.

Z62 Dennison, Sally. "Alternative Publishing: Its Role in the Development of Twentieth-Century English-Language Literature as Seen in the Publishing Histories of T. S. Eliot's THE WASTE LAND, Virginia Woolf's JACOB'S ROOM, James Joyce's ULYSSES, Anais Nin's WINTER OF ARTIFICE and UNDER A GLASS BELL, and Vladimir Nabokov's LOLITA." Univ. of Tulsa, 1982.
For abstract see DAI, 43 (1982-83), 443A.

Z63 DeSalvo, Louise A. "From 'Melymbrosia' to THE VOYAGE OUT: A Description and Interpretation of Virginia Woolf's Revisions." New York Univ., 1977.
For abstract see DAI, 38 (1977-78), 6140A. Also see J2.

Z64 DiBattista, Maria A. "The Romance of the Self: The Early Novels of Virginia Woolf." Yale Univ., 1973.
For abstract see DAI, 34 (1973-74), 7227A. Also see G18.

Z65 DiBona, Helene Rosenberg. "The Fiction of Virginia Woolf: A Quest for Reality." Univ. of California, Berkeley, 1970.
For abstract see DAI, 31 (1970-71), 6599A. Also see Novak (E11).

Z66 Dietche, Julia Phelps. "Virginia Woolf's THE WAVES: Portrait of the Author." Univ. of North Carolina, 1977.
For abstract see DAI, 38 (1977-78), 3479A.

Z67 DiGaetani, John Louis. "Wagnerian Patterns in the Fiction of Joseph Conrad, D. H. Lawrence, Virginia Woolf and James Joyce." Univ. of Wisconsin, 1973.
For abstract see DAI, 34 (1973-74), 7745A. Also see H62.

Z68 Disbrow, Sarah Kim. "To Lyricise the Argument: Virginia Woolf, Novelist and Feminist." Univ. of Nebraska, 1982.
On THE YEARS. For abstract see DAI, 43 (1982-83), 3601A.

Z69 Druff, James Hendrick, Jr. "Artistic Self-Consciousness in the Fiction of Sterne, Joyce and Woolf." Univ. of California, Berkeley, 1979.
For abstract see DAI, 41 (1980-81), 244A.

Z70 Dyrud, Marilyn Ann. "Rendering the Veil: Dreams in Five Novels by Virginia Woolf." Purdue Univ., 1980.
For abstract see DAI, 42 (1981-82), 224A.

Z71 Eiland, Howard Avery. "Double Vision in Conrad, Woolf, and Mann." Yale Univ., 1974.
For abstract see DAI, 35 (1974-75), 7300A.

Z72 Eirich, Susan Helen. "Lire au féminin: Une Étude du discours féminin dans les romans de Duras, Woolf, et Sarraute." State Univ. of New York, Buffalo, 1978. [In French.]
For abstract see DAI, 39 (1978-79), 1617A.

Z73 Eisenberg, Nora Gene. "'The Far Side of Language': The Search for Expression in the Novels of Virginia Woolf." Columbia Univ., 1976.
For abstract see DAI, 40 (1979-80), 247A.

Z74 Ferebee, Robert Steven. "Virginia Woolf as an Essayist." Univ. of New Mexico, 1981.
For abstract see DAI, 42 (1981-82), 4832A.

Z75 Flaherty, Luke. "Woman as Peacemaker in Virginia Woolf's Novels." Univ. of Iowa, 1977.
For abstract see DAI, 38 (1977-78), 4178A.

Z76 Fleming, Bruce Edward. "Modernism and its Discontents: Twentieth Century Literary Theory from Point of View of the Work of Art." Vanderbilt Univ., 1982.
Discusses VW. For abstract see DAI, 43 (1982-83), 1137A.

Z77 Flynn, Elizabeth Ann. "Feminist Critical Theory: Three Models." Ohio State Univ., 1977.
Discusses MD. For abstract see DAI, 38 (1977-78), 4842A.

Z78 Fox, Stephen Douglas. "The Novels of Virginia Woolf and Nathalie Sarraute." Emory Univ., 1970.
For abstract see DAI, 31 (1970-71), 5399A. Also see Novak (E11).

Z79 Freeman, Alma Susan. "The Androgynous Ideal: A Study of Selected Novels by D. H. Lawrence, James Joyce, and Virginia Woolf." Rutgers Univ., 1974.
For abstract see DAI, 36 (1975-76), 877A.

Z80 Frye, Joanne M. S. "Toward a Form for Paradox: Image and Idea in the Novels of Virginia Woolf." Indiana Univ., 1974.
For abstract see DAI, 35 (1974-75), 4518A.

Z81 Gairdner, William Douglas. "Consciousness in the Novels of Virginia Woolf." Stanford Univ., 1970.
For abstract see DAI, 31 (1970-71), 6055A.

Z82 Gallagher, Sarah Van Sickle. "The Fiction of the Self: Virginia Woolf and the Problem of Biography." State Univ. of New York, Buffalo, 1979.
For abstract see DAI, 39 (1978-79), 7339A.

Z83 Galton, John. "The Desertion of Character in Virginia Woolf's Novels." Univ. of Rochester, 1967.
For abstract see DA, 28 (1967-68), 1734A.

Z84 Gay, P. D. "Nineteenth-Century Ideas in the Novels of E. M. Forster and Virginia Woolf: Some Literary Sources." Univ. of London, Univ. College, 1975.

Z85 Gibson, Mary Virginia. "Event and Consciousness in Certain Novels of Henry James and Virginia Woolf." Univ. of Chicago, 1976.

Z86 Gillen, Francis X. "The Relationship of Rhetorical Control to Meaning in the Novels of Henry James, Virginia Woolf, and E. M. Forster." Fordham Univ., 1969.
For abstract see DAI, 30 (1969-70), 1525A.

Z87 Gleiter, Karin Jill. "Similes in Virginia Woolf's Fiction: THE VOYAGE OUT, TO THE LIGHTHOUSE, THE WAVES, BETWEEN THE ACTS." Univ. of North Carolina, 1977.
For abstract see DAI, 39 (1978-79), 295A.

Z88 Godwin, Janet Lynn. "Virginia Woolf: Moments of Vision in MRS. DALLOWAY, TO THE LIGHTHOUSE, and BETWEEN THE ACTS." Univ. of Texas, 1980.
For abstract see DAI, 41 (1980-81), 3102A.

Z89 Goetsch, Robert S. "Critical Methodologies: Jungianism and Structuralism." Univ. of Nebraska, 1978.
Discusses MD. For abstract see DAI, 39 (1978-79), 6745A.

Z90 Gohrbandt, Detlev. "Aspekte der Heldenfunktion in den Romanen von George Eliot, Henry James, und Virginia Woolf." Univ. of Saarbrücken, 1975. [In German.]
For abstract see DAI, 37 (1976-77), 3213C.

Z91 Goldman, Mark. "Virginia Woolf and the Art of Criticism." Univ. of Minnesota, 1959.
For abstract see DA, 20 (1959-60), 4111. Also see X1.

Z92 Goldsmith, Bonnie Zucker. "The Enormous Burden of the Unexpressed: Language as Theme in the Novels of Virginia Woolf." Ohio State Univ., 1978.
For abstract see DAI, 39 (1978-79), 4936A.

Z93 Goodenough, Elizabeth N. "Marvellous are the Innocent: A Study of Youth in Virginia Woolf." Harvard Univ., 1982. For abstract see DAI, 43 (1982-83), 2997A.

Z94 Gorsky, Susan. "'The Central Shadow': Dualism in Form and Meaning in THE WAVES." Case Western Reserve Univ., 1969. For abstract see DAI, 30 (1969-70), 3943A.

Z95 Gottlieb, Sidney Paul. "I. Textual and Contextual Revision in Herbert's THE TEMPLE; II. Criticism as Dialectics: Johnson and the Example of Dryden; III. 'Life and Death, Sanity and Insanity': A Reading of MRS. DALLOWAY." Rutgers Univ., 1974. For abstract see DAI, 35 (1974-75), 6666A.

Z96 Graham, John W. "The Mind and Art of Virginia Woolf." Univ. of Toronto, 1953.

Z97 Graves, Allen Wallace. "Difficult Contemporary Short Stories: William Faulkner, Katherine Anne Porter, Dylan Thomas, Eudora Welty and Virginia Woolf." Univ. of Washington, 1954. For abstract see DA, 14 (1953-54), 2067.

Z98 Grove-White, E. M. "The Uncommon Reader: Virginia Woolf's Aesthetic of the Novel." Univ. of Dublin, 1981. For abstract see DAI, 43 (1982), 689C.

Z99 Gupta, Linda R. "Fathers and Daughters in Women's Novels (Jane Austen, Gaskell, Charlotte Bronte, Kate Chopin, Edith Wharton, Woolf, Bowen, Atwood, Mary Gordon)." American Univ., 1983. Discusses TL. For abstract see DAI, 44 (1983-84), 1783A.

Z100 Hackenberg, Heide. "Das Wirklichkeitserlebnis in den Werken Virginia Woolfs." Friburg Univ., 1957. [In German.]

Z101 Hafley, James. "Virginia Woolf as Novelist." Univ. of California, Berkeley, 1952. See G31.

Z102 Haller, Evelyn Harris. "The Search for Life Itself: Characterization and its Relation to Form in the Novels of Virginia Woolf." Emory Univ., 1968. For abstract see DA, 29 (1968-69), 3140A.

Z103 Hamwee, L. A. "The Impact of English Post-Impressionism and the Aesthetics of Pure Form on Virginia Woolf's Fiction." Univ. of London, King's College, 1973.

Z104 Hanquart, Evelyn. "Trois Romanciers anglais contemporains: A la recherche d'un humanisme: D. H. Lawrence, V. Woolf, E. M. Forster." Sorbonne, 1970. [In French.]

Z105 Harakas, Theodore. "Dualism in the Novels of Virginia Woolf." Michigan State Univ., 1982. For abstract see DAI, 43 (1982-83), 1553A.

Z106 Haule, James Mark. "The Theme of Isolation in the Fiction of Dorothy M. Richardson, Virginia Woolf, and James Joyce." Wayne State Univ., 1974.
    For abstract see DAI, 35 (1974-75), 7905A.

Z107 Henig, Suzanne. "The Literary Criticism of Virginia Woolf." New York Univ., 1968.
    For abstract see DAI, 30 (1969-70), 328A.

Z108 Hill, Katherine Cicelia. "Virginia Woolf and Leslie Stephen: A Study in Mentoring and Literary Criticism." Columbia Univ., 1979.
    For abstract see DAI, 40 (1979-80), 1459A.

Z109 Hilsinger, Serena Sue. "Insubstantial Pageant: A Reading of Virginia Woolf's Novels." Univ. of Connecticut, 1964.
    For abstract see DA, 25 (1964-65), 4700.

Z110 Hungerford, Edward A. "The Narrow Bridge of Art: Virginia Woolf's Early Criticism, 1905-1925." New York Univ., 1960.
    For abstract see DA, 21 (1960-61), 2295.

Z111 Isenberg, Aloysia. "Studien zur Erzählkunst Virginia Woolf." Univ. of Mainz, 1952. [In German.]

Z112 Jewison, Donald Bruce. "Virginia Woolf: 'Reforming' the Novel Through Imagery." Univ. of Manitoba, 1974.
    For abstract see DAI, 35 (1974-75), 6142A.

Z113 Johnstone, J. K. "The Philosophic Background and Works of Art of the Group Known as 'Bloomsbury.'" Univ. of Leeds, 1952.
    See H126.

Z114 Julien, Hershey. "Virginia Woolf: Post-Impressionist Novelist." Univ. of New Mexico, 1968.
    For abstract see DA, 29 (1968-69), 4490A.

Z115 Kaplan, Sydney Janet. "The Feminine Consciousness in the Novels of Five Twentieth Century British Women." Univ. of California, Los Angeles, 1971.
    Discusses MD and TL. For abstract see DAI, 32 (1971-72), 4615A. Also see M43.

Z116 Katz, Judith N. "Rooms of Their Own: Forms and Images of Liberation in Five Novels." Pennsylvania State Univ., 1972.
    Discusses THE WAVES. For abstract see DAI, 34 (1973-74), 1283A.

Z117 Katz, Linda Sternberg. "A Rhetorical Analysis of Virginia Woolf's Feminist Tracts and Her Novels." Rensselaer Polytechnic Institute, 1976.
    For abstract see DAI, 37 (1976-77), 3266A.

Z118 Kelley, Alice van Buren. "Fact and Vision: A Study of the Novels of Virginia Woolf." City Univ. of New York, 1971.
For abstract see DAI, 32 (1971-72), 4615A. Also see Novak (E11) and G38.

Z119 Kenney, Susan McIlvaine. "Fin in the Water: A Study of Virginia Woolf." Cornell Univ., 1968.
For abstract see DA, 29 (1968-69), 4004A.

Z120 King, Merton Pruett. "The Price of Awareness: Virginia Woolf as a Practitioner-Critic." Univ. of Texas, 1962.
For abstract see DA, 23 (1962-63), 1704.

Z121 Kneubuhl, Barbara Jean. "Channel Crossings: Virginia Woolf in France, 1920-1977." Univ. of Massachusetts, 1979.
For abstract see DAI, 40 (1979-80), 1452A.

Z122 Kröger, Helmut. "Die Essays Virginia Woolfs." Univ. of Kiel, 1955. [In German.]

Z123 Kumar, Shiv K. "Bergson and the Stream of Consciousness Novel." Cambridge Univ., 1956.
See H133.

Z124 Kush, Katherine Davidson. "Virginia Woolf and F. H. Bradley: Metaphysical Idealism in Fiction and Philosophy." Univ. of Michigan, 1976.
For abstract see DAI, 37 (1976-77), 6500A.

Z125 Lampl, Nancy Williams. "The Decomposing Form: Studies in Faulkner, Woolf and Beckett." Case Western Reserve Univ., 1976.
For abstract see DAI, 37 (1976-77), 7735A.

Z126 Laskin, Miriam Meryl. "The Evolution of Virginia Woolf's Visionary Histories: THE YEARS and BETWEEN THE ACTS." State Univ. of New York, Stony Brook, 1979.
For abstract see DAI, 40 (1979-80), 833A.

Z127 Latham, Jacqueline E. M. "The Evolution of Virginia Woolf's MRS. DALLOWAY, With Special Reference to B. M. Add. MS. 51044-46." Univ. of London, King's College, 1968.

Z128 Laurans, Penelope. "Fictions about Fictions: The Study of a Modern Literary Development in the Novels of Virginia Woolf." Harvard Univ., 1975.

Z129 Leaska, Mitchell A. "The Rhetoric of Multiple Points of View in Selected Contemporary Novels." New York Univ., 1968.
Discusses TL. For abstract see DA, 29 (1968-69), 3145A.

Z130 L'Enfant, Julie. "Edith Wharton and Virginia Woolf: Tradition and Experiment in the Modern Novel." Louisiana State Univ., 1974.
For abstract see DAI, 35 (1974-75), 4531A.

Dissertations

Z131 Levenback, Karen L. "A Chasm in a Smooth Road: A Study of the Effect of the Great War on Virginia Woolf." Univ. of Maryland, 1981.
For abstract see DAI, 43 (1982-83), 809A.

Z132 Lewis, Edward William. "Frame and Axis: The Control of Psychological and Formal Levels of Meaning in MRS. DALLOWAY, TO THE LIGHTHOUSE, and THE WAVES." Temple Univ., 1977.
For abstract see DAI, 37 (1976-77), 7763A.

Z133 Lewis, F. C. "Significant Deformity: Art and Life in Virginia Woolf's Novels and Art Criticism." Univ. of Edinburgh, 1975.

Z134 Lilienfeld, Jane. "The Necessary Journey: Virginia Woolf's Voyage to the Lighthouse." Brandeis Univ., 1975.
For abstract see DAI, 36 (1975-76), 321A.

Z135 Limburg, Kay L. B. "ORLANDO: A BIOGRAPHY by Virginia Woolf: A Stylistic Analysis Based on Speech Act Theory, Case Grammar, and Women's Language Theory." Univ. of Tennessee, 1983.
For abstract see DAI, 44 (1983-84), 1011A.

Z136 Lindau, Bertha L. "Feminism in the English Novel: George Eliot, Virginia Woolf, Doris Lessing." Univ. of South Carolina, 1979.
For abstract see DAI, 40 (1979-80), 1483A.

Z137 Ludwig, Alvin Karl. "Lyric Form in the Modern Novel." Univ. of California, Berkeley, 1979.
Discusses MD and TL. For abstract see DAI, 40 (1979-80), 4028A.

Z138 Lukens, Cynthia Diane. "The Woman Artist's Journey: Self-Consciousness in the Novels of Virginia Woolf." Univ. of Washington, 1981.
For abstract see DAI, 42 (1981-82), 1648A.

Z139 Lyngstad, Sverre. "Time in the Modern British Novel: Conrad, Woolf, Joyce, and Huxley." New York Univ., 1960.
For abstract see DA, 27 (1966-67), 1374A.

Z140 Lyon, George Ella Hoskins. "The Dilemma of the Body in Virginia Woolf and E. M. Forster." Indiana Univ., 1978.
For abstract see DAI, 39 (1978-79), 873A.

Z141 Lyon, Mary Copeland. "Virginia Woolf as a Critic." Radcliffe College, 1957.

Z142 McClusky, Kathleen M. "Reverberations: Sound and Structure in the Novels of Virginia Woolf." Brandeis Univ., 1983.
For abstract see DAI, 44 (1983-84), 1083A.

Z143 McKillop, Laurence Terese. "The Process of Critical Articulation: Narrator, Character, and Symbol in Virginia Woolf." Univ. of Virginia, 1980.
For abstract see DAI, 41 (1980-81), 2125A.

Z144 McLaughlin, Ann Landis. "A Fin in a Waste of Waters: A Study of Symbolic Transformation in THE WAVES by Virginia Woolf." American Univ., 1978.
For abstract see DAI, 39 (1978-79), 298A.

Z145 McLaurin, Allen. "Aesthetics and Bloomsbury, With Special Reference to the Works of Virginia Woolf." Univ. of Wales, Cardiff, 1971.
See G48.

Z146 McNett, Jeanne M. "Virginia Woolf on Biography: Theory and Praxis." Univ. of Massachusetts, 1980.
For abstract see DAI, 41 (1980-81), 1065A.

Z147 Madison, Elizabeth Christen. "Reality and Imagery in the Novels of Virginia Woolf and Nathalie Sarraute." Indiana Univ., 1974.
For abstract see DAI, 34 (1973-74), 7765A.

Z148 Mahoney, Jeanne Noel. "The Vision of Unity: A Study of MRS. DALLOWAY." State Univ. of New York, Buffalo, 1978.
For abstract see DAI, 39 (1978-79), 1594A.

Z149 Majumdar, Robin. "The Critical Reception of Virginia Woolf's Novels, 1915-1960." Univ. of London, Queen Mary College, 1968.

Z150 Marder, Herbert. "The Androgynous Mind: Feminism in the Works of Virginia Woolf." Columbia Univ., 1964.
For abstract see DA, 28 (1967-68), 1440A. Also see G53.

Z151 Mares, Cheryl Jean. "'Another Space of Time': The Dominion of Painting in Proust and Woolf." Princeton Univ., 1982.
For abstract see DAI, 42 (1981-82), 4821A.

Z152 Marshall, Peggy Ann. "Private Vision Made Public: Style and Structure in Four Novels by Virginia Woolf." Indiana Univ., 1978.
For abstract see DAI, 39 (1978-79), 6779A.

Z153 Matro, Thomas Gaetano. "Life as Creative Activity in the Early Novels of Virginia Woolf." Rutgers Univ., 1975.
For abstract see DAI, 36 (1975-76), 905A.

Z154 Meisel, Perry. "Virginia Woolf: A Poetics of Character." Yale Univ., 1975.
For abstract see DAI, 37 (1976-77), 336A. Also see X3.

Z155 Mendez, Charlotte Walker. "Language Mystery and Selfhood in the Novels of Virginia Woolf." Syracuse Univ., 1972.
For abstract see DAI, 34 (1973-74), 1287A.

Z156 Meyerowitz, Selma S. "Class Perspectives and the Works of Virginia Woolf." Wayne State Univ., 1975.
For abstract see DAI, 36 (1975-76), 7442A.

Z157 Mor, Samuel. "An Inquiry into Madness: The Meaning of Madness in the Works of Virginia Woolf, André Breton, and Y. H. Brenner." Univ. of Southern California, 1979.
    For abstract see DAI, 40 (1979-80), 2049A.

Z158 Morgenstern, Barry Stephen. "Like a Work of Art: The Narrative Voices in the Novels of Virginia Woolf." Pennsylvania State Univ., 1971.
    For abstract see DAI, 32 (1971-72), 6443A.

Z159 Morris, Caryl Anne. "Motives for Metaphor in the Fiction of Marcel Proust, Virginia Woolf, and Robert Musil." Brown Univ., 1980.
    For abstract see DAI, 41 (1980-81), 5092A.

Z160 Naremore, James O. "The World Without a Self: Style in the Novels of Virginia Woolf." Univ. of Wisconsin, 1970.
    For abstract see DAI, 31 (1970-71), 1283A. Also see Novak (E11) and G59.

Z161 Neilen, Deirdre. "The Search for Intimacy: Feminist Reconciliations in the Fiction of Virginia Woolf." Syracuse Univ., 1980.
    For abstract see DAI, 41 (1980-81), 3594A.

Z162 Neubert, Albrecht. "Die Entwicklung der 'erlebten Rede' in bürgerlichen englischen Roman von Jane Austen bis Virginia Woolf." Univ. of Leipzig, 1955.

Z163 Novak, Jane. "The Search for the Razor Edge of Balance: The Shaping Principle of Virginia Woolf's Fiction and Criticism." Univ. of Chicago, 1971.
    See G62.

Z164 Olson, S. B. "The History of the Hogarth Press, 1917-1923: A Biographical Study, With Critical Discussion of Selected Publications." Univ. of London, Royal Holloway College, 1973.

Z165 Otte, George Frederick, III. "The Loss of History in the Modern British Novel." Stanford Univ., 1982.
    Discusses THE YEARS and BETWEEN THE ACTS. For abstract see DAI, 43 (1982-83), 1144A.

Z166 Overstreet, Linda K. "'This Globe, Full of Figures': An Archetypal Study of Virginia Woolf's THE WAVES." Univ. of Arkansas, 1982.
    For abstract see DAI, 43 (1982-83), 3316A.

Z167 Parasuram, Laxmi. "Virginia Woolf: The Treatment of Natural Phenomena in Six Novels." Univ. of Kentucky, 1972.
    For abstract see DAI, 33 (1972-73), 5741A. Also see G64.

Z168 Park, Hee-Jin. "The Search Beneath Appearances: The Novels of Virginia Woolf and Nathalie Sarraute." Indiana Univ., 1979.
    For abstract see DAI, 40 (1979-80), 5433A.

Z169 Paskoff, Louis. "The Artist-Hero in the Works of Six Modern Novelists." Univ. of Michigan, 1972.
Discusses TL. For abstract see DAI, 33 (1972-73), 5192A.

Z170 Peck, Ellen Margaret McKee. "Exploring the Feminine: A Study of Janet Lewis, Ellen Glasgow, Anais Nin, and Virginia Woolf." Stanford Univ., 1974.
For abstract see DAI, 35 (1974-75), 3761A.

Z171 Penman, M. E. "Moments of Apperception in the Modern Novel: A Study of Henry James, Virginia Woolf, E. M. Forster, and James Joyce Related to Psychiatric and Philosophic Developments in the Late Nineteenth and Early Twentieth Centuries." Univ. of London, Univ. College, 1966.

Z172 Peternel, Joan. "Doubling the Hero and the Bride: Four Modern Quest Novels." Indiana Univ., 1981.
Discusses TL. For abstract see DAI, 42 (1981-82), 3156A.

Z173 Phillips, Anne Heiberg. "'The Anonymous Self': A Study of Virginia Woolf's Novels." Stanford Univ., 1971.
For abstract see DAI, 32 (1971-72), 5801A.

Z174 Poirier, Suzanne. "Characterization and Theory of Personality in the Novels of Virginia Woolf." Univ. of Nebraska, 1978.
For abstract see DAI, 40 (1979-80), 275A.

Z175 Poresky, Louise Ann. "The Elusive Self: Psyche and Spirit in Virginia Woolf's Novels." Drew Univ., 1977.
For abstract see DAI, 38 (1977-78), 2779A. Also see G66.

Z176 Proudfit, Sharon L. "The Fact and the Vision: Virginia Woolf and Roger Fry's Post-Impressionist Aesthetic." Univ. of Michigan, 1967.
For abstract see DA, 28 (1967-68), 5066A.

Z177 Radbil, Alexandra. "Impressionism and Virginia Woolf." Florida State Univ., 1979.
For abstract see DAI, 40 (1979-80), 3292A.

Z178 Radin, Grace Pauline. "THE YEARS by Virginia Woolf: The Evolution of a Novel." City Univ. of New York, 1977.
For abstract see DAI, 38 (1977-78), 4161A. Also see R3.

Z179 Rahman, Shaista. "Virginia Woolf and Reality: The Artist, the Intellectual and the Mystic in the Novels." City Univ. of New York, 1973.
For abstract see DAI, 34 (1973-74), 3428A.

Z180   Raina, M. L. "The Use of the Symbol by English Novelists, 1900-1930, With Particular Reference to E. M. Forster, D. H. Lawrence, and Virginia Woolf." Univ. of Manchester, 1965.

Z181   Rakowsky, Christine Hirniak. "To Inhabit Eternity: Virginia Woolf's Coming to Terms with Death." Case Western Reserve Univ., 1978.
        For abstract see DAI, 38 (1977-78), 7315A.

Z182   Rea, P. S. L. "A Study of the Figure of the Artist in the Novels of Virginia Woolf." Univ. of London, Royal Holloway College, 1979.

Z183   Rettig, Cynthia Bestoso. "The Continuing Battle Against the Philistines: Virginia Woolf's Cultural Criticism." Univ. of Michigan, 1980.
        For abstract see DAI, 41 (1980-81), 682A.

Z184   Rey, Jean. "The Evolution of Mrs. Woolf's Technique and Style." Univ. of Lille, 1930.

Z185   Richardson, Robert O. "Virginia Woolf's THE WAVES: A Reading." Cornell Univ., 1969.
        For abstract see DAI, 30 (1969-70), 3955A.

Z186   Richter, Harvena A. "Modes of Subjectivity in the Novels of Virginia Woolf." New York Univ., 1967.
        For abstract see DAI, 31 (1970-71), 1239A. Also see G69.

Z187   Rigney, Barbara H. "Madness and Sexual Politics in the Feminist Novel: Studies of Charlotte Bronte, Virginia Woolf, and Doris Lessing." Ohio State Univ., 1977.
        For abstract see DAI, 38 (1977-78), 6749A. Also see M68.

Z188   Ringler, Susan Jane. "Narrators and Narrative Contexts in Fiction." Stanford Univ., 1982.
        For abstract see DAI, 42 (1981-82), 4821A.

Z189   Robinson, Deborah Sue. "'Frigidity' and the Aesthetic Vision: A Study of Karen Horney and Virginia Woolf." Univ. of Rochester, 1974.
        For abstract see DAI, 35 (1974-75), 2294A.

Z190   Rock, Marcia Lynn. "Electronic Storytelling: A Study of Narrative Techniques in the Novel and Video Adaptation of TO THE LIGHTHOUSE." New York Univ., 1981.
        For abstract see DAI, 43 (1982-83), 454A.

Z191   Rogat, Ellen. "The Lifted Veil: Virginia Woolf and Women's Consciousness." Stanford Univ., 1974.

Z192   Rosen, Amy. "The Pulse of Colour: A Study of Virginia Woolf." State Univ. of New York, Buffalo, 1981.
        For abstract see DAI, 42 (1981-82), 1650A.

Z193 Rubenstein, Roberta. "Virginia Woolf's Response to Russian Literature." Univ. of London, Birkbeck College, 1969.

Z194 Runyan, Elizabeth. "Escape for the Self: An Interpretation of E. M. Forster, D. H. Lawrence, and Virginia Woolf." Kent State Univ., 1970.
    For abstract see DAI, 31 (1970-71), 5423A.

Z195 Ruppel, James Robert. "Narcissus Observed: The Pastoral Elegiac in Woolf, Faulkner, Fitzgerald, and Graeme Gibson." Univ. of Toronto, 1977.
    For abstract see DAI, 39 (1978-79), 4249A.

Z196 Sacks, Majorie Consuelo Hamilton. "The Starling Pelted Tree: Image and Idea in the Novels of Virginia Woolf." Northwestern Univ., 1955.
    For abstract see DA, 15 (1954-55), 2534.

Z197 Samuelson, Ralph. "Virginia Woolf as Critic." Univ. of Washington, 1956.
    For abstract see DA, 16 (1955-56), 2459.

Z198 Satz, Murray E. "Virginia Woolf as a Literary Critic." Boston Univ., 1951.

Z199 Schaefer, Josephine O'Brien. "The Three-Fold Nature of Reality in the Novels of Virginia Woolf." Stanford Univ., 1962.
    For abstract see DA, 23 (1962-63), 238. Also see G75.

Z200 Scheiber, Howard Jeffrey. "Functions of Imagery in Virginia Woolf's THE WAVES: A Study of the Language and Rhetoric of the Text." New York Univ., 1978.
    For abstract see DAI, 39 (1978-79), 2263A.

Z201 Schlack, Beverly Ann. "Literary Allusions in Selected Novels of Virginia Woolf: A Study in Criticism." New York Univ., 1974.
    For abstract see DAI, 35 (1974-75), 3008A. Also see G76.

Z202 Schulkind, Jean. "Virginia Woolf, Novelist." Univ. of Sussex, 1971.

Z203 Schwartz, Nina E. "Dead Fathers: The Discourses of Modernist Authority." Univ. of California, Irvine, 1983.
    Includes Conrad, James, Hemingway, and VW. For abstract see DAI, 44 (1983-84), 488A.

Z204 Seltzer, Alvin J. "Chaos in the Novel: The Novel in Chaos." Pennsylvania State Univ., 1970.
    Discusses TL. For abstract see DAI, 32 (1971-72), 984A. Also see Novak (E11) and N88.

Z205 Sengelli, Nazan Feride. "Literary Continuity Traced through the Progression in the Use of Time in Wordsworth, Faulkner, Virginia Woolf, T. S. Eliot, and Yeats." George Peabody College, 1977.
For abstract see DAI, 38 (1977-78), 2766A.

Z206 Shabka, Margaret Collins. "The Writer's Search for Identity: A Redefinition of the Feminine Personality from Virginia Woolf to Margaret Drabble and Doris Lessing." Kent State Univ., 1981.
For abstract see DAI, 42 (1981-82), 3613A.

Z207 Shanahan, Mary S. "Order and Chaos in the Novels of Virginia Woolf." Univ. of Wisconsin, 1970.
For abstract see DAI, 31 (1970-71), 1292A. Also see Novak (E11).

Z208 Shields, Ellen F. "Characterization in the Novels of Virginia Woolf." Univ. of Illinois, 1966.
For abstract see DA, 27 (1966-67), 3880A.

Z209 Siek, Barbara L. "Virginia Woolf's Theory of Fiction." Univ. of Chicago, 1980.

Z210 Silver, Brenda R. "Virginia Woolf and the Elizabethans: A Study of her Elizabethan Criticism in the Context of her Growth as Critic and Novelist." Harvard Univ., 1973.

Z211 Simmons, Sarah Brey. "The Linguistic Analysis of a Literary Text: Virginia Woolf: 'The Russian Point of View.'" State Univ. of New York, Buffalo, 1979.
For abstract see DAI, 40 (1979-80), 5036A.

Z212 Smith, Michael Allan. "The Personality of the Essayist: Virginia Woolf and Thomas Mann." Univ. of Oregon, 1974.
For abstract see DAI, 35 (1974-75), 3772A.

Z213 Snow, Lotus. "Imagery in Virginia Woolf's Novels." Univ. of Chicago, 1949.

Z214 Spangler, Ellen Stewart. "The Book as Image: Medieval Form in the Modern Spatialized Novel of Marcel Proust and his Contemporaries." Univ. of New Mexico, 1976.
Discusses TL. For abstract see DAI, 37 (1976-77), 2865A.

Z215 Speltz, Ann Linda. "THE VOYAGE OUT and Virginia Woolf's Struggle for Autonomy: Imagery of Separation and Dependency." State Univ. of New York, Stony Brook, 1982.
For abstract see DAI, 43 (1982-83), 3606A.

Z216 Squier, Susan M. "The Politics of Street Haunting: Virginia Woolf and the City." Stanford Univ., 1977.
For abstract see DAI, 38 (1977-78), 5468A.

Dissertations

Z217 Steinberg, Lois. "Voice and Vision in the Lyrical Fiction of Virginia Woolf." McGill Univ., 1967.

Z218 Sterk, Kay Puttock. "Autobiographical Fiction: Virginia Woolf and D. H. Lawrence." Brandeis Univ., 1981.
    For abstract see DAI, 42 (1981-82), 699A.

Z219 Strong, Paul. "The Light in the Garden: Imagery in MRS. DALLOWAY, TO THE LIGHTHOUSE, and THE WAVES." Univ. of Wisconsin, 1973.
    For abstract see DAI, 35 (1974-75), 483A.

Z220 Stuber, Carol Ann. "Secular Immortality in Three Novels by E. M. Forster and Virginia Woolf." St. John's Univ., 1982.
    For abstract see DAI, 42 (1981-82), 5132A.

Z221 Studley, Grace MacFarlane. "THE VOYAGE OUT and THE WAVES: Revelations of the Structure of Being in the Novels of Virginia Woolf." Univ. of Southern California, 1976.
    For abstract see DAI, 37 (1976-77), 2206A.

Z222 Sudrann, Jean. "The Sea, the City, and the Clock: A Study of Symbolic Form in the Novels of Virginia Woolf." Columbia Univ., 1950.
    For abstract see DA, 11 (1950-51), 354.

Z223 Sukenick, Lynn. "Sense and Sensibility in Women's Fiction: Studies in the Novels of George Eliot, Virginia Woolf, Anais Nin, and Doris Lessing." City Univ. of New York, 1974.
    For abstract see DAI, 35 (1974-75), 4563A.

Z224 Swanson, Janice M. Bowman. "Speaking in a Mother Tongue: Female Friendship in the British Novel." Univ. of California, Santa Barbara, 1981.
    Discusses MD. For abstract see DAI, 43 (1982-83), 174A.

Z225 Taylor, Nancy McKeon. "Conscious Construction: The Concept of Plot in Five Novels by Women." Loyola Univ. of Chicago, 1977.
    Discusses THE WAVES. For abstract see DAI, 38 (1977-78), 2115A.

Z226 Thayer, Jacqueline Gaillet. "Virginia Woolf: From Impressionism to Abstract Art." Univ. of Tulsa, 1977.
    For abstract see DAI, 38 (1977-78), 1419A.

Z227 Tilberry, Joanne Howland. "The Literary Method of Virginia Woolf: A Phenomenological Approach." Case Western Reserve Univ., 1982.
    For abstract see DAI, 43 (1982-83), 1984A.

Z228 Tobin, Gloria Jean. "Virginia Woolf's THE WAVES and THE YEARS as Novel of Vision and Novel of Fact." Univ. of Wisconsin, 1973.
    For abstract see DAI, 35 (1974-75), 483A.

Z229 Transue, Pamela Jean. "Feminism and Fiction: The Aesthetic Dilemma: A Study of Virginia Woolf." Ohio State Univ., 1981.
For abstract see DAI, 42 (1981-82), 4463A.

Z230 Trivedi, H. K. "Virginia Woolf and the Tradition of the English Novel: A Study of Her Criticism." Univ. of Wales, Bangor, 1975.

Z231 Tudor, Kathleen. "The Androgynous Mind in W. B. Yeats, D. H. Lawrence, Virginia Woolf, and Dorothy Richardson." Univ. of Toronto, 1972.
For abstract see DAI, 35 (1974-75), 1126A.

Z232 Vanderwerff, Whitney Grove. "Virginia Woolf as Equilibrist: The Moment of Vision and the Androgynous Mind." Univ. of North Carolina, Greensboro, 1978.
For abstract see DAI, 39 (1978-79), 3606A.

Z233 VanHorn, Geraldine Kloos. "The Image of the City in the Early Twentieth-Century Novel: Studies of Conrad, James, Woolf, and Joyce." Ohio State Univ., 1978.
For abstract see DAI, 39 (1978-79), 4943A.

Z234 Venit, James S. "The Breakdown of Narrative Form and Authority in Modern Fiction: A Study of Some Texts of Conrad, Woolf, and Freud." Columbia Univ., 1976.
For abstract see DAI, 37 (1976-77), 3655A.

Z235 Vogelsang, John Daniel. "The Wave of Self in Time to Break: D. H. Lawrence and Virginia Woolf." State Univ. of New York, Buffalo, 1974.
For abstract see DAI, 35 (1974-75), 1677A.

Z236 Walter, Margot. "Strukturanalysen von Romanen Virginia Woolfs." Univ. of Bonn, 1952. [In German.]

Z237 Warner, E. D. "Some Aspects of Romanticism in the Works of Virginia Woolf." Oxford Univ., 1980.

Z238 Webb, Igor. "Sense and Sensibility: A Study of the Influence of English Aesthetics from Ruskin to Roger Fry on Ford Madox Ford and Virginia Woolf." Stanford Univ., 1971.
For abstract see DAI, 32 (1971-72), 4638A. Also see Novak (E11).

Z239 Weems, Benjamin Francis, III. "Virginia Woolf's Use of Imagery in her Search for Values." Columbia Univ., 1962.
For abstract see DA, 26 (1965-66), 2764.

Z240 Weinberger, Sylvia Zina. "Transition in Some Modern Novels: Gustave Flaubert, George Moore, and Virginia Woolf." City Univ. of New York, 1981.
For abstract see DAI, 42 (1981-82), 1139A.

Z241 White, Richard Lupton. "The Novelist as Critic: Conrad, Forster, Woolf, and Lawrence." Univ. of Pennsylvania, 1977.
For abstract see DAI, 38 (1977-78), 4856A.

Z242 White, Robert Finis, Jr. "The Literary Reputation of Virginia Woolf: A History of British Attitudes Toward her Work, 1915-1955." Univ. of Pennsylvania, 1959.
For abstract see DA, 20 (1959-60), 309.

Z243 Whitehead, J. "A Study of the Relationship between Virginia Woolf's Novels and the Intellectual Interests of her Time." Oxford Univ., 1979.

Z244 Wicht, Wolfgang. "Der isolierte Protest: Kunstkonzeptionen und Künstler bei Virginia Woolf, James Joyce, und T. S. Eliot." Univ. of Potsdam, 1978. [In German.]

Z245 Wilkotz, Jacqueline Norwood. "A Psychoanalytic Study of the Novels of Virginia Woolf." Univ. of California, Berkeley, 1973.

Z246 Wilson, Janice L. "'A House that Fits Us All': Search for Form in JACOB'S ROOM, ORLANDO, and THE WAVES." Univ. of California, Berkeley, 1969.
For abstract see DAI, 30 (1969-70), 4467A.

Z247 Winter, Günter. "Die Deutung von Virginia Woolfs Romanen (MRS. DALLOWAY, TO THE LIGHTHOUSE, und THE WAVES) im Lichte der Zeitung." Univ. of Aachen, 1977. [In German.]

Z248 Wirth-Nesher, Hana. "Limits of Fiction: A Study of the Novels of Henry James and Virginia Woolf." Columbia Univ., 1976.
For abstract see DAI, 37 (1976-77), 6469A.

Z249 Wong, Sau-Ling Cynthia. "A Study of Roger Fry and Virginia Woolf from a Chinese Perspective." Stanford Univ., 1978.
For abstract see DAI, 38 (1977-78), 7353A.

Z250 Woodcock, B. "Poetic Fiction: A Study in Representation, With Reference to Virginia Woolf and D. H. Lawrence." Univ. of Leicester, 1974.

Z251 Worrell, Elizabeth. "The Short Works of Virginia Woolf: A Study for the Oral Interpreter." Northwestern Univ., 1955.
For abstract see DA, 16 (1955-56), 345.

Z252 Worth, Fabienne André. "Historical Modes of Narration in Four Twentieth Century Novels: Marcel Proust's A LA RECHERCHE DU TEMPS PERDU, Alejo Carpentier's LOS PASOS PERDIDOS, Virginia Woolf's BETWEEN THE ACTS, Günter Grass's DIE BLECHTROMMEL." Univ. of North Carolina, 1979.
For abstract see DAI, 41 (1980-81), 239A.

Z253 Wyatt, Jeàn Murdy. "The Technique of Literary Allusion in the Novels of Virginia Woolf." Harvard Univ., 1969.

Z254 Yunis, Susan S. "Obligatory Pilgrimages: Garden Strolls, Train Rides, and Other Rituals in the Later Novels of Virginia Woolf." Case Western Reserve Univ., 1982.
  For abstract see DAI, 43 (1982-83), 3001A.

Z255 Zanotti, Lydia. "La Femme dans l'oeuvre et la vie de Virginia Woolf." Univ. of Nice, 1974. [In French.]

Z256 Zwiep, Mary Nelva. "The Late Fiction of Virginia Woolf, James Joyce, and Samuel Beckett." Univ. of Michigan, 1980.
  For abstract see DAI, 41 (1980-81), 2107A.

Indexes

AUTHOR INDEX

This index includes all authors, compilers, editors, and translators of the works entered in this volume. Also included are interviewers and interviewees, and contributors to collections and panel discussions who are named in annotations, but whose contributions are not otherwise entered and annotated in the bibliography.

Abel, Elizabeth M3
Adams, Robert M. H1
Ahrens, Rüdiger X18
Aiken, Conrad N6, P2
Albérès, René-Marill. See Marill, René
Albright, Daniel H2
Alexander, Jean G2, Z1
Alexander, Sally Jeanette. See Alexander, Jean and Brett, Sally Alexander
Alldredge, Betty Jean Edwards Z2
Allen, Walter H3, H4, S1
Alley, Henry M. F1
Alpers, Antony F2
Ameo, Kenneth J. M3a
Amorós, Andrés H5
Amoruso, Vito G3
Annan, Noel F3, F4
Apelt, Walter Z3
Apter, T. E. G4
Arakelian, Paul G. Q6
Araujo, Victor de T1
Arkin, Stephen E. Z4
Auden, W. H. U2
Auerbach, Erich N7
Aury, Dominique U3

Back, Kurt W. F5
Badenhausen, Ingeborg G5
Badt-Strauss, Bertha H6
Bagnold, Enid F6
Baillargeon, Gerald Victor Z5
Bain, Patricia Halligan Z6
Baisch, Dorothy R. Z7

Baldanza, Frank M4, N8, P3, Z8
Baldeshwiler, Eileen T2
Banti, Anna. See Longhi Lopresti, Lucia
Barnett, Alan Wayne Z9
Barrett, Michèle Z39, E1, X8, Z10
Barrette, Craig Richard Z11
Barzilai, Shulamith Q7, Z12
Basham, C. S2
Batchelor, J. B. H7
Battista, Maria Di. See DiBattista, Maria
Bauer, Gero T16
Bazin, Nancy T. G6, Z13
Beach, Joseph Warren H8, H9
Beaumont, Germaine U4, X9
Beck, Warren S3
Beckson, Karl H10
Beebe, Maurice E2
Beede, Margaret H11
Beer, Gillian H12
Beer, John F7, F94
Beja, Morris H13, N1, N9
Beker, Miroslav M5, X10
Bell, Anne Oliver B1
Bell, Barbara Currier X11
Bell, Carolyn Wilkerson Q8, Z14
Bell, Clive F8, H14
Bell, Millicent F9, H15
Bell, Quentin F10-F13, G1, S4, U5
Bell, Vanessa F14
Benedikz, B. S. Q56
Benford, Judith Lynne Z15
Benjamin, Anna M6
Ben-Merre, Diana Arbin Z16
Bennett, Arnold H16, L1
Bennett, Joan G7, U6

Bentley, Phyllis H17
Berets, Ralph Adolph Z17
Bernikow, Louise F15
Bertin, Célia U6
Bevis, Dorothy Q9
Billi, Mirella Mancioli. See
  Mancioli Billi, Mirella
Bisanz, Adam J. P4
Bishop, Edward L. J3, T3, Z18
Bishop, Morchard V1
Bizé, Paul Z19
Black, Naomi G52
Blackstone, Bernard G8, G9
Blanchard, Lydia X12
Blanchard, Margaret M7
Blanche, Jacques-Émile F16, H18
Blanchot, Maurice Q10, U7
Blöcker, Günter H19, S5
Bloomfield, Morton W. N15
Blotner, Joseph I. N10
Blumenthal, Helene Z20
Blunt, Katherine K. M8
Bodkin, Maud P5
Bogan, Louise W2, X13
Bokanowski, Hélène T19
Bollas, Sara Flanders Z21
Bonne, Rena Barbara Z22
Bonnerot, Louis H102
Bonnot, René M9
Boone, Joseph Allen Q11
Boorda, Timothy F. Z23
Borgal, Clément L2, Q12
Borgers, Wilhelm Z24
Borinski, Ludwig H20
Borker, Ruth N92, W9, X23
Bormann, Alexander von M30
Boshoff, Philip Peter Z25
Bourniquel, Camille U8
Bowen, Elizabeth H21, P6
Bowers, Susan Rae Belle Z26
Boyd, Elizabeth F. N11
Boyd, Michael Q13
Brace, Marjorie T4
Bradbrook, Frank W. H22
Bradbrook, Muriel C. H23, N12
Bradbury, Malcolm H24, Q22
Brady, E. T. Z27
Brandies, Ingeborg Weber-. See
  Weber-Brandies, Ingeborg
Brandt, Magdalene Q1

Brée, Germaine F17
Brenan, Gerald F18
Breton, Maurice Le H25, H59
Brett, Sally Alexander N13
Brewer, Wanda M. Z28
Brewster, Dorothy G10, G11, H26
Briffault, Herma G60, H27
Brochard, Lucien Z29
Brogan, Howard O. N14
Broner, E. M. H139, N25
Brooks, Benjamin G. H28
Brower, Reuben A. M10, N15
Brown, Alec H168
Brown, Carole O. J4
Brown, Dorothy Ann Duff Z30
Brown, Edward K. N16
Brown, Robert Curtis H29, Z31
Brownstein, Rachel M. M11
Brumm, Anne-Marie M12
Bryher, [Winifred] H30
Büchler, Franz H31
Buckley, Jerome H. L3
Buckley, William Kermit Z32
Buczek, Diane Z33
Bullett, Gerald H32
Bullock, Rebecca Roberts Z34
Burgum, Edwin B. H33
Burra, Peter H34
Burrell, Angus H26
Burt, John N17, W3
Butler, Susan Kirst Z35
Butturff, Douglas N87, Q42, W8

Caplan, Brina Z36
Carey, Gary M1
Carlo, Cordie F50
Carlson, Julia M13
Carroll, Bernice A. H35
Carruthers, John. See Greig,
  John Young Thomson
Carson, Sydney Z37
Caserio, Robert L. N18
Castagnino, Raúl Héctor P7
Cazamian, Louis Q14
Cecchi, Emilio N19, X14
Cecil, David H36
Celli, Rose U6
Chalfant, Thomas Haight Z38
Chambers, Richard L. G12

Chapman, Marjorie Dunn Z39
Chapman, Robert T. F19, F20,
    H37, T5
Charques, Richard D. H38
Chastaing, Maxime G13, Q15
Chattopadhyaya, Sisir H39
Chau, Nguyen van Z40
Chessman, Harriet Scott Z41
Chesson, Diane Marie Z42
Chevalley, Abel H40
Child, Harold T6
Church, Margaret H41, L4, L5,
    M14, Q16
Churchhouse, R. F. T27
Claro, Maria Elena G14
Cláudio, Mário J5
Clement, Walter H18
Clements, Patricia G15
Cohan, Steven M15, N20
Cohen, Keith N21
Cohn, Dorrit H42
Cohn, Ruby H43, N22
Collet, Georges-Paul F21
Collins, Arthur S. H44
Collins, Joseph T7
Collins, Robert G. Q2, Z43
Commenge, Béatrice Z44
Compton-Rickett, Arthur H45
Comstock, Margaret K1, R4, Z45
Condon, Thomas James Z46
Conklin, Anna Marie Z47
Conradi, Peter H46
Constein, Carl Frey Z48
Cook, Blanche Wiesen F22
Coombes, B. L. X41
Cordish, Penelope Sales Z49
Core, Deborah Lynn Z50
Cornillon, Susan K. N65
Cornwell, Ethel F. H47, X15
Corsa, Helen S. N23
Couch, F. A. Z51
Cousineau, Diane Levine Z52
Coveny, Peter H48
Cox, C. B. H49, N24
Crosland, Margaret H50
Culver, Sara Elizabeth Z53
Cumings, Melinda Feldt K2, Z54
Cunliffe, J. W. H51
Currier, Susan Z55
Curtin, Jeremy Francis Z56
Ćwiakała-Piątkowska, Jadwiga W4

Dahl, Christopher C. U9
Dahl, Liisa H52, H53
Daiches, David G16, H54, H55,
    U10
Dalgarno, Emily L6
Daniel-Rops, Henry H56
Das, G. K. F94
Dash, Irene G. H57, N25
Dataller, Roger. See Eaglestone,
    Arthur A.
Daugherty, Beth Rigel Z57
Davenport, William A. N2
Davidson, Cathy N. H139, N25
Davidson, Virginia Spencer Z58
Davis, Edward M16
Daziel, Bradford Dudley Z59
Dean, Michael P. Z60
de Gandillac, Maurice. See Gan-
    dillac, Maurice de
Deiman, Werner J. S6, Z61
Delattre, Floris G17, G34, H58,
    H59
Delbaere-Garant, Jeanne H60, T8
Delord, J. X16
Dennison, Sally Z62
Derbyshire, S. E. N26
DeSalvo, Louise A. C2, C11, F23,
    G52, J2, J6, P8, T9, U11, Z63
Deurbergue, Jean M17
Diamond, Arlyn M19
DiBattista, Maria G18, N27, Z64
DiBona, Helene Rosenberg Z65
Dick, Susan C7, N28, N29, Q17,
    U12
Didier, Béatrice H61
Dietche, Julia Phelps Z66
DiGaetani, John Louis H62, Z67
Disbrow, Sarah Kim Z68
Dobrée, Bonamy Q18
Dolch, Martin T23
Dölle, Erika G19
Donahue, Delia G20
Donaldson, Scott X17
Doner, Dean H63
Donovan, Josephine X11
Dottin, Paul H64
Dowling, David L7
Doyle, Esther M. N33, T30
Drabble, Margaret F24, G21
Drescher, Horst W. X18
Drew, Elizabeth A. H65

Druff, James Hendrick, Jr.   Z69
Durand, Régis   Q19
Dyrud, Marilyn Ann   Z70

Eaglestone, Arthur A.   X19
Eagleton, Mary   H66
Eagleton, Terry   M18
Edel, Leon   F25, F26, H67, P9, V2
Eder, Doris L.   Q20, U13
Edgar, Pelham   H68
Edwards, Lee R.   M19
Efron, Arthur   F27
Eiland, Howard Avery   Z71
Eirich, Susan Helen   Z72
Eisenberg, Nora   S7, X20, Z73
Elert, Kerstin   G22
Eliot, T. S.   F96, H69
Elkan, Lucy   H70
Ellis, Geoffrey U.   H71
Empson, William   N30
Endicott, N. J.   H72
Enfant, Julie L'.   See L'Enfant, Julie
Enright, D. J.   N31
Epstein, Edmund L.   N87, Q42, W8
Erlebach, Peter   P4
Erzgräber, Willi   M20, N32
Espinola, Judith   N33
Evans, B. Ifor   H74

Farwell, Marilyn R.   W5
Fassler, Barbara   F28
Faulkner, Peter   H75
Fawcett, Peter   F29
Fehr, Bernhard   H76, H77, Q21, R5
Ferebee, Robert Steven   Z74
Ferguson, Suzanne   N34
Fiedler, Leslie   F30
Finke, Ilse   G23
Fischer, Gretl Kraus   N35, T10
Fischer, Hermann   H78
Fishman, Solomon   X21
Flaherty, Luke   Z75
Fleishman, Avrom   G24, H79, H80, N36, P10, S8, T11, U14

Fleming, Bruce Edward   Z76
Floyd, Virginia H.   N33, T30
Flynn, Elizabeth Ann   Z77
Fokkema, Douwe W.   N37
Folsom, Marcia McClintock   W6
Ford, Boris   H22
Forrester, Viviane   F31, G67, W7
Forster, E. M.   G25, H81
Fortin, René   M21
Fouchet, Max-Pol   S9
Fourtina, Hervé   S10
Fox, Alice   G52, J7
Fox, Stephen D.   S11, T12, Z78
Francis, Herbert E.   H82
Frank, Armin P.   N32
Franks, Gabriel   H83
Fraser, G. S.   H84
Frazer, June M.   M22
Freedman, Ralph   G26, H85, H86, L8
Freeman, Alma Susan   Z79
Fremantle, Anne   H87
Freund, Philip   H88
Fricker, Robert   H89
Friedman, Alan W.   H80
Friedman, Melvin J.   H90, Q22
Friedman, Norman   M23, N38
Frierson, William C.   H91
Fromm, Gloria G.   X22
Fromm, Harold   H92, N39, S12
Frye, Joanne S.   J8, M24, Z80
Füger, Wilhelm   E3
Furman, Nelly   N92, W8, W9, X23
Fussell, B. H.   S13

Gadd, David   F32
Gaetani, John Louis Di.   See Di-Gaetani, John Louis
Gairdner, William Douglas   Z81
Gaither, Mary E.   P33
Gallagher, Sarah Van Sickle   Z82
Gállego, Cándido Pérez.   See Pérez Gállego, Cándido
Galton, John   Z83
Gamble, Isabel   M25
Gandillac, Maurice de   F34
Garant, Jeanne Delbaere-.   See Delbaere-Garant, Jeanne
García, Dámaso López.   See López García, Dámaso

Garnett, David F35, F36, V3
Gay, P. D. Z84
Gelfant, Blanche H. M26
George, W. L. K3
German, Howard N56, P11
Ghiselin, Brewster M27
Gibson, Mary Virginia Z85
Gilbert, Sandra M. M1a, N2a, P12, W10
Gill, Richard H93
Gillen, Francis M28, Z86
Gillespie, Diane F. F37, G52, N40, P13, S14
Gillet, Louis H94
Gillie, Christopher N41
Ginet, Sally McConnell-. See McConnell-Ginet, Sally
Gindin, James F39, F40, U15-U17
Ginsberg, Elaine G27
Gish, Robert X24
Giudia, Christine E6
Gleiter, Karin Jill Z87
Godwin, Janet Lynn Z88
Goetsch, Paul X25
Goetsch, Robert S. Z89
Gohrbandt, Detlev Z90
Goldman, Mark X1, Z91
Goldsmith, Bonnie Zucker Z92
Goodenough, Elizabeth N. Z93
Gorsky, Susan G28, Q23, Z94
Gottlieb, Freema G1
Gottlieb, Sidney Paul Z95
Grabo, Carl L9
Graham, John W. C6, H95, H96, P14, Q24-Q26, T13, Z96
Grant, Duncan F96
Graves, Allen Wallace Z97
Graves, Nora C. M29
Green, David Bonnell P3
Greene, Graham H97
Gregor, Ian H98, N42
Gregory, Horace X26
Greig, John Young Thomson H99
Griffin, Gail B. U18
Grindea, Miron H100
Grove-White, E. M. Z98
Gruber, Ruth G29
Grundy, Isobel G15
Grünewald-Huber, Elisabeth Q3
Guiguet, Jean A30, F34, F38, G30, H55, H101, H102, X27, X28

Gunsteren-Viersen, Julia van N43, W11
Gupta, Linda R. Z99

Hackenberg, Heide Z100
Hafley, James G31, H103, T14, Z101
Hagopian, John V. T23
Haller, Evelyn G52, Z102
Halpenny, Francess G. Q24
Halperin, John F41
Hamada, Koichi N44
Hamblen, Abigail Ann H104
Hamburger, Käte M30
Hampshire, Stuart N. H105
Hamwee, L. A. Z103
Hanquart, Evelyn H106, Z104
Harakas, Theodore Z105
Hardwick, Elizabeth H107
Hardy, John Edward N45
Harper, Howard G32, M31
Harrington, Henry R. N46
Harrod, Roy F. F42
Hartley, Lodwick R6
Hartman, Geoffrey H. H108
Hasler, Jörg H109
Haule, James M. D1, D2, Z106
Havard-Williams, Margaret H110, Q27, Q28
Havard-Williams, Peter H110, Q27, Q28
Hawkes, Ellen C8, F43
Hawkins, E. W. L10, M32
Hawthorn, Jeremy M2
Hayashi, Toshitaka M33, Q29
Hayman, Ronald F44
Heilbrun, Carolyn G. G52, H111, H112
Heine, Elizabeth H113, J9, Q30
Heinemann, Jan H114
Henderson, Philip H115
Henig, Suzanne A15, E4, F45, F46, T15, X29, X30, Z107
Henke, Suzette A. M34, N47
Herrick, Robert H116
Hessler, John G. M35
Hidalgo, Pilar H117
Higashida, Chiaki N107
Higdon, David Leon M96, S15

Hildick, Wallace M36
Hill, James S. W12
Hill, Katherine C. X31, Z108
Hilsinger, Serena Sue Z109
Himmelfarb, Gertrude N48
Hintikka, Jaakko H118
Hirsch, Marianne M3
Hoag, Gerald X2
Hoare, Dorothy M. H119, N49
Hochman, Baruch M37
Hoffman, Frederick J. H120
Hoffmann, A. C. N50
Hoffmann, Charles G. H121, M38, M39, N51, P15, R4
Holleyman, G. A. E5
Holliday, Terence N52
Hollingsworth, Keith M40
Holroyd, Michael F47
Holtby, Winifred G33
Hoops, Reinald H122
Hortmann, Wilhelm N32
Howarth, R. G. K4
Huber, Elisabeth Grünewald-. See Grünewald-Huber, Elisabeth
Hughes, Helen S. H144
Hulcoop, John F. U19, U20
Humma, John B. N53
Hummel, Madeline M. W13
Humphrey, Robert H123
Hungerford, Edward A. A38, M41, X32, Z110
Hunting, Constance P16
Hunting, Robert X33
Hyman, Stanley E. H242
Hyman, Virginia R. N54, U21, X34
Hynes, Samuel F48, H16, L1, X35

Ilford, Mary H154
Inglis, Anthony A. H. E6
Isenberg, Aloysia Z111
Isherwood, Christopher F49
Ishii, Koichi G35
Izzo, Carlo F50

Jackson, Gertrude H124, T16
Jacobus, Mary H12
Jaloux, Edmond M42
James, Rolfe A. Scott-. See Scott-James, Rolfe A.
James, Walter A31, X36
Jameson, Storm H125
Jardin, Claudine F51
Jardine, Alice Q31
Jehin, A. G78
Jelinek, Hena Maes-. See Maes-Jelinek, Hena
Jensen, Emily G52
Jewison, Donald Bruce Z112
Johnson, Manly G36
Johnson, Reginald Brimley J10, K5
Johnstone, J. K. H126, Z113
Jolas, Maria H212
Jones, Alan T27
Jones E. B. C. H127
Josephson, Matthew H128
Josipovici, Gabriel N69, U7
Joyner, Nancy N55
Julien, Hershey Z114
Juszczak, Wiesław G36a

Kaehele, Sharon N56, P11
Kahane, Claire N57
Kamerbeek, Jan Coenraad R2, W1
Kamuf, Peggy W14
Kaplan, Sydney Janet M43, N58, Z115
Kapur, Vijay G37
Katz, Judith N. Z116
Katz, Linda Sternberg Z117
Kellermann, Frederick P17
Kelley, Alice van Buren G38, Z118
Kelsey, Mary E. H129
Kendzora, Kathleen N59
Kennedy, Richard F52
Kenney, Edwin J. F53, X37
Kenney, Susan M. F53, S16, Z119
Kettle, Arnold N60
Keylor, William R. P26
Kiely, Robert H130
King, Merton P. Q32, Z120
Kirkpatrick, Brownlee Jean E7
Kneubuhl, Barbara Jean Z121
Kohler, Dayton H131

Kondo, Ineko F54, G39, H132
Koteliansky, S. S. A17
Koutsoudaki, Mary L11
Kreutz, Irving M44
Kreyling, Michael N61
Kristensen, Sven M. H198
Kröger, Helmut Z122
Kronenberger, Louis X38
Kuhn, Reinhard R8
Kumar, Shiv K. H133, Z123
Kush, Katherine Davidson Z124
Kushen, Betty H134, H135, P18
Kushner, Deena Dash N25

Lakshmi, Vijay H136, W15, X39, X40
Lalou, René Q33
Lampl, Nancy Williams Z125
Lange, Ludith P32
Langland, Elizabeth M3
Lanoire, Maurice M45
Laskin, Miriam Meryl Z126
Latham, Jacqueline E. M. G40, M46-M50, T17, Z127
Laurans, Penelope Z128
Laurenson, Diana E1
Lavin, J. A. N62
Lawrence, Margaret P19, W16
Lawson, Richard H. S17
Leaska, Mitchell A. C3, C5, G41, N3, R9, S18, Z129
Leavis, F. R. S19
Leavis, Q. D. W17
Le Breton, Maurice. See Breton, Maurice Le
Lee, Hermione G42
Lehmann, John F55-F58, G41, H137, X41
Lehmann, Rosamond F59, H138
Lemonnier, Léon G34
L'Enfant, Julie U22, Z130
Lesser, Simon O. F60
Levenback, Karen L. Z131
Lévy, Suzanne E6
Lewis, A. J. M51
Lewis, Edward William Z132
Lewis, F. C. Z133
Lewis, Thomas S. W. G44, T18, Y1

Lewis, Wyndham X42
Leyburn, Ellen Douglass X43
Lilienfeld, Jane H139, N63, N64, Z134
Limburg, Kay L. B. Z135
Lindau, Bertha L. Z136
Lipking, Joanna R10
Little, Judy G45, N65
Livi, Grazia H140
Lodge, David H141
Lohmüller, Gertrud G46
Lombardo, Agostino U23
Longhi Lopresti, Lucia P20
López García, Dámaso U24
Lopresti, Lucia Longhi. See Longhi Lopresti, Lucia
Lorberg, Aileen D. H142
Lorsch, Susan E. Q34
Lotringer, Sylvère H143, T19
Love, Jean O. F61, G47, P21
Lovett, Robert M. H144
Ludwig, Alvin Karl Z137
Lukens, Cynthia Diane Z138
Lund, Mary Graham Q35
Lyngstad, Sverre Z139
Lyon, George Ella Hoskins Z140
Lyon, Mary A37, Z141
Lyons, Richard S. S20

Maack, Annegret L12
Macaulay, Rose F96
MacCarthy, Desmond H145, P22
McClusky, Kathleen M. Z142
McConnell, Frank D. Q36
McConnell-Ginet, Sally N92, W9, X23
McDowell, Frederick P. W. J11
McFarlane, James Q22
McGavran, James Holt, Jr. Q37
McIntyre, Clara F. H146
McKillop, Laurence Terese Z143
McLaughlin, Ann L. G52, H147, Z144
McLaughlin, Thomas M. F62, H148
McLaurin, Allen E10, G48, G49, Q38, Z145
McNeillie, Andrew B1, E8
McNett, Jeanne M. Z146
McNichol, Stella A16, N31, T20

MacNiece, Louis X41
Madison, Elizabeth Christen
    Z147
Madsen, Henriette P1
Maes-Jelinek, Hena H149
Magny, Claude-Edmonde H150
Mahoney, Jeanne Noel Z148
Mais, Stuart P. B. K6
Majumdar, Robin E9, E10, G49,
    X44, Z149
Mancioli Billi, Mirella G50
Mandelkow, Karl Robert M30
Manning, Hugo H151
Mansfield, Katherine F63, K7,
    T21
Manuel, M. X45
Marcel, Gabriel M52, Q39
Marcus, Jane G51, G52, H152,
    K8, R11, R12, S21, W18, W19
Marder, Herbert G53, R13, Z150
Mares, Cheryl Jean Z151
Marill, René H153, Q40
Markovic, Vida E. M53
Marshall, Peggy Ann Z152
Martz, Louis L. N42
Masui, Jacques N66
Matro, Thomas Gaetano Z153
Maurois, André H154, X46
May, Keith M. H155, N67, Q41
Mayer, Louie F70
Mayoux, Jean-Jacques H156-H159,
    N68, P23
Medcalf, Stephen G1
Megata, Morikimi U25
Meisel, Perry X3, Z154
Melchiori, Giorgio H160
Mellers, W. H. H161, R14
Mendelson, Edward U2
Mendez, Charlotte Walker H162,
    H163, Q42, Z155
Mendilow, A. A. H164
Mepham, John N69
Mercier, Michel H165, X47
Merle, Gabriel F64
Merre, Diana Arbin Ben-. See
    Ben-Merre, Diana Arbin
Meyer, Doris F65, F71
Meyer, Kurt Robert H166
Meyerowitz, Selma S. F66, T22,
    Z156

Meyers, Jeffrey F67, F68
Middleton, Victoria S. F15, W20
Miles, Rosalind H167
Miller, David N. M54
Miller, J. Hillis M55, S22
Miroiu, Mihai G54
Mirsky, Dmitri H168
Moers, Ellen H169
Moloney, Michael F. H170
Monroe, Nellie Elizabeth H171,
    H172
Moody, Anthony D. G57, M56
Moon, Kenneth M57
Moore, Deborah Dash N25
Moore, Madeline C9, G87, J12,
    Q43, R16
Mor, Samuel Z157
Morgenstern, Barry L13, Z158
Morizot, Carol Ann F68a
Morra, Umberto H173
Morris, Caryl Anne Z159
Morris, Jill G58
Mortimer, Raymond P24
Moss, Roger L14
Muchnic, Helen Y2
Mueller, William R. M58
Muir, Edwin H174, H175, M59
Muller, Herbert J. H176
Müller, Wolfgang G. P4
Munro, John H. H10
Murry, John Middleton K7, L15,
    T21

Naremore, James G59, R17, Z160
Nashashibi, Pauline R. H177
Nathan, Monique G60
Neilen, Deirdre Z161
Neill, S. Diana H178
Nesher, Hana Wirth-. See Wirth-
    Nesher, Hana
Neubert, Albrecht H179, Z162
Neuschäffer, Walter H180
Newton, Deborah G61
Nicolson, Nigel B2, F69
Noël, Roger H181
Novak, Jane E11, F70, G62, X48,
    Z163

Oates, Joyce Carol H182, M96
O'Brien, Edna F70a
Ocampo, Victoria F71, P25, U1, W21
O'Connor, William Van S3
O'Faolain, Sean H183
Ogoshi, Tetsuya H184
Ohmann, Carol L16, X11
Okunishi, Akira Q44
Olsen, F. Bruce T23
Olson, Stanley F72, Z164
Oltean, Ştefan M60
Oppel, Horst M20
Osawa, Nimoru G63
Ottavi, Anne N70
Otte, George Frederick, III Z165
Overcarsh, F. L. N71
Overstreet, Linda K. Z166
Oya, Fukiyo N72
Ozick, Cynthia F73

Pacey, Desmond X49
Pachmuss, Temira H185
Page, Alex M61
Painter, George H186
Parasuram, Laxmi G64, Z167
Park, Hee-Jin Z168
Parkes, Graham N73
Parsons, Ian F89
Paskoff, Louis Z169
Pasternack, Gerhard G65
Paterson, John H187
Payne, Michael M62, Q45
Peck, Ellen Margaret McKee Z170
Pedersen, Glenn N74
Peel, Robert H188
Pendry, E. D. H189
Penman, M. E. Z171
Perazzini, Randolph M63
Pérez Gállego, Cándido N75
Peternel, Joan Z172
Phelps, Gilbert H190
Philipson, Morris M64, P26
Phillips, Anne Heiberg Z173
Picart, Yves G34
Pierce, David H66
Pillat, Monica H191

Pimienta, Louis G34
Pippett, Aileen F74
Pitt, Rosemary J13
Plomer, William F75, F76, F96
Plumb, John H. F3
Poirier, Suzanne Z174
Pomeroy, Elizabeth W. H192
Poole, Roger F77
Poresky, Louise A. G66, Z175
Porter, Katherine Anne H193
Pratt, Annis N76, N77
Price, Martin N78
Priestley, J. B. H194
Pritchard, William H. H195, N79
Proudfit, Sharon L. N80, R18, Z176

Quennell, Peter X4
Quick, Jonathan R. M65, S23
Quinn, Kerker T4

Rabinovich, Sacha U7
Rachman, Shalom M66
Radbil, Alexandra Z177
Radin, Grace R3, R19, R20, Z178
Rahman, Shaista Z179
Rahme, Mary H196
Rahv, Philip H197
Raina, M. L. Z180
Rakowsky, Christine Hirniak Z181
Ramløv, Preben H198
Ramsay, Warren H199
Rantavaara, Irma F78, G68, Q4, S24
Rea, P. S. L. Z182
Reade, Arthur R. H200
Redman, Ben Ray H40
Rest, Jaime X50
Rettig, Cynthia Bestoso Z183
Reuter, Klaus P4
Rey, Jean Z184
Reynders, Karen P32
Richardson, Robert O. Q46, Z185
Richman, David Y3
Richter, Harvena G69, H201, M67, U26, Z186
Rickett, Arthur Compton-. See Compton-Rickett, Arthur

Rickword, Edgell N30
Ridley, Hilda F79
Riesner, Dieter H78
Rigney, Barbara H. M68, Z187
Rigo, Giorgio de Q47
Rillo, Lila E. G70
Ringbom, Håkan S24
Ringler, Susan Jane Z188
Roberts, John H. H202, M69, N81, R21
Roberts, R. Ellis V4
Robinson, Deborah Sue Z189
Robson, W. W. H203
Rock, Marcia Lynn Z190
Rogat, Ellen H. F80, H204, Z191
Rohde, Peter P. H205
Rops, Henry Daniel-. See Daniel-Rops, Henry
Rosati, Salvatore H206, P27
Rose, Phyllis F81, N82
Rosen, Amy Z192
Rosenbaum, Stanford P. F82, F83, H207, N73
Rosenberg, Stuart M70
Rosenthal, Michael G71
Ross, Woodburn O. M40
Rousseaux, André J14, Q48, U27
Rowe, Margaret Moan M71
Ruas, Charles F84
Rubenstein, Roberta H208, H209, P28, Z193
Ruddick, Lisa N4
Ruddick, Sara L17, N83, Q49
Rudikoff, Sonya E12
Runyan, Elizabeth Z194
Ruotolo, Lucio P. Z36, M72-M74, Y4
Ruppel, James Robert Z195
Russell, H. K. N84

Sacks, Majorie Consuelo Hamilton Z196
Sackville-West, Victoria F96, P29, U28
Sagiyama, Yoko N85
Sakamoto, Kiminobu F85, G72, T24
Sakamoto, Koen H210

Sakamoto, Tadanobu G73, T25, X51
Salvo, Louise A. de. See DeSalvo, Louise A.
Samuels, Marilyn Schauer M75
Samuelson, Ralph H211, M76, P30, Z197
Sanna, Vittoria G74
Sarraute, Nathalie H212, H213
Satz, Murray E. Z198
Saunders, Judith P. T26
Savage, Derek S. H214
Schaefer, Josephine O'Brien G75, L18, V5, Z199
Schaubeck, Richard J., Jr. F14
Scheiber, Howard Jeffrey Z200
Schlack, Beverley Ann G52, G76, J15, M77, R22, U29, W22, Z201
Schneider, Daniel J. H215
Schorer, Mark H216
Schug, Charles M78, N86
Schuhmann, Kuno N32
Schulkind, Jean B3, U30, Z202
Schulz, Muriel R. N87
Schwank, Klaus G77
Schwartz, Nina E. Z203
Scott, George U31
Scott, Nathan A. H217
Scott-James, Rolfe A. H218
Sears, Sallie G52, R23, W23
Segura, Celia G78
Seltzer, Alvin J. N88, Z204
Sengelli, Nazan Feride Z205
Serefini, Guglielmo H219
Serreau, Geneviève G67
Seward, Barbara H220
Shabka, Margaret Collins Z206
Shanahan, Mary S. Q50, S25, Z207
Sharma, Kaushal Kishore X5
Sharma, O. P. K9, M79, N89
Sharma, Vijay L. X6
Shattuck, Charles T4
Shaw, Valerie U32, X52
Shibata, Tetsushi M80
Shibazaki, Yuko U33
Shields, E. F. M81, M82, Z208
Shoukri, Doris E. C. Q51
Showalter, Elaine H221
Siek, Barbara L. Z209
Silver, Brenda R. C1, C10, G52, S26, X53, Z210

Simmons, Sarah Brey   Z211
Simon, Irène   F86, H222, M83, N90
Sitter, Deborah A.   Q52
Sloman, Judith   X54
Smart, J. A. E.   H223
Smith, Logan Pearsall   F87
Smith, Michael Allan   Z212
Smith, Philip H., Jr.   D1, D2
Snider, Clifton   P31
Snow, Lotus   J16, M84, M85, N91, Q53, S27, Z213
Spangler, Ellen Stewart   Z214
Spater, George A.   F88, F89
Speltz, Ann Linda   Z215
Spender, Stephen   F90, H224
Spilka, Mark   G79, H225
Spivak, Gayatri C.   N92
Sprague, Claire   G80, H226
Squier, Susan M.   C11, G52, H227, R24, Z216
Stade, George   G88
Stadtfeld, Frieder   S28
Stamirowska, Krystyna   M86, N93
Stanzel, Franz K.   H228, T16
Starkey, Penelope Schott   W24
Starkie, Enid   H229
Steele, Elizabeth   P32, X7
Steele, Philip L.   P33
Steiger, Klaus P.   N94
Steinberg, Erwin R.   M87, M88, N95
Steinberg, Günter   H230
Steinberg, Lois   Z217
Steinmann, Theo   N96
Sterk, Kay Puttock   Z218
Stevenson, Lionel   H231
Stewart, Grace   N97, P34
Stewart, J. I. M.   Q56
Stewart, Jack F.   H232, N98, P35, Q54, Q55
Stewart, Jean   G30
Stouls, Pierre   G34
Strachey, James   B4
Strauss, Bertha Badt-.   See Badt-Strauss, Bertha
Stresau, Hermann   F91
Strong, Paul   Z219
Strouse, Louise F.   N99
Stubles, Patricia   H233
Stuber, Carol Ann   Z220
Studley, Grace MacFarlane   Z221
Stürzl, Erwin   U34
Sudrann, Jean   Z222
Sugiyama, Yoko   G81
Sühnel, Rudolf   H78
Sukenick, Lynn   Z223
Summerhayes, Don   S29
Swanson, Janice M. Bowman   Z224
Swartz, Mary Ann   Q57
Swingle, L. J.   S30, X55
Swinnerton, Frank   H234
Szladits, Lola   C5, V6

Tada, Minoru   M89
Tajima, Yoko   H235, H236
Takahashi, Kazuhisa   M90
Talamantes, Florence   H237
Tallentire, D. R.   T27
Tanger, Marilyn   Q58
Taylor, Nancy McKeon   Z225
Temple, Ruth Z.   N100
Thakur, N. C.   G82
Thayer, Jacqueline Gaillet   Z226
Tilak, Raghukul   M2a
Tilberry, Joanne Howland   Z227
Tindall, William York   H238-H240
Tobin, Gloria Jean   Z228
Toerien, B. J.   E13
Torgovnick, Marianna   Q59
Touber, Anthonius H.   M30
Toynbee, Philip   H241
Transue, Pamela Jean   Z229
Trask, Willard R.   N7
Trautmann, Joanne   B2, F92, F93
Trivedi, H. K.   F94, Z230
Trombley, Stephen   F95
Troy, William   H242
Tudor, Kathleen   Z231
Turnell, Martin   H243, H244

Upward, Edward   X41

Vanderwerff, Whitney Grove   Z232
VanHorn, Geraldine Kloos   Z233
Venit, James S.   Z234
Verga, Ines   G83

Verschoyle, Derek H127
Viersen, Julia van Gunsteren-. See Gunsteren-Viersen, Julia van
Vigne, Marie-Paule H245
Villanueva, Darío M91, N101
Villgradter, Rudolf T28
Villiermet, Laure V3
Vogelsang, John Daniel Z235
Vogler, Thomas A. N5, N102
Vowinckel, Ernst R. H246
Vukobrat, Slobodan V7

Wade, Michael M92
Wagenknecht, Edward H247
Wagenseil, Hans B. P36, X56
Walker, Cynthia J17
Wallace, A. Dayle M40
Walpole, Hugh F97
Walter, Margot Z236
Ward, Alfred C. H248
Warner, E. D. Z237
Warner, Eric R25
Warner, John M. N103
Warsi, Shaheen G84
Wasserman, Jerry Q60
Watkins, Renée S31
Watson, Robert A. T29
Watt, Donald J. F98
Watts, Janet F99
Webb, Igor Q61, Z238
Weber, Horst X27
Weber, Robert W. M93
Weber-Brandies, Ingeborg Q5
Weems, Benjamin Francis, III Z239
Weidner, Eva F. G85
Weinberger, Sylvia Zina Z240
Weiner, Dora B. P26
Weiser, Barbara E14
Wellek, René X57
West, Paul P37
West, Rebecca L19, W25
West, Victoria Sackville-. See Sackville-West, Victoria
White, E. M. Grove-. See Grove-White, E. M.
White, Richard Lupton Z241
White, Robert Finis, Jr. Z242

Whitehead, J. Z243
Whitehead, Lee M. N104
Wicht, Wolfgang H249, Z244
Wiget, Erik G86
Wild, Friedrich H250
Wildi, Max R5
Wiley, Paul L. E15
Wilkinson, Ann Y. S32
Wilkotz, Macqueline Norwood Z245
Williams, Aubrey N42
Williams, Margaret Havard-. See Havard-Williams, Margaret
Williams, Orlo H251
Williams, Peter Havard-. See Havard-Williams, Peter
Wilson, Angus H252
Wilson, Edmund X58, X59
Wilson, J. J. H253, P38
Wilson, James Southall H254
Wilson, Janice L. Z246
Winter, Günter Z247
Wirth-Nesher, Hana N105, Z248
Wolff, Erwin X18
Wong, Sau-ling Cynthia Z249
Woodcock, B. Z250
Woodring, Carl G88
Woolf, Leonard A26-A29, A32, B4, B6, F100, F101, K4
Woolmer, J. Howard F33
Worrell, Elizabeth T30, Z251
Worth, Fabienne André Z252
Wright, Nathalie M94
Wyatt, Frederick M95
Wyatt, Jean M. M96, N106, S33, Z253

Yoshida, Yasuo G89, N107
Yourcenar, Marguerite F102, G34, Q62
Yu, Sau-ling Cynthia V8
Yunis, Susan S. Z254

Zaccaria, Paola G90
Zaic, Frank T16
Zanotti, Lydia Z255
Zeman, Anthea H255
Zéraffa, Michel H256, H257, U35
Zorn, Marilyn S34

Zuckerman, Joanne P.   K10
Zwerdling, Alex   L20, M97, S35
Zwiep, Mary Nelva   Z256

TITLE INDEX

This index includes the titles of all books, essay collections, monographs, and pamphlets entered in this guide, as well as of all Woolf's major publications. Article titles are omitted. In all cases of identical titles, the author's or editor's name has been placed in parentheses after the title. The entry number(s) indicates the first, or, in a few cases, each complete listing of the title with full publishing data. An essay collection, therefore, will ordinarily have but one entry number, referring the user to the collection's full entry and its annotation where cross-reference numbers for its contents are provided.

Abinger Harvest H81
Absent Father, The X3
Accent Anthology T4
ADAM INTERNATION REVIEW G1
Afterjoyce H1
Age of Suspicion, The H212
Algo Sobre Virginia Woolf G14
"All That Summer She Was Mad" F95
Among Women F15
Annotated Critical Bibliography of Virginia Woolf, An E8
Antigone bij Virginia Woolf R2, W1
Apothecary's Shop, The N31
Appels, Les S9
Archetypal Patterns in Poetry P5
Archetypal Patterns in Women's Fiction N77
Arnold Bennett: A Biography F24
Art of Reading the Novel, The H88
Art of the Novel, The H68
Aspekte des Komischen bei Virginia Woolf G65
At Home F75
Attitudes to Class in the English Novel H66
Au pays du roman M42
Author in His Work, The N42

Author's Craft, and Other Critical Writings, The H16, L1
Authority of Experience, The M19
Autobiography of Leonard Woolf F100

Becoming a Heroine M11
Beginning Again F100
Bergson and the Stream of Consciousness Novel H133
Between Language and Silence G32
Between the Acts A9, S4
Beyond Egotism H130
Beyond Formalism H108
Beyond the Lighthouse H50
Bibliography of Virginia Woolf, A E7
Bibliography of Virginia Woolf, (Stephen), A E13
Bildstruktur und Romanstruktur bei Virginia Woolf G77
Bloomsbury F10
Bloomsbury: A House Of Lions F25
Bloomsbury Group, The: A Collection of Memoirs, Commentary, and Criticism F83
Bloomsbury Group, The: A Study of E. M. Forster, Lytton Strachey, Virginia Woolf, and Their Circle H126
Books and Portraits A37

230

Boy at the Hogarth Press, A F52
British Novel, The: Conrad to the Present E15
BULLETIN OF RESEARCH IN THE HUMANITIES: "Virginia Woolf Issue II" J1
BULLETIN OF THE NEW YORK PUBLIC LIBRARY: "Virginia Woolf Issue" R1

Captain's Death Bed, and Other Essays, The A28
Catalogue of Books From the Library of Leonard and Virginia Woolf E5
Cavalcade of the English Novel H247
Celebration of Life M58
Change of Perspective, A B2
Changing Face, The M53
Checklist of the Hogarth Press, A F33
Chaos in the Novel N88
Characters of Women in Narrative Literature H155
Classic British Novel, The M31
Closure in the Novel Q59
Cockney's Farming Experiences, A A15
Collected Essays, by Virginia Woolf A32
Collected Impressions H21
Comedy and the Woman Writer G45
Common Reader, The A19
Common Reader, The: Second Series A22
Computer in Literary and Linguistic Studies, The T27
Concordance to BETWEEN THE ACTS, A D1
Concordance to THE WAVES, A D2
Conscience et la vie dans le roman de Virginia Woolf, La H59
Contemporary Literature and Social Revolution H38

Contemporary Writers A30
Continuing Presences G76
Corruption in Paradise R8
Criticism of Society in the English Novel Between the Wars H149
Critics on Virginia Woolf G40

Days Before, The H193
Death of the Moth, and Other Essays, The A26
Death of the Moth, The: Stories T19
Diary of Virginia Woolf, The B1
Doctor Looks at Literature, The T7
Dostoevksy's English Reputation, 1881-1936 Y2
Dostojewskijs Einfluss auf den englischen Roman H180
Downhill All the Way F100

E. M. Forster: A Human Exploration F94
Écriture-femme, L' H61
Editing Twentieth Century Texts Q24
Edwardian Occasions F48, X35
Einfluss der Psychoanalyse auf die englische Litteratur, Der H122
Elusive Self, The G66
Ending in Earnest W25
Englische Dichter der Moderne H78
Englische Essay, Der X27
Englische Literatur der Gegenwart seit 1870, Die H250
Englische Literatur der Gegenwart und die Kulturfragen Unsererzeit, Die H76
Englische Literatur der heutigen Stunde als Ausdruck der Zeitwende und der englischen Kulturgemeinschaft, Die Q21
Englische Roman zwischen den Jahrzehnten, 1927-1935, Der H246
Englische und Amerikanische Literaturtheorie X18

English Historical Novel, The
  P10, S8
English Literature and British
  Philosophy H207
English Literature Between the
  Wars H74
English Literature in the Twen-
  tieth Century H51
English Literature of the Twen-
  tieth Century H44
English Novel in Transition,
  The H91
English Novel, The: A Short
  Critical History H3
English Novelists, The H127
Epiphany in the Modern Novel
  H13
Ere du soupçon, L' H212
Erlebte Rede H230
Esquisses anglaises H94
Essays and Studies in Commem-
  oration of Professor Shunichi
  Maekawa's Sixty-First Birth-
  day N72
Essays on Virginia Woolf:
  Theme and Style G89
Estructura y Tiempo Reducido en
  la Novela M91, N101
Études et recherches de lit-
  térature générale et comparée
  N70
Exhumations F49
Exiles and Émigrés M18
Experiment und Tradition in der
  Prosa Virginia Woolf G19
Experimentos Narrativos P7
"Extravagante Engländerin,"
  Eine E3

Faux pas Q10
Feminine Consciousness in the
  Modern British Novel M43,
  N58
Feminism & Art G53
Feminist Literary Criticism
  X11
Festschrift Prof. Dr. Herbert
  Kozoil T16
Feux d'automne H59

Fiction and Repetition M55, S22
Fiction and the Ways of Knowing
  N36
Fiction of Sex, The H167
Fields of Light, The M10
Fifty Years of English Literature
  H218
Figures of Autobiography H79, U14
Film and Fiction N21
Flight of the Mind, The B2
Flowers of the Forest F35
Flush A23
Forms of Modern British Fiction
  H80
Forces in Modern British Litera-
  ture A238
Forewords and Afterwords U2
Form and Meaning in Fiction M23,
  N38
Formes du roman anglais de Dickens
  à Joyce H222
Forms of Life N78
Forms of Modern Fiction S3
Frau im Werk Virginia Woolf, Die
  G46
Free Indirect Discourse H230
Free Spirit, The H49
Fremmede Digtere i det 20 Århun-
  drede H198
Freshwater A36
From Gautier to Eliot H229
From Parnassus P26

Gengo to Buntai N107
Georgian Literary Scene, The H234
Georgian Novel and Mr. Robinson,
  The H125
Geschichtlichkeit und Neuanfang
  im sprachlichen Kunstwerk P4
Glass Roof, The G31
Granite and Rainbow A29
Great Friends F36
Growing F100

Happy Rural Seat H93
Haunted House, and Other Short
  Stories, A A13
Henry James and the Criticism of
  Virginia Woolf X2

Histoire du roman moderne   H153
History of the English Novel, The   H231
History of the Novel in England, The   H144
Humanism in the English Novel   H75

Image and Idea   H197
Image of Childhood, The   H48
Images of Women in Fiction   N65
Importance of Imagination in Charles Morgan's Novels   G78
Impressionismus und Expressionismus in den Romanen Virginia Woolfs   G85
IMPRESSIONS: "Homage à Virginia Woolf."   G34
In My Own Time   F55
Insight II   T23
Intelligentsia   H168
Intelligentsia of Great Britain, The   H168
Interpretation of Narrative, The   N15
Introducción a la Novela Contemporánea   H5
Introduction to the English Novel, An   N60

Jacob's Room   A3
Jane Austen and Virginia Woolf   G39
Jessamy Brides, The   F92
Journey, Not the Arrival Matters, The   F100
Just this Side of Madness   F68a

Katherine Mansfield: A Biography   F67
Katherine Mansfield (1888-1923) and Virginia Woolf (1882-1941)   G70
Kew Gardens   A11

Language and Style   N107
Leave the Letters Till We're Dead   B2
Leonard Woolf   F66
Leslie Stephen   F4
Letter to Mrs. Virginia Woolf, A   X4
Letters of Virginia Woolf, The   B2
LETTRES FRANÇAISES   G43
Life of John Maynard Keynes, The   F41
Life of Katherine Mansfield, The   F2
Linguistic Features of the Stream-of-Consciousness Techniques of James Joyce, Virginia Woolf, and Eugene O'Neill   H53
Literary Biography   P9, V2
Literary Symbol, The   H239
Literary Women   H169
Literatur als Teilhabe   S5
Literature and Living   F44
Literature of Their Own, A   H221
Littérature et critique   H150
Littérature du vingtième siècle   J14, Q48, U27
Livre à venir, Le   U7
London Scene, The   A35
Lost Childhood, and Other Essays, The   H97
Lost Tradition, The   H139, N25
Loving Friends, The   F32
Lyrical Novel, The   H85
Lytton Strachey   F47
Lytton Strachey and the Bloomsbury Group   F47

Madness and Sexual Politics in the Feminist Novel   M68
Maekawa Shunichi Kyōju Kanreki Kinen-Ronbunshū   N72
Main Currents in Modern Literature   H200
Man in the Modern Novel   N45
Mark on the Wall, The   A10
Marriage of True Minds, A   F89
Married to Genius   F68
Meister des modernen englischen Romans   H20

"Melymbrosia," by Virginia
   Woolf   C2
Men Without Art   X42
Métamorphoses du roman   Q40
Mimesis   N7
Mind and Art of Virginia Woolf,
   The   G84
Miscellanea anglo-americana
   N32
Modern Age, The   H22
Modern English Fiction   H32
Modern English Literature   H203
Modern English Novel, The   H40
Modern English Novel, The: The
   Reader, the Writer and the
   Work   N69
Modern Fiction   H26
Modern Fiction: A Study of
   Values   H176
MODERN FICTION STUDIES "Virginia Woolf: A Special Number"   G55
MODERN FICTION STUDIES "Virginia Woolf Number"   G56
Modern Fictional Theorists   X5
Modern Literature and Christian
   Faith   H243
Modern Novel, The   H65
Modern Novel in Britain and the
   United States, The   H4
Modern Prose Style   Q18
Modern Psychological Novel, The
   H67
Modern Writer and His World,
   The   H84
Modern Writers and Other Essays
   H105
Moderne englische Roman, Der
   H89, M20
Modes of Modern Writing, The
   H141
Moment, and Other Essays, The
   A27
Moments of Being   B3
Monarch Notes on Woolf's MRS.
   DALLOWAY and TO THE LIGHTHOUSE   M1a, N2a
Monday or Tuesday   A12
More Portraits of a Lifetime
   H18

Mort de la phalene, La   T19
Mortal No, The   H120
Moth and the Star, The   F74
Movements in English Literature
   N41
Mr. Bennett and Mrs. Brown   A18
Mrs. Dalloway   A4, A20
MRS. DALLOWAY: Notes   M1
MRS. DALLOWAY (A Critical Study)
   M2a
Mrs. Dalloway's Party   A16

Neuen Wirklichkeiten, Die   H19
New Feminism of English Fiction,
   The   H189
New Feminist Essays on Virginia
   Woolf   G51
New Heaven, New Earth   H182
New Mythos, A   N97, P34
Night and Day   A2
Nineteen-Twenties, The   H248
Notes on Virginia's Childhood   F14
Novel and Society, The   H171
Novel and the Modern World, The
   H54
Novel and the World's Dilemma, The
   H33
Novel as Faith, The   H187
Novel Today, The   H115
Novels and Novelists   K7, T21
Novels of Virginia Woolf, The
   (Chambers)   G12
Novels of Virginia Woolf, The
   (Donahue)   G20
Novels of Virginia Woolf, The
   (Lee)   G42
Novels of Virginia Woolf, The:
   Fact and Vision   G38
Novels of Virginia Woolf, The:
   From Beginning to End   G41
Nurse Lugton's Golden Thimble   A14

Old Friends: Personal Recollections   F8
On the Novel   Q56
Open Night, The   H137
Opinioni   P20
Orlando   A6, P6
Out of the Maelstrom   Q41

"Pargiters, The" C3
Personality and Impersonality H2
Personne et personnage H256
Philosophie de Virginia Woolf, La G13
Plot, Story, and the Novel N18
Poets and Story-Tellers H36
Points of View H154
"Pointz Hall" C5
Portrait of a Marriage F69
Portraits and Personalities H45
Portraits of Women in Selected Novels by Virginia Woolf and E. M. Forster G22
Possibilities H24
Presumptuous Girls H255

Quatre études anglaises X46
Question of Things Happening, The B2
QUINZAINE LITTERAIRE, LA: "Virginia Woolf" G67

Rainbow and Granite G81
Razor Edge of Balance, The G62
Reader's Art, The X1
Reading a Novel S1
Readings in Modern Fiction M16
Realismus und Realität im modernen Roman Q1
Recollections of Virginia Woolf by Her Contemporaries F70
Reflection of the Other Person, A B2
Reflexive Novel, The Q13
Republic of Letters, The X38
Reviewer's ABC, A N6, P2
Rhythm in the Novel N16
Richard Wagner and the Modern British Novel H62
Roger Fry A25
Roman anglais de notre temps, Le H40
Roman et société H257
Roman féminin, Le H165, X47
Roman psychologique de Virginia Woolf, Le G17

Romantic Genesis of the Modern Novel, The M78, N86
Romanzo di Virginia Woolf, Il G74
Room of One's Own, A A21
Russian Novel in English Fiction, The H190

Scheherazade, or the Future of the English Novel H99
School of Feminity, The P19, W16
Scrittori Inglesi e Americani N19, X14
Scrutinies N30
Season of Youth L3
Second Common Reader, The A22
Seduction and Betrayal H107
Seeing Through Everything N79
Seen and the Unseen, The N4
Selected Criticism: Prose, Poetry W2, X13
Selected Essays (Troy) H242
Shores of Light, The X59
Short History of the English Novel, A H178
Short Season Between Two Silences, The J12
Sickle Side of the Moon, The B2
Siren's Song, The U7
Six Existential Heroes M72
Six Modern British Novelists G88
Sociology of Literature, The E1
Solitary Dialogue--V. Woolf's Literature and Circle G72
Some Contemporary Novelists (Women) J10, K5
Some Observations on the Art of Narrative H17
Some Studies in the Modern Novel H119
South From Granada F18
Sowing F100
Spirit of Time and Place X26
Sprache Virginia Woolfs, Die G5
Stavrogin's Confession and the Plan of the Life of a Great Sinner A17
Stephen versus Gladstone A33
Stilformem der "erlebten rede" im neueren englischen Roman, Die H179

"Still Point," The H47
Stream of Consciousness H90
Stream of Consciousness in the Modern Novel H123
Structure and Theme L5
Structure of the Novel, The M59
Studi in Onore di Vittorio Lugli e Diego Valeri F50
Studies in Honor of John Wilcox M40
Studies in Interpretation N33, T30
Studies in Social History F3
Stuff of Sleep and Dreams F26
Style and Text S24
Suga Yasuo, Ogoshi Kazugo H184, M89, M90, Q44, U33
Symbolic Rose, The H220
Symbolism: The Manichean Vision H215
Symbolism of Virginia Woolf, The G82

Technique of the Modern English Novel, The H39
Technique of the Novel, The L9
Test of Character, The M37
Testimonios I W21
Testimonios II F71, P25
Testimonios X F71
Three-Fold Nature of Reality in the Novels of Virginia Woolf, The G75
Three Guineas A24, W7
Thrown to the Woolfs F57
Tightrope Walkers, The H160
Time and English Fiction S15
Time and Reality H41
Time and the Novel H164
Time and Timelessness in Virginia Woolf G58
To the Lighthouse A5, N49, N52
TO THE LIGHTHOUSE N2
Towards Androgyny H111
Tozasarete Taiwa--V. Woolf no Bungaku to Sono Shuhen G72
Transcendental and the Transitory in Virginia Woolf's Novels, The G78

Transition H175
Transparent Minds H42
Trois guinées W7
Twentieth Century Interpretations of TO THE LIGHTHOUSE N5
TWENTIETH CENTURY LITERATURE: "Virginia Woolf Issue" C4
Twentieth-Century Novel, The H8
Twilight on Parnassus H71
Two Cheers for Democracy G25
Two Studies in the Contemporary Novel G78

ULYSSES: Cinquante ans après H102
Unknown Virginia Woolf, The F77

Vagues, Les Q62
Vanishing Hero, The H183
Venture of Form in the Novels of Virginia Woolf, The G2
Victoria Ocampo F65, F71
Virginia: A Play F70a
Virginia Woolf (Amoruso) G3
Virginia Woolf (Blackstone) G8
Virginia Woolf (Brewster) G10
Virginia Woolf (Daiches) G16
Virginia Woolf (Forrester) F31
Virginia Woolf (Forster) G25
Virginia Woolf (Gorsky) G28
Virginia Woolf (Holtby) G33
Virginia Woolf (Johnson) G36
Virginia Woolf (Mancioli Billi) G50
Virginia Woolf (Miroiu) G54
Virginia Woolf (Moody) G57
Virginia Woolf (Nathan) G60
Virginia Woolf (Newton) G61
Virginia Woolf (Osawa) G63
Virginia Woolf (Rosenthal) G71
Virginia Woolf (Woodring) G88
Virginia Woolf: A Biography F13
Virginia Woolf: A Collection of Critical Essays G80
Virginia Woolf: A Collection of Criticism G44
Virginia Woolf: A Commentary G9
Virginia Woolf: A Critical Reading G24

Virginia Woolf: A Feminist Slant G52
Virginia Woolf: A Personal Debt G21
Virginia Woolf: A Study G29
Virginia Woolf: A Study of Her Novels G4
Virginia Woolf: An Annotated Bibliography of Criticism E9
Virginia Woolf: Centennial Papers G27
Virginia Woolf--Colloque de Cerisy F34
Virginia Woolf: Her Art as a Novelist G7
Virginia Woolf: New Critical Essays G15
Virginia Woolf: ORLANDO P1
Virginia Woolf: Revaluation and Continuity G26
Virginia Woolf: Secrets of the Novel G73
Virginia Woolf: Selections From Her Essays A31
Virginia Woolf: Shosetsu no Himitsu G73
Virginia Woolf: Sources of Madness and Art F61
Virginia Woolf: The Critical Heritage G49
Virginia Woolf: The Echoes Enslaved G48
Virginia Woolf: The Emerging Reality G64
Virginia Woolf: The Inward Voyage G69
Virginia Woolf: THE WAVES: Eine textorientierte psychoanalytische Interpretation Q3
Virginia Woolf: THE WAVES: Emanzipation als Möglichkeit des Bewusstseinsromans Q5
Virginia Woolf: TO THE LIGHTHOUSE (Beja) N1
Virginia Woolf: TO THE LIGHTHOUSE (McNichol) N3a
Virginia Woolf and Bergson's Durée H133

Virginia Woolf and Bloomsbury G68
Virginia Woolf and Her Works G30
Virginia Woolf and Her World F58
Virginia Woolf and Intuition H133
Virginia Woolf & Lytton Strachey B4
Virginia Woolf and the Androgynous Vision G6
Virginia Woolf as Literary Critic X6
Virginia Woolf en su Diario U1
Virginia Woolf et le groupe de Bloomsbury F34
Virginia Woolf et son oeuvre G30
Virginia Woolf, James Joyce, und T. S. Eliot H249
Virginia Woolf No Sekai G35
Virginia Woolf par elle même G60
Virginia Woolf, "Pointz Hall" C5
Virginia Woolf Ronshu: Shodai to Buntai G89
Virginia Woolf, THE WAVES: The Two Holograph Drafts C6
Virginia Woolf, TO THE LIGHTHOUSE: The Original Holograph Draft C7
Virginia Woolf, Trama e Ordito di una Scrittura G90
Virginia Woolf, trois ou quatre choses que je sais d'elle F51
Virginia Woolf und die Konzeption der Zeit in ihren Werken G86
Virginia Woolf, Warp and Woof of a Writer G90
Virginia Woolf's Black Arrows of Sensation Q2
Virginia Woolf's First Voyage J2
Virginia Woolf's Lighthouse N3
Virginia Woolf's Literary Sources and Allusions X7
Virginia Woolf's London G11
Virginia Woolf's Major Novels G18
Virginia Woolf's MRS. DALLOWAY M2
Virginia Woolf's Novels and Their Analogy to Music G83
Virginia Woolf's Quarrel With Grieving G79
Virginia Woolf's Reading Notebooks C10
Virginia Woolfs Stellung zur Wirklichkeit G23

Virginia Woolf's THE WAVES Q4
Virginia Woolf's THE YEARS R3
Virginia Woolf's Vision of Life and Her Search for Significant Form G37
Vivants piliers H159
Vivants piliers II H158
Von Englands geistigen Beständen R5
Voyage In, The M3
Voyage Out, The A1

Wasserscheide zweier Zeitalter H31
Watershed Between Two Generations H31
Waves, The A7, Q62
Why We Should Read K6
Wissen aus Erfahrungen M30
Withered Branch, The H214
Woman of Letters F81
Women and Fiction H233
Women and Language in Literature and Society N92, W9, X23
Women and Literature, 1779-1982 H23, N12
Women and Writing A39
Women and Writing About Women H12
Women's Language and Style N87, Q42, W8
WOMEN'S STUDIES: "Special Issue: Virginia Woolf" G87
World of Virginia Woolf, The G35
World within World F90
World without a Self, The G59
Worlds of Consciousness G47
Writer's Diary, A B6
Wyndham Lewis H195
Wyndham Lewis: Fictions and Satires F20

Years, The A8

Zasłona w Rajskie Ptaki G36a
Zur erlebten Rede in Englischen Roman des zwanzigsten Jahrhunderts H166

SUBJECT INDEX

This index includes all historical and literary figures, literary and mythological characters, and titles named or discussed in the entries and annotations in this bibliography. Occasionally *implied* names and titles are also included (e.g., a discussion of the character Hamlet would be indexed under both HAMLET and Shakespeare, whether or not title and author are named). It also indexes literary and critical terms, kinds of criticism, and prominent themes and topics in Woolf criticism. Finally, it includes all references to cities and nations, cultures and languages, places and institutions.

For Virginia Woolf's works, see the concluding index to this volume. All remaining historical, literary, philosophic, or other titles are listed in this index, with the author's name provided in parentheses.

A LA RECHERCHE DU TEMPS PERDU (Proust) Z252
Abstractionism G87, H23, H59, H176, H214, H226, N79, S19, T7, Z226. Also see Subjectivism
Addison, Joseph A19
Adler, Alfred G84
Adolescence. See Childhood
"Adonais" (Shelley) T26
Adonis M46
Albee, Edward H57, H104, N35, T10
Allegory N71, N92, T29
Allusion G76, H80, H180, J7, J15, M8, M50, M96, N11, N27, N102, S28, S33, T26, X7, Z201, Z253
AMBASSADORS, THE (James) N34
America: Culture and literature E10, H124, M81, N62, X59. Also see Berg Collection, Washington State Univ., and individual American authors, by name
ANCILLA'S SHARE (Robins) W18
Anderson, Sherwood F91
Androgyny F28, G6, G66, G77, H111, H136, H221, M43, N77, N87, P1, Q5, Q32, Q35, W5, W11, X6, Z79, Z150, Z231, Z232
Antigone R2, W1
Anti-novel P38. Also see *Nouveau roman*
ANTIQUARY, THE (Scott) N20
APES OF GOD (Lewis) F20
Archetype. See Myth
Argentina: Culture and literature F65, F71, H237
Aristotle X6
Arnold, Matthew X6
Art F16, F21, G62, G77, G86, H14, H18, H232, K3, M69, N22, N32, N40, N47, N67, N68, N78, N80, N96, P21, S14, S20, S25, S26, S33, U7, X27, Z8, Z133, Z169, Z179, Z182. Also see Impressionism, Post-Impressionism, individual artists, by name, and below
Art and literature G77, G86, H14, H20, H232, J4, K3, L7, M69, N13, N32, N46, N67, N96, Q55, T6, Z151, Z177, Z226. Also see above
AS I LAY DYING (Faulkner) M12, Q22
Ashford, Daisy W24

Atwood, Margaret M68, Z99
Auden, W. H. U2
Austen, Jane A19, A37, A39,
  G17, G39, K7, K8, N6, N14,
  Z99, Z37, Z162
Autobiography. See sections
  B and U

Barnes, Djuna P12
Barthes, Roland W9
Beaumont, Germaine U3, U4,
  U7, U8
Beckett, Samuel Z125, Z256
Bell, Clive F8, F50, G1, G68,
  G77, H14, H114
Bell, Julian G67
Bell, Quentin F13, F22, F31,
  F39, F40, F45, F54, F73, F80,
  F99, G67
Bell, Vanessa F14, F15, F37
Bennett, Arnold A18, A28, A30,
  A31, F24, F48, G3, H16, H65,
  H72, H200, H202, L1, M44, X9,
  X15, X18, X22, X25, X35, X37,
  X42, X46, X56
Benson, Stella T7
Beresford, J. D. X32
Berg Collection, New York
  Public Library C2, C3, C5,
  C10, J2, J6
Bergson, Henri G17, G31, G74,
  G84, G86, H58, H95, H133,
  H172, L4, M52, M86, Z123
Berkeley, George G13
Bernard (in THE WAVES) Q3,
  Q10, Q11, Q59, Q61
Bertin, Célia U6
Bildungsroman H169, L3, M3,
  Q22, Z26
Biography. See section V
Blanche, Jacques-Émile F16,
  F21, G34, H18
BLECHTROMMEL, DIE (Grass) Z17,
  Z252
Bloomsbury Group, The B3, E8,
  F5, F7, F10, F11, F17, F19,
  F20, F25, F28-F32, F34, F35,
  F38, F41, F42, F47, F49,
  F62, F71, F75, F78, F82,
  F83, F85, F86, F98, G1, G3,
  G30, G42, G54, G60, G68, G71,
  G72, H78, H100, H107, H115,
  H126, H168, H198, U2, V7,
  Z113, Z145
BOOKS AND PERSONS (Bennett) X25
Bowen, Elizabeth Z41, Z99
Bradley, Francis Herbert Z124
Bradshaw, Dr. William (in MD)
  M66
Brenan, Gerald F18
Brenner, Y. H. Z157
Breton, André Z157
Briscoe, Lily (in TL) G66, G77,
  G79, N13, N25, N47, N51, N63,
  N67, N74, N78, N80, N83, N87,
  N96
British Museum M51, Z127
Bronte, Charlotte A19, G17, H221,
  M68, Z99, Z187
Bronte, Emily A19, G17, H60, P5
Brooke, Rupert A37
Browning, Elizabeth Barrett F95,
  V1
Browning, Robert H10
Brummell, Beau A22
Burke, Edmund G29
Butler, Samuel A30, G48
Byron, Lord [George Gordon] A38

Cambridge Univ. E8, N36
Cameron, Julia A36
Carpenter, Alejo Z252
Case, Janet F1
Cather, Willa H139, H169
Celli, Rose U6, X9
Cervantes, Miguel de L5
Cézanne, Paul N68, Q55
Characterization G22, G25, G46,
  G76, H9, H40, H43, H45, H63,
  H71, H101, H125, H139, H148,
  H155, H172, H175, H202, H203,
  H212, H246, H248, H256, H257,
  L1, L19, L20, M1, M2, M3a, M5,
  M24, M28, M30, M37, M39, M59,
  M71, M77, M79, M94, M96, N2,
  N45, N52, N78, N102, P14, P17,
  Q1-Q3, Q13, Q18, Q23, Q45, Q53,
  Q56, Q58, R11, T4, T5, T18, X5,

X15, X22, X37, Z1, Z23,
Z36, Z57, Z83, Z90, Z102,
Z143, Z154, Z169, Z172,
Z174, Z179, Z182, Z208.
Also see individual characters, by name
"Characters in Fiction" (Sarraute) X15
Chaucer, Geoffrey P38
Chekhov, Anton H168
Childhood and adolescence
A14, A15, A33, F13, F14,
F77, G54, H48, H79, H134,
M3, N99, R8, T15, U30, W24,
Z26, Z93, Z99
China: Culture and literature
V8, Z249
Chopin, Kate Z99
Christianity. See Religion and literature
CIVILIZATION (Bell) G68
Clapham Sect F5
Classicism F1, K1, L15, M22, M34, M50, N106. Also see Myth
Coleridge, Samuel Taylor A37, H47, H196, X6
Colette, Sidonie Gabrielle
Claudine H139, H154, H165, H169, N70, Z22
Comedy G18, G45, G65, H76, H142, H217, K1, K8, L18, L20, M34, N12, P23, R10, S13, V3, Z45. Also see Parody
Composition, Histories of.
See Textual studies
Compton-Burnett, Ivy Z41
CONDITION HUMAINE, LA (Malraux) A22
Conrad, Joseph A19, E15, H187, H215, J13, M25, X5, X10, Z67, Z71, Z139, Z233, Z234, Z241
"Conversation and Sub-Conversation" (Sarraute) H212, X15
COPAINS, LES (Romains) Q38
Craig, Maurice F95

D., H. See Doolittle, Hilda
Dalloway, Clarissa (in THE VOYAGE OUT and MD) G79, J16, M1, M3, M4, M7, M11, M29, M31, M35, M48, M53, M56-M58, M61, M66, M68, M72-M74, M79, M84, M85
Datchet, Mary (in NIGHT AND DAY) K1
DAVID COPPERFIELD (Dickens) A27
Davidson, Angus A34
Davray, Henry Z29
Death, Theme of F26, F61, G59, G79, H61, H120, H150, H163, J2, M15, M40, M53, M55, M82, N22, N23, N26, N99, N104, Q36, S2, U1, Z44, Z57, Z95, Z181
Death, Virginia Woolf's E3, E13, F31, F49, F71, F91, F96, G59, H151, H245, S9, S16, S29, U7, Z44
Defoe, Daniel A19, A22, X5
Delattre, Floris G33, H58, H59
Demeter N10, N97
DeSassure, Fernand W9
Dickens, Charles A27, H222, L3
Dickinson, Violet C8
DON QUIXOTE (Cervantes) L5
Doolittle, Hilda P12
DOORS OF PERCEPTION, THE (Huxley) U1
DosPassos, John Q6
Dostoevsky, F. M. A17, A37, H180, H185, Y2
Douglas, Norman A30, H37
Drabble, Margaret Z206
Dryden, John Z95
Dualism G6, G29, G37, G38, G42, G62, H60, H136, H149, H159, H215, K2, L8, M2, M19, M26, M71, N17, N41, N88, N103, S3, S22, S25, X21, Z94, Z105
Duras, Marguerite Q51, Z72

Education F1, G22, L16, Z1
Edward VII, King X37. Also see below
Edwardian period F48, G17, H222, X35, X37. Also see above
Eighteenth Century, The L14, M3a
Elegy G65, L14, L20, Z195

Eliot, George A19, G17, H12, H49, M15, Z90, Z136, Z223
Eliot, T. S. F31, F96, H47, H229, H249, L15, M88, P12, Q20, Q35, X1, X6, Z62, Z205, Z244
ELIZABETH AND ESSEX (Strachey) P24
Elizabethan period G52, H192, J7, S26, Z210
Emerson, Ralph Waldo A37
EMINENT VICTORIANS (Strachey) V7
Emotion G20, G57, G69, H23, H134, H172, J2, J8, K6, L17, M12, M19, M42, M57, N4, N39, W17, W18, X1, X13, Z25, Z42
Epic G32
Epiphany. See Moment of vision, The
Epistolary fiction W13
Eros N106
Existentialism G2, H150, M35, M72
Expressionism G84, G85, H8, H108, Q4
EYELESS IN GAZA (Huxley) Q14, Q33, Q48

"Fact in Fiction, The" (Sarraute) X15
FAERY QUEEN, THE (Spenser) A27
Fantasy P6, P7, P9, P14, P15, P22, P36, Q3, Q11, U1
Faulkner, William H19, H25, H170, L6, Q22, W12, Z2, Z17, Z97, Z125, Z195, Z205
Faust P34
Fehr, Bernhard E3, G5, G86, H76, R5
Feminism See section W. Also see A26, A29, A39, C3, F31, F43, F71, F79, G17, G29, G42, G45, G51-G53, G60, G71, G87, H7, H35, H70, H106, H112, H129, H146, H152, H155, H159, H167, H176, H189, H204, H221, H227, H233, H255, J12, K9, M7, M19, M43, M68, M79, N13, N40, N58, N65, N76, N83, N89, P1, P19, P30, Q31, R16, R18, R22, R24, S7, S14, T9, T22, U1, V6, X11, X23, X39, X53, Z1, Z30, Z45, Z57, Z68, Z72, Z77, Z115, Z116, Z136, Z150, Z161, Z170, Z187, Z191, Z206, Z224, Z229. Also see Women and Woolf's feminist tracts, A ROOM OF ONE'S OWN and THREE GUINEAS
Film and literature G13, G32, N21, Z190
Fitzgerald, F. Scott Z195
Flanders, Jacob (in JACOB'S ROOM) L3, L7, L11, L14, L17, L20, Z9
Flaubert, Gustav N34, Z240
Ford, Ford Madox Z7, Z238
Form and structure in fiction G2, G7, G9, G13, G19, G24, G28, G30-G33, G36, G37, G48, G62, G71, G75-G77, G81, G83, G87, G88, H8, H13, H20, H31, H37, H47, H85, H99, H108, H109, H113, H123, H171, H204, H212, H222, H240, H246, H254, H256, J2, J8, J11, K1, K2, K8, L5, L7, L8, L12, L20, M3, M5, M13-M15, M17, M20, M23, M30, M54, M55, M59, M63, M65, M67, M69, M83, M91-M94, M96, N2, N12, N14, N17, N18, N21, N26, N30, N32, N38, N46, N50-N53, N56, N57, N59, N68, N69, N75, N77, N80, N81, N88, N91, N92, N101-N105, Q1, Q2, Q4, Q5, Q8, Q30, Q34, Q37, Q45, Q52, Q57-Q60, R4, R10, R11, S6, S11, S20, S22, S23, S27, S28, S32, T1, T4, T8, T11, T20, T26, T28, W8, X5, X6, X18, X26, Z15, Z25, Z56, Z102, Z103, Z116, Z125, Z132, Z137, Z142, Z152, Z204, Z207, Z214, Z221, Z222, Z225, Z234, Z236, Z246
Forster, E. M. A26, A30, F7, F94, G22, H7, H36, H46, H49, H106, H113, H126, H127, H132, N31, Q1, V4, X1, X6, X24, X40, X46,

Z4, Z11, Z16, Z84, Z86,
Z104, Z140, Z171, Z180,
Z194, Z220, Z241
Frame, Janet   H60, Z170
France: Culture, language,
  and literature   E10, F16,
  F17, F21, F29, G30, G60,
  H10, H18, H59, H64, H69,
  H154, H181, H199, H230,
  H232, J14, L2, M52, Q33,
  Q62, S9, U3, U4, U6-U8,
  X9, Z121. Also see indi-
  vidual French artists and
  authors, by name
Freud, Siegmund   A30, F31,
  G82, G84, M40, M77, M87,
  M95, N27, N95, Q3, X32,
  Z234
Fry, Roger   A25, A27, F50, F86,
  G48, H138, J4, M69, S18, V2,
  V7, Z176, Z238, Z249. Also
  see Woolf's ROGER FRY

Galsworthy, John   A30, G68,
  H72
Garnett, Angelica   F37
Gaskell, Elizabeth Cleghorn
  Z99
Gautier, Théophile   H229
Georgean period   H51, H125,
  H234, K3
Germany: Culture, language,
  and literature   E3, G86,
  H76, H230. Also see indi-
  vidual German authors and
  figures, by name
Gibbon, Edward   G29
Gibson, Graeme   Z195
Gide, André   F17, F29, H85, U1
Gissing, George   Z22
Gladstone, William   A33
Glasgow, Ellen   Z170
Goethe, Johann Wolfgang von
  U34
GOLDEN BOWL, THE (James)   X48
GOLDEN NOTEBOOK, THE (Lessing)
  N55
Golding, William   L3
Goldsmith, Oliver   A28

Gordon, Mary   Z99
Grant, Duncan   F37, F96
Grass, Günter   Z17, Z252
Greece: Culture, language, and
  literature   L11, M22, M34, M50,
  N106, R12. Also see Classicism
Green, Henry   H212
Greene, Graham   H154
Greene, Nicholas (in ORLANDO)   P4
GUÉRILLÈRES, LES (Wittig)   Q31
Guillén, Jorge   H31

Hardy, Thomas   A22, H187, N14
Hawthorne, Nathaniel   N53
Head, Henry   F95
"Heart of Darkness" (Conrad)   J13
Hemingway, Ernest   X17
Herbert, George   Z95
Hesse, Hermann   H85
Hilbery, Katherine (in NIGHT AND
  DAY)   K1
Hilbery, Mrs. (in NIGHT AND DAY)
  K10
HILDA LESSWAYS (Bennett)   M44
Histories of composition and
  publication. See Textual
  studies
History and historical fiction
  C1, C11, G74, G87, P1, P4, P7,
  P10, P35, Q10, Q19, R17, S6,
  S8, S20, S22, S28, S31, T9,
  U20, X31, X54, Z47, Z62, Z126,
  Z164, Z165, Z242
Hitler, Adolf   R4
Hogarth Press   A10, A18, E4, F31,
  F33, F46, F52, F56, F57, F72,
  Z164
Homosexuality   F15, F22, F23, F28,
  H139
Horney, Karen   Z189
HOUSE OF THE SEVEN GABLES, THE
  (Hawthorne)   N53
HOWARDS END (Forster)   H46, H106
Humanism   H49, H75, H87, H106,
  H168, H171, H249, X6, Z104
Humbolt, Wilhelm von   G5
Hume, David   G13
Huxley, Aldous   A30, H37, H72,
  H219, L4, P27, Q14, Q16, Q33,
  Q48, U1, Z36, Z139

Huysmans, Joris-Karl Q22
Hyslop, T. B. F95

Ibsen, Henrik K8
Illness, insanity, and madness
  A27, F13, F26, F31, F47, F53,
  F60, F61, F68, F68a, F77,
  F95, H57, M12, M29, M31,
  M68, P18, Q50, U19, X37,
  Z95, Z157, Z187
Imagery. See Symbolism
Imagism N24
IMPERFECT MOTHER, AN (Beresford) X32
Impressionism G7, G54, G60,
  G84, G85, H5, H40, H52, H91,
  H128, H153, H179, H212, H232,
  H251, K3, L9, L10, N34, N66,
  P35, Q4, Q52, T1, X1, X13,
  X16, X25, X57, Z177, Z226.
  Also see Subjectivism
India M2a, N31
Insanity. See Illness
Interior monologue technique
  F16, G17, G46, G50, G59, G75,
  G84-G86, H3, H42, H52, H53,
  H56, H59, H67, H68, H71, H76,
  H88-H90, H108, H110, H120,
  H122, H123, H125, H133, H150,
  H166, H178, H179, H191, H217,
  H229, H230, H238, H246, H247,
  H250, L10, M32, M41, M42,
  M45, M52, M60, M91, N43, Q1,
  Q15, Q21, Q39, Q40, Q42, Q52,
  Q54, Z2, Z42, Z81, Z123,
  Z162. Also see Narrative
  technique
Irony G65, M3a, M34, M60,
  N34, Q45, S13, Z22
Italy: Culture, language, and
  literature H140, H173, N19

James, Henry A26, H47, H97,
  H182, H187, H188, H215, N34,
  N60, N107, Q1, X2, X6, X43,
  X48, Z52, Z85, Z86, Z90,
  Z171, Z233, Z248
James, William M86

JANE EYRE (C. Bronte) A19
Japan X30
Johnson, Samuel Z95
Joyce, James F46, G3, G17, G23,
  G32, G52, G74, G87, H1, H4,
  H19, H25, H27, H44, H48, H52,
  H53, H56, H59, H67, H69, H72,
  H76, H88, H89, H94, H102,
  H115, H122, H130, H150, H179,
  H183, H187, H194, H200, H205,
  H216, H218, H219, H222, H224,
  H229, H249, H250, H257, K3,
  L5, M9, M14, M45, N6, N7, P12,
  Q14, Q22, X18, Z2, Z20, Z42,
  Z62, Z67, Z69, Z79, Z106,
  Z139, Z171, Z233, Z244, Z256
Jung, Carl G6, G24, G82, G84,
  M64, N76, P31, Z89

Kafka, Franz P7
Keynes, John Maynard F35, F42,
  V3
Kilman, Doris (in MD) M57, M79
Kipling, Rudyard A37, H154
Koteliansky, S. S. A17, Y2

LADY CHATTERLEY'S LOVER (Lawrence)
  X12
Language and linguistics G5, H52,
  H53, H114, H162, H163, H199,
  H212, J3, M60, N33, N37, N44,
  N87, N92, Q3, Q4, Q11, Q19,
  Q39, Q42, R11, R23, S7, S10,
  S24, T30, W8, W9, W11, W20,
  X3, X20, X23, X59, Z18, Z34,
  Z41, Z72, Z73, Z86, Z92, Z135,
  Z155, Z200, Z211
LaTrobe, Miss (in BETWEEN THE ACTS)
  S7, S14
Lawrence, D. H. A27, A30, F7,
  F86, H2, H37, H47, H48, H69,
  H72, H130, H187, H211, H216,
  H218, H219, H224, H233, P12,
  X5, X12, X19, X29, Z7, Z36,
  Z42, Z67, Z79, Z104, Z180,
  Z194, Z218, Z231, Z235, Z241,
  Z250
Leavis, F. R. F86, G57

Lehmann, John F31, F55-F57
Lesbianism. See Homosexuality
Lessing, Doris H221, M68, N55, Z136, Z187, Z206, Z223
Lewis, Wyndham F19, F20, H37, H195, K3, X42
Lockridge, Ross H240
LOLITA (Nabokov) Z62
London A26, A35, E5, G11, G77, H55, M2, M5, M71, Q3, R24, X7, Z216
Louis (in THE WAVES) Q20, Q28
Love and marriage F15, F23, F32, F64, F66, F68, F69, F77, F89, F92, F100, G9, G22, G66, K1, M2, M26, M27, N64, N106, P5, P21, R24, S25
Lubbock, Percy Q1
Lyrical fiction G17, G32, G34, G50, G59, H67, H73, H76, H85, H141, H168, H224, M24, M78, M83, N15, N16, N19, N66, N68, P27, Q34, Q39, Q40, Q47, Q54, S1, T2, T6, X5, Z6, Z27, Z68, Z217, Z250. Also see Novel of sensibility

Macaulay, Rose F96
McCarthy, Mary X15
McTaggart, J. McT. E. G68, N36
MADAME BOVARY (Flaubert) N34
Madness. See Illness
MAGIC MOUNTAIN, THE (Mann) N104
MAISON DE CLAUDINE, LA (Colette) N70
Malraux, André Q22
MANHATTAN TRANSFER (Dos Passos) Q6
Mann, Thomas H2, N104, Z71, Z212
Mansfield, Katherine A39, F2, F15, F31, F44, F63, F67, G17, G52, G54, G70, H147, H155, K7, L10
Manuscript locations, VW's E7, E8, M51
Manuscripts. See section C. Also see Textual studies

Marxism and Marxist criticism E6, G54, H66, H152, H168, H249
Maugham, W. Somerset H72
Mauriac, François H97
Maxse, Kitty M48
Mayer, Louie F70
Melville, Herman A37
MEN WITHOUT ART (Lewis) F20
MERCURE DE FRANCE, LE (periodical) Z29
Meredith, George A22, H188, Z45
Metaphor. See Symbolism
MILL ON THE FLOSS, THE (Eliot) M15
Misogyny N20
Mistral, Gabriela F71
Modernism G19, G32, G42, H24, H27, H64, H97, H114, H144, H212, H238, N3, N37, P12, P37, Q22, T11, Z4, Z10, Z16, Z76, Z128, Z203
Moment of vision, The G50, G58, G87, H10, H13, H29, H39, H41, H47, H82, H153, H160, H251, H253, H14, M39, M65, M74, M90, N30, N49, N74, N84, N88, Q5, Q8, Q35, Q39, Q60, S12, S15, S23, S34, T16, U16, V5, X44, Z14, Z88, Z171, Z232
Monet, Claude H232, Q55
Moore, G. E. F50, F86, F98, G68, H83, H118, H207
Moore, George A22, Z240
Morality in literature G7, G12, G23, H83, H114, H126, H207, M19, M35, M82, M92, N45, N78, S29, S31, X5, X34, X49, Z239
Morgan, Charles G78, P7
Morrell, Ottoline M48
Motif. See Symbolism
MUR, LE (Sartre) M12
Murasaki, Lady X30
Murdoch, Iris H46
Music and literature G48, G83, G86, H62, H76, K8, N16, N39, N68, Q39, Z67. Also see Lyrical fiction
Musil, Robert Z159
Myth and archetype G24, G45, G47, G52, J12, K8, M34, M46, N10, N27, N77, N97, P5, P34, R8, Z34, Z166, Z195

Nabokov, Vladimir Z62
Narcissus H183, Z195
Narrative technique (point of
  view) G13, G18, G19, G32,
  G41, G57, G62, G66, H8, H32,
  H39, H43, H103, H121, H166,
  H179, H210, H228, H230, L6,
  L13, M17, M20, M28, M54, M55,
  M60, M63, M70, M78, N2-N4,
  N21, N33, N34, N43, N69, P1,
  Q1, Q5, Q13, Q26, Q46, S13,
  T12, U15, X5, X6, Z12, Z17,
  Z129, Z143, Z158, Z184,
  Z188, Z190, Z217. Also see
  Interior monologue
"Neo-Impressionism and Litera-
  ture" (Bennett) X25
NEW SIGNATURES (periodical)
  F55
NEW WRITING (periodical) F55
New York Public Library. See
  Berg Collection, and BULLETIN
  OF THE NEW YORK PUBLIC LI-
  BRARY and BULLETIN OF RE-
  SEARCH IN THE HUMANITIES
  in the title index
Nicolson, Nigel F69, F84, F93
Nin, Anais X12, Z62, Z170,
  Z223
Nouveau roman H24, H154, H181,
  H212. Also see Anti-novel
NOUVELLE REVUE FRANÇAISE (per-
  iodical) F17, F29
Novel of sensibility G16, H5,
  H28, H48, H87, H104, H109,
  H110, H119, H172, H188, H242,
  M16, M42, Q62, S5, Z36, Z223.
  Also see Lyrical fiction
  and Subjectivism

Oates, Joyce Carol X12
Ocampo, Victoria F31, F65, F71
Oedipus N10, Q3
O'Neill, Eugene H52, H53
OPTIMIST'S DAUGHTER, THE (Welty)
  N61
Orlando (in ORLANDO) G66, P33

Painting. See Art
Pargiter, Sara (in THE YEARS) R3
Parody P1, P14, S14
PASOS PERDIDOS, LOS (Carpentier)
  Z252
PASSAGE TO INDIA, A (Forster)
  N31, X46
Pater, Walter H10, Q61, X3
Penelope W14
Percival (in THE WAVES) L17, Q3,
  Q5
Persephone N10, N97
Philosophy and literature A30,
  E8, G2, G4, G5, G13, G31, G32,
  G46, G68, H57, H58, H95, H110,
  H114, H119, H133, H159, H185,
  H187, H207, J8, M86, N36, N50,
  N54, N73, N85, N106, P4, Q51,
  S20, S31, X21, Z113, Z124,
  Z171, Z227. Also see indi-
  vidual philosophers, by name
Pisarro, Camille
PLAN OF THE LIFE OF A GREAT SIN-
  NER, THE (Dostoevsky) A17
Plato N106
Plomer, William F75, F76, F96
Point of view. See Narrative
  technique
Politics and literature A31, E1,
  F11, F31, F76, G87, H7, H35,
  H38, H152, H249, J12, K1, K9,
  L16, M19, M68, M72, M73, R4,
  R23, R24, T22, W4, W8, W19,
  Z187, Z216. Also see Marxism
Pope, Alexander M3a
Porter, Katherine Anne X12, Z97
PORTRAIT OF A LADY, THE (James)
  N107
Portugal J5
Post-Impressionism N32, N46,
  X25, Z103, Z114, Z176
Pound, Ezra H10, Z7
Pre-Raphaelitism U4
PRINCIPIA ETHICA (Moore) F86,
  F98
Prometheus M46, S30, X55
Prose style G2, G5, G7, G17,
  G29, G32, G46, G48, G85, G89,
  H20, H23, H32, H43, H52, H53,
  H63, H64, H98, H121, H141,

H163, H171, H210, H232, H247,
K8, M20, N3, N24, N28, N30,
N44, N66, N68, N87, P1, Q4,
Q6, Q7, Q9, Q18, Q19, Q31,
Q34, Q39, Q42, Q47, R3, R15,
S22, S24, T27, W8, W14, W20,
X5, Z59, Z86, Z117, Z135,
Z152, Z184, Z200. Also see
Lyrical fiction
Proust, Marcel G1, G3, G17,
G54, G74, H4, H19, H27,
H41, H109, H115, H154, H270,
H172, H186, H188, H229,
H257, M52, N7, N100, Z151,
Z159, Z214, Z252
Psychology and psychoanalysis
A30, F26, F27, F60, F61,
F68a, F77, G4-G6, G17, G46,
G47, G54, G58, G66, G79, H5,
H25, H50, H67, H95, H110,
H122, H135, H164, H171, H180,
H200, H227, K9, M29, M31,
M40, M61, M64, M67, M68, M77,
M85-M87, M94, M95, N23, N27,
N36, N41, N52, N57, N66, N68,
N76, N95, N99, P5, P18, P31,
Q3, Q10, Q15, Q41, Q50, S31,
T5, U29, U35, Z21, Z89,
Z132, Z171, Z174, Z175,
Z245. Also see Illness,
Freud, and Jung
Publication, Histories of.
See Textual studies

QUEEN VICTORIA (Strachey) F64

RAINTREE COUNTY (Lockridge)
H240
Ramsay, Cam (in TL) U1
Ramsay, James (in TL) U1
Ramsay, Mr. (in TL) H29, N20,
N48, N54, N64, N65, N76, N87
Ramsay, Mrs. (in TL) G77, N13,
N25, N47, N63-N65, N70, N74,
N76-N78, N82-N84, N87
RAVISHING OF LOL STEIN, THE
(Duras) Q51

Realism and "reality" G3, G5,
G7, G13, G14, G17, G19, G23,
G29-G31, G37, G42, G46, G50,
G64, G75, H2, H19, H26, H47,
H76, H95, H99, H108, H110,
H116, H118, H124, H126, H141,
H144, H159, H161, H177, H180,
H187, H203, H205, H207, H209,
H217, H218, H222, H246, H249,
H254, J3, K2, L8, L12, M6,
M20, M37, M58, M70, M73, M86,
N4, N7, N17, N30, N41, N49,
N50, N57, N68, N73, N79, N84,
N93, P1, P15, P22, P26, P36,
Q1, Q2, Q19, Q27, Q28, Q36,
Q37, Q43, Q53, Q54, Q59-Q61,
R5, R7, R14, R17, S3, S25, S33,
T1, T16, T28, U1, U2, U16, U27,
X5, X9, X22, X27, Z31, Z36,
Z65, Z100, Z133, Z176, Z179,
Z199, Z228. Also see Abstractionism and Impressionism
Relativity Z48
Religion and literature H187,
H217, H243, M21, M26, M34, M58,
M67, M72, N71, S20
REMEMBRANCE OF THINGS PAST. See
A LA RECHERCHE DU TEMPS PERDU
Renoir, Pierre Auguste H232
REVENGE FOR LOVE, THE (Lewis)
F20
Rhea N10
Rhoda (in THE WAVES) Q10, Q27,
Q28
Richardson, Dorothy M. A30, A39,
G17, G52, G87, H76, H89, H155,
H179, H218, H250, K3, L10, N6,
Z106, Z231
RISE OF THE NOVEL, THE (Watt) Q1
Ritchie, Anne Thackeray K10
Robins, Elizabeth W18
ROBINSON CRUSOE (Defoe) A22
Romains, Jules Q38
ROMAN (periodical) U6
Romanticism G29, H11, H97, H144,
H224, M78, M86, S30, X55, Z3,
Z16, Z237
Ruskin, John A28, Z238
Russell, Bertrand G68, H118

Russia: Culture, language, and literature A17, A19, G17, G84, H168, H180, H190, H209, P28, Y2, Z193, Z211. Also see individual Russian authors, by name

Sackville-West, Vita F15, F23, F40, F69, F84, F92, F93, F96, P3, P8, P21, P29, U28
Saint-Beuve, Charles Augustin X31
Sarraute, Nathalie H43, H153, H181, H212, H213, Q40, X15, Z72, Z78, Z147, Z168
Sartre, Jean Paul M12
Sassoon, Siegfried A37
Satire. See Comedy
Savage, George Henry F95
Science N14
Science fiction P7
SCIENCE OF ETHICS, THE (Stephen) N54
Scott, Sir Walter A27, H66, N20, P10, S8
SCRUTINY (periodical) E6, W17
"Secret Sharer, The " (Conrad) M25
SENTIMENTAL JOURNEY, THE (Sterne) A22, L18
Seurat, Georges H232
Sex and sexuality F61, G6, G45, G46, G59, G66, H92, H167, H211, M57, M62, M87, N18, N65, N76, N77, N87, N92, N106, P21, R3, R23, S25, T26, U1, W10, W20, W21, W23, Z140, Z187, Z189. Also see Androgyny and Homosexuality
Shakespeare, William M10, M96, N27, T9
Shelley, Percy B. G29, T26
Sickert, Walter A28
SIDO (Colette) N70
Sinclair, May G17, H76, K3
Sisley, Alfred H232

Smith, Logan Pearsall F87, X58
Smith, Septimus (in MD) M1, M12, M23, M29, M46, M61, M68, M82, M85
Smyth, Ethel H152
Sociology and literature E1, F3, F11, F30, F76, G9, G45, G54, G66, G68, G75, G87, H7, H15, H33, H37, H38, H46, H48, H50, H54, H55, H66, H74, H76, H84, H115, H149, H151, H152, H159, H171, H200, H241, H249, H253, H255, H257, K1, K9, L16, M2, M4, M7, M12, M18, M34, M35, M56, M58, M92, M97, N65, N92, P7, P25, Q5, Q21, Q33, Q43, R17, R21, R22, S3, S26, S29, S35, T22, U1, U10, V7, W9, W24, X23, Z10, Z47, Z156, Z162, Z183, Z244. Also see Feminism
SOLDIERS' PAY (Faulkner) L6
Sophocles N19, R2, W1
SORROWS OF YOUNG WERTHER, THE (Goethe) U34
SOUND AND THE FURY, THE (Faulkner) Z17
Spain: Culture, language, and literature F18, H31, H117, J5
Spark, Muriel G45
Spender, Stephen F31, F90
Spenser, Edmund A27
STAVROGIN'S CONFESSION (Dostoevsky) A17
Stein, Gertrude H155, H169, Z37
Stendhal [pseud. of Beyle, Henri] A34
Stephen, Caroline Emilia G52
Stephen, Leslie A28, E5, F4, F79, H84, H159, H200, N8, N48, N54, P9, U1, U9, U21, X3, X31, X34, Z108
Stephen family, The F3, F4, F13, F26, F61, G79, H61, H139, H159, L17, N8, N57, N63, N82, N99, N100, Q49, U9, U21
Sterne, Lawrence A22, H29, L18, P27, X33, Z69
Stevens, Wallace H215
Storey, David H66
Storni, Alfonsina H237

Strachey, Alix F31
Strachey, Lytton B4, F35, F47,
  F62, F64, H126, P9, P24, V3
Stream of consciousness. See
  Interior monologue
Structure. See Form
Style. See Prose style
Subjectivism G5, G7, G19, G23,
  G64, G69, H2, H24, H97, H99,
  H159, H183, H217, H231, H257,
  J2, M16, M73, N24, N96, P27,
  Q36, S3, S17, T2, Z186.
  Also see Abstractionism, Im-
  pressionism, and Novel of
  sensibility
SUR (periodical) F65
Sussex, Engl. E5, F6
Sussex, Univ. of C10
Symbolism and imagery F31, G4,
  G24, G28, G45, G46, G59, G60,
  G64, G75, G77, G81, G82, G84,
  G87, H10, H13, H24, H37, H43,
  H47, H80, H93, H141, H156,
  H158, H184, H196, H197, H199,
  H201, H215, H220, H227, H239,
  H245, J7, J17, L17, M6, M8,
  M10, M21, M67, M75, M77, M83,
  M87, M92, M95, N2, N24, N30,
  N32, N38, N51, N56, N59, N67,
  N68, N71, N73, N76, N77, N80,
  N84, N90, N92, N95, N98,
  N103, N104, P1, P12, Q2-Q4,
  Q6, Q9, Q11, Q22, Q27, Q37,
  Q47, Q54, Q58, R11, R13, S11,
  S32, T1, T26, W15, X5, X22,
  X39, Z35, Z39, Z46, Z49, Z80,
  Z87, Z112, Z116, Z143, Z144,
  Z147, Z159, Z180, Z196, Z200,
  Z213-Z215, Z219, Z222, Z233,
  Z239. Also see Allegory and
  Myth
Symons, Arthur H10
SYMPOSIUM (Plato) N106

TALE OF GENJI (Murasaki) X30
"Tale of Sir Thopas" (Chaucer)
  P38
TEMPLE, THE (Herbert) Z95

Textual studies See section C.
  Also see G52, H121, J1, J2,
  J6, J7, J9, J15, K4, M36, M38,
  M47, M49, M51, M81, N28, N29,
  N62, P15, P29, Q17, Q24-Q26,
  Q30, R3, R7, R9, R11, R19, R20,
  R24, S4, S18, T13, U12, X7,
  Z62, Z63, Z95, Z127, Z211
Thackeray, William Makepeace
  K10
Thomas, Dylan Z97
Thoreau, Henry David Z37, X44
THOSE BARREN LEAVES (Huxley) L4
"Three Jews" (L. Woolf) A10
Time in fiction G6, G18, G31,
  G58, G69, G77, G86, H29, H41,
  H58, H95, H96, H109, H131,
  H133, H157, H164, H170, H172,
  H191, H246, H254, L4, L5, M9,
  M30, M33, M39, M45, M59, M67,
  M86, M91, M93, N4, N14, N21,
  N26, N36, N91, N101, P1, P11,
  Q1, Q10, Q14, Q16, Q29, Q42,
  Q48, R5, R6, R17, S6, S12,
  S15, S17, T18, U1, U18, X5,
  X26, Z40, Z139, Z205, Z222.
  Also see Moment of vision, The
TIME MUST HAVE A STOP (Huxley) L4
TIN DRUM, THE. See BLECHTROMMEL,
  DIE
Tolstoy, Leo H208
Tomas, Ann F31
Tragedy J10, M34, R2, U28
Translation A17, E7, E13, F102,
  H64, J14, L2, M52, N19, Q33,
  Q62, S9, U3, U4, U6-U8, X9,
  X30, Y2
TRISTRAM SHANDY (Sterne) H29
Turgenev, Ivan A28, H190

ULYSSES (Joyce) F46, H1, H59,
  H102, M9, M45, Q14, Q22, Z20,
  Z62
UNDER A GLASS BELL (Nin) Z62

Victorian period A36, E8, G15,
  G17, G54, L14, M37, N48, N64,
  U1, U9, U14, X3, X34

VILLAGE IN THE JUNGLE, THE (L. Woolf) G1
Vinrace, Rachel (in THE VOYAGE OUT) J2

Wagner, Richard H62, Z67
Waley, Arthur X30
Walpole, Hugh F97
WAR AND PEACE (Tolstoy) H208
Ward, Mrs. Humphrey [pseud. of Mary Arnold] G17
Washington State Univ. E5
WASTE LAND, THE (Eliot) L15, M88, Z62
Watt, Ian Q1
Waugh, Evelyn H37, Z11
Wells, H. G. A30, H72
Welty, Eudora N61, Z97
Werfel, Franz H185
Wharton, Edith Z99, Z130
Whistler, James Abbott McNeill N232
Whitehead, Alfred North H118
Whitman, Walt H200
WHO'S AFRAID OF VIRGINIA WOOLF? (Albee) H57, H104, N35
WILD PALMS, THE (Faulkner) W12
Wilson, Angus H49
WINTER OF ARTIFICE (Nin) Z62
WINTER'S TALE, A (Shakespeare) N27
WISE VIRGINS, THE (L. Woolf) U26
Wittig, Monique F31, Q31
Wollstonecraft, Mary A22
Women A26, A29, A30, A31, A39, C11, F9, F15, F80, G17, G22, G46, G52, G87, H7, H12, H23, H50, H61, H70, H84, H107, H129, H139, H165, H169, H189, H195, H221, H233, H255, J10, J12, K5, M2, M11, M43, M62, M79, N12, N25, N40, N47, N58, N65, N77, N82, N87, N89, N102, P5, P12, P19, P20, Q42, R18, R24, T9, T26, U13, V6, W2, W6, W8, W9, W16, W24, X8, X30, X47, Z22, Z26, Z50, Z57, Z72, Z75, Z115, Z135, Z138, Z170, Z191, Z224, Z255.
Also see Feminism
Woolf, Leonard A10, E5, F32, F33, F52, F56, F57, F66, F68, F77, F89, F95, F100, G1, M88, U1, U3, U26, X37
Wordsworth, Dorothy A22, Q37
Wordsworth, William Q37, Z205
World War I F35, H71-H74, H145, H149, H248, W10, Z131
World War II E3, F55, F91, G86, H71-H74, H149, S35
WUTHERING HEIGHTS (E. Bronte) A19, P5

Yeats, William Butler H47, Z205, Z231
YOUNG VISITERS, THE (Ashford) W24
Yourcenar, Marguerite F102, Q62

VIRGINIA WOOLF'S WORKS: INDEX OF COMMENTARIES

The following index includes, alphabetically by title, all the publications of VW found in the primary bibliography of this volume, listing the primary entry number for each title and the entry numbers for *all* substantive published commentaries concerning the title. Unless self-evident, the genre of each title is also identified.

In any guide such as this, it is not possible to indicate by organization into various topical sections, by sectional headnotes, or by annotations, either the complete extent of scholarship on a particular work, or the full range of coverage in a particular study of VW. Thus, when fully researching any of VW's publications, from one of the major novels to a brief essay, the user should turn first to the appropriate section of this guide concerned with the publication for commentaries largely or exclusively concerned with the title (e.g., THE WAVES, section Q), or its genre (e.g., the essays, section X), then review the section's headnote for references to the most significant commentaries entered in other sections of the guide. Finally, the user should consult this index for a *complete* listing of the entry-numbers for studies containing substantive discussions of the title.

This index has been compiled from a direct survey of the books and articles concerning VW, not from their annotations in this volume, and goes beyond the usual "subject" index in locating commentaries on specific works contained in general studies, even though the fact that these general studies consider various titles by VW might not and could not, in the interest of space, be indicated in their annotations. The unpublished dissertations (in section Z, above) are more selectively represented in this index. Only the entry numbers for dissertations concerned with specified works, as indicated by their titles or annotations, have been indexed.

"Addison" (essay) A19, X1, X7
"Ancestors" (story) A16, T11
"Anon" (essay) C1, G18, S7, X1, X20
ART DU ROMAN, L' (essay collection) X9
"Art of Biography, The" (essay) A26, G30, G59, X1, X7
"Art of Fiction, The" (essay) A27, G30, W9, X1, X5-X7, X21, X23

"Beau Brummell" (essay) A22, X7
BETWEEN THE ACTS (novel) S1-S35. Also see A9, C5, D1, F13, F31, F74, F77, F81, F100, G2-G4, G6-G13, G16, G18-G20, G24, G28, G30-G32, G36-G38, G41, G42, G45, G47, G48, G50, G52-G54, G57-G61, G64-G66, G68, G69, G71, G74, G75, G81, G82, G84, G86, G88, H1, H2, H21, H27, H28, H39, H50, H60, H80, H89, H90, H93, H96, H98, H101, H105, H109, H112, H113, H117, H126, H130, H135, H137, H140, H149, H154, H161, H163, H178, H188, H192, H214, H215, H231, H245, H247, H249, H252, H254, H256, U7, W7, X3, Z32, Z61, Z87, Z88, Z126, Z165, Z252
"Blue and Green" (story) A12, G30
"BOOKS AND PERSONS" (essay) X25
BOOKS AND PORTRAITS (essay collection) A37, U32, X52
"Broad Brow, The" (essay) A34
"Byron and Mr. Briggs" (essay) A38

CAPTAIN'S DEATH BED, AND OTHER ESSAYS, THE A28, C10, X5-X7, X13, X16, X53, X57, X58
"Captain's Death Bed, The" (essay) A28, X7

CHANGE OF PERSPECTIVE, A. See LETTERS OF VIRGINIA WOOLF, THE
"Character in Fiction" (essay) A18, F48, X35
"Cockney's Farming Experiences, A" (story) A15, T15
COLLECTED ESSAYS A32, C10, X1, X5-X7, X16, X53, X57
COMMON READER, THE (essay collection) A19, C10, F13, G7, G16, G17, G30, G54, G68, H18, H137, H175, H180, H244, P25, X1, X5-X7, X16, X21, X45, X53, X57
COMMON READER, THE: SECOND SERIES (essay collection) A22, C10, G7, G16, G30, G54, H18, X1, X5-X7, X16, X21, X45, X53, X57
CONTEMPORARY WRITERS (essay collection) A30, C10, X1, X5-X7, X28, X53, X57

"DAVID COPPERFIELD" (essay) A27, X1, X7
DEATH OF THE MOTH, AND OTHER ESSAYS, THE A26, C10, G30, H21, T19, V4, X5-X7, X14, X16, X21, X26, X38, X53, X57
"Death of the Moth, The" (essay) A26, G30, T19, X7
"Defoe" (essay) A19, X1, X5-X7
DIARY OF VIRGINIA WOOLF, THE B1, F12, F40, F57, F61, F77, F81, F84, F95, G28, G52, G79, H225, H245, R3, U5, U19, U20, U26, U32, X3
"Dorothy Wordsworth" (essay) A22, X7
"Duchess and the Jeweller, The" (story) A13, G30, T11, T23

"Essay in Criticism, An" (essay) X1, X17
"Experiences of a Pater-familias" (story) A15, T15

"FAERY QUEEN, THE" (essay) A27, G69, X7

FLIGHT OF THE MIND, THE. See
LETTERS OF VIRGINIA WOOLF,
THE
FLUSH: A BIOGRAPHY A23, C10,
F13, F95, G2, G8, G10, G11,
G16, G25, G28, G30, G36, G42,
G46, G48, G50, G71, G74, G81,
G88, H2, H34, H142, H231,
P26, V1, V5, V6, V8, X53,
Z11, Z35, Z146
FRESHWATER: A COMEDY (play)
A36, G28, Y1, Y3, Y4
"Freudian Fiction" (essay)
A30, Q3, X5, X6, X32
"Friendships Gallery" (essay)
C8

"George Eliot" (essay) A19,
G42, X7
"George Gissing" (essay) A22,
X7
"George Moore" (essay) A26, X7
GRANITE AND RAINBOW (essay col-
lection) A29, C10, G30, X1,
X5-X7, X16, X53, X57

"Haunted House, A" (story)
A12, A13, G10, G16, G30,
G54, G81, H103, T1, T11
HAUNTED HOUSE, AND OTHER SHORT
STORIES, A (story collection)
A13, G28, G30, G61, T4, T11,
T27, X3
"Henry James" (essay) A26, X2,
X7, X43, X48
"High Brow, The" (essay) A34
"Hours in a Library" (essay)
A29, G30, X1

"Introduction, The" (story)
A16, T11, T22
"Introduction to MRS. DALLOWAY"
(essay) A20

JACOB'S ROOM (novel) L1-L20.
Also see A3, F13, F74, F81,
F97, F100, G2-G13, G16, G17,
G20, G23, G24, G28-G33, G36-
G38, G41, G42, G45-G48, G50,
G53, G54, G57, G58, G60-G62,
G64, G66, G68, G69, G71, G74-
G77, G79, G81, G82, G84-G86,
G88, H2, H8, H14, H18, H20,
H22, H26-H28, H32, H44, H47,
H53-H55, H59, H61, H63, H65,
H76, H81, H85, H89, H90, H92,
H101-H103, H119, H121, H126-
H128, H130, H133, H137, H140,
H141, H157, H159, H166, H171,
H173, H174, H178, H180, H188,
H189, H201, H207, H208, H214,
H222, H223, H228, H231, H232,
H242, H247, H251, H253, H254,
H256, P27, U24, X3, Z21, Z62,
Z246
"Jane Austen" (essay) A19, G42,
G69, X7
"JANE EYRE and WUTHERING HEIGHTS"
(essay) A19, X1, X7
"Joseph Conrad" (essay) A19, X1,
X7, X10
"Journal of Mistress Joan Martyn,
The" (story) C11, T9

"Kew Gardens" (story) A11-A13,
F13, F74, F81, G8, G10, G11,
G16, G19, G30, G31, G33, G36,
G42, G54, G61, G62, G69, G71,
G84, H81, H103, H126, H134,
H177, T2, T3, T6, T7, T11, T16
T21

"Lady in the Looking Glass, The"
(story) A13, G18, G19, G30,
H227, T5
"Lappin and Lapinova" (story)
A13, G2, G30, T10, T11, T22
"Leaning Tower, The" (essay)
A27, A31, F13, F81, G18, G42,
H137, H151, Q5, U1, X1, X7,
X31, X41
LEAVE THE LETTERS TILL WE'RE DEAD.
See LETTERS OF VIRGINIA WOOLF, THE

"Legacy, The" (story) A13,
    G30, H130, T11, T22, T28
"Leslie Stephen" (essay) A28,
    X1, X7
"Letter to a Young Poet, A"
    (essay) A26, F13, G28, G30,
    G59, H137, H151, X1, X4, X7
LETTERS OF VIRGINIA WOOLF, THE
    B2, F40, F57, F61, F77, F81,
    F84, F87, G7, G10, G11, G24,
    G28, G30, G42, G50, G59,
    G69, G79, H245, R3, U13,
    U15-U17, U22, U25, U26, U29,
    X3, X12, X29
"Life and the Novelist" (essay)
    A29, X5-X7
LONDON SCENE, THE (essay collection) A35, C10, X53
"Low Brow, The" (essay) A34

"Man Who Loved His Kind, The"
    (story) A13, A16, G30, T11,
    T30
"Mark on the Wall, The" (story)
    A10, A12, A13, F13, F74,
    F81, G2, G10, G16, G19, G28,
    G30, G31, G33, G36, G42,
    G53, G54, G62, G71, G81,
    G88, H14, H29, H67, H81,
    H103, H119, H126, H207, T7,
    T8, T11
"Mary Wollstonecraft" (essay)
    A22, X7
"MELYMBROSIA," BY VIRGINIA
    WOOLF (manuscript) C2, F13.
    Also see VOYAGE OUT, THE
"Miss Janet Case" (essay) F1
"Modern Fiction" (essay) A19,
    A31, F81, G3, G4, G7, G17-
    G19, G28, G30, G31, G33,
    G42, G45, G46, G59, G69,
    G79, H16, H47, H54, H137,
    H209, H214, H243, H249, Q1,
    X1, X3, X5-X7, X18, X21,
    X22, X35, X47, X51
MOMENT, AND OTHER ESSAYS, THE
    A27, C10, G30, X1, X5-X7,
    X16, X53, X57
"Moment, The: Summer's Night"
    (essay) A27, G42, G69, H47,
    X2, X5-X7, X27

MOMENTS OF BEING (memoirs) B3,
    F77, F81, G28, G79, H61, H79,
    H140, H225, H227, H245, N78,
    Q17, U9, U11, U12, U14, U16,
    U18, U19, U21, U22, U30, U33,
    U35, X3
"Moments of Being: 'Slater's
    Pins Have No Points'" (story)
    A13, G30, G81, H13, T11, T14,
    T28, X3
"Monday or Tuesday" (story) A12,
    A13, G3, G8, G10, G16, G30, G33,
    G54, G81, H126, T11, T28
MONDAY OR TUESDAY (story collection) A12, F13, F67, G8, G28,
    G31, H103, H231, T7
MORT DE LA PHALÈNE: NOUVELLES
    (story collection) T19
"Mr. Bennett and Mrs. Brown" (essay) A18, A28, A31, F13, F24,
    F48, F81, G3, G7, G16, G19,
    G28, G30, G33, G42, G45, G46,
    G53, G54, G59, G69, G79, G84,
    H2, H3, H16, H19, H26, H43,
    H65, H74, H91, H99, H142, H145,
    H197, H202, H214, H217, H242,
    H244, H249, H254, L1, M44, Q1,
    Q5, X1, X3, X5-X7, X9, X15,
    X18, X21, X22, X25, X35, X37,
    X42, X46, X47, X56
MRS. DALLOWAY (novel) M1-M97.
    Also see A4, A20, F13, F15,
    F61, F64, F74, F77, F81, F95,
    F100, G2-G14, G16-G20, G22-
    G24, G28-G33, G36-G38, G41-
    G43, G45-G48, G50, G52-G54,
    G57-G62, G64-G66, G68, G69,
    G71, G74-G77, G79, G81, G82,
    G84-G86, G88, H1-H3, H8, H13,
    H18-H20, H22, H23, H25-H27,
    H32-H35, H37, H39, H42, H44,
    H46, H47, H50, H52, H53-H55,
    H59, H63-H68, H70, H71, H75,
    H76, H81-H83, H85, H88-H90,
    H94, H96, H97, H99, H101,
    H102, H107-H110, H117, H119,
    H120, H123, H125-H128, H130,
    H133, H141, H142, H150, H154-
    H159, H162, H164, H165, H170,
    H171, H173-H175, H178-H180,
    H188, H189, H197, H201, H202,

H207, H211, H214, H220-H222,
H227-H231, H239, H241, H245,
H247, H248, H251, H252,
H254-H256, P20, P27, T20,
T25, U24, X3, X38, Z20, Z21,
Z50, Z77, Z88, Z89, Z95,
Z115, Z127, Z132, Z137,
Z148, Z219, Z224, Z247
"Mrs. Dalloway in Bond Street"
(story) A16, F81, G10, G42,
G54, G62, G76, G79, M4, M38,
T17, T24-T26
MRS. DALLOWAY'S PARTY (story
collection) A16, G79, M4,
M38, T11, T20, T30

"Narrow Bridge of Art, The"
(essay) A29, G18, G69,
H47, X5-X7
"New Biography, The" (essay)
A29, A31, G59, X1, X7
"New Dress, The" (story) A13,
A16, G30, H104, T11, T22, T30
NIGHT AND DAY (novel) K1-K10.
Also see A2, F13, F15, F67,
F74, F77, F81, F95, F100,
G2-G4, G6-G11, G13, G16,
G17, G20, G22-G24, G28-G33,
G36-G38, G41, G42, G45-G48,
G50, G53, G54, G57, G60,
G61, G64-G66, G68, G69, G71,
G74, G75, G81, G82, G84,
G85, G88, H2, H14, H20, H22,
H40, H44, H49, H54, H75,
H80, H83, H101, H113, H119,
H121, H126, H128, H133,
H146, H149, H162, H173-H175,
H178, H180, H188, H189,
H208, H214, H215, H213,
H232, H247, H251, H254, U24,
X3, Z21
"Notes on D. H. Lawrence" (essay) A27, G69, X5, X7, X12,
X19, X29
"Novels of E. M. Forster, The"
(essay) A26, F94, X1, X7,
X24, X40
"Novels of George Meredith,
The" (essay) A22, X1, X7

"Novels of Thomas Hardy, The"
(essay) A22, X1, X7
"Novels of Turgenev, The" (essay)
A28, X1, X7
"Nurse Lugton's Golden Thimble"
(story) A14

"Oliver Goldsmith" (essay) A28,
X7
"On Being Ill" (essay) A27, G18,
G69, X1, X7
"On Not Knowing French" (essay)
X59
"On Re-reading Novels" (essay)
G69, X1
ORLANDO (novel) P1-P38. Also
see A6, C9, F13, F15, F23, F32,
F64, F69, F74, F81, F92, F93,
F100, G2-G11, G13, G16-G18,
G20, G23, G24, G28-G33, G36,
G37, G42, G45, G46, G48, G50,
G53, G54, G58-G61, G65, G66,
G68, G69, G71, G74, G76, G79,
G81, G82, G84-G86, G88, H2, H7,
H8, H20, H25, H29, H47, H54,
H61, H64, H70, H74, H76, H80,
H93, H94, H101, H109, H125-
H127, H129, H133, H142, H146,
H150, H157, H164, H165, H173,
H174, H178, H180, H188, H189,
H192, H201, H207, H231, H237-
H249, H254, U24, W7, Z58, Z135,
Z246

"PARGITERS, THE" (manuscript)
C3. Also see YEARS, THE
"Philosophy in Fiction" (essay)
A30, X5-X7
"POINTZ HALL." See VIRGINIA
WOOLF, "POINTZ HALL"
"Professions for Women" (essay)
A26, A31, C3, R3, X7

QUESTION OF THINGS HAPPENING, THE.
See LETTERS OF VIRGINIA WOOLF,
THE

"Reader, The" (essay) C1
REFLECTION OF THE OTHER PERSON, A. See LETTERS OF VIRGINIA WOOLF, THE
"Review of LES COPAINS" (essay) Q38
"Reviewing" (essay) A28, G30, X1, X7
"ROBINSON CRUSOE" (essay) H22, G69, X1, X7
"Roger Fry" (essay) A27, X1, X7
ROGER FRY: A BIOGRAPHY A25, C10, F13, G8, G10, G16, G25, G28, G30, G36, G42, G48, G50, G71, G74, G81, G88, H28, H112, H138, P26, X18, V2, V5, V7, X53, Z11, Z38, Z58, Z146
ROOM OF ONE'S OWN, A (feminist tract) A21, A31, C10, F13, F23, F31, F81, F98, G6, G8-G11, G16-G18, G25, G28-G30, G33, G41, G42, G45, G46, G50, G53, G59, G60, G66, G68, G69, G71, G76, G81, G84, H7, H23, H38, H61, H70, H92, H108, H111, H126, H129, H136, H142, H146, H152, H154, H155, H167, H189, H192, H204, H211, H221, H227, H233, H234, H244, H249, N83, P20, P25, T9, U1, W3-W6, W8, W9, W12, W14-W16, W18, W21, W24, W25, X1, X3, X53, Z117
"Ruskin" (essay) A28, X1, X7
"Russian Point of View, The" (essay) A19, G17, G30, G84, H180, H185, H190, H208, H209, X1, X5-X7, Y2, Z211

"Searchlight, The" (story) A13, G30, G42, G53, T11, T13
SECOND COMMON READER, THE (essay collection) A22. Also see COMMON READER, THE: SECOND SERIES
"SENTIMENTAL JOURNEY, THE" (essay) A22, X1, X7, X23

"Shooting Party, The" (story) A13, G30, G61, T11
SICKLE SIDE OF THE MOON, THE. See LETTERS OF VIRGINIA WOOLF, THE
"Sir Walter Scott" (essay) A27, X7
"Slater's Pins Have No Points." See "Moments of Being"
"Society, A" (story) A12, G16, G30, T7, T22
"Solid Objects" (story) A13, G19, G30, G61, G69, H2, H148, H152, T4, T11, T29
STAVROGIN'S CONFESSION AND THE PLAN OF THE LIFE OF A GREAT SINNER (translations) A17, G28, H180, Y2
"Stephen versus Gladstone" (essay) A33, X7
"Street Haunting: A London Adventure" (essay) A26, G11, G30, G42, H47, H126, X3, X7
"String Quartet, The" (story) A12, A13, F74, G8, G10, G16, G30, G54, H103, T11
"Summing Up, A" (story) A13, A16, G30, G81, T11, T30

"TALE OF GENJI, THE" (essay) X30
"Terribly Sensitive Mind, A" (essay) A29, F2, F15, F44, X7
"Thoreau" (essay) A37, X44
"Three Characters" (essay) A34
THREE GUINEAS (feminist tract) A24, A31, C10, F13, F23, F31, F77, F81, F95, G6, G8, G10, G16, G18, G28, G30, G41, G42, G45, G50, G52, G53, G66, G68, G71, G81, G84, H7, H35, H112, H126, H130, H140, H146, H211, H221, H223, P20, R3, U1, W1, W2, W4, W7, W10, W11, W13, W15, W17-W20, W22, W23, X3, X53, Z117
TO THE LIGHTHOUSE (novel) N1-N107. Also see A5, C7, F13, F23, F31, F41, F61, F64, F74, F77, F81, F100, G2-G10, G12-G14, G16-G18, G20, G22-G24,

G28-G33, G36-G38, G41, G42,
G45-G48, G50, G53, G54,
G57-G62, G64-G66, G68, G69,
G71, G74, G75, G77, G79,
G81, G82, G84-G86, G88, H1-
H3, H13, H19, H20, H22-
H26, H28, H29, H33-H35, H37,
H39, H42, H44, H46-H50, H52,
H54, H59, H64, H66, H68,
H70, H71, H75, H76, H79,
H82-H85, H89, H90, H93, H94,
H96-H99, H101, H106, H108-
H111, H113, H119, H123,
H125-H130, H133, H134, H137,
H139, H140, H148, H154-H167,
H171, H173, H174, H177,
H178, H180, H182, H188,
H189, H197, H199, H201,
H202, H207, H211, H214,
H220, H221-H223, H227,
H228, H230, H231, H238-
H242, H244, H245, H247,
H249, H251, H253, H254,
H256, M5, M37, P18, P20.
P25, P27, R13, S19, U1, U23,
U24, X3, X38, Z58, Z87, Z88,
Z99, Z115, Z129, Z132, Z137,
Z169, Z192, Z190, Z204,
Z214, Z219, Z247
"Together and Apart" (story)
A13, A16, G30, T11, T30

"Unwritten Novel, An" (story)
A12, A13, F13, F74, G3, G10,
G16, G19, G30, G36, G42,
G61, G69, G71, G81, H103,
T7, T11, T12, T18

VIRGINIA WOOLF, "POINTZ HALL"
(manuscript) C5. Also see
BETWEEN THE ACTS
VIRGINIA WOOLF'S READING NOTE-
BOOKS (manuscript) C10, X53
VOYAGE OUT, THE (novel) J1-
J17. Also see A1, C2, F13,
G64, G67, F74, F77, F81, F95,
F98, F100, G2-G4, G6-G10,
G13, G16, G17, G20, G22-G24,

G28-G33, G36-G38, G41, G42,
G45-G48, G50, G53, G54, G57,
G59-G62, G64-G66, G68, G69,
G71, G74-G76, G79, G81, G82,
G84, G85, G88, H2, H14, H20,
H22, H40, H49, H50, H54, H60,
H80, H81, H82, H101, H103,
H104, H113, H119, H121, H126,
H128, H130, H133, H134, H141,
H145, H149, H173, H174, H177,
H178, H188, H189, H199, H214,
H217, H231, H232, H242, H249,
H251, H254, K4, M3, M4, X3,
Z21, Z60, Z63, Z87, Z215, Z221

"Walter Sickert" (essay) A28,
X1, X7
WAVES, THE (novel) Q1-Q62. Also
see A7, C6, D2, F13, F23, F31,
F32, F56, F64, F74, F77, F81,
F95, F100, G2-G4, G6-G14, G16-
G20, G23, G24, G28-G34, G36-
G38, G41, G42, G45-G48, G50,
G53, G54, G57-G61, G64, G66,
G68, G69, G71, G74-G76, G79,
G81, G82, G84-G86, G88, H1-H3,
H8, H12, H18, H23, H26-H28,
H33, H34, H37, H42, H44, H45,
H47-H51, H54, H59, H60, H66,
H72, H79, H82, H85, H89, H90,
H96, H98, H101, H105, H108-
H110, H113, H116, H117, H119,
H122, H123, H126, H127, H130,
H133-H135, H137, H140, H150,
H154, H156, H158, H159, H161-
H164, H166, H170, H171, H174,
H178, H180, H187-H189, H199,
H201-H203, H207, H208, H214,
H216, H222, H223, H229-H231,
H238, H241, H242, H245, H247,
H249, H252-H254, H256, J11,
M37, P6, R13, S12, U23, U24,
U27, X3, Z15, Z17, Z24, Z43,
Z66, Z87, Z94, Z116, Z132,
Z144, Z166, Z185, Z200, Z219,
Z221, Z225, Z228, Z246, Z247
"Women and Fiction" (essay) A29,
X5-X7

WOMEN AND WRITING (essay collection) A39, C10, X8, X53
"Women Novelists" (essay) A30, X5-X7
WRITER'S DIARY, A B6, F31, G2, G7, G10, G14, G28, G30, G50, G59, G60, G69, G79, H140, H183, H189, H245, P20, U1-U4, U6-U8, U10, U19, U20, U23, U24, U27, U28, U31, U34, U35, X1, X3, X5, X29

YEARS, THE (novel) R1-R25. Also see A8, C3, F13, F74, F77, F81, F100, G2-G4, G6-G11, G13, G16, G19, G20, G24, G28, G30-G32, G36-G38, G41, G42, G45, G48, G50, G52-G54, G57, G58, G60, G61, G64-G66, G68, G69, G71, G74, G75, G79, G81, G82, G84, G86, G88, H2, H18, H35, H47, H54, H55, H60, H71, H101, H112, H126, H130, H135, H139, H149, H161, H171, H178, H187, H189, H190, H214, H215, H223, H231, H247, H254, H255, P25, S12, W13, W19, X3, Z68, Z126, Z165, Z178, Z228

For Product Safety Concerns and Information please contact our EU representative GPSR@taylorandfrancis.com
Taylor & Francis Verlag GmbH, Kaufingerstraße 24, 80331 München, Germany

www.ingramcontent.com/pod-product-compliance
Lightning Source LLC
Chambersburg PA
CBHW071811300426

44116CB00009B/1277